Jane Austen For Dummies®

W9-BRF-685

Doing Things Decently and in Order

Keep in mind the following kind of etiquette that dominated Austen's world:

- **Introducing and acknowledging people:** People lower in the social hierarchy waited to be introduced to those higher.

- **Speaking appropriately:** Group conversation did not include jokes about young couples' love interests, a woman's pregnancy, or a child's being born out of wedlock.

- **Courting:** Prior to their engagement, couples met at dances and dinner parties, where friends and family were also present and observing them.

- **Dancing the night away:** Dancing was not close-body dancing: Dancers held hands with their arms extended. Unless they were engaged or very serious about each other, a couple could only dance together for two dances (each dance consisted of two 15-minute dances).

Knowing How the Name Game Is Played

Below I list some of the titles you may come across in Jane Austen's novels:

- **Miss Last Name–Only:** the eldest daughter

- **Miss First Name–Last Name:** younger sisters

- **Mr. and Mrs. Last Name:** elders or husband and wife

- **Sir First Name–Last Name and Lady Last Name:** baronets, knights, and their wives

For Dummies: Bestselling Book Series for Beginners

Meeting the Cast of Characters

Here's a handy list of the main characters for each novel:

✔ *Northanger Abbey*
- Catherine Morland, heroine
- Henry Tilney, hero
- General Tilney, Henry's domineering and greedy father
- James Morland, Catherine's brother; in love with Isabella Thorpe
- John Thorpe, James Morland's thoughtless, rude, and lying college "friend"
- Isabella Thorpe, John's sister

✔ *Sense and Sensibility*
- Elinor Dashwood, the eldest of the three Dashwood sisters
- Marianne Dashwood, the middle Dashwood sister
- James Willoughby, a dashingly handsome and hunky young man
- Edward Ferrars, Elinor's love interest
- Lucy Steele, a poorly educated, pretty, and greedy young woman
- Colonel Brandon, becomes friends with the Dashwoods

✔ *Pride and Prejudice*
- Elizabeth Bennet, the clever, pretty, and athletic heroine
- Fitzwilliam Darcy, the extremely wealthy hero
- Jane Bennet, Elizabeth's beautiful eldest sister
- Charles Bingley, Darcy's best friend
- Lady Catherine de Bourgh, Darcy's control-freak aunt
- Mr. Collins, clergyman set to inherit the Bennets' property

✔ *Mansfield Park*
- Fanny Price, the quiet, dutiful heroine
- Edmund Bertram, younger son in a baronet's family
- Mary Crawford, a rich, attractive, and outspoken Londoner
- Henry Crawford, Mary's charming but unsettled brother
- Sir Thomas Bertram, Baronet of Mansfield Park

✔ *Emma*
- Emma Woodhouse, the handsome, clever, and rich heroine
- Mr. Knightley, close friend of the Woodhouse family
- Frank Churchill, Mr. Weston's handsome and charming son

✔ *Persuasion*
- Anne Elliot, strong minded and capable in a crisis
- Frederick Wentworth, engaged to Anne before the novel opens
- Sir Walter Elliot, Anne's vain, spendthrift father
- Louisa Musgrove, a good-natured somewhat self-centered woman

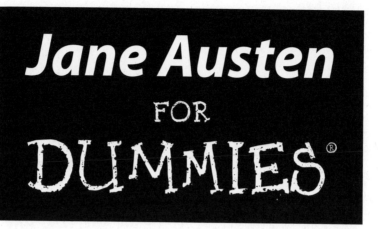

Jane Austen FOR DUMMIES®

by Joan Klingel Ray, PhD

Joan K. Ray

WILEY

Wiley Publishing, Inc.

Jane Austen For Dummies®

Published by
Wiley Publishing, Inc.
111 River St.
Hoboken, NJ 07030-5774
www.wiley.com

WILEY

About the Author

Joan Klingel Ray, PhD, is a *Janeite*: an admirer of the works of Jane Austen. Born and raised in New York City, she received her BA in English with Honors from S.U.N.Y at Stony Brook and her AM and PhD in 18th-century British literature from Brown University. After she received an offer for a tenure-track assistant professorship at the University of Colorado at Colorado Springs, Joan moved west. Having served the University in various administrative posts, she's a tenured professor of English and a President's Teaching Scholar — a University of Colorado Systemwide Lifetime Title.

Joan Ray is in her third term as President of The Jane Austen Society of North America (JASNA), making her, in the words of JASNA members, "the FDR of JASNA." (You can access information on JASNA at www.jasna.org.) In this role, Joan has lectured on Jane Austen around the world in England, Japan, Australia, and Canada; at The Library of Congress; and in numerous cities and at colleges and universities across the United States from Portland, Maine, to Portland, Oregon, and many cities in between. She's also discussed Austen on National Public Radio's (NPR) "The Diane Rehm Show," on the cable Biography Channel for the "Jane Austen" Bio, and in a variety of newspapers such as *The New York Times, Sunday Telegraph* (London), and *Philadelphia Inquirer.* Her refereed essays appear in *Studies in Philology, The Explicator, Studies in Short Fiction, The Dickens Quarterly, The George Herbert Journal, Notes and Queries,* and *Persuasions: The Journal of the Jane Austen Society of North America.* Joan also compiled the "Jane Austen Quotations Calendar," which comes out in 2007, for Rizzoli Publications and Universe Calendars (www.rizzoliusa.com).

Dedication

This book is dedicated to my mother, Jean Klingel, who always encouraged my dreams, and to my college professor, Professor Betty T. Bennett, who told me as a sophomore about graduate school and suggested that I go to one to become a college professor.

Author's Acknowledgments

I'd like to thank Janet Rosen of Sheree Bykofsky Associates for linking me to Wiley Publishing who was looking for someone to write this book. I am indebted to Stacy Kennedy, my acquisitions editor, who encouraged me to pursue the project; to Alissa Schwipps, my first project editor, whose patience and insights I've always appreciated; to Jennifer Connolly, my final project editor, whose generous help kept me going; to Carrie Burchfield, my copy editor, who assisted me with the *For Dummies* style; to my excellent students Dawn Pesut, Andrea Poss, and Margie Teals-Davis, who graciously assisted me with typing and research on the films; to Isabel Snowden, Jean Bowden, and Graeme Cottam for help with travel info for Austen visits; to Deirdre Le Faye for discussion on Tom Lefroy matters; and to Professor Laurie Kaplan, a great JASNA friend who served as the project's thoughtful and knowledgeable technical editor.

Publisher's Acknowledgments

We're proud of this book; please send us your comments through our Dummies online registration form located at www.dummies.com/register/.

Some of the people who helped bring this book to market include the following:

Acquisitions, Editorial, and Media Development

Project Editor: Jennifer Connolly

Acquisitions Editor: Stacy Kennedy

Copy Editor: Carrie Burchfield

Technical Editor: Laurie Kaplan

Editorial Manager: Michelle Hacker

Editorial Supervisor: Carmen Krikorian

Editorial Assistant: Hanna Scott

Cover Photo: © Rolinda Sharples/Getty

Cartoons: Rich Tennant (www.the5thwave.com)

Composition Services

Project Coordinator: Tera Knapp

Layout and Graphics: Claudia Bell, Andrea Dahl, Stephanie D. Jumper, Barry Offringa, Heather Ryan, Alicia South

Proofreaders: Laura Albert, Leeann Harney, Aptara

Indexer: Aptara

Publishing and Editorial for Consumer Dummies

Diane Graves Steele, Vice President and Publisher, Consumer Dummies

Joyce Pepple, Acquisitions Director, Consumer Dummies

Kristin A. Cocks, Product Development Director, Consumer Dummies

Michael Spring, Vice President and Publisher, Travel

Kelly Regan, Editorial Director, Travel

Publishing for Technology Dummies

Andy Cummings, Vice President and Publisher, Dummies Technology/General User

Composition Services

Gerry Fahey, Vice President of Production Services

Debbie Stailey, Director of Composition Services

Contents at a Glance

Table of Contents

Introduction

· ·

*J*ane Austen is everywhere! This early-19th-century, English, single author, who left only six completed novels, has inspired dozens of popular films, television miniseries, Broadway shows, and sequels to her books over the years and continues to do so. In fact, the use of her name alone appears in the titles of other books ranging from cookbooks to dating guides to modern romances, as well as shelves of academic literary criticism in college libraries. So even if you've never read a Jane Austen novel (and you don't need to in order to enjoy this book), her name probably rings a bell.

Austen is the greatest novelist in English. She mastered realism by presenting characters in familiar domestic situations. Her characters are recognizably human — they experience loneliness, love, frustration, humiliation, egoism, jealousy, confusion, and self-knowledge just like everyone does. So while her most-famous heroine, *Pride and Prejudice*'s Elizabeth Bennet, may be dressed in a column-shaped, high-waisted Regency muslin gown, Bennet experiences what many readers experience (gender aside): hurt pride, which leads to prejudices, which lead to misunderstandings and misjudgments, which lead to humiliation and finally to surprising insights about herself and others. This portrayal of a real person is why Hollywood's Amy Heckerling can take Austen's novel *Emma,* reset it in Beverly Hills in the late 1990s, call the character Cher, instead of Emma, and still be true to Austen's *Emma.* This is why Austen's novels are timeless and appeal to many different readers all seeking to get different meanings from Austen's words and all bringing different experiences to their reading.

About This Book

This book covers various aspects of Jane Austen's life, from her happy childhood in a supportive and intelligent family to her precocious youthful writing to her six completed novels that made her popular and admired. And in the great spirit of Austen's novels, I write this book for all readers, too. You don't need a degree in English to enjoy, or even love, Austen's novels. And you don't ever have to read any academic literary criticism to understand Austen's work. In fact, you can use this book in a number of ways:

✔ **To get some background info on the times and population about which Austen was writing:** Head to Chapter(s) 2, 5, 6, 9, 10, 11, and 12.

✔ **To supplement your appreciation of Jane Austen's novels:** Go to Chapters 2 and 4 for info on Austen's literary predecessors and to Chapter 16 for info on her literary descendents. Go to Chapters 5, 6, 11, and 12 to familiarize yourself with the manners, morals, and lifestyles of her times.

✔ **To determine why certain characters act the way they do:** For example, anyone who wonders why *Pride and Prejudice*'s Mrs. Bennet is so hysterically determined to get her daughters married needs to read the chapters on women's limited rights and marriage (Chapters 7 and 9), as well as the details of *primogeniture* (Chapter 10) — the eldest son's or living male relative's getting everything — and *entails* (Chapter 10) — documents limiting inheritance rights.

✔ **As a reference tool:** Although it's helpful to read some of the background material in Chapters 2 and 3 before you delve into some of the specifics about Austen's writing and times, you can jump around as you please, heading straight to the subject that most interests you.

The Table of Contents at the front of the book and the Index at the end are your best weapons to help you attack this book and find the info that you need or want.

Conventions Used in This Book

To make the text consistent and easier to understand, I use the following conventions:

✔ The full name *Jane Austen* is used occasionally throughout this book, but most frequently I refer to her as Austen. But when there are so many Austens in the picture that I need to clarify that Jane Austen did or said this or that, I refer to her with both her first and last name. When you see her as simply Jane, that is when I refer to her only when she was a child. Otherwise, I speak of her as Austen, just as I would speak of Shakespeare as Shakespeare, not William.

✔ When I feel Austen's voice is needed (and far better than mine I must say), I use her letters to allow "Jane" to be heard. *Jane Austen's Letters* (Oxford) were mostly edited by Deirdre Le Faye and published in 1995.

✔ When I quote from her novels, I cite volume and chapter number. So Volume 3, Chapter 11 of *Sense and Sensibility* is 3:11. If you're buying Austen's novels for the first time, even in paperback editions, be sure to buy an edition that comes in three volumes with new chapter numbering for each volume. ***Note:*** To clarify, the novel is in one paperback book but divided into three volumes within that book. (This was known in the 18th and 19th centuries as the three-decker novel!) The only two exceptions to this rule are *Northanger Abbey* and *Persuasion,* each of which contains only two volumes (but still contained within one book). If you're standing in a bookstore and you open an Austen novel to find that it has continuous chapter numbering from beginning to end, put it back and get one with the volumes.

While in Austen's day, her three-volume novels came out in three separate volumes, today all three volumes, say, for *Sense and Sensibility,* are in one volume. The exceptions are modern facsimile editions, where one novel, such as *Sense and Sensibility,* is printed in three separate volumes to imitate what the book looked like when it was published in Austen's day. But unless you're a meticulous collector of facsimile editions, buy the novel in *one* book. Thus, when you buy a paperback copy of *Sense and Sensibility,* flip through it and you'll find that all three volumes of the novel are in there in a handy, compact version.

✔ When I use a quotation from Austen's novels, I abbreviate the titles as follows: *Northanger Abbey* (NA), *Sense and Sensibility* (SS), *Pride and Prejudice* (PP), *Mansfield Park* (MP), *Emma* (E), and *Persuasion* (P). I refer to her incomplete works, *Sanditon* and *The Watsons,* as (S) and (W). *Lady Susan* is referred to as (LS). Any references to her youthful works, written as a child and teenager, have their full titles in quotation marks.

✔ All Web addresses and e-mail addresses appear in `monofont`. When this book was printed, some Web addresses may have needed to break across two lines of text. If that happened, rest assured that I haven't put in any extra characters (such as hyphens) to indicate the break. So, when using one of these Web addresses, just type in exactly what you see in this book, pretending as though the line break doesn't exist.

✔ New terms appear in *italics* and are closely followed by a straightforward definition or explanation.

What You're Not to Read

I've written this book so you can find information quickly and easily; when in doubt, check out the Table of Contents or Index. But I've also included extra information that you can skip over and still get the point of Jane Austen's life and art. This information includes

✔ **Text in sidebars:** Although interesting, sidebars aren't necessary to your understanding of the subject at hand. They're okay to skip — you won't miss anything you absolutely *need* to know. Sidebars appear in the gray boxes throughout the book.

✔ **Any text with a Technical Stuff icon:** You can also feel free to pass over anything with this icon (see the icon picture toward the end of this Introduction), which marks technical information — or as technical as reading literature ever gets. The information in this book doesn't compare with what's found in a book on rocket science, so there aren't many of these icons floating around.

✔ **Any text with the Trivia icon:** This icon flags the ins and outs of Austen info that you may not have known before. This info can be good to know if you're ever on a quiz show with Austen as a topic!

Foolish Assumptions

Every book has a specific audience in mind. In writing this book, I made some assumptions about you — the person holding this book right now (don't worry; I'm not watching you!)

✔ You've heard of Jane Austen, even if you've never read one of her novels.

✔ You're a reader of Jane Austen, but want more information about how her life and surroundings influenced her writing.

✔ You've read *Emma* twice but still don't get why it's such a big deal to Harriet Smith that Miss Woodhouse (whom Harriet never calls "Emma") shakes her hand.

✔ You're no longer confusing Jane Austen with *Jane Eyre*.

✔ You want to know more about Austen but want to find a lot of information in one reasonably priced and readable book.

✔ You've seen one or more Jane Austen–based films or TV miniseries and want to know if the novel is as good as or perhaps better than the screen version (the answer to that is that the novel is always better!).

✔ You're wondering why there are Jane Austen dating books, cookbooks, sequels, and books with her name in the title (instead of her name as an author).

✔ You want to know why Jane Austen is read and loved nearly two hundred years after her novels were first published and why she's both a popular icon on T-shirts and tea cups as well as the subject of highly serious academic study (and no, this book doesn't have a test at the end!).

How This Book Is Organized

This book is divided into five parts so you can easily find the information you want. Each part contains chapters relating to a particular topic about Austen and/or her world in relation to her writing. Use the Table of Contents or Index to help guide you to particular topics.

Part 1: Getting to Know Jane Austen, Lady and Novelist

This part speculates about the burning question on everyone's mind: "Why is Jane Austen everywhere today?" I discuss Austen's unique popularity, what she meant by using the byline "by a Lady" and what her contemporary readers expected from that byline. Then I talk about the ups, downs, and ups of her popularity, especially since World War I, when British soldiers read her novels in the trenches to remember why they were fighting for England.

Placing Austen in her world and what that means come next with explanations of the class system inherent in her day. I also explain who the gentry were (the gentry is a major term and focus in Austen's writing). She writes about ladies and gentlemen at a time when people were actually called that not just because they were polite. For details on Austen's life, head to Chapter 3, the biographical chapter. In Chapter 4, I discuss some of the key influences — literary and life — on Austen as a writer.

Part II: Austen Observes Ladies and Gentlemen

Austen's novels deal with the courtship of young ladies and gentlemen. This part explains her characters' behaviors when they dance, when they court, and when they decide to marry. "Dating" in Austen's day and in her novels was totally different from what we assume dating to mean nowadays. Finally, this part looks at some of Austen's wily and flirtatious females and seductive males — none of whom ever makes it to hero or heroine status.

Part III: Living Life in Jane's World

One of Austen's greatest skills is commenting on her world — socially, politically, and economically — with such subtlety that at times she doesn't call attention to her own dissatisfaction. But Austen wasn't only a writer of courtship novels; she was also a satirist — a satirist because she cared about what was going on in her world. One of Austen's most complex characters is *Mansfield Park*'s Mary Crawford, who says, "'I do not pretend to set people right, but I do see that they are often wrong'" (MP 1:5). The same could be said of Austen as she looks at her society. She comments on women's rights and wrongs, men's prerogatives, home life, manners, and morals and religion. Then she lets the reader draw conclusions.

Part IV: Enjoying Austen and Her Influence Today

While Chapter 1 deals with Austen's long-lasting appeal, this part offers some modest tutoring on reading Austen beyond readers liking her. You get information and evaluations of how and why her work has been adapted by other media (stage, screen, and television), and some suggestions about whom and how she influenced in terms of literature — both the serious stuff and the popular literature.

Part V: The Part of Tens

Every *For Dummies* book contains a Part of Tens. Here, you find some easy-to-reference information and my personal opinions about Austen's ten most memorable characters, the ten best Austenisms and what they mean, the ten best Austen places to visit and how to get there from London (or if you're at Jane Austen's House in Chawton, how to get to other nearby places from her house so you don't waste time and money going back to London and starting all over again!), and the ten best books (besides this one!) to read about Jane Austen and related topics.

Appendix

One last thing: If you want to check a date or historical event, the appendix provides a chronology of major events both in and around Austen's life.

Icons Used in This Book

This book uses different icons to point out different kinds of information:

This icon indicates memorable things regarding Austen, her work, and her times.

This icon alerts you to interesting, but not necessary, information. How technical can I get in a book about a novelist? And I'm not into fashionable literary jargon!

When you see this icon, you're alerted to fascinating and surprising information about Jane Austen.

Where to Go from Here

The only chronological chapter in this book is Chapter 3, which is about Austen's life. So you can move around in the book where you want. For example, if you want to find out more about the dancing that occurs in Jane Austen's novels, head to Chapter 5.

But if you want to place Austen's novels in the context of her times, start with Chapter 2 and move forward from there. And if you want to know why we're even publishing *Jane Austen For Dummies,* start with Chapter 1.

Part I

Getting to Know Jane Austen, Lady and Novelist

The 5th Wave　　By Rich Tennant

"Why is it when Jane Austen describes everyday events, it's literary genius, but as soon as I start talking about my gall bladder, your eyes glaze over?"

In this part . . .

An Austen blog claims that Austen is everywhere, and that's true. Austen's writings are studied and analyzed by scholars, yet also loved by ordinary folks — this part explores why. Chapter 1 speculates about why Austen's work, nearly 200 years old, continues to enchant and challenge readers. Granted, readers enjoy her novels for their charming heroines and good stories. But Austen also had certain expectations of her readers, readers who, like her, were a part of English society. Chapter 2 reveals the expectations of Austen as well as her contemporary readers by giving you a glimpse of what life was like in her world at her time. Chapter 3 gives you biographical info on Austen and her wonderfully witty and intelligent family who encouraged her writing from childhood on. And Chapter 4 discusses the writers she read who influenced her writing, as well as some of the persons she met who inspired her — after all, writers of fiction need to be somewhat voyeuristic!

Chapter 1

Introducing Jane Austen

In This Chapter

▶ Understanding why Jane Austen is so popular

▶ Examining Austen's critical reception

▶ Appreciating the many ways Austen is celebrated

*I*t's challenging to introduce someone who in a way "needs no introduction." Jane Austen isn't just the female writer from days gone by who writes love stories. Yet ironically (and Austen loved being ironic) she's the queen of the courtship novel and the originator of the *Regency romance* (courtship literature set specifically in England's Regency period, 1811–1820, during which Jane Austen actually lived, as opposed to authors today who write Regency romances, copying Jane Austen). She's a keen observer of her world (late-18th- and early-19th-century England), a subtle *satirist* (one who writes works that attempt to improve society or humanity), and a shrewd analyst of human behavior (a century before psychologists decided that observing human behavior was a reliable way to understand human beings).

Her small literary output of six major novels, two fragments of novels, about two dozen youthful pieces of fiction (later called her *Juvenilia*), and a *novella,* or short novel, is in inverse proportion to her popularity. Type her name into an Internet search engine, and within seconds you can explore nearly 13 million results. But reading a novel by Jane Austen is far more fun and enlightening than clicking through Internet Web sites. So, too, I hope, is reading this book.

Her novels are always selling. They inspire commercial films and television miniseries, as well as Broadway shows. Readers who can't get enough Austen buy dozens of sequels by authors who attempt to continue the events of her novels, which I believe she has already brought to closure. Her face, or the image that's believed to be an approximation of what she looked like, appears on tea mugs, T-shirts, computer mouse pads, and tote bags, prompting people who already own these items to buy more of the same items, but with Austen's face on them. Writers attach her name to dating guides, which always strikes me as ironic: Sure, guys have always been guys, but Austen's characters didn't date as we understand dating. (You can find more about how young people got to know each other in Chapter 6.) Writers also attach the Austen name to cookbooks, tea books, decorating books — anything writers and publishers can relate to Jane Austen. That's because she's hot stuff today.

Identifying the Lady Writer

The current blog that "Austen's everywhere" would undoubtedly shock Austen because during her most productive writing years (1809–1816), even her readers didn't know her name. Her first published novel, *Sense and Sensibility* (1811), appeared with the title page reading "By A Lady." And her second published novel was no help because *Pride and Prejudice* was published with the byline "By The Author Of *Sense and Sensibility*." You can guess how the bylines of her other novels read: "By The Author Of. . . ."

Do you see a pattern here? Being a lady meant more than being a courteous woman. A lady was a member of a social class called the *gentry*. This class owned land and was genteel. While some female (and note, I didn't write the word "lady" just now) novelists had their names in their bylines, they usually explained that they wrote because of financial distress — an ailing husband or wastrel husband with a brood of young children to support, and so forth. But a *lady* didn't write for money; she wrote for personal fulfillment — though Jane Austen enjoyed making the money, too! At the same time, the cryptic byline preserved her anonymity, which Austen desired. The byline identifying the author as a "Lady" also told the contemporary reader what to expect: a polite, well-mannered book with ladies and gentlemen as characters. And Austen didn't disappoint.

While Austen's identity as an author was leaking here and there, it was only after Austen's death at age 41 that the public finally discovered, through obituary notices, that Jane Austen was the "Lady" who wrote *Pride and Prejudice, Emma,* and so on. Her literary executor brother Henry prefaced a "Biographical Notice of the Author" with her name and the titles of her four previously published novels listed in the first paragraph to a two-volume set of her first and final completed novels, *Northanger Abbey* and *Persuasion,* which were published together in January 1818. Finally her reading public knew her name.

Keeping a Personal Record

Just because Austen published anonymously didn't mean she didn't care about her books. On the contrary, she wrote letters that served as her personal thoughts about her works. In her letters she specifically called *Sense and Sensibility* and *Pride and Prejudice* her children. She kept lists of friends' and family members' comments about *Mansfield Park* and *Emma*. She happily reported in letters to family members when a novel was going into a second edition or when someone praised one of her books. Austen also wrote to her naval brother Frank, who was at sea, to proudly report earning a total of £250 from her writing, £140 of that from *Sense and Sensibility,* which had sold out its first edition, plus getting the copyright to it back (Letter, July 3–6, 1813). (For info on Austen's writing and publishing, head to Chapter 3.)

But Jane Austen wasn't a publicity seeker. In another letter to Frank written the following October, she told him that the "Secret" of her novel-writing was spreading. What's worse, their talkative brother Henry, hearing *Pride and Prejudice* praised while in Scotland, blabbed in a moment of fraternal affection that his sister was the author. "I am trying to harden myself," she writes to Frank. Saying this, she means she's trying to strengthen herself intellectually and emotionally to endure any publicity that follows.

Getting Reviewed

Austen found herself reviewed by not only the critics of her time, but also her family, friends, and future readers.

Checking out the comments from the critics of her day

During her productive, publishing years, Austen preferred life in her native county of Hampshire, surrounded by a loving family and dear friends of both genders. But her books were starting to get noticed by the critics.

> ✔ In February of 1812, *The Critical Review* printed an unsigned *Sense and Sensibility* review, which praised the book for showing well-drawn, natural characters in realistic events and presenting instructive morality.

> ✔ The May 1812 *British Critic*'s reviewers were even more flattering of Austen's work, saying that they thought so highly of *Sense and Sensibility* that they wished they had room among the major articles in that issue to discuss the book. Commending the novel for having believable and consistent characters, the review recommends the novel to female readers for its conduct lessons.

While these aren't rave reviews, they were certainly encouraging to an author who'd been writing since her adolescence and was now finally published at age 36.

The same publications as abovereviewed *Pride and Prejudice* in 1813. This time the reviews more fully praised Austen's work. Calling it the best novel they had seen recently, the *British Critic*'s reviewer loved the way the author wrote the character of Elizabeth Bennet and praised the novel's energy. The review concludes by encouraging the author to continue writing — which she, in fact, was. Austen completed *Mansfield Park,* while her publishers issued second editions of *Sense and Sensibility* and *Pride and Prejudice* — all by the end of 1813. *The Critical Review* opened its evaluation of *Pride and Prejudice* noting that the author presented an entire family that interested the reader, and echoing the *British Critic* by calling this novel the best of any they'd recently seen that dealt with familiar, home life.

Commenting on the early reviewers

The two journals that reviewed Austen's first two published novels used the typical criteria for literary evaluation: the book's morality and probability. Today, Austen's work is considered realistic. That is, her characters represent human nature, which is always the same. Thus, the controlling Lady Catherine, the jealous Miss Bingley, and the manipulative Lucy Steele are all familiar because at one time or another, you've met someone who behaves just like they do. But Austen's characters aren't types; they're neither flat nor one dimensional. Each person is unique. So, while *Pride and Prejudice*'s Miss Bingley is jealous of Elizabeth, her jealousy manifests itself very differently from *Sense and Sensibility*'s Lucy Steele's jealousy of Elinor. Today Austen's novels may be called psychologically realistic, which is why readers of the present can relate and respond to characters created in 1812.

Getting the big review for Emma

While Austen's anonymous reviews in 1812 and 1813 were from respectable publications, getting a review of *Emma* by Sir Walter Scott, the most famous novelist and poet of the day, in the *Quarterly Review* (1815) was a real coup. Even though *Emma*'s publisher, John Murray, requested Scott to review the novel, Murray, the really big-time publisher of the period, did so because he knew he had something new, special, and unique in *Emma*.

Scott used the review to talk about the development of the novel, which was a comparatively new *genre* (form of writing). Noting that while recent novelists such as Henry Fielding *(Tom Jones)* and Fanny Burney *(Cecilia)* had been realistic and set characters in ordinary life, they still had extreme, unrealistic moments such as sword fights, dramatic illnesses, or the specter of poverty and ruin hanging over their characters. More recent novels had tried to be truer to everyday life, but they still found their excitement in well-worn ways such as heroic feats or excessive sentimentality. But then there was *Emma*. Scott praises *Emma*'s author (remember, he never heard the name "Jane Austen") for presenting original and spirited characters and actions while remaining within the boundaries of ordinary life — in other words, the book does not depend on heroic sword fights or dramatic illnesses to hold the reader's interest or arouse the reader's excitement. In accomplishing this, Scott said, the author of *Emma* was unique, or nearly so.

While there is much about Austen's work that Scott doesn't recognize, his high praise of *Emma* shows that he sees the writer's talent for doing something new in the novel form.

Glancing at later reviews

The important mid-19th-century critic, George Lewes, observed in 1859 that Austen's novels continued to be read, while many authors of her own day who surpassed her in reader-popularity had become neglected. (In other words, she was slowly becoming a classic in the sense that she was a writer whose works were outliving their author.) Lewes also praised Austen's artistic economy: She never wastes a word. But he also claimed that Austen was for the more "cultivated" reader. (La-de-dah!) This statement led to a certain snobbery because it suggested that you needed to be especially refined to read and appreciate Austen. By the later 19th century, some critics pointed to Austen's limitations, such as her not including showy scenes of great events, for which Scott had praised *Emma*. They complained, for example, that while she lived in the age of the Napoleonic Wars, she never really dealt with them. It would take later 20th-century critics to see all that is subtle in Austen: that she does deal with politics, social change, economics, and so forth. Likewise, modern critics fully recognized that perhaps Austen's greatest achievement was taking the incidents of everyday life, with which readers can identify, and treating them with humor, irony, sensitivity, and *élan* — a favorite word and desirable trait of Austen's meaning distinctive style or flair. Isn't her combination of realism, wit, and style the big reason that people still read Austen today?

Listening to Austen's current readers

Although Austen's novels inspire shelves of critical analysis by literary scholars, her main readership comprises people who don't pick up her novels professionally. They read Austen because they love her novels and find her work meaningful.

Between October and December 2003, BBC-2 television in England ran a reader's poll throughout the United Kingdom called "The Big Read." The goal was to determine the reading (and obviously TV-viewing) public's favorite 100 books of all time. Austen had three in the top 100, and she came in second overall with *Pride and Prejudice.* And what was number one? *The Lord of the Rings,* which was playing to box-office records in movie theaters just at the time of the poll. Now, I'm not saying "coincidence," but . . . to give you an idea of how the voting went, other titles in the top 21 were *Gone with the Wind, Winnie the Pooh,* and *The Wind in the Willows.* I'd speculate that of the five titles, Austen's is the only one that turns up regularly on college reading lists, unless you take a "kiddie lit" class. So regular folks who watch TV, enter polls, and read voted for *Pride and Prejudice.*

The following year, 2004, BBC-Radio 4's "Woman's Hour" ran a poll to determine the novel that women can relate to the most. Ninety-three percent of the respondents, presumably all female who listen to the show, named *Pride and Prejudice* (1813) as the book that not only maintains its relevance to them but also makes them proud to be women. (I love the Brits for doing these polls! They take reading seriously and popularly over there.)

The two polls point out that ordinary readers read Austen without being assigned it by a teacher — even though teachers and professors assign it for its literary value, too. Austen is a writer who inspires countless doctoral dissertations, as well as bumper stickers that proclaim, "I'd Rather Be Reading Jane Austen." Why? Keep reading to find out — and see if your reason for preferring to read Austen's works match those I suggest!

Getting Comfortable with "Jane"

For many Austen fans, reading one of her novels is taking an armchair vacation back to England in the early 1800s, known as the Regency. They see this period as a time of tea and etiquette. The Austen who conjures up such ideas may even inspire people to take up Regency dancing and Regency fashion. This is when Austen, the novelist, becomes to her readers "Jane," their friend. (For details on the Regency, go to Chapter 2.)

Hearing the friendly, welcoming narrator

Readers may love Dickens, but I never hear Dickens's fans calling him "Charles." Yet Austen fans easily call Austen "Jane." Jane is that wonderfully witty, wise, and well-spoken narrator who's a friendly and welcome companion as you read the novel.

For example, in Austen's early, frustrated attempt at getting published, the narrator in *Northanger Abbey* tells you of the marriage of the lovely and charming Eleanor Tilney to a presumably equally lovely and charming young Viscount, who never appears in the novel, but whose laundry lists do appear from Catherine Morland's snooping. Listen to the narrator:

> My own joy on the occasion is very sincere. . . . [Eleanor's] husband was really very deserving of her; independent of his peerage, his wealth, and his attachment, being to a precision the most charming young man in the world. *Any* further definition of his merits must be unnecessary; the most charming young man in the world is instantly before the imagination of us all. (NA 2:16)

The narrative voice you've just heard is attractive; it invited you into the book by saying "us all." Keep in mind the obvious — that it's only in a novel that you encounter a narrator in whose company you read for hundreds of pages. Can you point to a narrator who's more lovely and charming than Austen?

Hearing "Jane, the friend" become the witty, terse narrator

Sometimes, however, "Jane, the friend" gets a little terse, but never with the reader. Instead, Austen uses her characters as the butts of her jokes. For example, in *Persuasion,* she sets up a conversation between Mrs. Musgrove and Mrs. Croft. Mrs. Musgrove exclaims to her new friend, "'What a great traveler you must have been!'" and Mrs. Croft replies:

> Pretty well, ma'am, in the fifteen years of my marriage. I have crossed the Atlantic four times, and have been more than once to the East Indies and back again . . . But I never went beyond the Streights — and never was in the West Indies. We do not call Bermuda or Bahama, you know, the West Indies. (P 1:8)

Now "Jane," the narrative voice, enters: "Mrs. Musgrove had not a word to say in dissent; *she* could not accuse herself of having ever called them anything in the whole course of her life." So much for Mrs. Musgrove's knowledge of geography! Although this narrative voice sounds like it has quite a little bite to it, remember that in *Pride and Prejudice,* Mr. Bennet's delightful sarcasm has to come from someone. And that someone, of course, is Austen.

The sarcasm that appears in the narrator's quip about Mrs. Musgrove's ignorance of geography and throughout Mr. Bennet's speech first appeared coming from Austen, herself, in the first full publication of her remaining letters in 1932 under the editorship of R. W. Chapman. These letters reveal an Austen who could be cynical, nasty, cruel, and sarcastic. Here are some examples:

> Mrs. Hall, of Sherborne, was brought to bed yesterday of a dead child, some weeks before she expected, owing to a fright. I suppose she happened unawares to look at her husband. (October 27, 1798)

Poor Mr. Hall: He's now down in history as having such a frightening face that his wife's glancing at him caused her to immediately bear a premature dead baby.

She was only 22 when she wrote that. But she didn't soften with age. Here she is at 32:

> Only think of Mrs. Holder's being dead! — Poor woman, she has done the only thing in the world she could possibly do to make one cease to abuse her! (October 14, 1813)

Not only does Austen make jokes about dead babies, but about dead ladies, too! And even in speaking of Mrs. Holder's death, Austen shows neither kindness nor sympathy for the recently deceased.

Delivering the Hollywood goods

The same "Jane, the friend" who attracts armchair travelers to read and imaginatively travel back to "Jolly Olde England," also attracts filmgoers and television viewers and thus film and TV producers.

Austen's novels offer characters and events in lovely English settings with the people dressed in attractive costumes of a previous era. How comforting to get away from life's daily hassles with such well-dressed characters and charming settings! But her novels provide comfort in another way: by presenting logical stories, where all the loose ends are tied up at the end.

Logic is very comforting in an increasingly complex and often irrational world. Logic of this type — where everything is explained — is what makes television criminal investigation shows popular. Think about it: Character relationships on these shows are made secondary to solving the crime through the use of sophisticated scientific apparatus and forensic medical tests that uncover the guilty party. The solution of the crime returns temporary order to a disordered world. This is satisfying to the TV viewer.

What does a logically-presented story, with a beginning, a middle, and an end, do? It appeals to the natural human desire for answers, for security, for assuredness. And what does an Austen novel do? *Emma,* for example, provides a thought-provoking plot with a surprise at the end, rendered through interesting and articulate (except for poor Harriet!) characters, dressed in lovely Regency attire. A second reading reveals that all the clues to the surprise were there in the book all along. But in following Emma's thinking, which was wrong, you were led down the wrong path. And there's no need for even a finger-print test, though Frank Churchill's distracting Emma from her Weymouth questions by calling her attention to Ford's Store and going inside to buy new gloves certainly covers his romantic handiwork. The surprise is explained at the end of the novel. Emma was "duped." But she's wiser (or at least you hope so) and better for it.

Austen tells such a good story in *Pride and Prejudice,* where Elizabeth and Darcy begin as verbal sparring partners, that this novel, along with Shakespeare's Beatrice and Benedick of *Much Ado About Nothing*, provides the DNA for all those movies about antagonistic lovers who finally realize they belong together. Whether it's Tracy versus Hepburn or Jean Arthur versus Cary Grant, Austen's presence (and okay, Shakespeare's, too!) is hovering over the scene. And of course, Helen Fielding's *Bridget Jones* books and films are directly indebted to Austen's *Pride and Prejudice* — though Fielding's Bridget lacks all the self-possession, wit, and smarts of Elizabeth Bennet. Indeed, poor Bridget makes *Emma*'s Harriet Smith look like she's ready for rocket science!

Going back to Hollywood

Austen's attention to details makes her novels great sources for scripts. With her ear for conversational voice and the words she gives to a voice, the script writer can borrow pages of dialogue from the novel. Granted, the adapter must frequently add extra little scenes here and there to explain the story line. But the original dialogue is so right for the characters that it is not unusual to hear from the screen the exact, or almost the exact, words written in the novel.

Observing with Austen

Flip ahead to Chapter 3, and study Cassandra Austen's sketch of Jane Austen. Notice how sharp her eyes look and see her look of determination. But wait! There's something else. Her eyes aren't looking at the artist (her sister) but over her right shoulder. What could she be looking at or listening for? Whatever "it" is, "it" has her attention, and this portrait captures the astute observer that Jane Ascent was. No matter what she was doing, she was taking in all the little details of the world around her. Austen then used those details to masterfully write her novels, and those details make reading about her characters fun and insightful.

Writing dialogue and conversation

The observant Austen is a writer of witty dialogues that are the specialty of her novels. Each character's speech seems to match him or her perfectly. Austen puts those characters in conversations that you overhear in the reading. By doing this, she enables her readers to come to know the characters of her novels in the same way you know people in real life: by listening to what they say and picking up on how they say it. Sections of her novels read like little plays; for example, when Darcy, Bingley, Miss Bingley, and Elizabeth converse in *Pride and Prejudice* (PP 1:10), the pages of their conversation look almost like a script for a play. Even the first page of the same novel, with Mr. and Mrs. Bennet in dialogue, is filled with conversation, allowing the readers to make first impressions of the couple.

Putting Mark Twain and Jane Austen in the same paragraph

When Mark Twain was traveling on his lecture circuit, he was asked by a budding writer how to make characters seem real. Twain answered, "Don't say, 'The old lady screamed.' Just bring her on and let her scream." In other words, Twain was advocating writing dramatically, showing the story as much as possible through dialogue, instead of just telling the events. Austen does the same thing. So why should I warn you that I'm putting Twain and Austen in the same paragraph? Twain was notorious for making disparaging remarks about Jane Austen. For example, he said, "Every time I read *Pride and Prejudice,* I want to dig her up and hit her over the head with her own shin bone." *Every time* he reads *Pride and Prejudice*? What's wrong with this picture? How many times has he read the book, and if he hates it so much, why does he keep reading it? I would guess that, actually, Twain liked Austen. He made those nasty Austen jokes to annoy his great friend, the novelist William Dean Howells, who praised Austen's writing skills frequently and enthusiastically.

Having an ear for a character's voice

Showing the character in action, instead of telling the reader about the character, makes that character vivid. Austen lets her characters speak for themselves. For example, look at *Pride and Prejudice.* In the drawing room at Rosings, Elizabeth Bennet and Colonel Fitzwilliam are talking as they're seated at the pianoforte across the room from Lady Catherine. Lady Catherine abruptly interrupts them and calls out:

> What is it you are saying, Fitzwilliam? What is it you are talking of? What are you telling Miss Bennet? Let me hear what it is. [Fitzwilliam replies] We are talking of music, Madam. [Lady Catherine exclaims] Of music! Then pray, speak aloud. It is of all subjects my delight. I must have my share in the conversation, if you are speaking of music. There are few people in England, I suppose, who have a more true enjoyment of music than myself, or a better natural taste. If I had ever learnt, I should have been a great proficient. (PP 2:8)

Even if you've never opened *Pride and Prejudice,* you know what Lady Catherine is like from this brief excerpt of her speech: rude, arrogant, selfish, controlling, egocentric. You know all that without Austen saying "Lady Catherine is rude, arrogant, selfish, controlling, and egocentric." Austen shows Lady Catherine's personality through the action of the character.

Having an eye for details

Austen's observational skills and her eye for details give the readers characters who are as multifaceted as any of you are today. Here are a few examples:

- ✔ Within a page or two of *Emma,* the heroine can be helpful, conniving, and snide.

- ✔ In writing the jealous and ignorant Lucy Steele in *Sense and Sensibility,* Austen slips grammatical errors into her speech — not a lot, just enough to remind the reader that Lucy is no lady.

- ✔ Austen mentions Lucy's eyes several times, in order to suggest to the reader how closely and uncomfortably Lucy is scrutinizing Elinor.

Going onstage with Austen

Austen is everywhere — even off-Broadway. Chapter 15 provides details about the many screen and stage adaptations of Austen's novels, but at the time of this writing, a musical, "I Love You Because," very loosely based on *Pride and Prejudice,* is playing off-Broadway. The hero's name is Austin Bennet; his new girlfriend is Marcy Fitzwilliams (in the novel, the hero's full name is Fitzwilliam Darcy), and the girlfriend's best friend is Diana Bingley. The point of the show is advertised as "how to love someone because of his or her differences."

Tracing Austen's Popularity

Austen is now so popular that even non-novel readers recognize the name from seeing it in various, unexpected places like tea mugs and dating guides. Her immediate Regency siblings and her future Victorian collateral descendants would faint at seeing their sister and aunt depicted like this. For they presented her as a near saint. But Austen has also stepped off the pedestal into the trenches of World War I and classrooms ranging from high school to post-doctoral school seminars.

Starting the Saint Jane myth

When Henry Austen wrote his biography of his sister for the posthumous publications of *Northanger Abbey* and *Persuasion,* he presented a woman ready for sainthood:

> Faultless herself, as nearly as human nature can be, she always sought, in the faults of others, something to excuse, to forgive or forget. Where extenuation was impossible, she had a sure refuge in silence. She never uttered either a hasty, a silly, or a severe expression . . . She was thoroughly religious and devout; fearful of giving offence to God, and incapable of feeling it toward any fellow creature. . . .

Henry's notice, of course, is understandably influenced by his feelings of loss over his 41-year-old sister. Henry also had recently become a clergyman of the Anglican Evangelical persuasion, so this recent career move certainly affected his decision to write of his sister's religious devotion.

But imagine the shock when the edition of her letters came out in 1932. Here's another Austen one-liner from a letter that completely undercuts Henry's "incapable of feeling offence" line: "I do not want people to be very agreeable, as it saves me the trouble of liking them a great deal" (Letter, December 24, 1798). Yet 1932 was still a long way from 1818 when Henry wrote the biographical notice. And so the Austens had time to perpetuate "Saint Jane."

Victorianizing Jane Austen

Austen's next biographer was a beloved nephew, James Edward Austen-Leigh. By the time he published *A Memoir of Jane Austen* in December of 1869 (though dated as 1870 on the title page), he was a mutton-chopped Victorian. And so it's not surprising that he presented this type of Aunt Jane to the world with the help of his two sisters; all three of them, the children of Jane Austen's eldest brother James, knew their aunt well and still remembered her.

The *Memoir* opens by saying that Austen's life was "singularly barren" of events. This portrayal doesn't look too promising! And because the Victorian mindset is one of silence and coverup, the *Memoir* proceeds accordingly. Not that Austen has anything to hide. But the *Memoir* presents Aunt Jane as a simple woman who had "genius" and lived a happy Christian life without complexity. The sarcasm, cynicism, and satire that you've seen in her letters and even seen in some of her fiction are all missing. Nevertheless, the *Memoir* satisfied the appetites of a new generation of Austen readers for information on the author's life. And it boosted Austen's popularity!

Taking Austen to the trenches

In 1894, the English critic George Saintsbury coined the word "Janeite" to mean an enthusiastic admirer of Austen's works. But Rudyard Kipling popularized the term in a short story called "The Janeites," first published in 1924. Written in heavy cockney slang, the story isn't the easiest text in the world to read. But it's worth the effort. Here's the story in summary:

> Soon after WWI, the story's narrator goes to a Masonic lodge on cleaning day. One of the cleaners is Humberstall who'd been wounded in the head but who still returned to the western front as assistant mess waiter for his old Heavy Artillery platoon. A simple and uneducated man, he tries to explain how his boss, the senior mess waiter, was able to talk with the university-educated officers on equal ground because of their shared love of Jane Austen's novels. Humberstall is coached on the novels and is led to think that the Austen readers, or Janeites, are all members of a Masonic-like secret society. They scratch the names of Austen characters on the guns. Then all but Humberstall are killed by a hail of gunfire. When he

quotes *Emma* to a nurse, another secret Janeite, she saves his life by getting him on the hospital train back to England. Humberstall still reads Austen's novels as they remind him of his comrades back in the trenches. "There's no one to match Jane when you're in a tight place," he says, noting the comfort her novels provide. Yet her comfort isn't all healing, for as the other Masonic Lodge cleaner notes, Humberstall's mother has to come and take him home from the Lodge because he gets "fits."

WWI soldiers agreed that while they were overseas in the war, reading Austen was an effective mental escape from gas masks and bayonets. The Army Medical Corps advised shell-shocked soldiers to read Austen for the books' soothing effects. Supposedly, Mr. and Mrs. Rudyard Kipling found comfort in Austen's novels, which they read to each other after their son was killed in 1914 in WWI.

Taking Austen to school

Austen's novels became continuously available since 1833, when England's Bentley Standard Novel Series produced affordable editions of her works. In 1923, R. W. Chapman's edition of Austen's novels was published by Oxford University Press. This scholarly edition is one of the earliest of the works of any English novelist. While Austen had readership popularity before, she now had academic distinction. Scholars began to pay serious attention to her novels, proceeding with literary analyses. Austen's use of irony was especially appealing to American academic critics writing just after WWII because analyzing her verbal irony made use of a popular new critical approach that treated the text as an object in itself and studied that text in terms of how the author used language.

A study in 1997–1998 by the National Association of Scholars showed that in the 1964–1965 academic year, 25 liberal arts colleges surveyed in the United States still had no courses that cited Jane Austen in their catalogs. When those same schools were surveyed in the 1997–1998 academic year, however, Austen had moved into third place, just behind those old standbys Shakespeare and Chaucer. Austen's appearance in college catalogs' course descriptions is likely the result of the Women's Movement and the expansion of the *canon* (literary texts that authorities consider as the best representatives of their times). For along with Austen on the 1997–1998 lists were Virginia Woolf, Toni Morrison, Emily Dickinson, George Eliot, and Zora Neale Hurston. In the earlier list, no female writers were listed.

Translating Austen from English

Austen's novels began to be translated as early as 1813, with *Pride and Prejudice* going into French during the same year the book appeared in England. Within 11 years, all of her novels were available in French. But France hasn't quite caught the Austen craze like the United States and England. And one reason may be that the French found some of her characters alien to their culture. For example, the French found Elizabeth's behavior impertinent and unladylike. So in the French translations of *Pride and Prejudice,* the French read about a different Elizabeth Bennet than their English-speaking counterparts. Her character was changed. Be that as it may, Austen's novels have since been translated into Swedish, German, Russian, Arabic, Dutch, Greek, Hebrew, Japanese, Chinese, Italian, Persian, Polish, and numerous other languages. But like the French suppression of Elizabeth's sassiness, the translations may also make the female characters more in tune with the local culture. If you're interested in tracing translations, check out David Gilson's *A Bibliography of Jane Austen* (Winchester, 1997).

Becoming Today's Janeite

In 1940, the Jane Austen society of the UK was formed; sister societies appeared as The Jane Austen Society of North America (1979) and The Jane Austen Society of Australia (1988), as well as societies in non-English-speaking countries. The study of the so-called "cult" of Jane has become fashionable among academics who sometimes criticize the societies. But most members are not cult-creatures. They simply enjoy getting together to discuss and learn about Jane Austen. Yes, some of our members dress in Regency attire, but that's not a requirement of membership. Dressing up (or not!) and sipping tea are little harmless delights and escapes from the pressures of everyday life.

The Jane Austen Society of North America (JASNA), a nonprofit organization, can be accessed via the Internet at www.jasna.org. Over 60 regional groups offer periodic meetings, book groups, and related activities around the United States and Canada. Membership fees are reasonable and cover the production and mailing of three 32-page newsletters annually and an annual journal of Austen-related articles. The Society is run by volunteers, with the exception of a professional data bank manager. Students are welcome and have a reduced membership fee.

Jane Austen is so popular today that there are many ways to enjoy her after you've read and re-read the books and seen the films and television series:

- ✔ Take one of the many Jane Austen tours through Hampshire, England, which advertises itself as "Jane Austen Country."

- ✔ Visit the house in Chawton where Austen lived for the final eight years of her life. It's now a museum run by the Jane Austen Memorial Trust. Chapter 19 provides instructions on how to get there, plus its Web address.

- ✔ Buy or borrow from a library *The Jane Austen Cookbook* and create with friends and family a complete Jane Austen meal. Chapter 18 tells you about *The Jane Austen Cookbook*.

- ✔ Start a book club devoted to Jane Austen, and after you've read all of Austen, read Karen Joy Fowler's novel, *The Jane Austen Book Club*.

- ✔ As you read other novels, keep a list of how many times Jane Austen or one of her novels is mentioned casually. I was reading a mystery book last week in which one of the detectives saw an Austen novel in a room. I mentioned it to a friend who said she had noticed Austen's name popping up in many other novels.

- ✔ Encourage your school or local theater group to do a play based on an Austen novel. Chapter 15 gives you a start on finding such plays. Or have a class or another group write their own play. It can even be performed without costumes and settings in a reader's theater format.

- ✔ In 2005, Chicago picked *Pride and Prejudice* for its "One City, One Book" event. As President of the Jane Austen Society of North America, I had the privilege of speaking at the Chicago Public Library about Austen and the novel. Debates, discussions, and other events occurred in venues all over the city. Libraries offered the novel in numerous translations. Encourage your local leaders to do "One City, One Book," using an Austen novel.

- ✔ Schools have Jane Austen Days, when classes study the novels and students prepare food from Austen's time and dress in period costume.

Indeed, you may seem to be in a Jane Austen *daze,* but that's not so bad, is it?

Chapter 2

Visiting Jane Austen's Georgian World

*T*his chapter places Jane Austen in her historical context — Georgian England; her political context — Tory; and her social and economic context — the gentry. In so doing, the explanation also talks about the Georgian class system and the ongoing, real-world events that Austen expected her contemporary readers to understand immediately: Napoleon and the French Revolution, as well as the slavery issue. For Austen fans, perhaps the most important event in her lifetime was the development of the novel as a literary form or genre. Get those reading glasses on and prepare to immerse yourself in the current events of Jane Austen's day. Don't worry; there won't be a quiz at the end!

Asserting Austen's Georgian-ness

Because of the charm of her plots, their setting in merry old England, and the Victorian-styled costumes and 1850 setting used in the first film adaptation of *Pride and Prejudice* in 1940 (for more on screen adaptations of Austen's novels, see Chapter 15), you may view Austen as Victorian. (This is not your fault: The 1940 film misled you!) But Jane Austen lived between 1775 and 1817, and her novels came out between 1813 and 1818, the year after her death, which places her and her work in the Georgian period of English history. Figure 2-1 gives you a picture of Jane Austen's England.

Figure 2-1:
Jane
Austen's
England.

For over 100 years (from 1714 to 1830) the four kings of England were all named George, suggesting their parents had little imagination. So this was known as — guess what? — the Georgian period in British history. This period lasted until 1837 when Victoria became queen, which then began the Victorian era. (There was a brief stint with a king named William from 1830 to 1837, but the period was still named the Georgian period. Poor guy didn't even get a period named after him: the Willie period!) In Austen's lifetime, England's monarchs were George III — the king who lost the American colonies — and his eldest son, George, the Prince of Wales, who reigned as the father's regent or substitute when George III was severely ill.

Besides living when the two Georges, king and regent, reigned, Austen's work and personality display the satire, candor, and openness of the Georgian mindset — the prim and prissy days of the Victorian era came just two decades after Austen's death in 1817.

Examining Austen's Georgian satire

Like Fanny Burney, an earlier Georgian novelist whom Jane Austen admired, Austen writes about young women entering society and the marriage mart. (For more on ladies' "coming out," see Chapter 6, and for more on Burney's influence on Austen, head to Chapter 4.) Austen's novels also reflect the humorous satire and irony of Henry Fielding, whose contributions to the new novel form or *genre* are discussed in Chapter 4. *Satire* is a type of literature that aims to correct folly, vice, and stupidity, frequently through ridicule.

Understanding King George III: Tree-hugger or mad man?

George III was deemed to be mad: He was addressing trees as other European monarchs and displaying other demented behaviors. Today, scientists believe he suffered not from a mental illness, but from a metabolic one: *porphyria*, a rare disease caused by a malfunction in the production of hemoglobin. So it turns out that George III was neither crazy nor a tree lover.

George's condition caused chemicals called porphyrins to accumulate in the brain and damage it, along with the liver and skin (it itches), as well as the digestive and nervous systems. Symptoms, such as vomiting and various psychological disorders that mimic madness, can be triggered by the administration of certain drugs, such as the arsenic that was once given to George III to treat his mysterious illness. But what did the medical profession know in 1811? Frequently, doctors did more harm than good. So with his father running around in the park at Windsor Castle talking to trees, the Prince of Wales became the prince regent. In 1820 when George III died, the prince regent became King George IV.

To find out more about George III's illness and the Regency in a highly entertaining way, rent the 1994 film, *The Madness of King George*, directed by the great British showman Nicholas Hytner, and written by Alan Bennett, who also wrote the 1991 play, *The Madness of George III*, on which his film script is based.

Austen uses satire, a keynote of Georgian literature, a lot. For example, she ridiculed the patronage system that gave church ministries to sometimes undeserving, unsympathetic men through *Pride and Prejudice*'s stupid, lumbering Mr. Collins. He's full of himself and usually behaves like a pompous fool — unless he behaves like an agent of punishment disguised as a Christian clergyman. Austen shows Collins's lack of ministerial qualities just as Fielding showed Thwackum's in *Tom Jones*. (Thwackum, a clergyman, is excessively prone to corporal punishment: He likes to smack 'em — thus, Thwackum!) In Austen's novel, Collins's advice to Mr. Bennet that he "throw-off [his] unworthy child from [his] affection forever" (referring to Lydia, who has lived out-of-wedlock with Wickham), "leave her to reap the fruits of her own heinous offence" (meaning, cast her off or even let her become a whore!), and "never . . . admit [her] into [his] sight" again, leads Mr. Bennet to remark sarcastically, "'That is his notion of Christian forgiveness!'" (PP 3:6, 15).

Preferring candor over prudishness

In her personal life, Jane Austen was no prude. But neither was she indecent in speech — which, let's face it, is all too common today — nor in behavior. She was simply a realist, and with her Georgian openness, she acknowledged life as it was. For example, she reported to her sister that she was "disgusted" by the outright "indelicacies," such as those she saw in the first 20 pages of a French novel, *Alphonsine* (Letter, January 7, 1807). In this book a 15-year-old male character refuses to consummate his marriage to the girl he has married and then discovers that his wife has been sleeping with her 18-year-old page. But Austen wasn't too prim to include in *Mansfield Park* a vulgar joke about sodomy to emphasize the less-than-ladylike character of its teller Mary Crawford. Replying to a query about her orphaned youth, Mary explains her "acquaintance with the navy" through living with her uncle, Admiral Crawford:

> Certainly, my home at my uncle's brought me
> acquainted with a circle of admirals. Of *Rears,* and
> *Vices,* I saw enough. Now, do not be suspecting me
> of a pun, I entreat. (MP 1:6)

Austen has Mary make the remark as an example of the bad "education" that hero and heroine Edmund and Fanny ascribe to her upbringing — an upbringing that particularly pains the highly moral clergyman-to-be Edmund, who is in love with this "remarkably pretty" and lively young woman (MP 1:4).

A Victorian prude would never include a joke like that, but with two brothers serving as officers in the Royal Navy, Austen undoubtedly heard of the sodomy prevalent among a ship full of men sailing around the oceans for months at a time. Having read and reread Fielding's *Tom Jones* (1749), a bawdy novel with sex treated as a hearty roll in the hay without any disgust, Austen writes the sodomy joke to tell her readers something about Mary. (For more info on Fielding, see Chapter 4.) Likewise, Austen's novels also include other taboo topics of her day:

✔ Seduced young women

✔ Out-of-wedlock pregnancies

✔ Couples who live together out of wedlock

✔ Adulterers

Austen is a social realist, like Fielding, and she presents the temper, follies, and problems of the times in her fiction.

Surveying the Political Landscape

While Austen didn't intend her novels to be read as political or social reform texts, she was writing for her contemporary readers who, she naturally assumed, would know the news and culture of their times, which provide the settings of her work. She includes contemporary events as background to her novels without commenting on them overtly. This section clues you in on what Austen was assuming her readers understood about their own day, just as we, today, as readers would understand allusions to current events in contemporary novels.

Discerning Tories from Whigs

By the time that Jane Austen was in her late teens, England was at war with France under Prime Minister William Pitt, the Younger (1759–1806), who led the new Tory Party (the party which her family supported), representing land-owning country gentlemen and the establishment (the monarchy and the Church of England). With the war lasting until 1815, the social conservative or Tory view upheld patriotism and honor. And unlike the Tories of the early eighteenth century, these Tories were now strongly anti–Roman Catholic. The new, revived Whig Party, led by Charles James Fox (1749–1806), represented the reformers, supporting religious dissent (the nonconformists), and those wanting electoral and parliamentary change. Keep in mind that in Austen's day, only rich landowners could vote.

Anticipating trouble at home and across the channel

The combined forces of England, Holland, Belgium, and Prussia were at war with Napoleon for over 20 years. Because England was just a short boat trip across the English Channel from France, the British feared invasion on its southern shore. In addition to physical invasion, the English landowners and government cast a watchful eye and ear at the revolutionary ideas that were percolating during the French Revolution, which began in 1798. While Austen's novels never show soldiers at war or people protesting for political rights, they do show that she was well aware of these concerns.

Fearing French invasion

New fears arose in England with the rise of Napoleon Bonaparte. Napoleon threw out France's republican government and declared himself First Consul in 1799. Insisting that he wanted peace, France and England signed the Treaty of Amiens in 1802. Consequently, troops in the British army, marines, and navy disbanded. Even Jane Austen's naval brother Frank went on half-pay, meaning he was removed from his ship and given only half his salary. But Napoleon, though supposedly at peace, used this period to rebuild his forces, especially the French navy, and then declared war again in 1803. With Napoleon seeking to take over the world, in general, and England in particular, the British feared French invasion. Hence, the presence of the militia in *Pride and Prejudice,* which brings the ne'er-do-well character, George Wickham, on the scene. Wickham and the militia in which he serves move to Brighton, from where he and Lydia Bennet run off together. Austen uses the Brighton location for three reasons:

1. Brighton, a town on the southern coast, making it vulnerable to French invasion, is a logical place to send the novel's militia.

2. Brighton was a risqué place, full of sailors and militiamen who were looking for a "good time" while off duty.

3. Brighton was the prince regent's seaside home, The Prince's Royal Pavilion, which looks with its cream-puff façade like the Indian Taj Mahal, and the prince regent was known for his sexual escapades.

So what better place for Austen to send the morally careless Lydia when she flees with Wickham to live with him out of wedlock? Austen's contemporary readers knew all this — just as our radar today would perk up about a wild and over-sexed (Lydia's "high animal spirits," meaning both energy and physicality, PP 1:9) young female character in a novel who heads to Las Vegas.

Jane Austen had a personal knowledge of the French Revolution from its beginnings: Her beautiful and glamorous older cousin Elizabeth (called "Eliza") married a French count in 1781 who was guillotined in 1794. Eliza fled Paris for England and spent time at Steventon with her uncle, George Austen, and his family. In 1797, she married Jane's brother Henry, who was ten years her junior. (For more on cousin Eliza, see Chapter 3.)

Reeling from revolution and riots at home

Even before the threat of Napoleon, England was troubled by fears of revolution and riot at home during Austen's teenage years and early twenties:

- **The Gordon Riots:** On June 2, 1780, about 50,000 people, carrying signs saying "No Popery," marched on Parliament in opposition to the Roman Catholic Relief Act of 1778. This act removed some of the more extreme discriminatory measures officially taken against Catholics, especially requiring military recruits to swear an oath to the Church of England. The number of rioters grew as the original crowd headed to Parliament. The rioters tried to force their way into the House of Commons, virtually destroyed Newgate Prison, attacked the Bank of England, and destroyed many Roman Catholic churches. The army was dispatched on June 7, and nearly 300 rioters were killed. Austen may be referring to the Gordon Riots in *Northanger Abbey* (1:14), when Henry Tilney mentions a mob in St. George's Fields, which was, in fact, an assembly point for the Gordon Rioters. She might also have been thinking of the anti-government riots that were also held in St. George's Fields in January, 1795, discussed in the next bullet.

- **London Riots in 1795, organized by the London Corresponding Society (LCS):** Comprised mainly of small craftsmen (shoemakers, tailors, clockmakers, and so on) in 1792, this Society was founded to oppose the war with France, fight hunger, and compel parliamentary reform. In 1795, LCS members, joined by other workers, stoned the coach of George III as he went to open Parliament. At other times, the Society's meetings drew thousands of members of the working class. This frightened the government and led to the passage of Acts forbidding Seditious Meetings. Knowledge of meetings like the Gordon Riots and the LCS activities frightens Eleanor Tilney, who has a brother in the army. So Eleanor misunderstands Catherine Morland's allusion to news from London about events "'uncommonly dreadful'" (NA 1:14). Eleanor thinks Catherine is speaking of political riots, but Catherine actually is referring to the publication of a new horror novel!

- **The Spithead and Nore Naval Mutinies of 1797:** First at Spithead (April–May), a port near Portsmouth, England, and then at Nore (May), in the Thames Estuary, sailors mutinied over their terrible living conditions on board ship and low pay, which was not keeping pace with the high inflation rates of the late 18th century. These mutinies frightened the government and ruling class because England's main fighting force was the Royal Navy, and England was at war with France. Unfortunately, we have no letters by Austen for the year 1797. But with two brothers serving as navy officers at this time, she was undoubtedly concerned that the seamen's anger would spread from the ports to the ships — which actually occurred in the West Indies, off the Cape of Good Hope, and off the Irish coast. The Spithead Mutiny was resolved with the Admiralty's pardoning the crews and agreeing to pay raises and better living conditions on ship. But after the Spithead resolution, the government was in no mood to make further conciliations to the Nore mutineers, who had blocked the London port. Ultimately, the mutiny failed, because of deserters and lack of food. But this was a nervous time for Austen and her countrymen regarding the Royal Navy and the war with France.

✔ In 1794, Parliament suspended Habeas Corpus, which meant that people could be jailed without being officially charged. Government suppression was so successful that the radicals were silenced.

Ruling the waves with the Royal Navy

Napoleon was winning on land because of the vast superiority of the French Army. But when it came to the seas, England ruled. The superiority of the British navy was shown as they ruined Napoleon's plans by chasing and attacking his ships. The Battle of Trafalgar clinched the British victory on October 21, 1805.

Jane Austen's brother Frank was terribly disappointed to miss the action at Trafalgar. Having chased the French ships in the West Indies, Frank Austen's ship, the *Canopus,* was ordered to Gibraltar and then Malta. His ship was unable to reach Trafalgar in time for the battle.

With two of her brothers, Frank and Charles, serving in the Royal Navy, Austen pays homage to naval officers in her final novel, *Persuasion*. She praises both the professional skills and the personal loyalty of navy men in the characters of Admiral Croft and Captains Wentworth and Harville.

Protecting the home front (and dancing a lot) in the militia

Between 1797 and 1805, England faced serious danger that France would invade British soil. This fear created a need to expand England's homeland defense force, the militia, and at least 300,000 men stepped up to serve. Henry Austen, another of Jane's brothers, was one of them: He joined the Oxfordshire Militia as a lieutenant in 1793 and remained in it until 1800.

Austen's most famous militia is the –shire that arrived in Meryton and then headed to Brighton in *Pride and Prejudice* (1:15). This militia's fighting skills are questionable because instead of performing military exercises, the troops spend their time off walking around Meryton and talking to young women, attending parties, or dancing, all while showing off attractive red coats. Obviously, they have no fear of a French invasion. Or maybe they'll challenge the French to a dance contest!

By the way, if you're wondering about the –shire militia in *Pride and Prejudice,* Austen's using a dash before the term "shire," which means county or borough (also "country," which meant the same thing), such as Hertfordshire, was an early convention of the novel to give the illusion that the novelist was writing about a real militia; this added to what critics call the "verisimilitude" of the novel. In plain English, the novel appears to be a true story.

Sugaring tea from the slave trade

Most of us probably think of England as a nation of tea drinkers, politely asking, "One lump or two?" In Austen's day, that sugar came from the West Indies as a result of slavery's Transatlantic Trade Triangle, which means:

- ✔ Goods were shipped from British ports to the west coast of Africa, where they were exchanged for slaves.

- ✔ The slaves were taken to the New World (a horrid ocean journey called The Middle Passage).

- ✔ Slaves were then traded for agricultural goods like cotton and sugar that went back to England.

Jane Austen had personal connections with folks who in one way or another had involvement in this Triangle. She also lived in the early age of Abolition. And while Austen certainly wasn't writing in the vein of the future famous American anti-slavery novel, *Uncle Tom's Cabin* (1852), she either refers directly to slavery or alludes to it in her fiction with great disapproval.

Austen was familiar with the slave trade and slave workers on plantations in British colonies through ways that are far more personal than reading about slavery and abolition in books and newspapers:

1. Her father was a trustee for a plantation in Antigua owned by his old classmate at Oxford, James Nibbs, who was also the godfather of Mr. Austen's eldest son, James (possibly named for James Nibbs?).

Mr. Nibbs's eldest son, George (possibly named for Jane's father, George Austen?), became a student at Mr. Austen's school run at the Steventon Rectory, the Austens' home, which even had a portrait of Mr. Nibbs hanging on a wall (Letter, January 3–5, 1801). Thus, plantation talk would have been common when Jane Austen was growing up. No wonder in *Mansfield Park,* she places Sir Thomas Bertram's plantation in — of all the locations in the West Indies — Antigua.

2. Her mother's brother's wife (Jane's aunt, Jane Cholmeley Leigh-Perrot) was from a family that held investments in Barbados, another slave-holding location.

3. Her younger brother, Charles, spent several years of his Royal Naval career in the Americas, searching ships and stopping trade between France and the Americas. While serving in the West Indies, a group of islands, he married the daughter of a former attorney general of Bermuda (1807). Charles certainly was an eyewitness to slavery during this period.

4. Her favorite poet, William Cowper, was active as an Abolitionist and wrote two important anti-slavery poems that she would surely have known, "The Negro's Complaint" (1778) and "Pity for Poor Africans" (1787).

Austen was horrified by the slave trade, and she shows it in several places in her novels:

✔ In *Emma,* she has Jane Fairfax, who is facing life as a governess, refer to offices in London that place young women in governess jobs as places that sell "'not quite . . . human flesh — but . . . human intellect'" (E 2:17).

✔ Again in *Emma,* she has the dreadful Mrs. Elton come from a merchant family in Bristol, which was a major port for the slave Triangle. Thus, Austen suggests that Mrs. Elton's money and the wealth of her brother-in-law, who lives near Bristol, are tainted from slavery. This is a subtle and clever way for Austen to degrade both the boastful Mrs. Elton and her pride in her in-laws' riches.

✔ As already noted, Sir Thomas of *Mansfield Park* has a plantation in Antigua. The moral illness of many of the Bertrams can be connected to their slave-holding wealth.

So Jane Austen wrote with a full social awareness of slavery. She shows her anger about it in a ladylike, subtle way that nevertheless should register with her readers. While Jane Austen does not appear in any list of Abolitionist writers, it is intriguing to speculate that perhaps she should be!

Understanding the Class System

Jane Austen's England was class oriented, dating back hundreds of years. Austen made sure to put each of her characters in a social and economic place. She also saw that people of a lower class wanted to move to a higher one, which was something new in her day. Understanding the class system deepens your insight into Austen's novels.

Recognizing class

Austen shows in her novels a clear understanding and even support of a need for change: longtime, careless, wealthy landowners fell down on the job, and the new business class rose as they were needed in society. Class notwithstanding, women were virtually nothing in a legal or economic sense. But in terms of class, one woman could rank higher than another.

Identifying the nobility

The social pyramid of Jane Austen's day followed a certain order:

- Royal Family
  - King
  - Queen
  - Prince(s)
  - Princess(es)
- Nobility or Aristocracy (the hereditary peers of the realm)
  - Dukes
  - Marquises
  - Earls
  - Viscounts
  - Barons

The men of nobility sat in the House of Lords. So when a man is addressed as a Lord, he's a peer or noble or the son of a peer. A peer's daughters are Lady First Name. So in *Pride and Prejudice,* Lady Catherine de Bourgh is called "Lady Catherine" because her father was one of the three higher ranks of peers: a duke, marquis, or earl. (Later, we learn that her brother is an earl, so their father must have been an earl, too [PP 2:10].)While she is the widow of Sir Lewis de Bourgh, he was only a knight, and knights are commoners and not noble. So rather than being merely Lady de Bourgh, which is what a knight's wife is called (using the husband's last name), she shows her higher rank as Lady Catherine. Austen's readers of her day would know immediately that Lady First Name comes from the nobility — unlike Lady Lucas, in the same novel, who is only the wife of a lowly knight. (You can find more on the "Ladies" a little later in this section.)

Unless the title was a life peerage, which meant it died with the holder, the title was hereditary, meaning it went to the peer's eldest son. If the peer had no male children, the title went to his eldest brother. If he was an only child, the closest and oldest male relative got the title and accompanying estate. A lady who married a peer assumed his noble rank. In *Persuasion,* Austen introduces the Dowager Viscountess Dalrymple. She's a Dowager because she's a widow. And her late husband was Viscount Dalrymple. Their unmarried daughter is the Honourable Miss Carteret. Carteret is the family name; Dalrymple is the title name.

Austen comments on the aristocracy (nobility) by the way she treats them in her novels. Lady Catherine is rude, bossy, and controlling; her behavior even embarrasses her nephew, Darcy (PP 2:8). The Dowager Viscount Dalrymple is snobby and has no direct speech; her daughter never says a word. This is Austen's way of showing a useless and vulgar or bland effete aristocracy.

Separating aristocrats from commoners

If Lady Catherine is called by her first name, preceded by the word "Lady," then why are Lady Lucas in *Pride and Prejudice,* Lady Russell and Lady Elliot in *Persuasion,* and Lady Bertram in *Mansfield Park* called Lady, but with their last names? Lady Catherine, as explained earlier, takes her nobility from her father, Earl Fitzwilliam, and so she gets to call herself, as an earl's daughter, Lady Catherine. Likewise, her sister, Darcy's mother, is called "Lady Anne," and not Mrs. Darcy, to show her noble paternal lineage (PP 1:16). But all of the other women called "Lady Last Name" are the wives of either knights or baronets. Knights and baronets aren't part of the nobility or aristocracy; they're *commoners.* Sir Thomas Bertram and Sir William Elliot are baronets, abbreviated Bart., or Bt.

A baronet's title is hereditary, but baronet is the newest titled rank, having been invented by King James I in 1611, in order to raise money: In his day, one paid dues to be a baronet. The titles of knights weren't hereditary, and a knighthood was granted to a gentleman for special services rendered to the Crown — and still is.

Sir William Lucas was originally just plain Mr. Lucas, a merchant in the town of Meryton and its mayor. In Volume 1, Chapter 5 of *Pride and Prejudice,* we learn that Mr. Lucas had made "a tolerable fortune" in his trade and had "risen to the honour of knighthood by an address to the king, during his mayoralty." So far from earning a knighthood by wearing armor and riding a gallant steed, Mr. Lucas became Sir William Lucas by making a speech of thanks to the king for visiting the town. Austen ridicules the effect that the knighthood has had on him: "The distinction had perhaps been felt too strongly. It had given him a disgust to his business and to his residence in a small market town; and quitting both, he had removed his family to a house about a mile from Meryton, denominated from that period Lucas Lodge," a comical sign of how the knighthood has flattered his ego (PP 1:5). To add to Austen's poking fun at Sir William, her contemporary readers knew that during the period in which this novel is set, 1811–1812, and until 1815, the awarding of knighthoods was common. So for all of Sir William Lucas's kindness to others, Austen shows he has let his knighthood go to his head by making him somewhat ridiculous. After all, the novel is called *PRIDE and Prejudice*! And Austen wants us readers to see that Darcy is not the only proud character.

Defining a gentleman and the gentry

The part of the population on whom Jane Austen focuses her attention is the landed gentry (generally one who owns at least 300 acres of property, and most gentry owned much more). The gentry is a long-established and highly respectable class.

Male members of the landed gentry, along with noblemen and those with the lesser titles of baronet or knight, were officially considered gentlemen (from the word "gentry"). Jane Austen was a gentleman's daughter. While her maternal ancestors were truly wealthy gentry, her father was at the lower end of the gentry. Most of the company that the Austens associated with were gentry, who blended well with the lower titled class of baronets and knights — all of whom are commoners and characters in her novels carrying major roles. Being familiar with this class is probably why she wrote about it as vividly and realistically as she did. The gentry was the bedrock of society of her day, and Austen respects them. All of her heroines and most of her heroes are members of the gentry — whether at the lower end, like the Dashwood ladies (SS); more towards the middle of gentry, like the Morlands (NA), Colonel Brandon (SS), and the Bennets (PP); or at the higher end like Darcy (PP), Henry Tilney (NA), the Bertrams (MP), Emma and Mr. Knightley (E), and Anne Elliot (P). From this list, you can also see that the gentry is a wide class, with people of less wealth at the lower end of the class. But they're all gentry.

Many readers of Austen's novels observe (and are sometimes even confused) that the gentlemen, who are men of the gentry, don't go to work. But they're not "lazy bums," as one of my students claimed at the beginning of the term! Gentlemen lived off the money earned by their land, which they've inherited. For example, in *Pride and Prejudice,* gentlemen range from Darcy, with his magnificent estate, Pemberley, and annual income of £10,000, to Mr. Bennet, with his smaller estate and far lower annual income of £2,000.

Discovering a new kind of gentleman

While nowadays we admire people who make their money by earning it, in Austen's day the more genteel way of making money was to inherit it and get it from your land or estate, which a gentleman also usually inherited: You rented out land to tenant farmers, or perhaps your estate had valuable timber, which you sold for profit. But a new and upwardly mobile group of people who weren't gentry — they didn't own land — were slowly being recognized and accepted as gentlemen. And Jane Austen knew it! These newly recognized group of gentlemen included

- **Businessmen:** These individuals earned their way in business. For example, in *Pride and Prejudice,* Elizabeth's uncle, Mr. Gardiner, is a well-educated businessman in London. He earns his money "in a respectable line of trade" (PP 1:7). While the Bingley sisters make fun of him and his family for living in Cheapside, a commercial part of London, both he and Mrs. Gardiner are intelligent, modest, courteous, and charming. Even Darcy is impressed — and somewhat surprised — by them when he meets them at Pemberley, and Elizabeth proudly notes that he "'takes them for people of fashion'" (PP 3:1). The Gardiners' demeanor is intelligent and genteel. They represent what we, today, think of as a lady and a gentleman. But this was just starting to occur in Austen's time.

Charles Bingley, also in *Pride and Prejudice,* represents a variation on this situation. In his case, he inherited nearly £100,000 from his late father, who made a fortune "in the north of England . . . by trade" (PP 1:4). Austen's contemporary readers would immediately pick up that the Bingleys come from a manufacturing city up north like Manchester. Such wealth did not immediately grant status. But the late Mr. Bingley planned to buy an estate in order to become a member of the gentry. Not living long enough to do that, Bingley Senior left it up to his son Charles Bingley to use his inheritance to buy an estate. Charles's status-conscious sisters urge him to do so, for as rich as they are, they want the status that comes with being members of the gentry — even through their brother.

In Austen's day, the type of wealth that had the highest regard was land (property). This idea went back to the Middle Ages, and would continue into the 19th century.

✔ **Army and naval officers:** Younger sons of members of the gentry needed to have respectable careers in which they would still be regarded as gentlemen, but also make money. Why only younger sons? Their elder brothers inherited the family estate, and so younger sons needed to supplement any money they inherited from the mothers by earning it. (For maternal money, see Chapter 7, the section on "marriage settlements.") Society considered army and naval officers gentlemen. Austen also had a special respect and affection for the Royal Navy because two of her brothers were naval officers. (For more on the Austen family, see Chapter 3.)

In *Persuasion,* Captain Wentworth fought the French on the seas and returned home with £20,000 in prize money for capturing enemy ships and their cargo (P 1:9, 2:12). If he continues to win battles and gain more prize money, he'll be able to purchase an estate, too, thus making him an actual member of the gentry.

✔ **Anglican clergymen:** Clergy were also considered gentlemen, even if they had little or no property. This was out of respect for the profession, which required a university degree from Oxford or Cambridge. As with the army and navy, many younger sons of families of the gentry became Anglican clergymen. In Austen's novels, Henry Tilney (NA), Edward Ferrars (SS), and Edmund Bertram (MP) are all younger sons of the gentry; their elder brothers (or in Edward's case, his younger brother, because their mother is angry at Edward and disinherits him!) inherit the family property.

Persuasion's snobbish Sir Walter Elliot is confused when his lawyer mentions that a "gentleman," who turns out to be a clergyman, lives in a neighboring village: "'You misled me by the term gentleman. I thought you were speaking of a man of property,'" with property meaning land (1:3).

Austen recognized that her social world was changing, and that people could honorably earn their way "up" the ranks of society. She scorns only those who forget their origins and behave like snobs.

Austen makes fun of the social-climbing Bingley sisters by observing that they think well of themselves and meanly of others and forget that their money comes from trade. But she thinks well of people who earn their fortunes but who don't let that fact go to their heads. The Coles in *Emma* have made their money in trade and now live in Highbury in a style close to Emma Woodhouse's and her father's. But they are — unlike the Bingley sisters — "friendly, liberal, and unpretending" (E 2:7). Emma is a snob for looking down on them.

Dealing with everybody else

Austen's books are realistic because she gives her readers an entire community. While focusing on the gentry and gentlemanlike, she includes secondary and minor characters who're merchants, physicians, apothecaries, farmers, schoolmistresses, household help, and the militia (the militia protected the homeland, while the army fought abroad). Some of these characters never say a word, but they walk in and out of the pages of their novel and add to its social world.

An example that portrays the wide range of Austen's characters is Mr. Perry (the apothecary, a pharmacist, and more!), in Highbury, who cares for Mr. Woodhouse, Emma's hypochondriac father.

Apothecaries served the medical needs of most of the ordinary people of the day. Jane Austen, herself, was treated mostly by apothecaries. As their name suggests, they dispensed medicines and also made diagnoses, referring only their most serious cases to physicians.

Characters in and readers of *Emma* know Mr. Perry; he attends Miss Taylor's wedding and gives his children wedding cake; he visits Mr. Woodhouse almost daily. He's an important part in Highbury society. Yet he never utters a word. One of Austen's many skills as a novelist is her ability to flesh out her main characters' world without having too many actors crowd the stage with speaking parts.

Defining "condescension"

Keep in mind that the English class system was accepted as a fact of life in Austen's day. A nobleman who acted pleasantly toward a social inferior was considered admirable and courteous. In other words, the aristocrat, though higher in rank than the person he or she is addressing, doesn't pull rank. This concept is known as condescension — being nice to those who rank lower than you do.

But the characters in Austen's novels didn't always follow this notion. If you take a look at Lady Catherine in *Pride and Prejudice,* you see her acting in the worst condescending way: She gives Mr. Collins his orders to marry, tells him what kind of woman he should marry, and then tells the new Mrs. Collins how to care for her poultry. Lady Catherine's behavior is anything but pleasant. Mr. Collins idiotically observes that Lady Catherine "'. . . likes to have the distinction of rank preserved'" (2:7). His inability to see the difference between friendly condescension and the snobbish superiority that Lady Catherine displays is another mark of his stupidity.

Through Lady Catherine's behavior, Austen reminds us that even titled folks could let their titles and status go to their heads. Instead of behaving the way she should—with "condescension" that is pleasant — Lady Catherine is proud, overbearing, and never lets anyone forget that she is the daughter of an earl.

An example of proper condescension is seen in *Emma*'s Mr. Knightley. The richest man in Highbury and from an old and distinguished family of the gentry, Mr. Knightley, while not titled, behaves with kindness and generosity to those below him socially and economically: He quietly sends apples to the poor Bates family; he advises the young farmer Robert Martin who seeks him out; and he even dances with Harriet, a young woman of uncertain parentage, when she is left as the only wallflower at the Crown Inn Ball. Mr. Knightley understands and practices condescension in the best possible way.

Growing the Novel

The novel was a new literary genre that Jane Austen was familiar with growing up. In a letter to her sister, she reminds Cassandra that "'our family . . . are great Novel-readers & not ashamed of being so'" (December 18–19, 1798). "Not ashamed of being" novel readers? Why would someone have to be ashamed of reading novels?

Well, as the novel developed in England, it was sometimes viewed suspiciously because imagined characters and plots were presented as real people and situations. England had enough problems with overactive imaginations in the 17th century, when Puritan soldiers, fueled by intense emotionalism or fancied inspirations, marched against the king. (This was England's Civil War, 1642–1649.) Thus, some people viewed novels, works of the imagination that are presented as realistic, as a throwback to that dangerous "fancy" that caused England to have a king beheaded in 1649. It may seem a stretch to connect political unrest with literature, but many folks felt that the fancy or imagination that caused the first event (political unrest) contaminated the second event (the appearance of novels, which are works of the imagination that are presented as if they were realistic and true). The imagination was viewed with so much suspicion, that Dr. Johnson's popular fictional work of 1759, *Rasselas,* contains a chapter called "The Dangerous Prevalence of Imagination" (Chapter 44). To avoid having their books appear as products of the imagination, early experimenters in novel writing presented their fiction as "true stories" that the authors claimed to have merely found and edited. For example, in 1722, Daniel Defoe offered *Moll Flanders* as the "Memorandums" of an actual woman who used the name Moll Flanders as a guise because she is so well known, and himself as the mere editor who fixed up her immodest language. But Defoe actually invented the character and plot; he's the author.

This section highlights other forms of writing that preceded and influenced the development of the novel in England. Notice that the word "novel" also means "new"—as in the phrase, "What a novel idea!"

Influencing the creation of the novel

A novel has several characteristics:

- ✔ It presents realistic, breathing characters, which are products of the author's imagination, who live their lives on the pages as we read.
- ✔ It is a fictional prose narrative.
- ✔ The novel's length is considerable, say at least 200 pages.
- ✔ Its characters and actions represent real life of past or present times in a plot with varied complexity.
- ✔ It brings us into the lives of characters who are learning how to live through trial and error — characters try something else and finally (hopefully!) learn from their mistakes.

The novel didn't develop spontaneously and fully grown like Athena did from the head of Zeus. A variety of sources contributed to the growth of the novel as we know it today.

Newspapers

One of the earliest influences on the development of the novel was the newspaper. Newspapers offer the latest news: News is set in reality and occurs here and now. Events in a novel occur here and now on the page of the book! Newspapers went from hand to hand: One person bought it and would pass it on. Thus, newspapers had wide circulations beyond the original purchasers. So many readers were familiar with newspapers. Reading newspapers taught them to be novel readers.

The first English daily newspaper, *The Daily Courant,* founded in 1702, obviously couldn't bring up-to-the-minute news reports to its readers the way newspapers can today with faxes, e-mails, and cell phones. Also, the newspaper was printed by hand, a time-consuming process. The *Courant* and its followers did offer readers actual news of new events occurring in different parts of the world, even though the news was several days (if it was carried by horseback rider), weeks, or months (if it was carried by ship) old. But to readers of the 18th century, this was news because they just learned about it in the newspaper. It was *new* information.

Personal guide books

Another early influence on the formulation of the novel included personal guides or conduct books, which were highly popular in the early 18th century: They had titles like *A Young Man's Guide* or *The Whole Duty of Man.* (And you thought self-help books were a phenomenon beginning in the 1990's!) As a new and growing middle class learned how to live, they sought all sorts of conduct and guide books about customs and manners. Many folks moved from the country to the city, experiencing a whole new lifestyle, a whole new world, requiring new modes of behavior. Novels introduce us to new characters and lifestyles, and the characters in novels usually have something new to learn. Moreover, unless a character is living an isolated life on a remote island (like Defoe's Robinson Crusoe), he or she must learn how to live in society and deal with all types of social interactions. Thus, personal guides provided a basis for characters' experiences in the novel.

Pamphlets and tracts

During the 17th century, readers enjoyed pamphlets and tracts about true accounts of murders, fires, and robberies. They also enjoyed reading about travel to exotic places. Lots of these pamphlets told sensational tales. Reading these works entertained people and took them out of themselves and to another world. Has that ever happened to you while reading a novel?

Because a novel merely *represents* real life, the lives of Elizabeth Bennet or Mr. Knightley in their novels may not be factually true, but their life experiences certainly represent reality and the truth.

Diaries, biographies, and autobiographies

Diaries, biographies, and autobiographies were three other favorite nonfiction reading materials, which all shared a common characteristic: recording an individual's life experiences and the responses to the experiences. When reading a biography, personal dairy, or journal, we're examining the subject's life; the text is full of day-to-day details, including drama and conflict. Everyone likes to read about other peoples' experiences because they take us out of ourselves. In the days before the novel, reading diaries, biographies, and autobiographies did that. Novels do that, too.

Some early novel titles include *Joseph Andrews, Tom Jones, Belinda, Evelina, Cecilia, Pamela,* and *Clarissa.* What do they all have in common? The titles are names of people, thus promising the reader a story of the title character's life. You may be able to name dozens of novels, old and new, that use characters' names for the titles. Centralizing a story on one character provides the reader with focus. The reader follows that character for hundreds of pages, and through many important events in his or her life. As readers, we come to relate to that character, whose life experiences draw us in. Can you name any novel you've enjoyed that doesn't have a central character?

Writing for middle-class readers and women

With the growth of industry and the movement of people from the country to the town, individuals had time to read. People were freed of everyday chores:

✔ Spinning cotton to make cloth for clothing: The cotton mills in Manchester and other northern cities took care of that work, first with water-powered and then steam-powered machinery.

✔ Growing and tending to the crops or animals: People could go to the shops where they could buy food.

✔ Performing time-consuming household tasks such as making soap: You just went to town to buy your supplies.

So women, especially, with their newfound freedom (because they were the ones mostly performing the daily chores), had time to read. Women of the landed gentry class, as well as the growing middle class (wives of tradesmen and businessmen) were looking for new reading material. They needed something that they could do and enjoy on their own. With the boys away at school and the girls with their governesses, solitaire became a boring option. And let's face it: There is only so much country dance music that one wants to play! (For more on the daily lives of men and women in Austen's day, see Chapter 11.) Is there any wonder, then, that early novels were written with a female readership in mind?

If you remember the titles of the novels using person's names that I offered a few paragraphs back, you'll have noticed that all but two of the names were female names. While women certainly read fiction by male authors, they particularly liked to read about other women's experiences. And that is precisely what those novels offered. Female novelists who preceded Austen include Aphra Behn, Elizabeth Inchbald, Eliza Heywood, Charlotte Smith, Amelia Opie, Fanny Burney, and Maria Edgeworth (called "the Irish Jane Austen" for her depiction of Irish life). If we jump ahead a few decades in literary history to Jane Austen, we recognize that this is what Austen writes about, too.

While many of the female writers who preceded Jane Austen have been long out of print, their works are being republished and reissued.

We're now at the point in English literary history when the novel — with its many contributing influences (newspapers, diaries, conduct books, and so forth) — is born. Austen read the fiction by many of her female and male predecessors. To learn more about the major literary influences on Austen, as well as how people and events influenced her writing, head to Chapter 4. But remember, the novel in England is a Georgian English baby and the product of its times.

Chapter 3

Being Jane Austen (1775–1817)

*J*ane Austen grew up experiencing most of the same events as her heroines: going off to school, as well as learning at home; rolling down hills; reading those new works of literature called *novels;* acting in family plays; laughing with her sister; and being teased by her brothers. And also like her heroines, in her adult life she enjoyed dancing at local balls; paying visits and calls to friends; playing cards, charades, and piano; selecting new fashions; attending the theater; and writing letters to friends and family (for she lived in the great age of letter writing).

But unlike her heroines, Jane Austen, by age 13 or 14, was doing something else, something unique: writing little vignettes and stories that unquestionably showed that she understood how fiction worked. This chapter explores her life and calls your attention, as well, to her writing, which was a major part of her life from later childhood until her death.

Meeting the Austens

Jane Austen's parents and siblings formed a happy, educated group who provided Jane with a wonderful, encouraging family circle that appreciated her early writing just as they did her mature novels. The Austen brothers (with the exception of George, who, because of illness, lived apart from the family), all rode horses, hunted, fished, and played games — sometimes even with their sisters. As they grew older, the boys also danced with their sisters and discussed literature, especially with Jane. With a mild, intelligent father, a witty but hypochondriac mother, and lively siblings who loved her, young Jane grew up in a happy and supportive environment and grew into a cheerful, witty, and bright young woman.

Introducing the Rev. Mr. and Mrs. Austen

While George Austen (1731–1805) hailed from an old and distinguished family in Kent, his early years were marked by misfortune. Orphaned and left with no money at age 6, he moved in with an aunt. But young George was a clever and diligent student, and he eventually won a university scholarship.

Educated at St. John's College, Oxford University (B.A., B.D., M.A.), he was known as a young man for his pleasant personality, strong academic ability, and good looks — the last item leading to his title of "The handsome proctor" (a proctor is a supervisor). In fact, even at the end of his life, people spoke of the tall clergyman's good looks and full head of (by that time) white hair.

He was ordained a deacon in The Church of England in 1754 and a priest the following year. Recognizing that he needed a wife (unlike the clergyman Mr. Collins in *Pride and Prejudice* who marries on orders from his patron, Lady Catherine!), George courted Miss Cassandra Leigh (1739–1827).

The couple married in the Walcot Church (still standing) in Bath on April 26, 1764, and moved to the Steventon rectory in Hampshire in 1768. Jane was born at the rectory seven years later. Jane's father was given the church living of Steventon, along with the rectory, by a rich relative. (For more on church livings, see Chapter 13.)

Getting to know Jane and her siblings

Jane was very close to her six brothers for her entire life, and she and her only sister, Cassandra Elizabeth (or Cassy) were best friends from childhood until Jane, her head resting on a pillow on Cassy's lap, peacefully breathed her last breath at the age of 41. The following list introduces Jane and her siblings in birth order:

✓ **James Austen (1765–1819):** As the eldest brother, James was 10 when Jane was born. A reader, hunter, rider, and writer of verse, James went off to Oxford and eventually in 1801 succeeded his father at Steventon rectory as an Anglican priest. James's son, James Edward, would publish in December 1869 his important *Memoir* of Jane Austen, a basic source for much of our knowledge about his aunt to whom he was very close. His sisters helped him with information.

- **George Austen (1766–1838):** This son was named for his father and was the brother of whom little is known. As an epileptic, George didn't live at the Steventon rectory; instead, he lived with nearby family but was always looked out for by the Austens. Many of his siblings saw to this care after their parents' deaths.

- **Edward Austen (1767–1852):** If any Austen lived the life of a fairy-tale character, it was this third Austen son. Polite, sweet-looking with blond hair and pink-cheeks, and smart, Edward, familiarly known as Neddy, was adopted at age 12 by Thomas Knight II, Mr. Austen's distant cousin. See the "Understanding Edward the inheritor" sidebar for details about this life-changing event and how it eventually affected Jane.

- **Henry Austen (1771–1850):** Henry was Jane's favorite brother. He was very tall, handsome, and witty, and like James, Henry went to Oxford and received his M.A. in 1796. As an optimist and extrovert, Henry found that it took a while for him to settle down. He joined the militia and became an army agent and a banker, but then in 1816, he was bankrupt. After that, Henry spent the rest of his life in holy orders, serving in various clerical capacities.

  When Jane died in 1817, Henry was Jane's literary executor and first biographer. He wrote, in December 1817, a "Biographical Notice of the Author," which was appended to Jane Austen's posthumously published *Northanger Abbey* and *Persuasion* in a four-volume set.

- **Cassandra Elizabeth (1773–1845):** Named for her mother, Cassandra treated Jane like her new "plaything." Though just two years younger than Cassandra, Jane followed her sister around so much that their mother commented that if Cassandra were to have her head cut off, Jane would want hers cut off, too (*The Family Record*, 47). Far more prim than Jane, Cassandra was her sister's first literary audience. Visitors to their house later recalled hearing the sisters laughing upstairs as Jane read aloud some of her latest writing long before it went to the publisher. As both sisters remained unmarried, they lived together for Jane's entire life.

- **Francis (Frank) Austen (1774–1865):** Called "Fly" by his family because of his active nature, the curly-haired boy, at the age of 12, went off to the Royal Naval Academy at Portsmouth. Entering Portsmouth at 12 wasn't that unusual.

  Frank had a distinguished career in the navy, including his promotion to Admiral of the Fleet in 1863. He was also known for his devoutness and identified as "*the* officer who knelt in church."

✔ **Jane Austen (1775–1817):** Jane was born at home in the Steventon rectory on December 16, 1775. She was named for her mother's sister, Mrs. Jane Leigh Cooper as well as for her father's uncle's wife, Mrs. Francis (Jane) Austen.

Families loved repeating names from generation to generation. But life was like that in Austen's day: Families regularly named their children after a relative either out of the desire to secure that person's patronage and favoritism or just to show plain, sincere love and respect for that relative.

✔ **Charles Austen (1779–1852):** Following his brother Frank's footsteps, Charles entered the Royal Naval Academy at Portsmouth in 1791 at the age of 12. Charles, too, had a successful naval career and became rear admiral in 1846. Had he not died of cholera while on active duty in Burma in 1852, Charles, too, might have become admiral of the fleet, like his brother Frank, who outlived him by 13 years. (Attaining the rank, admiral of the fleet, was based on seniority of admirals, and so the admiral who lived the longest normally secured that rank.)

Understanding Edward the inheritor

While Anglo-Saxon England had its King Edward the Confessor, the Austen family was lucky to have as their third son, Edward, who became the heir to two great estates: one in their native Hampshire and another in Kent. Edward's (and Jane's) father's wealthy cousin, three or four times removed, Thomas Knight II, of the Godmersham estate in Kent, had married, on May 8, Miss Catherine Knatchbull, who was also from an old and important Kentish family. (Thomas Knight's father had given George Austen his church livings or benefices, Deane and Steventon, in Hampshire.) Traveling on their honeymoon, Mr. and Mrs. Knight stopped at Steventon, where they saw Edward, age 12, and of course his siblings, including Jane, not yet 4. When they left Steventon to continue their honeymoon, Edward accompanied them. Yes, this strikes us as unusual today. But not so much in Austen's day.

In Austen's day, not only was it common for children to be adopted by rich relatives, it was also traditional — if the bride and groom desired

it — for a companion to go along on the honeymoon so that the couple did not *look like* honeymooners, thereby avoiding a shivaree (a mock celebration with horns and pans for a newly married couple, a sample of which you can see in the movie and play *Oklahoma!* when Curlie and Laurie marry). The Knights returned Edward to his family a few weeks later. But they remained both childless (perhaps Mrs. Knight knew from the outset that she would not be able to bear children; hence, the Knights' taking Edward on the honeymoon to get to know him as soon as possible) and impressed with this charming boy, whom they invited to spend school holidays at their beautiful Kentish estate, Godmersham, though Mr. Austen was worried about Edward missing his Latin lessons at home. The Knights became so fond of him that they formally adopted him, making Edward their son and heir. This adoption probably occurred in 1783, for a silhouette bearing the date 1783 made by William Wellings shows Mr. Austen presenting Edward (looking short for age 16) to the Knights.

be adopted
common in
Austen was
eman in the
come a true
who lived in
ter of a large
a man of prop-
Knights. The
ts chose wisely
herited estates
t Edward had a
lso had a good
th his birth family
2, upon the death
widower, and his
e Knight.

birth family to live
s may well have
Austen to include
ters who grow up in
rents'. This practice
asons:

ld give a poor niece,
even a close friend's
n life than the child's
ember from Chapter 2
a very class-oriented
society. Who wouldn't want to see a son or
daughter get a chance to move to a higher
class? Letting a wealthy relative adopt a
child meant a huge improvement in their
child's prospects, their grandchildren's
prospects, and so on.

2. Wealthy members of the gentry with rich,
large estates wanted to be sure that their
money and land stayed in the family. For
this, they needed a male heir. (For information on the tradition and laws of male inheritance, see Chapters 7 and 10.) If they had
no children of their own, adopting a nephew

or male cousin (Edward) would keep the
estate in the family. Everybody recognized
the need for male heirs in Austen's time.

Jane Austen deals with both reasons in her
novels. In *Mansfield Park,* the heroine Fanny
Price leaves her poor birth family to join the
household of her rich and titled aunt and uncle;
she becomes a gentlewoman who marries well.
In fact, when Fanny visits her birth parents, she
disappointingly finds they are too poor, too har-
ried, and too distracted with their brood of
younger children to have ever missed her!
Emma's Jane Fairfax, orphaned by the early
deaths of both parents, leaves the home of her
kind but poor aunt and grandmother to be raised
by her late father's dear friends, Colonel and
Mrs. Campbell, who have their own daughter,
Jane's age. The Campbells raise both girls as
young ladies, with all the masters and training
required for a daughter of the gentry, enabling
Jane to associate with the gentry and make a
genteel marriage. In the same novel, the widowed Mr. Weston allows his brother-in-law and
his wife, the wealthy but childless Churchills, to
raise his son Frank from childhood; they adopt
Frank, who will succeed to the Churchills'
estate and money. When Isabella Knightley
recalls the story of little Frank's departure from
his father, she exclaims, "'I never can compre-
hend how Mr. Weston could part with him. To
give up one's child! I really never could think
well of any body who proposed such a thing'"
(E 1:11). But Jane Austen appears to have been
far more practical than her distressed character
Isabella. For she saw that her own brother
Edward's good fortune filtered into his birth
family. As she grew up, Austen visited many
great estates, including Edward's, which
enabled her to depict the country life of the
gentry accurately in her novels. But she also
enjoyed the luxury of visiting him and his family,
too! In 1809, Edward provided his widowed

(continued)

(continued)

mother and two unmarried sisters with a place to live: Chawton cottage, which is now the Jane Austen Museum, a popular tourist site in England and a veritable shrine to Jane Austen's fans and admirers. (For details on the museum and instructions on how to get there after you arrive in London, see Chapter 19.)

Photo by Adrian Harvey, Courtesy of the Jane Austen Society of North America

Growing Up Gentry: Jane's Formative Years

The Austens were gentry, but they occupied the lower end of the gentry class. The Austens had less land and less money than the characters from Jane Austen's novels, but rather than owning a magnificent country house at the center of a huge estate with a working farm, the Austens lived at the rectory, which had a farm that produced enough food to sustain them.

The farm was away from the Austen's house, not next to it as the 2005 film version of *Pride and Prejudice* erroneously shows the Bennets' farm.

Austen was later able to write so eloquently and so knowledgeably about life on the large country estates owned by richer gentry. The Rev. Mr. Austen's clerical profession and excellent education opened the doors of the homes of richer neighbors of the gentry with whose children his children could associate. Back then, like today, a good education opened many doors.

But Jane rarely longed for playmates or entertainment.

Living and learning at the rectory

The Steventon rectory was a busy place. To help make ends meet, the Rev. Mr. and Mrs. Austen boarded four or five young boys — frequently from wealthy and even titled families — as students, who lived with Jane's brothers in the rectory's attic. The Rev. Mr. Austen taught the boarding students, along with his own sons, such subjects as Latin, Greek, and literature, thereby preparing them for Eton or the other elite public schools. (Such schools are still called public schools even though they're private. For more information on elite English public schools, see Chapter 9.)

Mrs. Austen supervised what women of that time supervised: the busy household, which included the cooking, washing, and mending. Like Cassy, Jane was nursed by their mother and then sent to live with a local farmer's wife until she more or less turned from baby to little girl — able to walk, talk, and do those other things that make us say, "She's not our little baby any-more," probably between ages 2 and 3. Of course, Jane's parents and family would see her at the neighboring farm daily, but Mrs. Austen was spared the chores of changing, dressing, feeding, and watching a crawling baby when she had all those boys running around the rectory.

Between the ages of 7 and 11, Jane began to split her time between Steventon and two boarding schools that she attended with her sister. (You can read more about her time at boarding school in the "Surviving boarding school" section later in this chapter.) While at Steventon, Jane enjoyed a happy childhood in the Hampshire countryside playing outdoors and also learning from her father and reading the books from his well-stocked library of 500 volumes. From Shakespeare and Milton (the very works that many of today's college students fret over reading) to the popular new novels that were being published, young Jane Austen was absorbing literature. But even more important, she was listening to the intelligent, witty conversation carried on by her clever parents and big brothers.

Eighteenth-century England is called "The Great Age" of many things. Among those "greats" was the Great age of Conversation. Jane Austen's overheard conversations during her childhood were an education that included the discussion of the literature, including the novels that her brothers, sister, and parents had read. Later Jane would read them, too, and share in those lively and intelligent family conversations.

With her own family, a couple of servants, and the boarding students all in residence at the rectory, little Jane was now living among 16 or 17 people! Is it any wonder that she clung to her big sister, Cassandra? The two Austen girls — as their father called them well into their adulthood — were very close as the only two little females in a world of boys at home.

Surviving boarding school

At the ages of 7 and 9, respectively, Jane and her sister went off with their cousin (Jane Cooper) in 1783 to Mrs. Cawley's boarding school in Oxford. The experience wasn't only an educational fiasco (Mrs. Cawley let her students have a free reign), but also more frighteningly, a health disaster for the three girls. The girls would probably have died of typhus while at school, but the timely arrival of their mothers saved them: They nursed the girls and as soon as they could travel, took them to Steventon. Alas, poor Mrs. Cooper eventually died of the fever.

Alas, more boarding school was in Jane's future. But this time, it was a happier and healthier experience. The Austens felt that Cassandra needed more formal schooling and planned in the spring, 1785, to send her to the Abbey School (still standing) in Reading. When Jane, age 9, heard that her big sister was heading to school, she insisted on going along. So their parents gave in — parents can only take so much insistence, right? — and off the girls went. The school's headmistress was Madame la Tournelle, whose most fascinating quality, besides her name, especially for girls aged 10 to 12, was having a cork leg. She provided the girls with a little spelling and sewing instruction in a friendly (and thankfully, non-pestilence-ridden) environment, but not much else. And certainly no French. For it turned out that her real name was the very un-French Sarah Hackitt. But happy memories of the Abbey School stayed with Austen. For when she wrote *Emma* decades later, she undoubtedly thought of those school days when she said of Mrs. Goddard's school that it was "a real, honest, old-fashioned Boarding-school, where . . . girls might be sent out of the way and scramble themselves into a little education, without any danger of coming back prodigies" (E 1:3).

Getting bitten by the writing bug: Austen's "Juvenilia"

When Jane wasn't springing over puddles or playing ball with her friends and siblings, young Jane was writing fiction to entertain her family during the evening when the Austens would read aloud. A voracious reader with a large memory for what she read, the adolescent Jane was inspired to try her own hand at fiction. Between the ages of 12 and 18, she wrote short pieces of fiction as gifts for her brothers, sister, and others. Little did the recipients know that the young writer who presented them with presents of fiction would some day be considered both the world's greatest novelist and the world's favorite novelist.

But even Austen's works from her early years show that at a young age she understood how fiction worked; how characters should be presented; how dialogue operates; how the plot should be constructed; and how all this could occur in a way that made entertaining, thought-provoking, and highly workable fiction.

Fortunately for posterity's sake, Austen copied many of her literary gifts in three notebooks. Better yet, all three volumes survived. The volumes aren't in chronological order, suggesting that Austen sorted and copied works to suit her tastes. While volume two has the earliest date, 1790, (14- to 15-year-old Jane), Austen scholars concur that some of the writing goes back to when she was 12 (1787). She obviously cared a lot about these works, because she corrected "typos" and revised certain entries here and there through 1809. The writing in the three volumes is called Austen's "Juvenilia." In December 1794 — perhaps as a gift for her 19th birthday — Jane's father bought her a mahogany writing desk at Ring Brothers in Basingstoke, the big market town near Steventon. (See Figure 3-1.) As you can see in the photo, the writing desk is actually a writing slope, designed so the user could write without bending over. Being ergonomically correct is not just a 21st-century concern! The angled top is hinged so it can be raised to store paper, glasses, and so on inside. A glass ink-stand appears at the top. The desk sits on a table and is portable, allowing a writer to put her papers inside the desk and take both desk and writing with her. Austen's writing desk remained in the Austen family until October 29, 2001, when Joan Austen-Leigh, Austen's great-great-grandniece, donated it to the British Library, where it is on permanent display in the Treasures Room, which also holds the *Magna Carta* — pretty good company.

Austen's youthful works are divided as follows:

✔ *Volume the First:* With a mischievous sense of humor and ironic foresight, she pompously called the initial calf-bound notebook *Volume the First*. While it's quite worn, it's preserved in Oxford University's Bodleian Library. The "novels" — as she called the short pieces in this volume — combine a precociously shrewd undercutting of sentimental fiction, a cartoonist's sense of humor and absurdity (where characters get their legs caught in traps or jump from high windows, only to carry on as if nothing happened), and a knowledge of how a novel should be structured. Two of the better-known pieces from this volume are

• **"Jack and Alice":** This "novel" consists of only nine chapters, each of which is only about two printed pages. It's a youthful and giggly work, with a heroine, Alice, who's a drunk, and her brother Jack, who is finally introduced in Chapter 7, only to be dismissed after a few lines because, he, too, is a drunk and "never did anything worth mentioning." Imagine young Jane laughing her head off over a family of drunks! (Had she lived in Victorian, rather than Georgian England, her parents would have been mortified. For more on Georgian England, see Chapter 2.)

- **"Henry and Eliza":** Another short "novel," this piece, dedicated to her cousin Jane Cooper, deals less with Henry (who dies soon after he is introduced!) than with his wife, Eliza, whose children eat her fingers when they are hungry, but who carries on anyway.

✔ *Volume the Second:* The second notebook, along with the third in the British Library, is of higher quality (vellum) than the first, and in it Austen wrote "*Ex dono mei Patris,*" meaning, from my father. Perhaps Papa Austen liked what he heard her read from the first volume so much that he bought his daughter a better notebook — and at a time when paper was expensive — so that she could continue her writing. One work that stands out from this volume is

- **"Love and Freindship":** And yes, that is how Austen spelled "friendship"! Her most well-known work in the second volume is "Love and Friendship" (dated June 13, 1790, when Jane was 14). This work is a hysterical, brilliant burlesque of the sentimentality that was extremely popular in contemporary fiction. An example, the loaded title, *The Man of Feeling,* tells the whole story of this tear-evoking 1771 bestseller! The ability to create an original burlesque of sentimental novels requires the writer to understand the style and use her talent to take the texts that inspired her to a laughable extreme.

As you've already seen, Austen had trouble spelling "friendship." Apparently, she couldn't remember "i before e, except after c." She also misspelled niece as "neice." So there's hope for bad spellers to become great novelists — especially nowadays with spell-check on the computer!

- **"The History of England":** Inspired to make fun of Oliver Goldsmith's fact-filled *History of England,* which young Jane, along with just about every other schoolchild in England was forced to read, the 16-year-old Austen presents her own history "By a partial, prejudiced, and ignorant Historian."

✔ *Volume the Third:* This volume is also bound in vellum, and on the inside cover in her father's handwriting are the words "Effusions of Fancy by a very Young Lady Consisting of Tales in a Style entirely new." This volume contains just two pieces:

- **"Catharine; or, The Bower":** This piece (dated August 1792, when Jane was just 16½) is an impressive work because it reveals a mature understanding of how realistic fiction operates. The fiction contains a believable set of characters in probable situations, rendered largely through dialogue.

- **"Evelyn":** Described as "the best of men," Mr. Gower arrives in the village of Evelyn and reveals himself to be anything but!

Photo by Adrian Harvey, courtesy of the Jane Austen Society of North America

Becoming a Professional Writer

Encouraged by her family's reception of her juvenile works and undoubtedly encouraged by her father, Jane Austen continued to touch up what she had written in her childhood and adolescence and experiment with the writing of new, full-fledged novels.

Beginning a life of letter writing

Letters were the primary form of communication between people who lived quite a distance from each other. In her lifetime, Jane Austen wrote thousands of letters, of which only about 160 remain. The earliest surviving letter by Jane Austen is dated January 9–10, 1796, just a few weeks after she had turned 20. She most frequently wrote to her sister, Cassandra. Whenever they were separated, Jane and Cassandra wrote to each other the way close sisters today would telephone or e-mail each other. She also wrote to her brothers in the navy, as well as to her other brothers. Indeed, she came from a letter-writing family in a letter-writing culture. Even some of the earliest novels were written in the form of letters between the characters, known as the epistolary style. (For more on the early novel, see Chapter 2.)

Experimenting with epistolary novels

After Jane Austen started the three volumes of "Juvenilia," she knew that she wanted to be a novelist. In 1794 and 1795, Austen began writing in the epistolary style. (Her favorite novelist, Samuel Richardson, wrote in the epistolary style, and Austen was influenced by his writings. For more information on Richardson, see Chapter 4.) Telling a novel through letters (epistles) supposedly written by varied characters allows the writer to experiment with different characters' voices. Each of us — yes, you, too — has his or her own personal tone of voice and writing style in a letter, or indeed, in anything we write. Austen experimented with the epistolary style in *Volume the Second* of her juvenile works.

Austen wrote other novels in the letter-writing style:

- ✔ *Lady Susan* **(1794–1795):** This novel is particularly remarkable because the title character — a beautiful, conniving woman and seductress — is also a sociopath! The letters written by the various characters certainly show Austen's increasing skill in giving her characters' voices that are uniquely their own. While she put this work aside to start another, she returned to *Lady Susan* and completed it in 1803.

- ✔ **"Elinor and Marianne" (1795):** Austen began a manuscript called "Elinor and Marianne" — we know it as *Sense and Sensibility,* which is what Austen titled this work when she revised it first in November 1797 and again between 1809 and 1811. While the 1795-manuscript is gone, scholars agree that she also wrote this as an epistolary novel.

- ✔ **"First Impressions" (October 1796):** Austen wrote "First Impressions" as an epistolary novel, but later she reworked it into what would become her most famous novel: *Pride and Prejudice.* When reading this novel, note how many letters appear in it — possible holdovers from the early epistolary version. She worked on this manuscript until August of 1797. Her father read it, thought it worthy of publication, and on November 1, 1797, sent it with a letter to London's most famous publishers: Cadell and Davis. The publishers never even opened the package; they simply wrote on it "declined by Return of Post." So for Jane, it was back to "Elinor and Marianne."

Seeing the Personal Side of Jane

Jane wasn't all work and no play. While her collected letters only began in January, 1796, we can reasonably assume that she enjoyed going to dances and being social from the age of 16 — the usual age for a girl's coming "out." (For more on dancing and a young lady's coming out, see Chapter 6.)

Having a sophisticated grown-up friend

Probably nothing is more flattering to a clever young girl than finding an adult female friend who respects your intelligence and cleverness. Mrs. Anne Lefroy, known as Madam Lefroy (1749–1804), was such a woman for young Jane Austen. The Rev. Mr. George Lefroy and his beautiful, intelligent wife lived at Ashe and were the Austens' closest neighbors.

When Jane Austen was about 11, the Lefroys invited her to play with their eldest child, Jemima, who was 7 years old. Madam Lefroy immediately recognized that young Jane was special. A great lover of literature herself, she talked seriously with Jane about her favorite poetry and plays (Shakespeare's). Jane must have shared her own reading, as well as her writing with her new, much older friend, who applauded her work. Jane soon came to see Mrs. Lefroy as a mentor who represented grace and goodness. Austen mourned deeply when Mrs. Lefroy died prematurely in 1804 in a riding accident.

Flirting with a new friend, Tom Lefroy

The earliest existing letter by Jane Austen was written over the winter holidays of the 1795–1796 season and focused on a new acquaintance, an Irishman named Tom Lefroy. Tom was the nephew of young Jane's much admired older friend and mentor, Mrs. ("Madam") Lefroy. (See "Having a sophisticated grown-up friend" for more on this relationship.)

Tom was a law student in London, preparing for a career at the Irish Bar. In fact, he eventually became Lord Chief Justice of Ireland. One of his professors at Trinity College, University of Dublin, wrote to his guardian and sponsor that Tom was deeply religious, highly principled, and very devoted to his goal to serve in the Irish courts (*Memoir of Lord Chief Justice Lefroy*, 13–14). This young man had a professional plan and the temperament to pursue it.

In Austen's letter, she told Cassandra that she and her "Irish friend" behaved in a "most profligate and shocking . . . way [by] dancing and sitting down together" (Letter, January 9–10, 1796). As explained in Chapter 5, dancing manners required that a couple dance only twice together or they would be looked upon as a serious couple heading for engagement. So Jane was teasing her elder sister about her spending, perhaps, a suspicious amount of time with Tom at a ball. But while the two shared a few dances and a few laughs, another woman kept young love from blossoming. Her name was Mary Paul. She was the only sister of Tom's close college friend back in his Trinity days (beginning 1790). He had met her when he joined his friend's family in visits to their fine home in county Wexford, south of Dublin, Ireland. By 1797, the young Irish couple, Tom Lefroy and Miss Mary Paul, was engaged to marry, which they did two years later. Jon Spence, in his biography of Austen, which is the inspiration for a film, *Becoming Jane,* speculates that when Jane Austen and her brothers Edward and Frank stayed with Tom's uncle in London in August 1796 while traveling from Steventon to Kent, that she once again encountered Tom Lefroy. (Spence is advising on the film *Becoming Jane,* in production in Ireland in 2006.) But Lincoln's Inn, where Tom "kept terms," as the saying went, for "studying" the law, was not in session during Austen's London visit. The term dates for 1796 show that Trinity Term ended June 15, and the Michaelmas Term only began November 6. So it's unlikely that Tom was even in London during August 1796. It's more probable that he went home to Ireland — perhaps to visit Mary Paul!

Notice that I wrote "studying" the law in quotations when discussing Tom Lefroy's time at Lincoln's Inn. Neither Lincoln's Inn nor any of the other law Inns offered formal law classes as law schools do today. All a Lincoln's Inn student back then had to do was to dine at the Inn a minimum of five days, revolving around "Grand Day," in order to "take" a certificate. Jo Hutchings, the Archivist at Lincoln's Inn Library, kindly replied to my enquiry of April 3, 2006, that legal "training was entirely a matter of self-help — attending the courts, studying standard textbooks, reading in barristers' chambers, or working in an attorney's office" (e-mail reply, April 11, 2006). Thanks also go to Ian Warr, Information Services Administrative Office at the Law Society in London for his help on Lincoln's Inn's terms for the year 1796 (e-mail reply, April 7, 2006). Spence's book cites no records of Tom Lefroy's legal studies or time spent at Lincoln's Inn; nor does it mention using the *Memoir of Chief Justice Lefroy,* written by his son.

Remaining unmarried

Perhaps Jane's inability to present a would-be husband with a dowry affected her chances of attracting a husband, as it is a fact that without a dowry, a woman's chances of marrying well, if at all, were nonexistent. (See Chapter 7 for more on dowries and other financial elements of marriage.) She did have several casual admirers, but nothing came of any of them. But the writing young woman had many female friends, including her sister, whose company she enjoyed. Attending dances and even frequently spending several nights at Manydown (the country estate of her good friends, the Biggs sisters) and other great country houses belonging to friends who were rich members of the gentry, Jane wasn't only having fun but also gleaning additional information about country-house life that she included in her novels.

Given Jane's single status, you may be wondering what she looked like. Ironically enough, she's the most famous member of her immediate family and also the only member of the family who never sat for a professional portrait or silhouette.

Some published descriptions from both Austen herself and those who knew her do exist. Here are some details that float around about Miss Jane Austen:

- In a letter written on January 25, 1801, to her sister, she asks her to buy material for a gown for her, noting that she needs enough fabric for "a tall woman."

- A niece, Anna, recalled her aunt's being "tall and slight," with "bright hazel eyes."

- Her biographer-nephew, James Edward, remembered her as being very attractive, tall and slender, with a small and nicely-formed nose and mouth.

- A neighbor recalled her high cheekbones and sparkling and intelligent eyes.

- Her brother, Henry, described her posture as "graceful" and her complexion as "of the finest texture" with naturally reddish cheeks.

- An old family friend said she was pretty.

Figure 3-2 gives you an idea of what Jane looked like through her sister's eyes.

Figure 3-2: A pencil and watercolor sketch of Jane Austen, around age 30, by her sister Cassandra.

Courtesy, National Portrait Gallery

Softening Jane Austen

This popular image of Jane Austen was first seen in 1870 as the frontispiece for James Edward Austen-Leigh's *Memoir of Jane Austen*. It is actually an engraving by a Mr. Lizars from a portrait that Austen-Leigh commissioned a Mr. Andrews to create, basing it on Cassandra's portrait, with input from Austen-Leigh and his sisters. Thus, the engraving you're looking at is a copy of a copy of Cassandra's work, shown in Figure 3-2. It is perhaps softened for Victorian tastes: A woman who, as a child, saw Jane Austen many times at Chawton, observed that the face shown here was too broad and plump.

JANE AUSTEN

Courtesy, A Room of One's Own Press

In addition, James Stanier Clarke, a talented amateur artist, spent time with Austen in 1815, when he hosted her visit to Carlton House. His small pencil and watercolor depiction of a woman (see Figure 3-3) is, very likely, Jane Austen. This conclusion is based on the study of several professional forensic artists who have compared Cassandra's portrait of her sister with Clarke's, using the technology found in police labs.

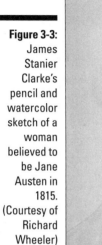

Photo by Simon Wheeler, Courtesy of Richard Wheeler

Experiencing New Places, New Faces, New Feelings: Moving to Bath

When her parents unexpectedly announced her father's decision to retire and move with his wife and two unmarried daughters to Bath, it is rumored that Jane promptly fainted. After living in the country and in the same house for 20 years, Jane must have found the idea of moving to Bath, a city that was second only to London in importance and activity, a real shocker! The move also meant condensing to a smaller rental, city property: Her father's 500-volume library and her pianoforte would be sold, along with all the family furniture, except for their beds. But with her cheerful personality and love of the ridiculous, if only to satirize it as she had in her "Juvenilia" and would continue to do in her mature novels, Jane bucked herself up and prepared for the move.

Living and lulling in Bath

The four Austens — parents and daughters — moved to Bath in May 1801. By the end of September, after much looking, they found a lovely house to lease at No. 4 Sydney Place, just opposite the lovely Sydney Gardens. Today the house bears a plaque that Jane Austen once lived there.

Living in Bath, Austen occupied herself doing what any young lady in Bath would do:

- Attended the theater
- Accompanied her uncle, James Leigh Perrot (her mother's brother), to the Pump Room (where Bath's mineral water was and is dispensed, and in Austen's day, it was believed to be good for what ailed you — in her uncle's case, gout; the water has a slight metallic flavor)
- Took long walks with new acquaintances (none of whom would ever replace her old Steventon friends)
- Meandered on drives in the surrounding neighborhood
- Enjoyed Bath gossip

But we have no literary composition from this period. Austen scholars vary on the reasons:

- Austen was too busy having fun in the city.
- Austen was unhappy being out of the country and thrown into the busy streets of Bath.
- Austen disliked not having a real home, only leased quarters.

Take your pick. Many things could have kept her uninspired and from writing.

Accepting and rejecting a proposal

In late November 1802, Jane and Cassandra Austen had the great pleasure of visiting their old Steventon friends, the Biggs sisters, at their beautiful home, Manydown, where as younger women they had enjoyed many balls. Catherine Bigg and her sister Alethea — nearly the same ages as Jane — had long been among Jane's closest friends. So this reunion was to be especially happy for both sets of sisters.

Harris Bigg Wither, who like his father had assumed the additional surname Wither when the father inherited the Manydown estate, was Catherine and Alethea's brother and the heir to Manydown. (For more on inheritance and primogeniture, see Chapter 10.) Poor Harris stuttered badly and was, reportedly, large and clumsy. Because his sisters were good friends with Jane Austen, he knew Jane, too, and must have felt comfortable around her. Imagine Jane's surprise, while staying at Manydown during this November–December visit, when her friends' brother Harris, six years her junior, proposed to the 27-year-old family friend on the evening of December 2, 1802! And even more surprising, imagine her accepting the offer!

At age 27, Austen was pretty much over the hill when it came to marriage in her day. So to have an offer at age 27 was unusual. Besides, such a proposal would relieve her parents' economic concerns, and she was great friends with the Manydown family. However, although marriage without love wasn't unusual or unsatisfying in Austen's day when women depended on husbands to support them, she still found herself miserable at the thought of being Mrs. Harris Bigg Wither.

Thirteen years later, when she would write to her beloved niece Fanny, then 21, "Anything is to be preferred or endured rather than marrying without affection," she personally knew how true those words were (Letter, November 18–20, 1814). For after accepting Harris's proposal, the next morning, December 3, 1802, she retracted her acceptance and with Cassandra immediately left Manydown for her brother's home in Steventon to rehearse the events of the last 24 hours with her brother and sister-in-law, Cassandra, and friend Madam Lefroy.

Keep in mind Austen's words to her niece and remember that her heroines never marry for money: They marry for love, but being practical young women, they love men who at least have more money than they have and who will be able to support them nicely. In fiction, you *can* have it all.

Losing a father and a friend

On January 21, 1805, Jane Austen's father died. While he had been ailing for some time, his death came after a short sickness. In a sweet letter to her brother Frank, Jane wrote, "Our dear father has closed his virtuous & happy life, in a death almost as free from suffering as his Children could have wished" (Letter, January 21, 1805). His death came just a little more than a month after that of Jane's longtime friend, Madam Lefroy, a highly experienced equestrienne who died after being thrown from a horse on Jane's 29th birthday: December 16, 1804.

The shock and pain of the two losses coming so close together may have stopped Jane Austen's writing *The Watsons,* her only work of fiction named for the central family. The fragment certainly contains the makings of a courtship novel, with a lovely and intelligent heroine, Emma Watson, plus Austen's only charming child character in all of her fiction, the dancing 10-year-old Charles Blake.

The grief over Mr. Austen's death was worsened by his family's knowing that his church living (income) died with him. This loss meant that his widow was now down to an annual income of about £140 — an amount that clearly threatened the women's lifestyles and put them in genteel poverty.

Relying on the kindness of sons and brothers

Jane Austen's life between 1806 and 1809 was one of extended visits to brothers and their families. In 1808, she stayed at least a month at Godmersham, Edward's estate in Kent, where she wrote that "It seems odd to have such a great place all to myself" (Letter, June 15–18, 1808). Edward's wife, Elizabeth, was pregnant with child number 11.

Elizabeth would die on October 10, 1808, of childbirth problems 12 days after the birth of her 11th child, a son. Living in Southampton, Mrs. Austen and Jane immediately took charge of caring for and entertaining Edward and Elizabeth's two grieving older boys, Edward (14) and George (12), who were students in nearby Winchester, while Cassandra went to Godmersham to be with Edward and the rest of the children. At this terrible time, to help the boys raise their spirits, their Aunt Jane taught them a card game they loved, one that she would later use in *Mansfield Park:* Speculation.

Shortly after Elizabeth's death, Edward invited his mother and sisters, along with their friend Martha Lloyd, to live in a brick cottage of six bedrooms belonging to his Chawton Estate in Hampshire. Here they would be close to their first home, Steventon Rectory, where James Austen and his family now lived. The ladies happily accepted Edward's offer.

Exploring the Highs and Lows of Being a Writer

The years between the appearances of her first two published novels had their share of pain (for example, Edward's generous benefactor and adopted mother, Mrs. Knight, who had always been kind to Jane, died in 1812, and Henry's wife, Eliza, who had been ill for some time, died in April, 1813), as well as the joy she took in being published. This section takes you through the ups and downs Austen experienced as a writer.

Getting MAD and getting even

In 1809, just a few months before moving to Chawton, Austen had written to Crosby & Company to inquire about their failure to publish *Susan,* which they had now owned for six years. To preserve her anonymity and to show her feelings about the publishers' failure to act, she closed her letter, writing, "I am Gentleman &c &c MAD.—" The name on the return address was Mrs. Ashton Dennis, in care of the Post Office in Southampton (Letter, April 5, 1809). Three days later, Crosby replied that she could have the manuscript back if she paid them the ten pounds that they had paid her for it (Letter from Richard Crosby, April 8, 1809). Not having that sum to spare, Austen just bided her time. Finally, in early 1816, Jane had four published novels out, so her brother Henry went to Crosby and paid the ten pounds to buy back the manuscript and receive Crosby's resignation of all copyright claims. Only then did Henry have the fun of telling Crosby that the author of *Susan* was also the author of *Pride and Prejudice,* and so on. Some things *are* worth the wait!

Getting published for the first time

In her first three years at Chawton, Jane Austen had taken three of her early works, *Susan, Elinor and Marianne,* and *First Impressions,* reworked the last two, and had the huge satisfaction of seeing herself a published writer of popular novels. The following briefly details that journey:

- ✔ **Susan:** In 1803, her brother Henry saw to it through his agent that *Susan* (forerunner of *Northanger Abbey*) was sold to London publisher, Crosby & Company, for ten pounds, which was a great price for an unpublished writer in those days. The publisher advertised that the book would appear in 1803 or thereabouts. Jane Austen was thrilled! But it never appeared.

  Crosby & Company was the publisher of Ann Radcliffe's widely popular Gothic mystery novels, of which *Susan* made fun. Crosby publishers couldn't undermine its most popular seller, so Jane had no hope of earning anything from that novel, other than the ten pounds Crosby & Company had originally paid for the manuscript.

- ✔ **Sense and Sensibility:** Seeing that the epistolary novel had gone out of style and applying the maturity that came with the passing of 12 years, Jane Austen first set out to revise *Elinor and Marianne,* which she had last touched in 1797, changing its title to *Sense and Sensibility.* Working as her literary agent, her brother Henry took the manuscript to the London publisher Thomas Egerton. Because the book was by a previously unpublished and untried author, Egerton published the novel on commission, meaning the author paid for the book's publishing and gave the publisher a commission for selling the book. Henry undoubtedly helped her pay for all this.

Advertised in the newspaper as an "Extraordinary Novel," it finally appeared with a byline reading "By a Lady" on October 31, 1811; by 1813, it was out in a second edition. Austen made £140. What a happy — though silent — published author she was, for she requested her family members to keep the identity of the "Lady" mentioned in the byline hush-hush. In those times, if a lady put her name to the byline, society frequently assumed she was writing because of poverty. And Jane Austen was still a *lady* of the gentry.

✔ ***Pride and Prejudice:*** Besides starting *Mansfield Park* in 1812 while at Chawton, Austen was working on *Pride and Prejudice.* In 1797, her father had offered the original manuscript, *First Impressions,* to the London publisher Cadell and Company only to have it immediately declined. But having already brought out one novel of Austen's that sold well, publisher Thomas Egerton gave her £110 for the copyright to her second. He made money on this, for a second edition of *Pride and Prejudice* was needed in October of the same year (1813), and a third edition in 1817. The byline read, "By The Author of *Sense and Sensibility.*"

Writing as a mature novelist

Austen scholars consider *Mansfield Park, Emma,* and *Persuasion* Austen's mature novels. While her first three novels (including *Northanger Abbey,* though it was only published after her death) are certainly thought provoking, sensitive, and intelligent, the final three are more complex in terms of characterization and plotting.

Mansfield Park

Mansfield Park, finished in June of 1813, wasn't a reworking of an earlier manuscript. Setting the novel almost entirely at a grand country house and its accompanying estate, Austen used her earlier experiences of staying at the Bigg Withers family's Manydown Park and Edward's Godmersham to flesh out this world. Her now widowed brother Henry escorted her to London and brought her new novel to her publisher — Egerton. Despite the popular success of *Pride and Prejudice* and Egerton's praising the new novel for its "Morality" and having "No weak parts," he published it on commission, instead of buying the copyright as he had for *Pride and Prejudice* (Works 6:433). Published in May of 1814, again with a the cryptic byline, "By The Author of *Sense and Sensibility* and *Pride and Prejudice,*" the edition sold out by November. Even with the commission, Austen made £350.

Meanwhile, with Napoleon's resignation in April, 1814, Frank Austen was home, living on Edward's Chawton estate in the Chawton Great House, just a short walk from Austen's Chawton cottage. This proximity allowed her to consult Frank about the naval maneuvers she describes in the Portsmouth section of *Mansfield Park* in preparation for its second edition.

Dealing with an unwanted Royal invitation

Henry Austen fell seriously ill in October of 1815, during the Murray negotiations, and couldn't complete them as he wished. His illness kept his sister, Jane, in London, where she had come to participate in the Murray business. She stayed at Henry's longer than she had planned in order to nurse him. Being with the ailing Henry brought Jane Austen to the attention of the prince regent (later King George IV).

In his illness, Henry Austen was attended by Dr. Matthew Baillie, one of the prince regent's physicians. While Austen kept her identity as a novelist a secret from everyone other than her mother, sister, and brothers (and their wives), Henry was so proud of Jane that he once in a while let her authorship slip. So the identity of the "Lady" in the cryptic bylines was getting around. While seeing Henry for his illness, Dr. Baillie told Austen that the prince regent read and admired her three novels and had a set of

them at each of his residences. Furthermore, Dr. Baillie admitted telling the prince regent that their author was currently in London. The prince then invited Austen, through his chaplain and librarian (the Rev. Mr. James Stanier Clarke), to tour his library at Carlton House, his London palace. (For more about the prince regent and Regency England, see Chapter 2.)

On November 13, 1815, Clarke escorted the author through the luxurious royal residence. And during the tour, he told her that she was invited to dedicate her next book to the prince regent. Rejecting this invitation wasn't an option. And so *Emma* opens with the official dedication. But while the dedication was an honor for Austen, it wasn't a pleasure. For like many of her contemporaries, Austen scorned the prince regent for his blatant immorality, sexual escapades, and financial extravagance.

Emma

Awaiting the publication of *Mansfield Park,* Austen began the year 1814 writing *Emma,* a novel with a heroine of that name and of whom she said, "I am going to take a heroine whom no one but myself will much like" (*Memoir,* 157). Yet Emma, along with Elizabeth Bennet, is one of Austen's most endearing characters for many readers precisely because she's intelligent and funny, but she thinks too well of herself, making many errors in judgment that compel her to undergo a tough learning experience.

Working again through her brother Henry, Austen switched publishers to John Murray, the publisher of Byron. Murray offered Austen $450 for the novel's copyright, but as it turned out this was another commission publishing. *Emma* was published at Austen's expense with profits going to her after Murray's 10 percent commission was met.

Persuasion

Having completed *Emma* in March 1815, Austen began writing *Persuasion* in August; this would be her last completed novel. Austen finished *Persuasion* in July 1816, after revising the final chapters. She thought this novel would be called *The Elliots,* after the family of heroine Anne Elliot. (See the section, "Reacting to her death," which explains why this is known as *Persuasion.*)

Having her naval brothers home and showing English pride in the final victory over Napoleon at the Battle of Waterloo in June 1815 (albeit an army victory), she made the heroes of her last novel naval heroes. *Persuasion* deals with two books:

- The *Baronetcy,* listing those who have inherited their titles and wealth
- The *Naval List,* naming those who have earned their ranks and riches

The novel is the most romantic of her novels, being the story of Anne Elliot, who at age 27, has "lost her bloom" because she lost her one true love — a naval officer whose proposal she had rejected eight years earlier, in 1806, on the grounds that his having a wife would not be good for him. But then he returns on the scene, in 1814, still handsome and now wealthy. What's a girl who has lost her bloom to do?

While writing *Persuasion,* Austen was also beginning to feel ill.

Sanditon

As the summer of 1816 progressed, the physical decline that Austen experienced became worse. In January 1817, Austen began a new novel, which she knew as *The Brothers* but which came to be known as *Sanditon.* At the time she began the book, she was feeling somewhat better. But as time went on, the symptoms returned. Though ill herself, she writes about a new spa town, Sanditon (think Sandy-town) and the hypochondriacs who visit it and live there. It was her most slapstick writing since "Juvenilia," filled with physical humor. But she couldn't write to bring herself back to health. Leaving off writing with the quill pen, she surrendered to writing with a pencil (no more having to dip the quill into ink), and her regular strong handwriting grew weaker. And in March, at Chapter 12, she stopped writing, period.

Some people attribute Austen's physical decline to her busy last visit to London in the winter of 1815, including her nursing Henry there. Did she catch an infection? No one knows. But she certainly felt increasingly weaker and intermittently suffered gastrointestinal problems (*"Bile,"* as she called it) and backaches (Letters, September 8–9, 1816, January 24, 1817).

Succumbing to Illness

Although her family remained hopeful because Austen's condition alternated periods of weakness with periods of seeming recuperation, the author, herself, sensed that she was declining. On April 27, 1817, she wrote a will, leaving everything to her sister, except for a legacy of £50 to her bankrupt brother Henry, who'd helped her greatly with the business of getting her manuscripts to publishers, and an equal amount to Henry's housekeeper. She didn't have the will witnessed, probably to keep up the spirits of those close to her. After paying her legatees, funeral costs, and a few small debts, Austen's estate gave Cassandra £561 and change.

Seeking help in Winchester

Agreeing to the desires of her family, she decided to go to Winchester, 16 miles from Chawton, where Giles King Lyford, a highly respected surgeon at that city's County Hospital, practiced. (Lyford had helped relieve her symptoms earlier.) Accompanied by her sister, Austen traveled to Winchester on May 26, 1817, using James's carriage, while Henry rode on horseback next to it. She would never again see Chawton. Her old Manydown friend, Catherine and Alethea Biggs' big sister, the widowed Elizabeth Bigg Heathcote, lived in Winchester, and arranged for the Austen sisters to live near her at No. 10 College Street. In June, they were joined by James's second wife, Mary (Martha Lloyd's sister), who came to assist Cassandra in her nursing of Jane.

Lyford knew that Austen was beyond help. In early June, Austen's death seemed inevitable, so several of her brothers and James's wife came to be with her in her final moments.

Dying at age 41

On July 17th, Jane Austen looked the weakest she had ever appeared and slept a lot. When Cassandra asked her if she wanted anything, her sister replied that she wanted only death and asked her sister to pray for her. Lyford came and gave her something to comfort her, causing her to grow completely tranquil by 7:00 p.m. She died peacefully the following morning, July 18th, her head in the lap of her sister, who closed her eyes.

Writing to her niece Fanny, Cassandra mourned, "I have lost a treasure, such a Sister, such a friend as never can have been surpassed,— She was the sun of my life . . . I had not a thought concealed from her, & it is as if I had lost a part of myself" (Letter, July 20, 1817).

At the time of her death, with an illness that manifested symptoms for more than a year, Austen would've been thought to have died from "a slow decline" — the vague phrase that newspapers used to identify a drawn-out, undiagnosed illness. (A death from a brief undiagnosed illness was called "a rapid decline.") But history has identified a cause — doctors and scholars agree that Austen likely died from Addison's disease, a malfunction of the adrenal glands, which affects every tissue and organ in the body.

Visiting a tombstone with a major omission

Since the 19th century, Jane Austen's tomb has been a shrine — a pilgrimage site for visitors to Winchester Cathedral. But when they come to her tomb and look down to the stone floor to read the epitaph engraved in bronze covering her resting place, they read only of her Christian virtues and goodness. The reason for their visiting her grave is missing: The epitaph says nothing of her writing novels. Only after 1870 did a brass memorial tablet appear on the north wall of the nave, near Jane Austen's grave, telling the viewer that "JANE AUSTEN, known to many by her writings" is "buried in this Cathedral." Her nephew James Edward Austen-Leigh had the tablet placed in the Cathedral, using the profits of his *Memoir* of his aunt to pay for it.

In 1900, a public fundraiser provided a memorial stained-glass window with St. Augustine, whose abbreviated name is Austin (with an i), at the head; David plays the harp in the top center; St. John holds a Bible opened to his Gospel in Latin at the center of the bottom. Other figures in the window carry scrolls that have quotations from Psalms. All of these figures represent Jane Austen's religious character. A Latin inscription reads (in English translation): "Remember in the Lord Jane Austen, who died 18 July, A.D. 1817."

Winchester, home to the historic Winchester Cathedral, was, in Austen's day, the major city in her native borough or county of Hampshire. Because of her family's Hampshire clerical connections, she was laid to rest in the north aisle of the Cathedral's nave on the morning of Thursday, July 24th.

Reacting to her death

Henry Austen prepared obituaries for the press, acknowledging his sister as the author she was. As her literary executor, he also prepared for the press *Susan,* on which his sister had clearly worked since its original completion. After seeing an anonymous novel called *Susan* out in 1809, Austen changed her heroine's name to Catherine. Henry must've changed the title to *Northanger Abbey.* Likewise, he probably changed *The Elliots* to *Persuasion,* and indeed, both the word "persuade" in various forms and the concept of persuading are strikingly evident in the novel. The two novels, her first completed work and her final completed work, appeared as a two-volume set on December 17 (the day after her birthday), 1817, published by John Murray. Henry's "Biographical Notice" prefaced the novels and identified the author as Jane Austen. It sold briskly.

Cassandra returned to Chawton Cottage and cared for her mother. After Mrs. Austen's death, Cassandra visited her brothers and their children, also inviting them to visit her at the Cottage. To Cassandra we owe most of the information existing about her sister, for she made sure that her nieces and nephews learned about their aunt. But to Cassandra we also owe the loss of much information. For before her death, she burned possibly 3,500 letters written by her sister. Deirdre Le Faye, the world's expert on Austen's letters, suggests that the destroyed letters were full of information Cassandra deemed too personal for others to read.

Chapter 4

Inspiring the Aspiring Novelist

*W*riters may well be born. But they're also certainly made. As Dr. Johnson, Jane Austen's favorite moralist said, "The greatest part of a writer's time is spent in reading, in order to write; a man will turn over half a library to make one book." Fortunately, Jane Austen grew up in a family of enthusiastic readers of all kinds of literature: histories, biographies, newspapers, plays, poems, and novels. While the novel genre was still new (and therefore lacking critical stature that poetry and drama had) when Austen was growing up, Austen observed that her family was a group of enthusiastic readers of novels and "not ashamed of being so" (Letter, December 18–19, 1798).

Being inspired to write by what one has read is a frequent occurrence. Original creativity is also a great part of a novelist's craft. So, too, is observational power, especially for a novelist like Austen, who focused on the world in which she lived and wrote realistically about people and events that were familiar to her contemporaries. Not that the Meryton Assembly (a public ball) in *Pride and Prejudice* is a replica of the Basingstoke Assemblies that Austen, herself, attended and where she danced many an evening. But she knew the manners and customs of assemblies and the ladies and gentlemen who attended them. This chapter suggests some of the writers, people, and events that inspired Jane Austen.

Growing Up in a Family of Novel Readers

Probably the most intriguing part of Austen's comment about being part of a family of novel readers is her adding that they're "not ashamed of being so." Ashamed of reading novels? Actually, yes, some people were at the time she wrote that letter. The novel was still a new form of literature. Poetry and drama had been around since the Ancient Greeks and Romans. But as explained in Chapter 2, the British novel was conceived and developed in the 18th century. And so under the leadership of Jane's father, the Austens were a progressive and sophisticated group in terms of their literary tastes because they read and enjoyed novels. (For details on the early novel, see Chapter 2.)

Absorbing the style of The Book of Common Prayer

As the daughter of an Anglican clergyman, Austen read the Bible in the King James Version and *The Book of Common Prayer* of the Church of England. These books were practically required reading for all young people of the gentry class (particularly if your father was a clergyman). Austen doesn't quote Scripture in her novels; as Chapter 13 explains, she was quiet about religion in her personal life, but as someone who read her *Prayer Book* regularly, she absorbed its writing style. A keynote of that style is the repetition of words and/or phrases or the gradual escalating of words and/or phrases for rhetorical effect. (Rhetoric means the effective use of language.)

Austen knew how effective rhetorical repetition could be, when used for both serious and comic effects. For the former effect in a scene in *Mansfield Park,* she writes in nearly consecutive phrases that escalate in intensity, separated only by six lines. Speaking of Edmund Bertram and Fanny Price, she says: "Edmund proposed, urged, entreated it — " and then ". . . she could not, would not, dared not attempt it" (MP 1:18). This is the style of repetition one hears in "The Order for the Administration of the Lord's Supper, or Holy Communion in the 1662 version of *The Book of Common Prayer,* which is the edition Austen would've owned and known intimately.

Jumping to Dr. Johnson for instruction in morality and prose

It may seem jumpy to move from religious prose to secular prose. But in the case of Dr. Samuel Johnson (1745–1789), the jump is appropriate because he was Austen's favorite moralist and a great influence on her prose. Literature's Age of Sensibility, which is discussed later in this chapter, is also known as the Age of Johnson because he was the dominant literary figure of the period. Dr. Johnson was a complete realist. He fought hard for self-knowledge and believed everyone should do the same. The greatest danger, he felt, was filling one's mind with illusions. A devout Christian with deep faith in God, he also championed reason, believing that thinking reasonably meant thinking morally. Turn to Austen and she, too, emphasizes self-knowledge and reason.

Those who dwell in illusion (like Marianne, Elizabeth, and Emma do for some time in their respective novels) find themselves misled and must, instead, come to know themselves, even if it causes anguish. His prose style can also be compared to the *Prayer Book*'s balanced and parallel phrases and sentences. So Austen inherited her phrasing from both the *Prayer Book* and Johnson's secular writing, demonstrated in such works as his *Rambler* essays and short fictional piece, *Rasselas,* all of which she read repeatedly and absorbed.

Finding Shakespeare in Austen's "constitution"

In the evenings when Mr. Austen or other family members read aloud to the others, they often read Shakespeare. In *Mansfield Park* (3:3), Fanny reads *Henry the VIII* aloud to Lady Bertram, who later tells Henry Crawford, who takes over the reading and reads with great dramatic effect, that Fanny "'often reads to me out of those books'" — those books being either a collection of Shakespeare's plays or plays by Shakespeare and other hands. As Henry Crawford states in the same chapter, Shakespeare "'is part of An Englishman's constitution.'"

Austen's earliest use of Shakespeare cites him as a source in her mock *History of England,* written when she was about 16, showing she had his work at her fingertips. But while Austen, as an Englishwoman, had Shakespeare in her constitution, her writing doesn't overflow with direct references to his plays. In fact, when she does cite Shakespeare in her novels, it's in a more subtle way. For example, *Mansfield Park* is thought to be her most "Shakespearean" novel. In this novel, Henry Crawford reads *Henry the VIII* to Fanny and Lady Bertram with great dramatic effect (MP 3:3). The play was a good choice for Henry Crawford's reading, for like Henry the VIII with his six wives, Henry Crawford has real trouble being constant to one woman. References to Shakespeare appear here and there in her novels, including *Julius Caesar* in *Mansfield Park* (1:13), *A Midsummer Night's Dream* in *Emma* (1:9), and *Romeo and Juliet* in *Sense and Sensibility* (1:12).

Shakespeare's chief influence on Austen is seen in her ability to capture human nature in the way Shakespeare does, as well as in the dramatic character of her writing (that is, presenting her plot largely through characters' talking, through dialogue). These characteristics have traditionally led critics and readers alike to view Shakespeare and Austen together. Indeed, Shakespeare and Austen are two of England's greatest literary exports and symbols of "Englishness." (For more on Austen's "Shakespearean" quality, see Chapter 1.)

Mining Milton

The second great English classic writer whom Austen read was John Milton — the superb mid-17th-century poet. His most famous work is the epic poem *Paradise Lost.* This book-length poem imaginatively renders the creation of the earth and Adam and Eve, life in the Garden of Eden, Adam and Eve's fall, and their expulsion from Paradise. Milton's goal in the epic was to "justify the ways of God to man." While Austen's literary aims weren't nearly so high, she uses Milton's epic in her work in varied ways.

If *Mansfield Park* is Austen's most Shakespearean novel, it is also her most Miltonic. Once again, Henry Crawford first brings up Milton by deliberately putting the accent on the wrong word in a line from *Paradise Lost.* Protesting his sister's efforts at marrying him off to one of the Bertram sisters, Henry quotes *Paradise Lost* and calls marriage "'Heavens *last* best gift'" (MP 5:19). In the line's original context, Adam awakens to find the newly created Eve and calls her "Heav'n's last best gift," with the implied accent on the word "best." It is even possible to think of Henry as *Mansfield Park*'s serpent, tempting both Bertram sisters and attempting to tempt Fanny.

A Miltonic temptation motif also underlies many of Austen's books. Consider *Northanger Abbey:* Frederick Tilney tempts Isabella Thorpe, who loses the innocent James Morland because of succumbing to the temptation of Frederick's money and future as an elder son who is in line to inherit substantial property. Catherine Morland succumbs to the temptation of thinking that a Gothic mystery and murder occurred at the Abbey. She's ejected from the Abbey paradise because General Tilney falls for the lies of John Thorpe.

Learning from Drama

Jane Austen's eldest brother James enjoyed producing plays or "theatricals" in the Austens' barn or dining room when he was home from the university for the holidays in the 1780's. The Austen family, and occasionally some of the boys who boarded at the Steventon Rectory as Mr. Austen's students, assumed roles. The family probably acted Shakespeare, or at least read his plays aloud, and often turned to recent plays for their productions, some of which are listed next:

- ✔ **The Rivals:** They performed Richard Brinsley Sheridan's comedy *The Rivals* in the summer of 1784, when Jane was 9 years old. Though young when she saw it at home, aspects of this still wonderfully humorous, laugh-filled play must have stayed with her. Satirizing 18th-century sentimentality, *The Rivals* is a comedy of manners, a realistic presentation of the customs and fashions of the day, usually in a satirical way. The hero and heroine frequently engage in witty repartee, and the satire is typically aimed at would-be wits and dandies.

✔ ***The Way of the World:*** Another famous comedy of manners from an earlier time (1700) that Austen must have known is William Congreve's brilliant *The Way of the World.* The hero and heroine, Mirabell and Millamant, engage in clever conversation in which one sometimes *caps* (completes or surpasses) the other's remark in the vein of Elizabeth and Darcy in *Pride and Prejudice.*

✔ ***The Wonder—A Woman Keeps A Secret:*** Over the Christmas holidays of 1787, the Austens acted this comedy by Susanna Centlivre, dating back to 1714, as well as David Garrick's (1717–1789, the greatest actor in 18th-century England) adaptation of John Fletcher's ***The Chances.*** Both comedies deal with ladies and gentlemen in love and the jealousy love can prompt.

✔ ***The Tragedy of Tragedies; or, The Life and Death of Tom Thumb the Great:*** *Tom Thumb* was Austen's last major production, performed in spring, 1788. More famous today as the novelist who wrote *Tom Jones,* Henry Fielding was also a playwright, and this is his most famous and brilliant farce: A farce is a comedy that arouses laughter from ridiculously improbable situations and coincidences, slapstick humor, and coarse jokes. *Tom Thumb* (1730) satirizes both the linguistic absurdity (pompous dialogue) of the previous century's "heroic" drama and the "greatness" of courtly life. Fielding's play, complete with the villainous parents and thwarted lovers typical of heroic drama, concludes with the characters ludicrously killing each other off. Just picture 13-year-old Jane laughing hysterically at such nonsense!

"Heroic" drama, usually in the form of tragedies, appeared on the British stage from around 1660 to the end of the 17th century. Known for its elaborate scenery and grandiose language used to express extravagant emotions, as well as the character types mentioned in the previous paragraph, heroic drama was easy for Fielding to parody and mock.

As both a viewer and reader of plays, Austen learned a great deal that she would apply to her fiction writing. The next section considers how she applied what she learned from drama to her writing.

Presenting characters dramatically

Just as in a play, where the audience doesn't have a narrator to tell them about characters and so learns about characters from what they say and how they say it, Austen lets characters tell about themselves. In turn, you assess the characters as you read what they say.

Consider how Austen presents Wickham, along with Elizabeth's initial response to him, in *Pride and Prejudice:* He appears shortly after the hero-to-be, Darcy, has behaved badly to Elizabeth Bennet and hurt her pride, causing her to form a prejudice against him. Into her life comes Wickham: handsome, charming, and an old acquaintance of Darcy. Having been insulted by Darcy,

Elizabeth is flattered by Wickham. Because Darcy refused to dance with Elizabeth at the Meryton Assembly, claiming she was not pretty enough, Wickham chooses to sit with Elizabeth at her Aunt Phillips's supper party (PP 1:16). Five points for Wickham! Elizabeth sees that the other young ladies in the room desire Wickham to choose them, but he has selected her. She goes from being rejected to being preferred. Elizabeth had earlier seen Darcy and Wickham barely acknowledge each other on the street — and Austen shows what a great writer she is by observing that "Both changed colour, one looked white, the other red" (PP 1:15). And so Elizabeth, having witnessed this little scene, is curious about the men's relationship.

Wickham quickly obliges by asking her how long Darcy has been in town. Answering him, she lets her negative feelings about Darcy surface when she says, "'I think him very disagreeable.'" This is all Wickham needs to hear — though first-time readers don't know why. He says, "'I have no right to give *my* opinion . . . as to his being agreeable or not . . . I have known him too long . . . It is impossible for *me* to be impartial.'" But he soon goes into a long (and it turns out, false) story about how Darcy has mistreated him. Having picked up on Elizabeth's animosity toward Darcy, Wickham feeds her prejudice against him and gains her favor. The clever Elizabeth Bennet (and frequently even the clever reader who has witnessed Darcy's earlier poor behavior toward Elizabeth) falls for Wickham's story of being misused and abused by Darcy. Oblivious to Wickham's prefacing it by saying that he wouldn't give his opinion of Darcy, Elizabeth proceeds down a path of misinformation until, learning the truth, she berates herself, saying, "'How despicably I have acted! . . . I who have prided myself on my discernment! . . . How humiliating is this discovery! . . . Till this moment, I never knew myself'" (PP 2:13).

As readers of the page, you see Austen's characters on the stage of your imagination; you listen to their words and watch their behaviors in an effort to understand them. You discover the truth about the characters as the other characters do. Austen usually doesn't have to narrate the facts about them. She shows her readers the characters and lets you hear them in dialogue.

Creating effective entrances

A good playwright knows how to bring characters onto the stage. Austen does, too. Having Darcy and Wickham reunite in a chance meeting on the street is an effective way to bring them together in front of the other characters. Their cool greeting indicates that something has happened between them in the past, but Austen can hold back her hand and arouse interest because meeting as they do in public, neither raises the past with the other. Indeed, in *Pride and Prejudice,* Austen brings four strangers into town — Darcy, Bingley, Wickham, and Collins — and each will in some way upset the equilibrium. Give each of the men a cowboy hat, and you'd have the setting for the conflict in a western movie!

Another great entrance occurs in *Sense and Sensibility* in the way she brings Willoughby into Marianne's life. A reader of romances and a young woman of excessive feeling, Marianne wants to meet the man of her dreams. She goes walking up a hill, ignoring the warnings of imminent rain. When the sky begins to pour, Marianne runs down the hill and slips on the mud, twisting her ankle. And there, in the mist, hunting, with his dogs and gun, appears Willoughby, handsome and strong, ready to rescue Marianne from the rain and mud and carry her home. The fairy-tale entrance of Willoughby turns him into Marianne's prince charming: From her reading, she was ready for him, and with the accident, he had the perfect opportunity to enter as her hero. This incident makes Marianne only more vulnerable to his charm and to the pain he will inflict by later rejecting her for the very un-heroic reason of wanting more money.

My two personal favorite entrances occur in *Mansfield Park:*

- ✔ The first occurs when the young Bertrams and their friends are about to start the full rehearsal of their play. With the unexpected absence of Mrs. Grant, they've pressured Fanny to act. Though highly reluctant, she finally agrees to read Mrs. Grant's part. But as they're about to begin, Julia Bertram, who isn't in the play, comes rushing in to announce, "'My father is come! He is in the hall at this moment'" (MP 1:18). Sir Thomas has been overseas in Antigua, and he will neither approve the play they've chosen nor like what they've have done to his house. But more important, Fanny is unexpectedly saved from acting.

- ✔ The second great entrance in *Mansfield Park* occurs moments after Sir Thomas's arrival home. The "actors" have used Sir Thomas's "dear room" — probably his study — and the connecting billiard room for their green room and theater. Finally home after his long time in the West Indies, Sir Thomas desires to see "his own dear room" (MP 2:1). Hearing someone "almost hallooing" in the billiard room, he immediately enters, finds himself on a stage, and is almost knocked backwards by "a ranting young man" (Mr. Yates), who's still practicing his role and in so doing gives "the very best start he had ever given in the whole course of his rehearsals."

Ranting and starting were familiar acting styles of the day. As opposed to natural acting, acting in the 18th-century was so highly mannered that it would look preposterous today. Actors ranted or declaimed their lines with real extravagance as they "started": gestured with their hands extended forward, the right to affirm, the left to negate. Thus, Mr. Yates starts and nearly knocks Sir Thomas off the stage when he unexpectedly interrupts Yates's rehearsing.

Rising Sentimentalism and Sensibility in Society

The desire for morality and sentimentality on the stage reflected the desires of society in real life. The period between roughly 1745 and 1789 in England is known as the Age of Sensibility. This name acknowledges the emergence of feeling (as opposed to reason or sense) as a guide to behavior. People of refinement were encouraged to show sympathy and even empathy for their fellow human beings: Showing such fellow-feeling came to be known as shedding "the sympathetic tear." Sentimental drama and novels were an outgrowth of this.

Based on the philosophy of Anthony Ashley Cooper, the third earl of Shaftesbury, sensibility grew out of his idea that people have an inborn capacity for doing good and for feeling the pain of others. (For those of you English majors reading this, the Age of Sensibility was the precursor to Romanticism.)

Austen's youthful reaction to sensibility

Austen's juvenile works mentioned in Chapter 3 include pieces ridiculing sentimental novels — fiction that pulls out all the stops to get the reader's sympathetic tear ducts flowing. Just the titles of such works give you an idea of their contents: *The Man of Feeling* and *A Sentimental Journey*. The most notable example of Austen's reaction to titles like those is her *Love and Freindship* (spelled just like that!), where the sentimentality of the characters borders on the absurd as young people fall in love literally at first sight and fall (literally, on the ground!) into hysterics. Written in 1790, two yeas after the Austens performed Fielding's farcical comedy *Tom Thumb,* in which the then 12-year-old Jane may have even acted, *Love and Freindship* is clearly influenced stylistically by Fielding's play, described under the major header "Learning from Drama." As with Fielding's farce, ridiculing heroic drama, so is Austen's youthful send-up of sentimentality. For heroic tragedy and sentimental novels shared certain traits:

- ✔ **Characters speaking in pompous language:** "'But never shall I be able so far to conquer my tender sensibility as to enquire after him'" (Letter the 13th). "'Victuals and Drink . . . and dost thou then imagine that there is no other support for an exalted Mind . . . than the mean and indelicate employment of Eating and Drinking?'" (Letter the 7th).

- ✔ **Cruel parents:** "'No! Never shall it be said that I obliged my Father,'" announces Lindsay (aka Edward) in response to his father's encouraging his marriage to Lady Dorothea (Letter the 6th). To add to the absurdity, even though Lindsay/Edward loves the beautiful and charming Dorothea, he insists he won't marry her just to defy his father, who approves their marriage!

> ✔ **Thwarted lovers:** Sophia and Laura are cruelly separated from their hus-
> bands, Augustus and Edward. Laura reports, "'[W]e could not support
> it—we could only faint'" (Letter the 10th).

Austen's mature reaction to sensibility

Sense and Sensibility is a serious treatment of excessive emotionalism in the
character of 16-year-old Marianne Dashwood, whose total loss of control
when she loses her beloved Willoughby caused her to become ill. (Austen
attributes her illness in the novel to walking in long wet grass and then failing
to change her stockings when she comes indoors. My students and I have
decided that Marianne suffers a situational depression when Willoughby
ignores her, wherein she spends nights not sleeping and days not eating. Our
class decided that this lack of care for herself leads to a depressed immune
system that leaves her open to infection.) Instead of mocking sensibility as
she had in her youthful *Love and Freindship* (remember, that's how Austen
spelled it!), she now tells a serious story to remind the reader that a healthy
psyche needs a balance of sense and sensibility. (For more info on the treatment of sense and sensibility in this novel, head to Chapter 14.)

Sensing Sensibility in Samuel Richardson

Chapter 2 mentions that the novel developed as a specific literary form with
identifying characteristics in Georgian England. One of the key figures in the
novel's development was Samuel Richardson (1689–1761), who wrote the
youthful Jane Austen's favorite novel, *The History of Sir Charles Grandison*
(1759). Richardson's life was a success story: He was apprenticed to a
London printer, whose daughter he eventually married. Nothing like marrying
the boss's daughter, right? Soon Richardson had his own business and pros-
pered as the printer of the report for the House of Commons. As a lifelong
letter writer, he was delighted when the prominent publishers, Rivington and
Osborn, asked him to create a guidebook of model letters for country readers
who couldn't compose a good letter on their own. The intended audience for
this book also included folks whose education wasn't as rich as the fortunes
they had earned in trade.

Richardson decided to write a model letter book that not only trained his
readers in the art of letter writing but also taught them moral lessons. His
guidebook came out in January 1741. Each model letter was based on a situation. Here are two examples from the book:

> ✔ From a Son reduced by his own Extravagance, requesting His Father's
> Advice on his Intention to turn Player [become an actor].

> ✔ From a Maid-Servant in Town, acquainting her Father and Mother in the
> Country with a Proposal of Marriage, and asking their Consent.

Developing the epistolary novel

Letters are also called epistles (as in the New Testament's Paul's Epistle to the Romans), so writing a novel where the plot is rendered through letters makes the novel an *epistolary novel.*

Richardson's epistolary style was based on an episode that he recalled hearing 20 years before he was asked to compose the model letter book. The story was of a 12-year-old girl whose poor parents had fallen on even harder times and so had to send their daughter to be the personal maid of an old woman. The son of this woman attempted to seduce this girl. But she successfully resisted the man's numerous attempts through varied "innocent" strategies; her virtue impressed the rich young man so much that he turned honorable and married her.

Richardson was so impressed with this story that he created two letters (#138 and #139) for his book: "by a father to a daughter in service, on hearing of her master's attempt on her virtue," and her model reply. Given that the novel had yet to be fully developed as a genre of literature, Richardson decided to use this episode for a full-length book of letters written between his fictional character, Pamela Andrews, and her parents, as well as a series of extended journal entries written by Pamela when she no longer has access to mail. He called this "writing to the moment" because Pamela demonstrates a fabulous skill of being able to transcribe entire events in a letter, complete with verbatim conversations, immediately after they occur. The result in 1740 was a very thick book: *Pamela; or, Virtue Rewarded.*

What was especially important about *Pamela* to the development of the novel form was that Richardson paid very close attention to the thoughts and feelings of Pamela, the heroine, as she goes through her numerous trials. Readers, male and female, became totally absorbed by the character; they worried through her dilemmas, cried when she cried. Readers' sensibilities were aroused: They felt for her! The novel evoked readers' sympathetic tears. And when she and Mr. B., the young man who has been trying to seduce her, married, church bells rang all over England. Thus, Richardson made this character real to his readers so that they felt both her pain and triumph! He did this by getting the reader into Pamela's emotions and thoughts as events happened through her supposedly transcribing those feelings and ideas in her letters moments after the events that evoked those emotions and thoughts occurred. He called this "writing to the moment." Granted, the ability to transcribe events verbatim — and one after the other — is a stretch! But by having his heroine do this, he puts the events in the present as his heroine gives her readers her immediate reactions to them. Austen would take Richardson's value in the feelings of a young woman to a new level, without resorting either to letters or to sentimentality.

Austen's inheritance from Richardson

Reading Richardson taught Austen that writing about the feelings and experiences of a young woman could be the stuff of a novel. All of Austen's novels deal with this topic. When in 1795 Austen began her first full-fledged novel (as opposed to the short pieces, mainly ridiculing current sentimental novels, in her juvenile work), *Elinor and Marianne,* she used Richardson's epistolary style. She did the same in 1796 when she wrote *First Impressions.* While neither manuscript exists, we can infer from the books that each eventually became — *Sense and Sensibility* and *Pride and Prejudice* — that Austen was using the epistolary style for the same reason as Richardson used it in *Pamela:* to convey the thoughts and feelings of her heroines. Although she eventually made major revisions to both epistolary manuscripts to turn them into the novels we know today, it's interesting to observe how Austen uses letters in *Pride and Prejudice,* a non-epistolary novel, to convey the feelings and personalities of various characters. Even before Collins appears on the scene, his letter to the Bennets tell them and the reader a lot about him, as do his letters to the Bennets after Lydia's scandal (PP 1:13, 3:6, 3:15). And Darcy's lengthy letter to Elizabeth allows him to explain himself in detail to her (PP 2:12). But she also surpassed Richardson in finding a new way to let her readers into the emotions and thoughts of her characters: by using free, indirect discourse as a method of narration. (For Austen's achievements in this area, head to the last section in this chapter, "Bringing It All Together: The Genius of Jane Austen," and to Chapter 16.)

Austen's departure from Richardson

As the discussion of *Pamela* showed, Richardson's novel aroused its readers' sensibility. One way he achieved this was putting the innocent Pamela into terrifying situations that placed her virginity at risk. Pamela's terror became the reader's terror. Yet for today's reader, most of these situations are now embarrassingly laughable: having Mr. B. dress in a maid's nightgown to get into bed with Pamela is totally ridiculous, even though Richardson wrote the scene with complete seriousness. (Don't worry — nothing happens because Pamela faints, and Mr. B. is not interested in her when she faints!) Austen never puts her heroines in excessive physical danger from another person, never threatens them with melodramatic villains, nor does she evoke in her readers strong feelings about her characters by placing them in tear-inducing situations. (In fact, she's tough on Mrs. Musgrove's sentimentality in *Persuasion* [1:8].) Austen stays within the confines of the probable and the familiar. And among her many great talents is giving the probable and familiar a witty, original, and thoughtful turn.

Maturing the Novel with Henry Fielding

While Richardson was Austen's favorite novelist, we can also conclude that she knew Fielding's *Tom Jones* (1749) very well. In her first collected letter, she mentions that Tom Lefroy, with whom she has been dancing, is "a very great admirer of *Tom Jones,* and therefore wears the same coloured clothes, I imagine, which *he* did when he was wounded" (January 9–10, 1797). To remember the color of Tom Jones's coat means Austen read and certainly re-read the book with care. Fielding was also the author of the comical play *The Tragedies of Tragedies; or, The Life of Tom Thumb the Great,* which the Austens performed in 1788, and which may well have inspired her style of ridiculing sentimental novels as discussed earlier in this chapter.

Educated at Eton and then at the University of Leyden (Holland), Fielding had a far more extensive acquaintance with the world than Richardson did. His first novel was actually a parody and satire of *Pamela* called *Shamela,* which proposes that Shamela is actually an artful manipulator of men, out to snare Mr. B. by holding back, rather than protecting her virtue for the sake of her honor and moral good. His later novels, *Joseph Andrews* (another swipe at *Pamela,* as Joseph is Pamela's virtuous brother!) and *Tom Jones,* take his characters all over England, where they meet all kinds of people. Dr. Johnson said of Fielding that he wrote characters of manners — characters that can be understood by a more superficial observer — as opposed to Richardson's characters of nature, whose psychology we come to understand. While Fielding's characters are shown with less depth than Richardson's, Fielding more fully surveys the world around him and comments upon the follies and vices of society, which he satirizes. Among his many contributions to novel's formation, Fielding brought society at its broadest into its pages.

Fielding wrote as a man of the world: Young Tom Jones has numerous sexual encounters with all types of women, from the good-natured country girl to the dangerous sophisticate in London he meets on his travels. Tom meets fine gentlemen, drunken squires, country poachers, and city thugs. His journey teaches him a major lesson: the need for prudence. While Austen's characters have less worldly experiences than Tom Jones — after all, as Chapter 1 stressed, Austen wrote as a "Lady" — she, too, sets her heroines on journeys through which they learn more about themselves and the society in which they live. Even Austen's least-traveled heroine, Emma, reaches both sexual maturity and mature self-knowledge by the conclusion of he novel. Also in the tradition of Fielding, Austen criticized what she thought needed correction: vanity (*Pride and Prejudice*'s Lady Catherine, Mr. Collins, and Miss Bingley), greed (*Northanger Abbey*'s General Tilney and *Sense and Sensibility*'s Lucy Steele), and human cruelty (*Mansfield Park*'s Aunt Norris), to name a few traits and characters. But while Fielding painted with a broad brush, Austen painted with a fine one.

Reading Fanny Burney

If Richardson showed in *Pamela* and *Clarissa* that the thoughts and feelings of young women were important, albeit in extreme circumstances (Pamela fears rape and Clarissa is raped), Fanny Burney in her three most famous novels, *Cecilia* (1782), *Camilla* (1796), and *Evelina* (1778), brought to the novel the experiences of young women of contemporary society in realistic circumstances involving interpersonal relationships with family members and friends. In each of the novels mentioned, Burney presents the experiences of intelligent young women entering the world of society. In so doing, Burney brought the comedy of manners — in which Austen would excel — from the stages of the theaters to the pages of the novel. Moreover, she made novel writing for women respectable.

Austen actually took the phrase *Pride and Prejudice* from the final chapter of *Cecilia,* where the phrase appears three times in capital letters on one page.

Critics have studied *Cecilia*'s specific influence on *Pride and Prejudice.* Burney's *Camilla* was published by subscription, meaning the publisher would issue a prospectus for a book and people would sign up to buy the book, sometimes putting money down. In this way, the publisher had a good idea of who was buying the book and how many would be sold. Among the subscribers to *Camilla* (and there were many, including some of the most famous names in England) was "Miss. J. Austen, Steventon," who at the time would have been 20 years old. Turning again to literary critics who look at "intertextuality" — a fancy way of saying how one book influences another — I note that they see *Camilla*'s influence on *Sense and Sensibility,* as *Camilla* involves two sisters in their courting days, and Camilla's suitor is Edgar, while Elinor's is Edward. That Austen admired the novel is clear from her commenting in a letter about an acquaintance whose two most pleasing traits were not putting cream in her tea and liking *Camilla* (Letter, September 15–16, 1796).

Being Influenced By Real People

Jane Austen said that she never modeled a character on a real person. But as an astute observer of people, she occasionally found a personality trait here and there to flesh out a fictional character.

Meeting an exotic "French" cousin

One of the most influential people Jane Austen ever met was her grown-up cousin (14 years Jane's senior), Eliza, the only daughter of her father's sister. Born of English parents in India, Elizabeth Hancock, called Betsy as a child, was educated in London and France. By the time, as a teenager, she and her widowed mother went to France, she had rid herself of Betsy and renamed herself Eliza. Eliza visited Versailles and saw King Louis XVI and his queen, Marie-Antoinette. The young woman was thrilled with the court and everything French, particularly the fashions. She was obviously also thrilled with the captain's uniform for the Queen's Dragoons. For this was the uniform of Captain Jean Capot de Feuillide, to whom Eliza became engaged during the summer of 1781. While the captain's family was not royal — his father was the mayor of Nerac — the captain liked to be called Comte (Count). And so when he and Eliza married, she became Eliza, Comtesse de Feuillide. That name was a long way from Betsy.

Imagine being 11 years old, living in a little English village, and having a glamorous 25-year-old cousin, dressed in the latest French couture, who spoke French with you (Jane was better at reading French than speaking it) and was called Comtesse in your house! And not just once, but again over the holidays of winter 1787! During the latter visit, Eliza participated in the Austen family tradition of producing and performing in plays at home under the supervision of big brother James. She likely took the lead female roles in two comedies. The lovely, petite, and stylish Eliza, with her big round eyes, flirted happily with her male cousins, Jane's elder brothers. Everything about Eliza must have fascinated the 12-year-old Jane. Among the brothers most taken with Eliza was the tall (over 6 feet), charming Henry, a decade her junior. This crush wasn't short-lived on Henry's part. Three years after Eliza's husband, the so-called Comte, was guillotined in 1794 during the French Revolution, Henry married his 36-year-old widowed cousin, with whom he lived happily until her death, probably from breast cancer (which also took her beloved mother, Philadelphia Austen Hancock) in 1813.

It is certainly possible to see some of Eliza in *Mansfield Park*'s pretty, lively, and flirtatious Mary Crawford. And perhaps even some of Elizabeth Bennet's incredible self-possession came from Jane's "French" cousin. What can be said with assurance is that the 12-year-old Jane Austen, living in the Steventon Rectory, had never seen anyone quite like Eliza de Feuillide.

Running across other memorable personalities

One of the most intriguing activities to do while reading Austen's letters is to play detective and note people she meets who turn up in one form or another in her novels. Seeing a personal trait of someone mentioned here and there in a letter turn up in a character shows that Austen was a real people-watcher.

Here are a few examples:

- ✔ On September 15–16, 1796, Austen wrote of 17-year-old Lucy Lefroy's failing to write a letter because "everybody whom Lucy knew . . . in Canterbury, has now left it . . . By *Everybody,* I suppose [she] means that a new set of Officers have arrived there — " Sounds like Lydia Bennet and her redcoats in *Pride and Prejudice.*

- ✔ On January 22, 1799, Austen observed that the Miss Coopers are "fine, jolly, handsome, ignorant girls." Are *Mansfield Park*'s Bertram sisters lurking nearby?

- ✔ On October 12, 1813, Austen met Mrs. Britton — an "ungenteel woman with self-satisfied and would-be elegant manners." I think I hear *Emma*'s Mrs. Elton.

- ✔ In the same letter in which she mentions Mrs. Britton, Austen also mentions having breakfast at her brother's home with Robert Mascall, who eats a lot of butter. In *Sanditon,* Arthur Parker slathers his toast with butter.

Bringing It All Together: The Genius of Jane Austen

Like the novel genre, itself, Austen's skills as a novelist grew over time. Austen intellectually absorbed the novel form by

- ✔ Starting to write at age 12
- ✔ Sharing her writing with her well-read family
- ✔ Having an unquenchable reading habit in her father's excellent library
- ✔ Discussing what she read with her family of readers

Creating living, breathing characters

Using a third-person, omniscient, or all-knowing, narrator (the voice that tells the story), Austen is able to present the interior workings of her characters' minds without resorting to Richardson's device of letter writing. And while she said that she never modeled a character on Mr. A. or Mr. B., her letters show how closely she observed human behavior — taking one character facet from here, another from there, and still others from her own creative imagination to present vivid characters: characters like the nosey Mrs. Jennings, the restrained Elinor Dashwood, or the clueless Emma Woodhouse. In her own way, Austen combines the characters of nature with the characters of manners that she knew from reading Richardson and Fielding.

Austen's characters are so realistic that many of her readers go to sequels written by other authors to fill their need to learn the future of the characters' lives! (For more on the sequels, see Chapter 1.)

Setting her characters in society

Like Fielding, Austen is a satirist. She looks around her world and sees both the charming and the correctable. Like Mary Crawford in *Mansfield Park,* Austen could say of herself, "'I do not pretend to set people right, but I do see they are often wrong'" (1:5). The characters in her novels show us that:

- Noble titles and rich estates don't necessarily make true ladies and gentlemen.
- Family life is far from guaranteeing what today is called "family values."
- Father doesn't always know best and neither does mother.
- Social and economic times were changing.
- Greed frequently operates in people when you least expect it.
- First impressions will always leave us clueless.

She achieves the above points with wit, irony, and sensitivity to human nature, so her characters remain with us long after the novel is closed.

Part II
Austen Observes Ladies and Gentlemen

The 5th Wave   By Rich Tennant

In this part . . .

*E*ver wonder while reading *Pride and Prejudice* why Mrs. Bennet is thrilled that Bingley has danced twice with her eldest daughter, Jane, but there's no talk of their dancing together three times? Or why in *Sense and Sensibility*, Elinor is shocked that her sister, Marianne, isn't engaged to Willoughby, even though Marianne has written letters to him? Austen's ladies and gentleman danced and courted according to certain rules. Although characters' actions may seem strange to you, they were or weren't following the protocol of the times for persons of their class. Even marrying meant arranging legal "settlements" and "articles." Part II clues you in on all this. Plus, there's a chapter on Austen's ladies and gentlemen who don't — for shame — act like ladies and gentlemen!

Chapter 5

Practicing the Politics of Dancing

*I*n Austen's day, young people did not date in the way we think of dating. So when young people of the gentry, the only social class that concerns Austen, were looking for a fun-filled evening — and a possible spouse — dances were the best places to be. Attending dances was the primary way for young people to meet and get to know each other socially. In fact, even if a young lady was interested in the young gentleman whose family were lifelong friends of her family and who resided at the neighboring estate — an estate that was many miles across the field! — dancing was the occasion where she could actually hold his hand for several minutes! Pretty hot stuff, yes? (For more information on the gentry, the class that interested Austen and to which she belonged, see Chapter 2.)

Austen enjoyed dancing, and so do the characters in her books. Austen wrote to her sister, Cassandra, about her grand plans to attend dances and the dances she'd already attended. Her letters to Cassandra included the names of her partners and descriptions of their looks, personalities, and dancing abilities. After all, one of them might end up being her marriage partner, so she may as well give her only sister a full report about a young man who might someday be Cassandra's brother-in-law!

The ability to dance — and to dance well — was a social requirement in Austen's day. Whether you were a male or female dancer, finding yourself with a partner with two left feet usually meant two things:

▸ The partner with whom you were dancing wasn't really genteel.

▸ You would likely write that partner off as a potential spouse.

The exception to the second bullet, of course, was if your partner was swimming in money, you were really desperate, or you were a gold-digger — in which case, Jane Austen would never cast you as a hero or heroine. But interestingly enough, Jane Austen's heroines never married for money, but they never married without getting a piece of the pie, either. Even though Austen's characters married for love, they were still realistic.

This chapter familiarizes you with the customs and rules of dancing in Austen's day. Dances could be public or private, formal or informal, and people attending these soirees had certain expectations about what would occur and how to behave.

Looking for Love on the Dance Floor

Children of the gentry were taught how to dance the latest steps so they could participate readily in social dancing as they grew up. Dances in Austen's day were either informal or formal.

Rolling up the rugs to dance at home

Informal dances were spur of the moment ideas that occurred when a musician and enough dancers gathered for home entertainment. But wherever young people gathered to dance, the event was an opportunity to meet new friends, dance with old and new friends (and even siblings), and initiate or continue a romantic relationship.

Impromptu, informal dances at home were both family evening entertainment and social events and were more characteristic of country life than city life in Austen's day. While city dwellers could find evening entertainment outside the home at such places as the theater, opera, or even the circus, country families had to make their own after-dinner fun, especially in the winter, when weather problems meant staying home.

Keep in mind that even though Londoners might look down on impromptu after-dinner dancing at home, these occasions weren't country hoe-downs. Country gentry families still dressed for dinner and had great fun dancing after the meal. For guests who weren't dancing, watching was enjoyable. And for those who didn't care for the dancing at all, cards and other games were always available at the other end of the drawing room. A popular card game requiring no prowess, just luck, was "lottery tickets," which engrosses Lydia in *Pride and Prejudice* (1:16). (Using a deck of cards, lottery tickets involved the players' betting on and receiving random cards; they bet with "fish," similar to little poker chips but fish-shaped.) See "Amusing the Non-Dancers: Finding the Card and Tea Rooms" later in this chapter.

Having a spontaneous dance involved just the right ingredients:

- ✔ Someone to play the music
  - A willing pianist-mother
  - The wallflower, keyboard-playing sister
  - The violinist-servant
- ✔ A room with enough space to dance
- ✔ Plenty of willing friends and family

After that, you'd just roll up the rug and voilà! The sudden thought of an evening of dancing became a reality.

Attending formal balls

Formal dances, requiring advance planning, took two forms: private balls and public balls (also called assemblies). Because a gentry lady would never settle for a formal ball in a dingy location, formal balls occurred in varied locations:

- ✔ **Assembly rooms:** Large ballrooms located in buildings built for that purpose; market towns and cities had such rooms.

- ✔ **Ballrooms in country inns** (like *Emma*'s Crown Inn): The size and elegance of these venues varied depending on the size of the village, market town, or city.

- ✔ **Large rooms in home or country homes:** Because large houses usually had formal ballrooms or lovely rooms large enough to serve as ballrooms, their owners or residents hosted formal balls (evidenced in *Pride and Prejudice* with Mr. Bingley and Netherfield Park, and in *Mansfield Park,* when Sir Thomas hosts a ball). (For more information on the splendid country houses of Austen's day, see Chapter 11.)

Jane Austen, being a member of the gentry, attended all types of formal balls, allowing her to write about them knowingly. (For information about the term *gentry,* see Chapter 2.)

The private ball

When the owner of a large country house decided to host a private formal ball, the first step was creating the guest list and sending out invitations. But how did you get on that guest list? Knowing the *right* people and being in the *right* circle of friends, just as it helps today, helped the people in Jane Austen's time get invitations to desirable events.

What to wear, what to wear?

Austen's novels are set in a period of ladies' fashion known as the Regency period (or in France, the Empire period). England borrowed the style from the French, ever the fashion leaders. Dresses were straight, sometimes called tube-shaped or columnar (like a column on a building) — but full enough to accommodate dancing. The waistline was high — known as the Empire waist (again, the French influence) — coming just under the bosom, and the neckline was low. When the 1995 television special *Pride and Prejudice* appeared, the joke going around regarding the young actresses' Regency gowns was that the production had bought all the push-up bras in England! Modest young women shy about revealing cleavage could tuck gauze into the neckline — really the bosom line.

The favorite material for making these gowns was muslin, a fine cotton fabric, sometimes beautifully embroidered with floral designs. This was especially true when England was at war with France (relative to Austen's novels, 1793–1815): silk, a former favorite fabric, came from France, but the English mills could produce cotton. *Northanger Abbey*'s Henry Tilney, having a sister, teasingly shows off his knowledge of muslins in a conversation with Catherine Morland and her chaperone, Mrs. Allen, saying he "'understands muslins,'" "'Particularly well . . . and my sister has often trusted me in the choice of a gown'" (NA 1:3). White was a favorite color for muslin gowns for two main reasons: It looked very classical, as seen in the marble statues from ancient Greece and Rome, which were in vogue; and it indicated that the wearer was wealthy enough to have maids to keep the gowns clean. Henry Tilney's sister Elinor "'always wears white'" (NA 1:12), while *Mansfield Park*'s Aunt Norris compliments the housekeeper at Sotherton for turning "'away two housemaids for wearing white gowns,'" which is dressing above their class (MP 1:10).

Other favorite colors were pale yellow, pink, and blue. Sleeves were short.

Because muslin is a flimsy, sheer material, the young lady wore at least one petticoat under the gown, as well as long underpants called "drawers," which were long. The petticoat, which had a decorative binding at the bottom, sometimes extended a bit below the gown's hemline. Over the petticoat sometimes went the chemise, a long linen or cotton short-sleeved shirt. But risqué young women wore their muslin gowns with neither petticoat, nor chemise, nor drawers — obviously providing quite an eyeful! I am relieved to report to my readers that Elizabeth Bennet definitely wore a petticoat: Recall that when she walks across the wet fields to Netherfield, Mrs. Hurst criticizes "'her petticoat, six inches deep in mud . . . and the gown, which had been let down to hide it, not doing its office'" (PP 1:8). Undoubtedly, the moral Elizabeth Bennet wore a chemise and drawers, too!

The big, tall hair look for women of the 1770s and 1780s had thankfully been replaced in the 1790s by simpler styles, also imported from France and influenced by classical statuary. No longer sporting the ridiculously high, pomaded (covered with ointment) and powdered hair that was pulled over padding and ornamented with ribbons, miniature boats, and birds, women now wore their hair short in the front with curls framing the face and relatively short in the back. With shorter hair, women were no longer walking around with creepy, crawly things in their hair. But their hair still needed to be curled and arranged. A simple ribbon and/or a feather ornamented the hair. In *Northanger Abbey*, the well-dressed Eleanor Tilney wears "'white beads round her head'" at a ball (NA 1:8).

To top off her ball gown, the young lady would put on a paisley shawl and some simple jewelry. When Fanny Price attends the ball in her honor at Mansfield Park, she wears a white gown with a simple gold chain to hold her amber cross around her neck, as well as a more ornate gold necklace (though less to her taste), in order not to embarrass the latter's giver, Mary (really Henry!) Crawford (MP 2:9).

The young lady also carried a delicate fan, good for both flirting and keeping oneself cool! (Country dances could be quite lively, and with the heat of all the people in the room, the dancers became hot.) Ladies' gloves went up to the elbow and could be sheer. Both men and women wore gloves while dancing.

The party host normally sent invitations to families with young ladies and gentlemen, knowing that their parents would consider the ball a wonderful place for their marriageable daughters and sons to meet and further their acquaintances. But the ball's guest list also included whole families with interaction for all the guests — old and young.

Invitations had to be sent early enough to give the guests sufficient time to prepare to attend, which usually suggested that an invitation to a formal ball, private or public, meant that young ladies participated in new experiences:

- Buying a new and fashionable dress made with fabric and patterns from the nearest market town or city

- Securing fashion accessories such as new shoes and shoe ornaments

- Getting their hair done professionally or by a maid who had hairdressing talent to save the expense

Young men — depending on how vain they were — also made preparations for attending balls. But mostly, they had others take care of the arrangements:

- A gentleman's butler or "man" had his suit, shoes, and gloves in order.

- The groom or stableman made sure the carriage or horse was ready.

In only one of Austen's works does the man actually take care of getting ready himself: *Catherine; or The Bower*. The young man in this story spends over half an hour doing his hair. In fact, the average gentleman, himself, needed to be sure of doing only one thing: ask the lady of his choice for the first dance. If he didn't, he risked losing that dance to someone else. The men sure had it easy, wouldn't you say?

When attending a private ball, the evening usually had a certain schedule:

- **8:00 p.m.:** Evening began

    Private balls began in the evening around 8:00 p.m. and usually began with mingling and dancing to the music of several string players. Sometimes the host went so far as to hire musicians from a nearby city. And if he really wanted to impress his friends and neighbors, he might even have musicians from London, the capital of the nation, as well as the capital of fashion and taste.

Tradition held that the gentleman who danced with the lady just before supper joined her at the supper table. This time gave the couple more opportunities for talking, flirting, and being together. For example, during the formal ball at Mansfield Park, Fanny suspects that Henry Crawford inquires "about the supper-hour . . . for the sake of securing her [Fanny] at that part of the evening" (MP 2:10). Henry is leaving nothing to chance: Having opened the ball as Fanny's partner, he'll time his *second dance* with her to be just before the supper hour so he can sit with her at the dining table. (Read more about the two-dance rule in the aptly titled "Observing dancing etiquette" section later in this chapter.)

✔ **12:00 a.m.:** Supper served

Now this might seem late. But they ate a hearty breakfast around 10 a.m.; morning lasted until around 3 p.m., and they ate a multicourse dinner anywhere between 5 p.m. and 7 p.m. — perhaps a bit earlier than 7 p.m. on the night of a dance that began around 8 p.m.

A sit-down supper was traditionally offered to the guests at a private, formal ball. (Curious what items were popular fare? See the "What's for supper?" sidebar.) The importance of the supper was social as well as nutritional

✔ **3:00 a.m. to 4:00 a.m.:** Head home

Jane Austen herself enjoyed dancing at private balls, mostly held in the large country homes of friends. For example, she danced at Manydown Park (home of her good friends Catherine and Alethea Biggs) and Ashe House (home of the Austens' good friends the Lefroys). At one winter ball held at Ashe, the 20-year-old Austen danced and flirted with her friends' Irish nephew, Tom Lefroy, who aroused her romantic interest. (For more on Tom Lefroy, Jane Austen, and her letters, see Chapter 3.)

The public ball

Public balls (or assemblies) were open to anyone who could afford a ticket — though I've come across no stories of a very poor soul who scrimped and saved for a ticket to a ball! While this sounds certainly snobby today, in Austen's time, people knew and accepted their place in society. A season's worth of tickets for public balls might cost anywhere between one pound in the country and around ten guineas (London) — the value of which is difficult to calculate today because the buying power has changed dramatically. But let's give it a try! A British pound (£) contained 20 shillings, and 1 guinea was 21 shillings, or 1 shilling over a pound. In the year 2004, it took $1.84 to buy £1. And in 2004, £1 from 1810 had the purchasing power of £49 (or $90.16). So this will give you an idea of the purchasing power of a season ticket in 1810 in today's money. A pound in 1810 was worth a lot. But remember, the ball ticket also included supper! A season's worth of balls could run for just three or four months in the country. In London, the social season ran from about February to June and September to pre-Christmas.

What's for supper?

Formal balls always included a supper. To understand this, you need to know that even if a person rose early in the morning, he or she ate a big, hot breakfast around 10 a.m. Morning lasted until around 3 p.m. Then the family ate their main meal, dinner, anytime between 4 p.m. and 6 p.m. — with the really fashionable eating dinner between 7 p.m. and 8 p.m. Because of the dinner hour, supper at home, if it was eaten at all, tended to be a snack of cold meats or something hot and light (like soup) eaten late in the evening in the drawing-room, not in the dining room, which was reserved for dinner. But a sit-down supper was necessary at balls mainly because dancers worked up an appetite! The menu often included such delicious items as

- ✔ White soup, made with cream and eggs and chicken stock, was always a hit.

- ✔ If a cold supper was served, it could include ham, chicken, scalloped oysters, or sandwiches.

- ✔ If a hot supper was served, roasted or boiled chicken, beef, or veal could be on the menu.

- ✔ To supplement the meat, poached or boiled eggs, asparagus, cheese, pickles, bread, and butter were on the table.

- ✔ And to drink, party goers enjoyed wine and *negus* — a popular hot, spicy drink.

Most public balls such as the Basingstoke Assemblies, which Austen attended quite regularly, were held monthly to coincide with a full moon. This isn't because the planners assumed that the dancers were more likely to fall in love under moonlight. Instead, a full moon made it easier and safer for attendees to travel. In fact, whether scheduling a private ball or an assembly, the organizers always checked their almanacs to see when a full moon would be visible. In a time when country roads were rough and the only artificial light came from the candle-lit lamps in front of the carriage, it was important for everyone's safety and comfort to be sure that dance attendees could travel when the natural light was at its brightest at night. Of course, this travel was *to* the ball. With country balls, especially private balls, sometimes lasting until 5:00 or 6:00 a.m., people could travel safely in their carriages, driven by their coachmen, at the dawn's early light.

The ticket price for the ball was usually worth it because assemblies attracted dancers from beyond one's immediate neighborhood, and attending these events enabled you to see new faces and increased your chances of meeting a mate. But you couldn't always count on a big crowd of new faces. In the country, gentry families who normally attended the assemblies in the nearest market town might have gone to Bath or London for the social season, which ran February to June and September to December prior to Christmas, to attend even more glamorous balls.

Socializing for a season

Bath, located in Somerset, England, was a fashionable spa city in Austen's day, attracting thousands of annual visitors. Because of its popularity and social elegance (just about anybody who was anybody spent some time in Bath), Bath was the perfect place to go to check out eligible young women and gentlemen as future marriage partners.

Bath, built on a hill, had two splendid assembly rooms, the older Lower Rooms located near Bath Abbey in the lower part of the city (built in 1709), and the Upper or new Assembly Rooms located near The Circus and Bennett Street in the upper part of the city (built between 1768 and 1771 because the Lower Rooms did not provide enough space). The Lower Rooms were destroyed by fire in 1820, but the Upper Rooms, though bombed in World War II, have been refurbished and are a popular tourist site as well as a beautiful venue for social functions.

To avoid competition, the Upper and Lower Rooms arranged their respective event schedules to allow people to take advantage of dancing at both assembly rooms on different evenings. Because Bath was a haven for the ill (who came for the mineral waters, which provided a colonic irrigation), as well as the healthily social, the balls in the rooms began at 8:00 p.m. and ended much earlier than the private balls that Jane Austen and Fanny Price attended in the country. Not that the sick were attending balls. This earlier time was in consideration of them, probably causing the streets to be quieter at night.

The exterior of the Upper Rooms, which means the entire building, is quite plain. But once inside, the vestibule and the four interconnected social rooms are breathtakingly splendid:

✔ **The Ballroom:** Decorated with five glass chandeliers and mirrors, the elegant high-ceiling Ballroom was 100 feet long, 42 feet wide and high, with a capacity of 1,200 people (no wonder Catherine Morland and Mrs. Allen were nearly crushed in it on a packed night). The Ballroom includes a balcony, known as the Musicians' Gallery, for the players of mostly stringed instruments.

✔ **The Tea Room:** Guests took tea in this magnificent room (hence the name), but it was also used as a concert venue. The room was adorned with chandeliers, pillars, statues, carved scrolls, and a wrought-iron balcony.

✔ **The Octagon Room:** This central room, with its beautiful domed roof and sculptured wall painting, served as a meeting place, as well as a music room. *Persuasion*'s Dowager Viscountess Dalrymple hosts a concert of Italian singing in the gorgeous green and gold Octagon Room (2: 7, 8). It is also here that the novel's heroine and hero, Anne Elliot and Captain Wentworth, have an emotionally important reunion, causing Anne to wonder, "How was the truth to reach him?" (P 2:8).

✔ **The Card Room:** This handsome room provided a space where guests could play cards; today it's a bar. When Catherine Morland and the Allens arrived at the Upper Rooms, Mr. Allen "repaired directly to the card-room, and left them to enjoy a mob by themselves" (NA 1:2).

In fact, Austen attended a country assembly in Basingstoke on Thursday evening, November 22, 1798, that had "but seven couples, and only twenty-seven in the room" (Letter, November 25, 1798). Notice that the date of the ball falls within the social season, when many wealthy people from the country went to London or Bath. So even the best laid plans for attending a public ball, hoping to meet new and old friends, could be disappointing. In fact, on January 8, 1801, Austen wrote that the "Basingstoke Balls are certainly on the decline." Five months later, on May 12, 1801, after attending an assembly in Bath, Austen wrote to her sister that even with a "shockingly" thin crowd in Bath's Upper Rooms' ballroom, "there were people enough . . . to have made five or six very pretty Basingstoke assemblies." When the Austens moved to Bath in 1805, Jane and Cassandra, aged 25 and 28, respectively, were unmarried and hitting the social scene pretty hard, but unfortunately, Jane's existing letters reveal no romantic prospects for either, larger assemblies notwithstanding. And they even lived there when the season was full.

But one of Austen's fictional couples did meet in Bath. Austen's heroine, Catherine Morland, of *Northanger Abbey,* is simply introduced to Mr. Henry Tilney by the Master of Ceremonies in the Lower Rooms, and the rest is history.

As with private balls, whole families attended assemblies. Whether in country towns like Basingstoke or busy cities like Bath, parents accompanied their sons and daughters to these public balls. And when a parent wasn't available, an older woman serving as chaperone accompanied the group of youngsters (see the "Having fun under a watchful chaperone's eye" section later in this chapter). Parents wanted to have fun too, but they (and the chaperones) attended the assemblies mainly to keep an eye on their daughters who were of marrying age (at least 16 years old) or "out" — see Chapter 6 for details. While no young lady (including Austen) could attend an assembly on her own, a gentleman could go solo. But with the young lady's chaperone or parents keeping an eye on her, his behavior was always that of a gentleman!

Unlike private balls, assemblies or public balls didn't serve suppers; tea was served about halfway through the night instead. Similar to the tradition at formal private balls, where the gentleman sat at supper with the young lady with whom he danced just before the supper, so at public balls the gentleman sat with the lady with whom he danced just before the tea service. Thus, Henry Tilney sits with his dancing partner, Catherine Morland, for tea during the dancing recess at the Lower Rooms (NA 1:3). This, of course, gave the couple additional time to talk, flirt, or do whatever else a couple can do sitting at a table with her chaperone or parents and surrounded by hundreds of other tea drinkers.

With assemblies lasting until the wee hours of the morning, Austen and others would frequently stay overnight at a friend's family home after the ball. This wasn't only because of weather concerns, but also because traveling without a male escort was considered improper for young ladies. So Austen would have to wait until a brother or someone from a friends' family, like the father, could take her home. Another reason for her spending the night with friends is that the Austens didn't keep a carriage after 1798. This, too, meant that Austen needed to rely on her host's family, her own brother, or even her older sister or sister-in-law to drive her home. But like her most athletic heroine, Elizabeth Bennet in *Pride and Prejudice,* the young Austen could also spend the night with friends and then walk home to Steventon through the fields the next day — something she would not do, of course, at 3:00 a.m. when the ball ended.

Facing the challenges of dancing

Now what about the young ladies present who had a bad track record for getting asked to dance? Mary Bennet in *Pride and Prejudice* was in her late teens and, unfortunately (I hate to say it, but I must speak the truth), a little nerdy. But, in fact, all gentry ladies, nerdy or not, were expected to play their share of dance music on the *pianoforte,* the predecessor to the modern piano, sounding more like a harpsichord with soft (piano) and loud (forte) tones. So, for Mary Bennet, providing the dance music at an informal dance gladdens her heart and ego, saving her, of course, from the humiliation of not being asked to dance.

Another factor for avoiding dancing was age (not that there was a definite cut-off age for dancing). A letter dated January 30, 1809, reports the unmarried, 33-year-old Jane Austen dancing at a ball. But in a letter to her sister written on November 6–7, 1813, Austen, now nearly 39 years old, says, "By the bye, as I must leave off being young, I find many Douceurs in being a sort of Chaperon for I am put on the Sofa near the Fire & can drink as much wine as I like." Staying at Godmersham, her brother Edward's estate in Kent, she is probably referring to attending a ball in Canterbury with her nieces, nephews, and their friends the previous Thursday evening (Letter, November 3, 1813).

Austen's characters also shied away from dancing as they got older. At the Musgroves' informal dances, Anne Elliot is a pretty, "elegant little woman" of 27, who in her happier, younger days undoubtedly enjoyed her share of dancing (P 2:8). When Captain Wentworth dines with Anne and the Musgroves and the evening ends with dancing, he asks if Anne ever dances anymore. Someone answers, "'Oh, no; never. She's quite given up dancing'" (P 1:8). At 27, Anne Elliot would still be dancing if it weren't for her poor spirits. You will, though, have to finish *Persuasion* to see if Anne's future holds any promise of dancing again!

So while we have no records to say that ladies stopped dancing at age 39, Austen's reports of dancers and dancing indicate that it is the younger folks who fill the dance floor.

Gentlemen, however, kept their dancing shoes on for as long as they were able. In *Emma,* for example, Mr. Weston, who is probably in his 40s, dances. That his wife, who is probably in her early 30s, isn't dancing should not be seen as a sign of any particular rule, for Mrs. Weston is pregnant and taking it easy.

Finding a Desirable Dance Partner (Possibly for Life!)

Before you became part of a couple, you were, of course, single. This section explains how one went from being by yourself to being one half of a couple. While at an informal dance or formal ball at someone's home, the host could go around encouraging young gentlemen to ask seated young ladies to dance (as Sir William Lucas does when he hosts a party in *Pride and Prejudice,* 1:6); at assemblies and public balls, young ladies had the help of Masters of Ceremonies. The young gentlemen at a dance or ball could not plead ignorance of dancing, for they were expected to know how to dance, period. Indeed, one had to know specific dance steps for specific dances, or else become the person with whom nobody wished to dance! (Think: Mr. Collins in *Pride and Prejudice!*)

Getting help from the Master of Ceremonies

While private dances, whether formal or impromptu, were made up of people who were friends, family, and neighbors who — like Mrs. Weston — encouraged idle young gentlemen to ask seated young women to dance, the large assemblies, such as those held at the Upper and Lower Rooms in Bath, employed Masters of Ceremonies (MC). The responsibilities of the MC included the following:

- Oversaw the protocol of the ball
- Introduced young ladies and gentlemen to each other so they might dance together

✔ Sized up the people whom they introduced

✔ Had knowledge of the people's backgrounds

In *Northanger Abbey*, the MC of the Lower Rooms introduced Henry Tilney to Catherine Morland, who eventually marry. As Henry and Catherine converse, Henry mentions that Mr. King introduced them. Mr. James King was the MC for the Lower Rooms from 1785 to 1805 and then moved to the Upper Rooms. While not every couple matched by the MCs ended up married the way Catherine and Henry did, the MCs still played a successful role as cupid (at least some of the time).

Taking a turn with family and friends

Aside from meeting a potential marriage partner, one went to a ball simply to dance and have fun! So it wasn't uncommon to see young ladies dancing with friends and family members. Women dancing with women, especially at private balls and impromptu dances at home, was common because the female attendees usually outnumbered the men. Some public assemblies, however, had a rule that same-gender dancing was allowed only when no gentlemen partners were available and only with the MC's permission.

Jane Austen clearly loved dancing and happily wrote to her sister in her letters of December 24–26, 1798. She stated that she attended a ball where "There were twenty Dances & I danced them all, & without any fatigue." In the same letter, she numbers her male partners: "Of the Gentleman present You may have some idea from a list of my Partners. Mr. Wood, G. Lefroy, Rice, a Mr. Butcher (. . . a sailor & not of the 11th Light Dragoons) Mr. Temple (not the horrid one of all) Mr. Wm Orde . . . Mr. John Harwood & Mr. Calland." Clearly, she mentioned men that her sister knew. They are friends, neighbors, or friends of friends or other family members familiar to both sisters. (Jane Austen had several brothers, and having brothers usually gets one introduced to their male friends.)

But on November 1, 1800, the 24-year-old Jane Austen wrote to her sister about attending a different ball the previous Thursday evening: "It was a pleasant Ball . . . for there were nearly 60 people. . . . There was a scarcity of Men in general, & a still greater scarcity of any that were good for very much. . . . There was commonly a couple of ladies standing up together." In fact, Jane Austen performed four dances with her good friend Catherine Bigg at this ball.

Putting Those Childhood Dance Lessons to Good Use

Children of the gentry were expected to perform even the liveliest dances with grace and style. Sometimes dancing masters were brought from the town or city to the country estate to instruct the boys and girls in the graceful skill of dancing. Dancing was also taught in school. When Jane Austen's brothers, Frank and Charles, went at age 12 to the Royal Naval College in Portsmouth, part of the curriculum was dancing for these young gentlemen-in-training.

Just think: British naval officers in the Napoleonic Wars could order cannon fire at the French ships while doing their Scotch steps to avoid the bullets being fired at them — which was exactly what happened, because the ships were very close to each other. In fact, Admiral Nelson died from an enemy sniper's bullet fired at him when he was on deck, though whether he was practicing dance steps at the time is doubtful!

Jane Austen also made sure that her two most famous heroes, *Pride and Prejudice*'s Darcy and *Emma*'s Mr. Knightley, could dance extremely well, despite each man claiming to dislike dancing — exactly what one would expect from a gentleman who isn't a total klutz.

And what about the ladies? Daughters of the gentry also had dancing lessons as children. When Jane and Cassandra, at ages 9 and 12, respectively, attended The Abbey School as boarding students, dancing was part of the curriculum. They also danced at home, even as children. *The Family Record* tells the charming anecdote of a Christmas Holiday gathering at Steventon Rectory in 1786, the Austens' home until Jane was 25, when she (having just turned 11 on December 16), her sister Cassandra, their brothers Henry, Frank, and Charles, and their cousins Jane and Edward Cooper were joined by their grown cousin, the Comtesse de Feuillide, who provided music on the pianoforte for "a very snug little dance" in the rectory's parlor for all the children under Mrs. Austen's direction (53–54). As children of the gentry, Jane Austen's heroines know how to dance. Even her least lively heroine, *Mansfield Park*'s Fanny Price, dances in a manner that pleases her uncle Sir Thomas, who observes her and reflects that "education and manners she owed to him" (2:10). Her childhood education, which she shared with her wealthy cousins, Maria and Julia, Sir Thomas's daughters, included learning how to dance.

Dancing up the set

In Austen's novels, the dance form that most frequently appeared is the English Country Dance — so called because the dancing couple stood opposite *(être contre)* each other in a line. Thus, *contre*-dancing became Anglicized as country-dancing. A variation on forming the line was standing in a square or in a circle, but with the gentlemen and ladies still standing opposite each other.

Dancing was a group activity (no tangoing together across the dance floor). In fact, when the first one-on-one dance, the waltz, was introduced to England from the Continent around 1812, it was viewed as too risqué. Although Almack's, one of London's most exclusive assembly rooms, introduced the waltz in 1814, it took quite a while for the waltz to become acceptable, and none of Austen's characters waltz.

Thus, with no one-on-one dancing (in other words, alone as a couple), that's why the characters in Austen's novels are always dancing with other couples or looking for other couples to dance with them. (For more on the waltz, see the sidebar, "What about the waltz," later in the chapter.)

Because couples standing in parallel lines (or a *set*) was the most popular dance formation, ballrooms were rectangular in shape. (See the sidebar "Socializing for a season.")

Understanding the most basic rudiments of English Country Dancing helps readers of Austen's novels understand how this form of dancing enabled dance partners to further their relationship — even though the couple's physical contact while dancing was limited to occasionally holding hands. The dancing involves skipping and walking steps that include weaving in and out of one's lines in order to go from the bottom of the line or set to the top of the line or set. Couples remain in line, standing opposite each other, waiting their turns to dance again and move up the set to the top, which is the position closest to the musicians.

Because the English Country Dance is a type of dancing that includes numerous specific dances, the dancers must master many variations of the basic country dance movements and steps. Otherwise they risk messing up a line or set. This type of dancing was hard, if not impossible, to ad lib.

At times in the country dance, the choreography requires couples to stand and wait their turn to dance up the set. So they used the waiting time to talk with their partners, who stood just about two feet across from each other. They could even flirt verbally. A single dance was actually two dances, lasting a total of 30 minutes — about 29 minutes too long if you were on the dance floor with a person not exactly light on his feet, as poor Elizabeth is with Mr. Collins at the Netherfield Ball (PP 1:18). But having the same partner for 30 minutes offered an extended period for conversation with an individual you were truly interested in.

What about the waltz?

Because dancing in Austen's day involved minimal physical contact — holding hands with arms extended — people, especially country people, no matter how rich, were horrified of the waltz. Introduced to England from Germany in 1812, the waltz had a catchy rhythm, but it required the partners to be in close physical proximity, with the male partner's arm around the female's waist. Four years after its introduction, the scandalous waltz was approved by England's great dancing arbiter, Thomas Wilson.

Even then, the waltz was only approved for married couples who were dancing together! Jane Austen never has her characters waltz. In fact, the key dance scenes in an Austen novel occur when the couple stands opposite each other, waiting their turn to dance up the set. When Mrs. Weston begins playing an "irresistible waltz" at the Coles' dinner party in *Emma,* the music serves only to establish a rhythm for a country dance (2:8).

Knowing other popular dances

While the English Country Dance became the most popular dance form in Austen's day, people also had to know the steps and movements for other dances, including

- **A minuet:** If people were going to a very formal assembly, the first dance would likely be a minuet, dating from the early 18th century — a slow, stately dance with little steps.

- **The quadrille:** A popular dance was the *quadrille* — a five-part dance for four couples standing in a square.

- **The cotillion:** This was a lively dance usually performed by four couples and including the tiny, dainty minuet steps from the minuet. Dancers also sometimes clapped their hands while doing the *cotillion.*

- **A Scottish reel:** An impromptu dance at home, as well as a dance at a ball, might include the quick-stepping, lively Scottish reel, a folk dance with gliding steps and jumps.

Observing dancing etiquette

The dance floor was the perfect place to observe the good manners that characterized Austen's England. But while these elements are wonderful to practice, they sometimes made courting on the dance floor a little difficult.

Because dancing was a communal activity, certain rules enhanced the feeling of community. Check out the following examples of proper dancing etiquette:

✓ **Rescue the wallflowers:** While dances usually had more young women than young men present, the gentlemen were expected to ask the young ladies who were seated without a partner to dance. Failing to do this was ungentlemanly and went against the community. Missing these moments in Jane Austen's novels is also to miss the first of the "do's and don'ts" of ballroom etiquette: Gentlemen should ask seated young ladies without partners to dance.

- **The good example:** *Emma's* Mr. Knightley is ever the gentleman. Although he has been standing with the older men while others are dancing, he immediately steps forward and asks Harriet Smith — "the only young lady sitting down" — to dance (3:2).

- **The bad example:** When at the Meryton Assembly, Darcy, "catching [the] eye" of Elizabeth Bennet, who "had been obliged, by the scarcity of gentlemen, to sit down for two dances," turns back to Bingley and says he is "'in no humour at present to give consequence to young ladies who are slighted by other men.'" He behaves badly in two ways (PP 1:3). Obviously, he deliberately insults Elizabeth, making sure she hears him, but he also sees a young lady who is sitting out two dances for lack of a partner and does nothing about it.

✓ **Respect one's partner and don't bother another man's partner:** Another rule of community is the attentiveness of the partners to each other while dancing. Even while in the "standing and waiting to dance" part of a country dance, partners are supposed to pay attention to each other.

- **The good example:** When, in *Pride and Prejudice,* Darcy and Elizabeth dance together for the first time at the Netherfield Assembly, they converse only with each other, and she tells him that she is "'trying to make . . . out'" his character. When they part after their dance ends, Darcy feels "a tolerable powerful feeling towards" Elizabeth (PP 1:18). He is well on the road to love!

- **The bad example:** In *Northanger Abbey* (1:10), Henry Tilney solicits Catherine Morland for a dance. No sooner has the couple found their way into the dance set when John Thorpe arrives and stations himself behind Catherine, badgering her for a dance.

✓ **Show up for the dance you requested:** Respect and attentiveness for one's partner also includes the gentleman showing up for the dance he asked for.

- **The good example:** At the Netherfield Assembly, Darcy asks Elizabeth to dance, and returns promptly when the dance begins "to claim her hand" (PP 1:18).

- **The bad example:** John Thorpe engages Catherine prior to the ball for the first two dances, but when the music begins, he is nowhere in sight (NA 1:8).

✔ **Decline a gentleman's invitation to dance with grace:** The only way a lady could politely decline an invitation to dance — if she was not already pre-engaged for the dance by another partner — was to claim tiredness or indisposition, which meant that she could not dance with another partner later in the evening.

- **The good example:** When John Thorpe, having stood Catherine up for the first two dances for which he had engaged her, returns and asks to dance again, she thanks him and says that "'our two dances are over [as in, he failed to show up for them!]; and besides, I am tired, and do not mean to dance any more'" (NA 1: 8). While Catherine probably would have loved to dance with any other partner, she does not dance again.

- **The bad example:** When James Morland leaves Bath, his fiancée Isabella Thorpe, declares — insists, even — that she will not dance while he is away. But she not only goes to the dance, but dances with Captain Tilney (NA 2:1)

✔ **Adhere to the two-dance rule:** A couple was expected not to dance with each other more than twice. The idea was to spread out among the crowd in order to meet and dance with other people to get to know the group. Indeed, dancing more than twice with the same partner was viewed as a serious interest in matrimony!

- **The good example:** In *Pride and Prejudice,* Mrs. Bennet, with the marriages of her daughters always on her mind, is thrilled that Bingley has asked Jane for two dances, a sure sign of his romantic interest in her.

- **The bad example:** Marianne and Willoughby's being "partners for half the time" of an impromptu ball at Barton leads people to suspect an engagement or at least a pending engagement between them (SS 1:11). They are *not* engaged nor have they planned an engagement.

Having fun under a watchful chaperone's eye

When a young lady attended a ball, whether a private affair or a public assembly, she was dancing in front of her parents, siblings, neighbors, and friends. If her mother was unavailable, she was accompanied by an older woman serving as her chaperone.

Chaperones for young ladies had several responsibilities:

✔ Accompanied their charges wherever they went in public

✔ Ensured the young lady's safety

- Reminded her charge about protocol — the rules of dancing, general conduct, and adherence to the customs of the day
- Advised her young woman about clothing, courtship, men, and manners
- Ensured that the two-dance rule was followed
- Protected the young lady from fortune-hunting men

As noted earlier in this chapter, Jane Austen, herself, eventually saw herself as a chaperone. When at her brother Edward's huge country house in Kent, Godmersham, she accompanied her nieces, nephews, and their friends to a ball in the nearby city of Canterbury and enjoyed her wine as she observed the dancers from the sofa!

Amusing the Non-Dancers: Finding the Card and Tea Rooms

A ball, whether private or a public (an assembly), always had activities for the older male and female non-dancers (as opposed to the young women who were sitting, waiting to be asked). A ball was a social event for all who attended — dancer or not.

Both the Upper and Lower Assembly Rooms in Bath had Card Rooms, where many of the older men (fathers, uncles, and husbands of chaperones) in Austen's day went to spend the evening of an assembly. At private balls, a card room was always available for the older guests, male and female, to head off for games of whist, quadrille, casino, and other card games.

Look at the characters who head to the card rooms in Austen's novels, and you'll see that card rooms aren't places of romance!

- **Mr. Allen:** The gouty Mr. Allen goes to the card room when he accompanies his wife and Catherine Morland to the Upper Rooms, leaving them in the ballroom (NA 1:2).
- **John Thorpe:** The card room is also where John Thorpe talks of trading dogs when he should be dancing with Catherine, whom he has engaged for the first dance (NA 1:8).
- **Mrs. Norris:** When Mrs. Norris isn't moving the chaperones around the Mansfield Park ballroom, she is "making up card tables" for the older guests (MP 2:10).

- ↙ **Tom Bertram:** During the earlier, impromptu ball at Mansfield Park, Tom Bertram asks his cousin Fanny to dance simply to avoid having to make up a card table for the older people at the request of their aunt, Mrs. Norris, who's always busy doing something (MP 1:12).

- ↙ **Mr. Elton:** When Mr. Elton is shamed for refusing to dance with Harriet by Mr. Knightley's dancing with her, he retreats to the card room provided at the Crown Inn ball (E 3:2).

So with card games being played, dogs being traded, and people hiding from humiliation, the card room was a busy place. But not for young couples!

While the young people danced at the balls and assemblies, the non-card-playing parents could simply observe the dancers and chat with friends. The balls were opportunities for people to meet, and those meetings didn't have to be on the dance floor between the dancers. Simple socializing among the older folks was a pleasant way to pass the evening.

As observed earlier, Jane Austen as a chaperone enjoyed drinking wine as she watched the younger people. Mrs. Allen liked having her old friend Mrs. Thorpe as a companion during the assemblies in the Upper Rooms because Mrs. Thorpe provided her with a fellow tea-drinker in the Tea Room. This was a pleasant change from her first visit to the Upper Rooms, when Mrs. Allen and Catherine found themselves in the Tea Room with "no party to join, no acquaintance to claim, no gentleman to assist them" (NA 1:2). Their experience is probably familiar to many of us: attending a social event, even a dance, where you know nobody! Nowadays, we can introduce ourselves to others. But unfortunately for Mrs. Allen and Catherine, the ball was so crowded that apparently they could not even find the Master of Ceremonies to introduce Catherine to a partner — the only way strangers could be introduced at a ball unless they had mutual friends to introduce them.

Chapter 6

Playing the Dating Game: Courtship, Austen Style

In This Chapter

▶ Dating in an age of many rules

▶ Limiting "alone time"

▶ Figuring out how to flirt

▶ Securing a proposal at last

*J*ane Austen's novels are frequently called *courtship novels* because they trace one or more young woman's courtship experience(s). Courting followed various rules and protocols that made getting to know each other far more difficult for young couples than it is today. Just spending too much time together led to gossip and speculation. But what is especially intriguing about reading an Austen novel is seeing how the author, while completely aware of the etiquette of courting, also respects the common sense and good morals of her characters as they deal with society's strict and often unreasonable, even hypocritical, notions about male-female relationships. (In this chapter, you experience the process of courting and what it really meant to "date" in Jane Austen's day.) Despite the difficulties involved, though, young couples met, courted, married, and lived happily ever after — or not. (Developing a relationship needed more than just conversing on the dance floor — see Chapter 5 for information on dancing.)

Defining Eligibility

In the world of the gentry and thus in Austen's novels, the reader meets young ladies who go to dances and dinner parties and meet young gentlemen who are slightly older than the ladies. This was not unusual because men of the gentry had to establish themselves so that they could present marriage-able prospects financially, especially if they were not eldest sons in line to inherit the grand family country estate. Gentlemen looked for younger wives (usually 27 was the top age!) to ensure that children (read: *sons!*) would be born. This is the old "heir and a spare" concern. So with this mind, let's go courting. (For information on the class system and the gentry, a particular class, see Chapter 2.)

"Coming Out" as a Young Lady

Until a gentry girl turned 16, she lived a quiet, protected, isolated life at home and school. Demure in company, she wasn't to call attention to herself, nor were adults, especially young gentlemen, meant to afford her any attention socially. But when the girl reached the magical age of 16, she officially became a young lady, and it was time for her *coming out* — a formal introduction to society for a woman who was mature enough to be a gentleman's bride. (No, we're not in the film "Deliverance" here! Remember, a woman married at a young age in Austen's day because she was expected to secure her financial future through marriage, thus relieving her father from supporting her — explained in more detail in Chapter 7.) She was also expected to produce sons to inherit paternal property.

A young lady's coming out occurred at a formal ball marking the momentous occasion: she was now marriage material! For those readers who know what getting ready for the senior prom was like, imagine how you felt during your big night. Young ladies in Austen's day felt the same — they were coming out and making their society debut! With a fashionable new dress, jewelry, and the latest hairdo, the girl was ready — or hoped she was ready — to be the center of attention. Her parents hoped that her fine clothes, elegant manners, dancing skills (for which they had paid a moderate fee to a dancing master), and, of course, dowry, would secure their daughter a good match. Among all the guests, whether family, friends, neighbors, or new acquaintances, the young gentlemen were of the main interest to the girl. She wanted to be noticed and find a gentleman with elegance and manners as well as husband potential (financial and other ways).

After the official coming out event, the young teenager could now participate in the adult social world by attending balls, assemblies, and dinner parties: all good places to meet marriage-minded gentlemen. The more balls and dinner parties she attended, the better, because these occasions provided more chances for gentlemen to see her, as well as for her to assess the young men as potential husbands. And at those dinner parties, the newly "out" female actually was allowed to participate in the conversation. (Prior to coming out, if a girl happened to be at the dinner table with adults, she was expected to remain quiet and to speak only when asked a question, to which she responded only "yes" or "no.") The year of coming out was full of new social adventures, including talking!

Joining one's older sister

When Elizabeth Bennet visits Lady Catherine de Bourgh, she receives the third degree on her sisters' social positions: "'Are any of your younger sisters out, Miss Bennet?'" (PP 2:6). Elizabeth, at age 20, is the second eldest of five sisters, all unmarried, and the youngest, Lydia, is 15 at this point. When Elizabeth replies that all of her sisters are out, Lady Catherine bristles, "'What, all five out at once? Very odd! — . . . The younger ones out before the elder are married!'" Elizabeth sympathetically observes, "'I think it would be very hard upon younger sisters, that they shouldn't have their share of society and amusement because the elder may not have the means or inclination to marry early.'" The five Bennet sisters range in age from 15 to 23.

The strain on younger sisters who are kept in is also mentioned in *Pride and Prejudice* regarding the Lucas sisters. When Charlotte Lucas, age 27, agrees to marry Mr. Collins, her younger sisters are thrilled and form "hopes of coming out a year or two sooner than they might otherwise have done" (PP 1:22). With an unmarried daughter in her late twenties, parents could deliberately delay their younger daughters' coming out to lessen the competition for the older daughter. While not exactly Cinderellas sweeping up the ashes, the restrained younger sisters must have felt like her, staying home from the balls even though they were of age!

But Elizabeth's sympathy for her younger siblings notwithstanding, Lydia is the most man-crazy, self-indulgent, and morally irresponsible of the group. Perhaps more time "not out" might have helped her mature. On the other hand, given Lydia's loud and forward personality — and her love for dancing — the Bennets would never have heard the end of it if they hadn't let Lydia come out early. And even if she had waited another year to come out, Mrs. Bennet would never have restrained her favorite daughter. So it's not surprising that Lydia causes the most man-trouble for her parents and sisters by fleeing and living with Wickham.

But don't forget that the young lady still had to have a chaperone looking out for her and accompanying her to social affairs. (For more information on chaperones, check out Chapter 5.) The difference between before and after a young lady's coming out is that men could look upon the lady with marriage in mind. When she married, she lost the chaperone and gained the husband.

Of course, it must have been hard for a 15-year-old girl to see her 16-year-old sister "out" and attending dances, when she had to stay home with her governess and younger siblings. Sometimes, then, parents with daughters close enough in age permitted both the younger and older girls to come out at the same time. But this could be a good or bad idea, as Austen illustrates in *Pride and Prejudice* (see the "Joining one's older sister" sidebar).

Eligible gentlemen were expected to pay attention *only* to the young ladies who had come out. But sometimes they couldn't tell the difference and on first meeting a young woman could mistakenly give her the time and attention that weren't due to her, leading to embarrassment all around. Austen writes about such embarrassing moments in *Mansfield Park* (1:5). (See the "Strolling with social disaster" sidebar nearby.)

To tell if a young woman was out, you had to pay attention to the following clues:

- A young lady who *was* out would
  - Engage in conversation with young gentlemen
  - Display gracious confidence in social situations
  - Attend formal dances and dinner parties
  - Be allowed to walk alone with a young gentleman, assuming he was not a total stranger
- A young lady who *wasn't* yet out would
  - Wear when outside a "close bonnet," a hat with a deep brim that hid most of the face unless the wearer and the observer were actually face to face
  - Be quiet, retiring, and modest
  - Not attend formal dances and dinner parties
  - Normally be accompanied by her chaperone or governess, and not walk alone with a young gentleman unless he was a relation

The clever Mary Crawford from *Mansfield Park* makes a good point about girls coming out when she insists that "'the alteration of manners on being introduced into company is frequently too sudden.'" As Mary then explains, some young ladies "'pass in . . . very little time from reserve to quite the opposite—to confidence!'" In other words, they go from being the demure, quiet young lady who is not "out" to acting as if they know everything, to being over confident. This is not the graciousness that a young lady should display in social situations. Tom Bertram speaks up, corroborating Mary's assessment, and tells an anecdote of sitting in a room with a young lady who hadn't yet come out and enduring her awkward silence: Awkwardness aside, the young lady in question behaved properly by remaining quiet in his company. But then a year later, just after coming out, she approached Tom at a party, "'claimed [him] as an acquaintance . . . and talked and laughed till [he] did not know which way to look'" (MP 1:5). Coming out appears to have so gone to her head that she embarrasses Tom with her overly familiar, forward behavior. In fact, her laughing and talking up a storm in public with a man she barely knows is just plain impolite, whether a young lady is out or not! In chapter 12, you will read an excerpt from John Gregory's *A Father's Legacy to his Daughters* (1744), which was the young ladies' guide to conduct. He stipulates that young ladies should always converse with young gentleman showing "easy dignity" (28). Obviously, the young lady whom Tom Bertram met needed to review her copy of that book!

Strolling with social disaster

A gentleman failing to recognize if a young lady is "out," or not — or worse yet — a young lady behaving as if she is out and she's not, can lead to a total social fiasco.

In *Mansfield Park,* Tom Bertram tells the story of visiting a friend's family and taking a walk with his friend's sisters and mother (1:5). He strolled with one of the sisters who was "'perfectly easy in her manners, and as ready to talk as to listen.'" But at the end of the walk, Tom learned that he had been in the company of the younger sister, whose coming out wasn't for another six months. He also had ignored the elder sister, who had already come out, and this behavior was a major social no-no. Tom Bertram isn't exactly Mr. Sensitivity, but even he's disturbed and embarrassed for giving an ineligible girl his attention.

When Mary Crawford hears Tom's story, she's quick to blame the mother: "'But it was entirely the mother's fault. Miss Augusta should have been with her governess.'" An attentive, proper mother would have the younger daughters under her wing or under the girls' governess's charge.

Not all young ladies caused the embarrassment that Tom Bertram experienced with the forward young woman who inappropriately laughed and talked up a storm with him, assuming he would remember her from her pre-out days. Austen's paragon of propriety is *Mansfield Park*'s heroine, Fanny Price. When her uncle, Sir Thomas, hosts a ball to honor her coming out, the guests who observe her note that she is "attractive . . . modest . . . Sir Thomas's niece . . . and soon said to be admired by Mr. Crawford. It was enough to give her general favour" (MP 2:10). Had they been asked, both Mary Crawford and Tom Bertram would approve Fanny's behavior, as well. For though she is now officially "out," she retains her modesty and courtesy. Recognized by all the guests as the honoree of the dance, Fanny does not have to call attention to herself.

Austen's coming out

There's no reason to doubt that Austen was out and attending formal and informal dances when she reached 16, the normal coming-out age, though only sketchy records of her social life at that age exist. She had a sister who was just two years older than she was. So why wouldn't the practical Mrs. Austen allow the 16-year-old Jane to join Cassandra at neighboring dances and dinners? Elizabeth Bennet's sympathy for her mother's letting Lydia come out early may well have come from Austen's own experience.

We do know that the 18-year-old Austen and her elder sister joined their married cousin in Southampton in December of 1793 at an Assembly Ball. And we know she attended balls the previous year, 1792, because that was the year of marriages: Her brother James married Anne Mathew; her cousin Jane Cooper was married; and Margaret Bigg, the eldest sister of Jane Austen's good friends Catherine and Alethea Bigg, married. It's reasonable to speculate that in a year when engagements and marriages were flourishing, formal and informal dances were, too. So Jane Austen would have been "out" by this time.

But Austen makes her feelings about the "coming out" process clear through her characters' experiences. For example, as she approached age 16, Austen wrote jokingly about young women coming out in one of her juvenile pieces, "A Collection of Letters," dedicated to her cousin Jane Cooper and copied in Volume 2 of her youthful works. (For more on Austen's early writing and her cousin Jane, see Chapter 3.)

In the first letter, addressed "From A Mother to her friend," the fictional mother, A.—F.—, writes of bringing her two daughters out through a series of teas with close friends, visits, dinners, and a private concert — much less exciting than coming out at a ball — "How they will bear so much dissipation I cannot imagine," Austen has the mother say ridiculously; "of their spirits I have no fear, I only dread their health." At a tea? (Picture the teenage Jane Austen smirking as she wrote those lines!) Heading to tea at their mother's friend's house, the two daughters "trembled with fear & expectation," as they "prepared to find a World full of things to amaze and shock them." (Should they select Darjeeling or Earl Grey tea?!) As they arrive at their first tea-drinking challenge, the elder sister, age 17, "could hardly breathe," while the younger, age 16, "was all Life & Rapture," as she said, "'The long-expected Moment is now arrived, and we shall soon be in the World.'" Getting through the tea experience, the girls — now young ladies who are "out" — "returned [home] in raptures with the world, its inhabitants, and its manners."

Clearly, the young writer thought the whole thing was ridiculous. Sip a cup of tea and voilà, a girl became a woman, ready to become a wife! She must have felt that dancing at a "coming out" ball was equally stupid as a mark of maturity.

No wonder at age 38, Austen, reviewing her teenage niece's novel-in-progress, commented that what one of her characters "says about the madness of otherwise sensible Women, on the subject of their Daughters coming out, is worth its' [sic] weight in gold" (Letter to Anna Austen, August 10–18, 1814). By this time, Austen had undoubtedly witnessed numerous coming out events with an amused smile on her face.

Identifying the eligible gentlemen

While gentlemen could look for those overt clues of the close bonnet, demure demeanor, and accompanying governess or chaperone to help them know if young ladies were "out" or not — if the young ladies were not out, they wouldn't be at the dance or dinner party! — young gentlemen, themselves, displayed no overt signs. Gossip, of course, told young ladies which men were available: They knew older brothers, cousins, and so on. And even when the stranger Darcy enters the Meryton Assembly, the gossip soon circulates that he's eligible and has an income of £10,000 a year (PP 1:3). Furthermore, only the brothers, cousins, and so on, who were eligible or looking for wives would be at the balls and dinners. Their younger brothers were at school, learning geography *and* dancing, as they waited their turns to attend balls!

Young gentlemen became eligible for marriage at a later age than the young ladies for the very simple reason that they had to be able to afford marriage. Twenty-one was the age of coming of age for men, and they could not enter into any contracts before 21 without their parents' consent. This included marriage. Thus, it should not surprise readers of Austen's novels to come across young women marrying older men. If the young gentleman did not inherit property and wealth as an eldest son, or have the prospect, as an eldest son, of inheriting his father's property, he had to find a genteel occupation, such as an Anglican clergyman or an army officer, in order to support a wife and family in a genteel style. He needed time to establish himself, and as a younger son, he would then need to look for a rich wife. Colonel Fitzwilliam, the younger son of an earl, makes this clear to Elizabeth Bennet, saying, "'I may suffer from the want of money. Younger sons cannot marry where they like'" (PP 2:10). The Colonel is clearly planning to marry a rich young lady who will supply him and their family with money.

Getting to Know Each Other

It's fine for a couple to meet on the dance floor or at a dinner. But first impressions in a crowded room could be very misleading, because all one had to go on was the other person's appearance, and at a social event everyone would be dressed well and intent on appearing elegant and charming. So couples needed time to get to know each other. One-on-one conversations, however, could be a problem because young ladies and gentlemen who weren't related weren't supposed to be left alone together in private. And if a young gentleman and a young lady danced too many dances together or spent too much time alone in public and people noticed — which was very likely, given that the ballroom and other social venues were full of lookers-on and gossips — it was assumed that the couple was serious about marriage. So going from getting to know each other to feeling enough about each other to be engaged was a tricky and subtle road filled with many roadblocks.

The courtship do's of Austen's day

With rules and traditions restricting the time that young ladies and gentlemen could be together, couples had to use what time they had well.

Dancing in a crowd

Young ladies and gentlemen appreciated dancing because it gave them an opportunity to talk. For this reason, young people looked forward to balls. Granted, this rather public business of conversation was better than nothing. But the young lady and gentleman who were mutually interested had to grab opportunity as it came because even dancing and then dining or drinking tea together at the ball didn't give a couple that much time to get to know each other. The rule was no more than two dances: each dance consisting of two separate dances, for a total of 30 minutes on the floor. So two dances gave the couple an hour. (For more on dancing and how it relates to courtship, see Chapter 5.)

Being together at home . . . with the parents, of course

Obviously, young people who had a romantic interest in each other couldn't always be in the ballroom. A young gentleman might be invited to a young lady's home (but with her parents looking on), yet ways existed for the couple to be together:

- **Acting:** *Home acting* — acting out a popular play with other family members and friends taking part — was very popular. The parents might be the audience. In *Mansfield Park,* Maria Bertram and Henry Crawford get to show their feelings for each other through their roles of long-separated mother and son — the hugs and affectionate poses they strike as a reunited family enable them to have considerable physical contact on the stage. No wonder they like to rehearse the reunion scene a lot!

- **Singing duets:** With young ladies expected to be musical, a traditional evening entertainment included having them play the pianoforte and sing. But if her young gentleman was also musical, he might go to the pianoforte after a while and watch her play or even sing with her. He might even learn ahead of time the male part of her favorite songs. While Darcy gives no indication of having any musical talent enabling him to break into harmony, he does go over to the pianoforte to listen to Elizabeth play at Lady Catherine's (PP 2:8).

- **Playing card games:** Because card playing was a popular evening pastime for both men and women at home, the young couple could join the parents and other guests. The couple might be partners in the game or at least sit at the same table, enabling them to use the time to talk. When Austen writes in *Mansfield Park* that Henry Crawford has "his hands full of business" as he plays the card game Speculation with Fanny Price and others, her phrase is a loaded one (2:7). Henry isn't only busy with the cards; he is busy trying to arouse Fanny's interest in him. Even more in his favor, Fanny is sitting at the table close to him.

Meeting at the theater

If the families of both the lady and gentleman happened to be in London, Bath, or another city that boasted a theater, the couple had another chance to meet and talk. During the intermission or after the play's conclusion, the gentleman could go to the lady's theater box, sit down, and chat with the lady of his interest. Henry Tilney does this at Bath's Theatre Royal when he sees Catherine Morland seated in a box with the Allens (NA 1:12).

The don'ts (unless done on the sly)

The hurdles faced by couples trying to get to know one another as a potential spouse led to their finding ways to spend time together, if only to talk. But Austen also questions the existing stringent rules for male-female relationships, showing in her novels characters of excellent morals enjoying each other's company alone.

Walking together

Taking a walk on a quiet path together is always a good way for a couple to talk together, too. But because a young lady and gentleman weren't to be alone in private taking long, romantic walks weren't an option. (This shouldn't be confused with instances when a gentleman sees a young lady he knows alone on a public street, for some reason, and then gallantly escorts her home.) Yet in Austen's novels, her very proper heroines and heroes sometimes do manage to walk together for long periods of time in even the most remote places! In *Pride and Prejudice,* when Elizabeth visits Rosings, she enjoys taking long walks in Rosings's beautiful park. Darcy often arranges to accidentally meet her on her rambles, even though she tells him where she likes to walk to discourage his meeting her. (The clever Elizabeth can't figure out why he keeps showing up on her walks!) Meeting her as she walks, of course, gives him time to talk with her. So there were ways to get around the "no time alone in private" rule, and Darcy was aware of it.

Driving together

If a young lady and gentleman walking together in private for a long period of time was viewed suspiciously, driving together in a carriage was surely worse. After all, an unscrupulous young man, up to no good, could get away quickly with the young lady in a carriage. And let's not even think about what could occur in a closed carriage.

A good example that shows the stigma of riding in carriages as a "couple" can be seen in *Northanger Abbey*. Catherine Morland is rightly stunned when she discovers that her chaperone, Mrs. Allen, permits her to go for a drive with John Thorpe in his carriage. When she returns to the Allens' house, she hears the sensible Mr. Allen speak of the incident:

> These schemes are not at all the thing. Young men and women driving about the country in open carriages! Now and then it is very well; but going to inns and public places together [which Thorpe had planned for a meal]. . . . Do not you think it has an odd appearance, if young ladies are frequently driven about . . . by young men, to whom they are not even related? (1:13)

When Mrs. Allen agrees with her husband on the impropriety, Catherine is distressed and asks Mrs. Allen, "[W]hy did not you tell me so before? I am sure if I had known it to be improper, I would not have gone with Mr. Thorpe at all; but I always hoped you would tell me, if you thought I was doing wrong.'" Mrs. Allen's mistakes as a chaperone along with Catherine's social innocence could've exposed the young lady to public criticism. Austen lets the reader know what the social norm is, and when a character acts inappropriately, she wants the reader to scrutinize the behavior and the consequences.

Riding horseback together

Going for a nice, leisurely horseback ride together is another no-no, especially into the deep, dark woods. Alone — in the woods — together? See how difficult proper courting was?

In the 1995-film version of *Sense and Sensibility,* Elinor and Edward, who are interested in each other, go for a long ride together at Norland Park. And it sure looks like they're heading towards the woods! But if the proper Elinor chastises Marianne for the curricle drive with Willoughby, it's hard to believe that she would ride in the park alone with Edward. Taking a film-maker's latitude, Emma Thompson, who wrote the screenplay, needed to quickly show the film's audience that Elinor and Edward enjoy each other's company. Perhaps, too, Thompson like Austen, when she sends her characters walking together, trusts her characters to behave properly when they ride. (For more on the film versions of Austen's novels, see Chapter 15.)

A "couple's" riding scene that does occur in an Austen novel is *Mansfield Park*'s "teaching the city-girl, Mary Crawford to ride" episode (1:7). Mary and Edmund are both on horseback, "riding side by side." Mary then begins to canter, and Edmund follows. Soon, however, they stop and Edmund is "close to her, he was speaking to her, he was evidently directing her management of the bridle, he had hold of her hand." The way Austen builds the sexual tension of the scene is quite remarkable: He simply holds Mary's hand as she holds the bridle. And these two aren't even in the deep, dark woods! But the sexual tension between the two is high through just his touching her hand.

Corresponding by letter

Austen lived in the great age of letter writing in England. Jane Austen's letters are important documents of her busy life in Georgian England. Austen called the true art of letter writing . . . "[an expression] on paper exactly what one would say to the same person by word of mouth" (January 3–5, 1801). (See the nearby sidebar, "Letter-writing mechanics.") While Austen's letters don't include courtship letters, they do provide a glimpse into the way Jane Austen viewed the people and the world around her, and they offer the closest example possible of what she sounded like when she spoke.

But as far as love letters go, in Austen's day, a young man and woman who weren't related to each other and who wrote letters to each other were assumed to be engaged. In other words, a would-be couple, not yet engaged, was prohibited from writing to each other — yet another roadblock to reaching the altar! So even though England started to observe Valentine's Day in the 1600's, forget sending that Valentine's card in Austen's time unless you were engaged to the recipient.

Jane Fairfax and Frank Churchill break the letter-writing rules in *Emma.* They're secretly engaged — a social *faux pas,* as engagements were meant to be open with parental or guardian approval — and write letters to each other. Because they are pretending to be virtual strangers when they are visiting Highbury, the only way they can communicate is through letters. In their secret letters, Jane and Frank also exchange little tidbits of news. Because of their letter-writing campaign, Jane adamantly insists on collecting her own mail from the post office despite Mrs. Elton's pressuring her to let her servant pick up Jane's mail when he gets the Eltons' mail (2:16).

The "no letters" rule caused difficulties of all sorts in Austen's books. Because of the rule, Jane Bennet can't write to Bingley to inform him of her visit to London when she goes to visit her aunt and uncle (PP). Instead, she must write to his obnoxious sisters, hoping that they'll tell their brother that she's in the city. Of course, Bingley's sisters hide Jane's letter and their knowledge of her being there from their brother. If Jane *had* been able to write directly to Bingley, their marriage could've occurred on about page 80 of the book, instead of about 300 pages later!

Another letter difficulty occurs in *Sense and Sensibility.* Because Marianne writes to Willoughby as soon as she and her sister arrive in London, Elinor assumed the two must be engaged. Marianne writes again and again to him. Surely, this is a secret engagement between the two. So Elinor is shocked when, upon Willoughby's returning Marianne's letters to her, Marianne admits that there was no engagement (SS 2:7). In *Emma,* Jane Fairfax and Frank Churchill secretly exchange letters: On the one hand, they are secretly engaged, and so as an engaged couple, they can write to each other; on the other hand, the engagement is a secret one — they have gone against society's norms.

Letter-writing mechanics

Letters in Austen's day looked like little books of folded paper containing four pages. On page 4, the back page, the writer left a rectangular space blank for the address, also known as the direction. People used goose-quill pens and ink to write. Just as people today have preferences for pen point type, so did writers who used quill pens; they shaped and repaired the nib of the quill with a pen knife. To relay as much as possible, folks often used cross writing, or turning the letter around at a right angle and writing either across the original or writing between the lines. Obviously, this is hard to read! Jane Austen, herself, commented to her sister that their brother Charles used red ink when he crossed to contrast with the black ink originally on the page (Letter, November 6–7, 1813). When the letter was complete, the writer then sealed the letter with wax or a wafer (a thin disk of dried paste used to seal a document). If using wax, the writer let the wax melt over the fold to seal it; a signet ring or seal pressed into the wax secured the paper seal.

Mail was usually sent from and delivered to a post office. But in the country, where Austen's novels are mainly set, the post office wasn't always the official building that we think of today. So people had letters delivered in other ways:

✔ The post office was frequently located in an inn or tavern in town. When Jane Austen's family lived in Steventon, they collected and sent their mail at the nearby Wheatsheaf Inn.

✔ Some people sent their letters and parcels via friends or employees who were traveling the direction of the mail. Austen, herself, advised her sister against this practice: "It is throwing a Letter away to send it by a visitor, there is never convenient time for reading it—& Visitor can tell most things as well" (Letter to Cassandra, October 26, 1813).

✔ Private messengers were also enlisted to deliver particularly important pieces of mail.

Unlike today, the addressee paid the postage due on the letter. The exception to this was in London, which had a Penny-Post service requiring the sender to pay the postage. In 1801, the cost rose, and the service became the Two-Penny Post.

Members of Parliament were the only folks who until 1840 were allowed to frank a letter to send it for free (so they could carry on Parliamentary business by mail at no personal cost). *Franking* involved writing the MP's name and the date by the address of a letter weighing no more than an ounce. But this privilege often was abused — even by (take a big breath) Jane Austen herself. In six of her letters, she mentions either securing a frank or seeking a frank for a letter she wished to send. But even the greatest defender of postal laws would not prosecute the penniless, 10-year-old Fanny Price for accepting her cousin Edmund's offer to have his father frank her letter to her equally penniless brother William, also a child (MP 1:2). Franking, however, was abused by people who did not have the excuse that Fanny Price had.

Mastering the Fine Art of Flirting

The limited opportunities for conversation between ladies and gentlemen made every chance to communicate important. Thus, they frequently expressed themselves with looks. Subtle smiles in Austen's works often serve as communication between her heroes and heroines. Sometimes the smiles are so subtle that they even fail to register with the person to whom they're aimed. Likewise, the conversations between the hero and heroine are sometimes misleading because they don't sound anything like what we would take to be emotionally-charged words of love. But frequently the witty banter shows that the banterers are meant to be together, for who else could keep up with one's verbal skills and cleverness except the other, who's equally skilled and clever?

When people in Austen's day used the phrase "making love," it had no physical or sexual overtones. The phrase simply meant verbal flirting or flashing interested looks at the other person. Yet when Mary Crawford enters the room at *Mansfield Park,* wondering who will play the male part opposite hers in a play they're doing, and asks, "'What gentleman among you am I to have the pleasure of making love to?'", the next line reads, "For a moment no one spoke" (MP 1:15). Her bluntness shocks her auditors, comprised of mixed company.

Austen also uses the phrase "making violent love" in *Emma,* when Emma, alone in a carriage with Mr. Elton, finds herself the object of his amorous overtures, "actually making violent love to her" (1:15). But while Elton is talking up a storm of passion, he goes no further than seizing her hand. He then drops it and tries to take her hand again, but fails. This is *not* an X-rated carriage ride! So again, "making violent love" simply means that Mr. Elton is telling Emma how much he loves her, and so on.

"Looking" the feelings of love

Having to express one's romantic interest in another without the possibility of using verbal communication wasn't conducive to spoken intimacy. So a lot had to be communicated between a couple by looks, smiles, and blushes flashed across the room. Smiles between potential lovers in Austen's novels vary in character. Smiles can convey sincere romantic interest. *Pride and Prejudice*'s Darcy smiles at Elizabeth Bennet quite a bit. The reader knows these aren't scornful smiles because when Elizabeth observes the "'finer, larger picture'" of Darcy in the family portrait gallery, she beholds "a striking resemblance of Mr. Darcy, with such a smile over the face, as she remembered to have sometimes seen, when he looked at her'" (PP 3:1). What if the young woman was too modest to flash those pearly whites? She could lose her man. In *Pride and Prejudice,* Jane Bennet, uniting "a composure of temper and a uniform cheerfulness of manner, which would guard her from the suspicions of the impertinent," unfortunately also prevented Bingley from seeing her real feelings for him (PP 1:6). While looking lovingly across the room at a gentleman might seem sappy, looks were frequently the only way that young women could convey their interest in a gentleman, given the limited chances they had to talk alone. And of course, a proper young lady or gentleman wouldn't flash those looks to a stranger. The looks would come after the couple had been formally introduced.

Reading and misreading body language

Body language may seem a modern phenomenon, but it was as common in Austen's day as it is in ours. Frequently, her characters misread such language, leading to mistaken ideas about romantic feelings. For example, Emma observes Mr. Elton observing her sketching Harriet Smith. He moves closer to Emma's easel and positions himself "where he might gaze and gaze again" (E 1:6). The problem arises because Emma misreads Mr. Elton's body language, assuming that he is gazing at Harriet and Harriet's portrait. However, he is really gazing at the artist, Emma. Another misreader of body language is Darcy, who admits to discouraging Bingley's romantic interest in Jane Bennet because he saw only that "Her looks and manners were open, cheerful and engaging . . . but without any symptom of peculiar regard" for Bingley (PP 2:12). Darcy's observation of Jane Bennet's body language reminds the reader that earlier in the novel, Charlotte Lucas said of Jane's composed, placid temperament and demeanor that "'a woman had better shew *more* affection than she feels'" (PP 1:6).

With other characters, however, body language is obvious and unmistakable as they work to attract one another. Fanny Price, an astute observer of those around her, sees that Maria Bertram's eyes are "sparkling with pleasure" and hears her speak "with great animation" when Henry Crawford comes near with his partner — even though Maria is dancing with her fiancé, Rushworth (MP 1:12).

Speaking the language of love

Jane Austen's true lovers are plain-speaking men and women who speak from the heart and brain. Frequently, their conversations are witty, showing that their marriage will be a marriage of people who truly belong together. Being able to engage in lively repartée may not sound romantic, but in *Pride and Prejudice,* Austen shows how this works in the same way that playwright William Congreve did in *The Way of the World,* a play Austen knew well. (See Chapter 4 on writers who influenced Austen.) Austen perfectly matches the verbal skills of Elizabeth and Darcy to the dismay of Miss Bingley but to the delight of readers, who witness Darcy and Elizabeth conversing together at length, while Miss Bingley grows "tired of a conversation in which she ha[s] no share" (PP 1:11).

Having Darcy and Elizabeth matching wits is Austen's way of showing their psychological compatibility. This novel presents two highly articulate young people, Elizabeth and Darcy, who show that they belong together through their language. They are the only couple who converse aloud (we never hear Jane and Bingley in conversation), and they are an intellectual match. Ironically, the reader senses this before Darcy and Elizabeth do! Elizabeth is known for her intellectual "quickness," and Darcy is "clever" and naturally enjoys "conversation" (1:1, 1:4, 1:6). So when they talk to each other at Netherfield Park (or anywhere else, for that matter), their conversation speeds along briskly with each capping the other's statement. *Capping* means to follow up with something good or better in a conversation. While Darcy is attracted to Elizabeth physically — he notices her "beautiful . . . dark" eyes, her pretty and "intelligent" face, and even her body size (he compares his sister's height to Elizabeth's after only knowing her for a short time!) — he also admits that he admires her "For the liveliness of [her] mind'" (PP 3:18). Austen reminds her readers that compatibility can work in many areas: physical, emotional, and intellectual. And all of these can lead to love.

Even nonwitty couples managed to get to know if they were compatible, but Austen portrays these characters as secondary. While the reader never hears the quiet and modest Jane and Bingley in a conversation of any substance, we do read that during the supper at the Netherfield Ball, they sit together talking "very composedly" (PP 1:18). And as the Bennets await the arrival of their carriage at the end of the ball, Elizabeth sees "Mr. Bingley and Jane . . . standing together, a little detached from the rest, and talked only to each other." They share no witty banter the way Elizabeth and Darcy do, which makes them the secondary characters of the novel.

Getting Engaged (Finally!)

It may be hard to believe, but in spite of all the roadblocks and difficulties that society placed in the way of a young lady and gentleman getting to know each other, engagements still happened.

Making the proposal

The one time when a couple was allowed to be alone together was when the gentleman proposed to his lady. In *Pride and Prejudice,* Mrs. Bennet hurries Kitty out of the room so that Collins has a clear and open field for attacking Elizabeth with his proposal of marriage (PP 1:19). I use the word "attacking" advisedly, because Collins's proposal is trite and cliché-filled, using the proposal he had designed for Jane to propose to Elizabeth after Mrs. Bennet tells him that Jane is already spoken for (in her dreams at this point of course!). (He probably used most of the same speech to Charlotte when he proposed to her two days later!)

Later in the novel, Mrs. Bennet is at it again: She clears the drawing room of her other daughters so that Bingley and Jane can be in a proposable situation, and her plan works: Bingley proposes to Jane, and she accepts (3:13).

In Austen's novels, the proposals offered by the heroes tend to be plainspoken and honest: in other words, the exact opposite of Collins's proposal. When the heroes propose, they do not kneel on one knee, nor do they give engagement rings in her novels — though engagement rings go back to the 15th century. (But the history of engagement practices is for another *For Dummies* book!) Consider Darcy's first proposal to Elizabeth: "'In vain have I struggled. It will not do. My feelings will not be repressed. You must allow me to tell you how ardently I admire and love you'" (PP 2:11). While his fourth sentence about his ardent love for her is pretty romantic, his first sentence, while sincere, candid, and concise, hardly conveys sentiments that will win the lady. He has been struggling against his love and admiration for her. But at least he's honest. Darcy's second proposal to Elizabeth is much better, as well as concise "'If your feelings are still what they were last April [when she rejected his insulting proposal], tell me so at once. My affections and wishes are unchanged . . . '" (PP3:16). Likewise in *Emma,* when the heroic, gallant Mr. Knightley proposes to the heroine, he begins, "'I cannot make speeches, Emma. . . . If I loved you less, I might be able to talk about it more'" (E 3:13).

But one passionate love speech does appear in Austen's work, and that is in *Persuasion.* Captain Wentworth expresses his passion in a secret letter to Anne "I must speak to you by such means as are within my reach. You pierce my soul. I am half agony, half hope" (P 2:11). Wow! Yes, Wentworth is breaking the "no letter unless you're engaged" rule. But this is a desperate man who is unwilling to risk losing, for the second time, the woman he loves!

Securing father's approval

With the lady's acceptance, the next step is for the gentleman to secure her father's approval. Proper marriages had the approval of both the bride's and groom's parents. Obviously, after seeing the young man at all those balls asking his daughter to dance twice, coming to dinner, playing cards with her and her parents, and so on, Dad isn't going to be too surprised to hear the request for her hand. If the young lady's father was deceased, the fiancé could make the request for her hand to her mother, brother, uncle, or guardian.

A short and direct "conference" between Bingley and Mr. Bennet seals the deal in *Pride and Prejudice* (3:13). And when Darcy, having Elizabeth's acceptance, meets with Mr. Bennet, he emerges from her father's library smiling (3:17).

Exchanging gifts

Austen never tells us of any gifts exchanged between her heroine and hero either before, at the time of, or after the engagement. But she does show us the social "no-no" of unengaged couples exchanging gifts. In *Sense and Sensibility,* Marianne accepts Willoughby's gift of a horse, which Elinor immediately tells her she must reject, though her disapproval is couched more in the language of the expense of keeping a horse than the gift's outright impropriety.

A man's offering a lady to whom he is not yet engaged a gift always goes sour in Austen. *Mansfield Park*'s Henry Crawford, with the help of his sister, gives Fanny Price a gold necklace "prettily worked" to hold the amber cross that William, her brother, had given to her (MP 2:8). Notice that Henry works it so that Mary is the actual giver, thus enabling him to circumvent the "no gifts" rule. But his plan backfires: The ring of the cross will not fit the ornate necklace (MP 2:9). The most elaborate gift given in an Austen novel is *Emma*'s Frank Churchill's anonymous present of a very fine forte-piano (or pianoforte, the predecessor of the modern piano) to Jane Fairfax. The source of the gift puzzles everyone in the book because no one knows of Jane and Frank's secret engagement. But Frank can speak cryptically about the instrument in a way that only Jane understands. For example, he says in front of Emma and Jane that sending the pianoforte, along with sheet music, to Jane "'shews [the gift] to have been so thoroughly from the heart. . . . True affection only could have prompted it'" (E 2:10). When Jane hears this, she immediately blushes and forms "a smile of secret delight." Emma, misled into thinking that the instrument was sent by the man who married Jane's friend, of course, misreads the object of Jane's smile, even though the gift is compromising because the engagement is not known.

Breaking an engagement

Breaking an engagement, once approved by the parents, was a sticky issue. A gentleman, who was engaged at the age of 21 or over, didn't break an engagement. But if he was a minor and had been taken in by a female fortune-hunter, the Court traditionally sided with the young man's family and released him from the engagement. A young woman, however, whatever her age, could break the engagement, though it was still a serious thing to do. Jane Austen, herself, accepted at age 27 a proposal from an old family friend, Harris Bigg Wither, and then ended it early the next morning. While this caused temporary embarrassment to Jane, especially as Harris was the younger brother of her dear friends, Catherine and Alethea, she was not going to marry a man she did not love just because he was rich. And as to break-ups, she told her niece that "it is no creed of mine . . . that such sort of Disappointments kill anybody" (Letter, November 18–20, 1814). For more information on marriage and divorce, head to Chapter 7.

Chapter 7

Marrying: A Serious Business for Jane Austen and Her Characters

In This Chapter

▶ Discovering the ins and outs of marriage

▶ Revealing the practices of unmarried people

▶ Succumbing to failure: Knowing when to divorce

Marriage was a paradox in Austen's day — a paradox because marriage ideally secured a woman's financial security and social importance even as marriage meant her legal and financial rights simply went from her father to her husband. She had no rights of her own.

This chapter takes you through the whirlwind process of planning a wedding, stopping here and there to explore why women chose to marry, what the premarital business arrangements were; why men chose to marry; how women prepared for their weddings; what the Church of England wedding service involved; why couples eloped; and what happened when marriages went sour. Have you caught your breath yet?

This chapter examines marriage in Austen's day, which was financially necessary for almost all women and desired by most men. Because Austen lived in a world with neither pensions nor insurance and no career opportunities for women, the couple had much to consider in terms of money. This sounds crass, but it was necessary to ensure the fiscal stability of both the bride and groom. Couples and their parents entered premarital legalities to effect this stability. Austen mentions such legal agreements as "marriage settlements" and "articles" casually in her novels because she expects her contemporary readers to know what she's talking about. Read this chapter, and you will, too.

Exploring the Main Motivations for Marrying

Because a lady had virtually no individual rights or options, legal or financial (like having a career to support herself), she had to attract a good husband. What was a good husband? He was a gentleman who could support her as a member of the gentry, as well as one who was not cruel. (Remember: She has no rights!) The gentleman, if he's smart, wants a wife who will bring him both money and sons. Notice the use of the word "attract" in the first sentence. He's doing the asking.

Jane Austen explains the roles and motivations of men and women in the marriage relationship through the hero of *Northanger Abbey,* Henry Tilney. He likens marriage to a country dance, saying that "'in both, man has the advantage of choice, woman only the power of refusal; that in both, it is an engagement between man and woman, formed for the advantage of each'" (1:10). The advantages he speaks of are financial as well as personal, as the following sections explain.

Landing a loving husband . . . with a sizeable estate

Pride and Prejudice would be a very different novel if Jane Austen was writing it today. Yes, the romance and witty repartee between its heroine and hero, Elizabeth and Darcy, would still be there. But Elizabeth Bennet would not be in the same weak financial position that limits her choices in the novel.

Today a woman as clever and bright as Elizabeth Bennet from *Pride and Prejudice* would be in law school, heading to a well-established firm with a six-figure salary in view. The modern Elizabeth might wait to marry or not marry at all; after all, romance aside, she could certainly support herself quite well, and in today's world, she would have her own legal identity. But in Austen's day, financial and legal security for Elizabeth and her sisters only came with one option: marriage.

Securing her place in society

Women of the Bennets' class — the landowning gentry class on whom Jane Austen focuses her authorial attention — had no rights to speak of and no occupation open to them, no matter how smart, clever, diligent, and well-read they were. (See Chapter 2 for a discussion on social class.) This was true for Austen's female characters, as well as for Austen herself.

It's worth repeating that a daughter's legal identity belonged to her father; and a married woman's legal identity was secured by identifying her with her husband. This role identity was both good and bad.

- ✔ **Good:** The husband protected the wife and secured her place in society. It was better to be married with a house of your own than to be a spinster responsible for running a brother's household.

- ✔ **Bad:** The wife could virtually do nothing without her husband's approval — enter a contract, buy property, write a will. Legally, then, a married woman ceased to have her own existence.

Marriage also secured the woman's financial place. A gentry woman's finances, pre-marriage, were, of course under her father's care and control. If she was lucky, her parents' marriage also secured some money for her, usually from her mother's side, when she came of age. But unless her mother's parents were extremely rich, the young woman didn't get that much money from her mother. In order to live the gentry life to which she was accustomed, she needed to marry a man who could give her the lifestyle she had with her parents or an even better one. In *Pride and Prejudice,* Elizabeth Bennet's sensible and kind Aunt Gardiner seriously advises her niece on connecting herself with Mr. Wickham — and on marriage in general (2:3).

In Austen's novels, readers come across many female characters who are looking for financial security through a good marriage. While they are gentry women, they don't have much money of their own. What they have is the result of arrangements made by their parents for them and/or by their husbands for them at the time they married. Because the bulk of an estate normally went to the eldest son or nearest male heir, the women in the family were left with comparatively little.

For example, in *Sense and Sensibility,* the widowed Mrs. Dashwood and her three daughters do not inherit the great Dashwood estate, Norland, because the owner, Uncle Dashwood, suddenly changes his will and leaves it to his grandnephew. He does this for two reasons: The grandnephew is cute, and he will carry on the Dashwood surname, keeping Norland in Dashwood hands.

So the four Dashwood women now must live on £500 annually (SS 1:2). Now while this does not put them on the street, this sum doesn't give them the life they lived at Norland Park, a beautiful and spacious gentry estate with a large house attached to it. They must move to a cottage with moderate rent. And their social life is limited to where their feet can take them because they can't afford a carriage and horse. A visit to London is out of the question financially, unless a friend covers their expenses. And their chances of landing a financially stable marriage are lessened by the daughters each having a dowry of only £1,000, their Uncle having given each girl that amount (and their inability to get out often to meet people).

Figuring out the Dashwood's finances

How much money would the Dashwood ladies have today?

While converting money from Austen's time to ours and then from British pounds to U.S. dollars is always a contentious question, I've found a Web site that helps: "How Much Is That Worth" at www.eh.net/hmit/ppowerbp/. Accordingly, I entered £500, the Dashwood ladies' annual income, for the year 1811 (when *Sense and Sensibility* was published) and asked what its purchasing power would be in British pounds for the year 2004: The answer was £24,162 and 41 pence. I then found that in July

2004, £1 was worth $1.94. Multiply £24,162 and 41 pence by $1.94 and the result is $46,875.05 in 2004. Keep in mind that prices were much lower in 1811: The Dashwood ladies have a cottage at a very moderate rent; they have two maids and a man servant, whose pay would have been quite low; they have neither carriage nor horse; the four Dashwoods probably have limited wardrobes; and they appear to get quite a bit of food from Sir John Middleton, on whose estate they live. This amount would allow them to live in a minimally genteel way.

At the other extreme, a wealthy heiress needed to take great care in choosing a spouse. Unless someone (a father, brother, uncle, or other male in the position of guardian) was really looking out for her finances, all of her money went to her husband. And if he was an irresponsible man, the more pity for her. Fearing a fortune-hunter in Wickham, relatives of a young heiress, Miss King, remove her from his presence purview because they fear that he's interested in her only because she has £10,000 (PP 2:2). If he took her off and married her, that money could become his to do with as he wishes. Lucky Miss King to have such observant relatives!

Marrying for love and money

In Austen's day, marriages weren't forced. Not that this didn't happen, but this type of forced marriage — where parents prearranged things for monetary reasons and assumed the bride would eventually learn to love, or at least endure, her husband — was getting more and more rare.

In fact, literature — both novels and plays — that stressed marrying for love helped change society! Even in the decades before Austen wrote, literature was showing that couples marry more happily when love brings the couple together. So no more of that Montague-Capulet stuff from *Romeo and Juliet*!

Austen's novels always show the heroines marrying for love. But being the smart young women that they are, they also never marry without money. Women had to be careful whom they chose to marry. Because all of the wife's rights were controlled by the husband, a poor choice in a husband could mean his spending all her money frivolously, unwisely, and selfishly.

Taking a husband when love has nothing to do with it

In Austen's day, single women who weren't wealthy were scorned as spinsters, so marriage conveyed status for a woman — whether or not she liked her husband. If a gentry woman found herself unlucky in securing a husband in England, she could take a huge step: travel by ship in a hazardous journey to a British colony where lonely European men awaited wives. A frequent site for this journey was India. Jane Austen knew about this option personally because her father's sister, Miss Philadelphia Austen, did just this.

Traveling to India in 1752 at the age of 22 by herself on board the ship *Bombay Castle,* Philadelphia arrived in Madras seven months after departing from England. After being there for six months, she married an English surgeon, Tysoe Saul Hancock, who was 20 years older than she was. He worked for the East India Company. They had a daughter, Elizabeth, who was born in Calcutta. Thirteen years after leaving England, Philadelphia Hancock, her husband, and daughter sailed to England, arriving in the summer of 1765. Jane's father went to London to reunite with the sister he hadn't seen for over a decade and to meet his brother-in-law. But in 1768, Tysoe Hancock had to return to India to make enough money to support the lifestyle he and his wife had adopted in England. Not only did he fail in this endeavor, but he never saw his wife and daughter again. It has been suggested that Philadelphia's voyage to India and marriage to Hancock had been prearranged by some of her family members. But arranged or not, her experience doesn't sound like a very happy one.

Philadelphia's story stayed with young Jane Austen, who being born in 1775, never met her uncle Tysoe. Jane uses the story of her Aunt Philadelphia in her unfinished fiction, *Catharine; or, The Bower.* The 16-year-old writer includes a character, Cecilia Wynne, whose parents' deaths left her poor. As a result, Cecilia is "obliged to accept the offer of one of her cousins to equip her for the East Indies." Cecilia's experience sounds much worse than Philadelphia's: "Her personal Attractions had gained her a husband as soon as she had arrived at Bengal, and she had now been married. . . . Splendidly, yet unhappily married. United to a Man of double her own age, whose disposition was not amiable, and whose Manners were unpleasing. . . ." (MW 194). Unfortunately, because marriage was the accepted means of securing a young woman's future and her place in society, the experiences of both Philadelphia and Cecilia weren't unusual.

One didn't have to travel to India to marry without love. In *Pride and Prejudice,* Charlotte Lucas asserts her reasons for marrying Mr. Collins. At the age of 27, Charlotte obviously worries about ending up a spinster without any place of her own. She tells Elizabeth, "'I am not romantic. . . . I never was. I ask only a comfortable home'" (1:22). So she marries the very unpleasant Mr. Collins, relieving her younger brothers "from their apprehension of Charlotte's dying an old maid." And of course, if Charlotte hadn't married, as time went on, her brothers would have had to support her and perhaps even bring her into their homes. Charlotte recognizes that marriage "was the only honourable provision for well-educated young women of small-fortune, and however uncertain of giving happiness, must be their pleasantest preservative from want" (1:22).

Choosing a willing wife . . . with a decent dowry

While the young woman was hoping to find a husband whom she loved and who could offer her financial security, the young man hoped to find a wife to love as well (and who had a decent dowry, too).

Providing for his family

A *dowry* is the amount of money that a woman brings to the marriage. Not that men were money grubbers, but when a young man looked for a wife, in addition to personal attraction, he hoped that the bride could bring some money with her to supplement what he had to offer. The dowry, if wisely invested, could significantly help the young married couple and their children; the husband might even be able to use some of the dowry money to buy more property to add to his estate. Wise investment of the wife's dowry would improve the lives of generations to come.

Why all this worry about money? Birth control didn't exist in Austen's day (other than separate bedrooms). So when a gentleman asked a lady for her hand, it was expected that he would be able to support her and their ever-growing family.

In some cases, the couple had to postpone their marriage until the man could secure more money. After all, that day and age weren't a time when genteel couples could decide to be a two-income family, with the wife having her own career and sharing in the household upkeep! In Austen's work, the insufficiency of the gentleman's finances to marry occurs most dramatically in *Persuasion*.

> ✔ Captain Benwick and Fanny Harville remain engaged until he earns enough money for them to marry. Long engagements for this reason were not at all unusual. And because the woman surrendered her fiscal, physical, and legal rights to her husband upon marriage, she had also to be sure that he was honest, responsible, kind, reasonable, and able to support her. In the Benwick/Harville case, poor Fanny dies before they can afford to marry.

> ✔ Anne Elliot rejects the proposal of Frederick Wentworth, a young naval
> officer, even though she loved him and knows that he loved her. While
> her godmother advises her against the marriage because of Frederick's
> lack of financial security at the time, the prudent Anne consults her own
> feelings and judgment, deciding that for *his* good, she must reject him
> (1:4). I suggest that the reasons are again financial: As a naval officer
> during the Napoleonic Wars, Frederick is constantly in harm's way.
> Should he be wounded and put on half-pay, and she pregnant, he would
> be under a terrible burden in trying to support his wife and child.

Safeguarding his assets and lineage

Although the legal and financial rights of a married couple were really the
husband's rights, the gentleman still had to be sure that he selected the right
woman. The selection process was especially important for the wealthy
young gentleman, or the heir to or owner of a great estate, who faced the
same problems as the wealthy heiress: beware the fortune hunter. For example, in *Pride and Prejudice,* young women danced pirouettes of admiration
around the handsome and wealthy Darcy, so he needed to be sure that he
selected the right woman to become the mistress of his incomparable estate.

A wealthy young gentleman like Darcy was in the marriage-market for not only
a well-meaning wife, but also one who could bear a male heir and, if possible,
a spare so that his property could be passed down within the immediate
family. Frequently, the distribution of property was stated in documents that
went back many generations. If the property was designated to go to males,
sons were important. So a woman knew she was destined for pregnancy, possibly many pregnancies until a son was born, to ensure that the property
stayed in the family. (For more on property inheritance, see Chapter 10.)

Jane Austen saw two phenomena resulting from both the need for sons and
the lack of effective birth control. In her youth, her brother Edward was
adopted by their father's cousin and his wife, Mr. and Mrs. Thomas Knight II.
Wealthy but childless, the Knights wanted their extensive property to remain
within the family, even through cousins. But the need for sons also led to the
early deaths of wives. Because of primitive and unsanitary birthing conditions, the infant mortality rate was high, as was the death rate of wives from
childbirth problems, whether in quest of an heir or not. Austen's wealthy
brother Edward and his wife, Elizabeth, had 11 children, including 6 sons.
Poor Elizabeth, age 35, died in 1808 shortly after the birth of child number 11
(son number 6). They really could have stopped sooner to ensure an heir. Is
it any wonder that hearing of her niece Anna Lefroy's miscarriage, Austen
wrote to her sister, "Poor Animal, she will be worn out before she is thirty.—I
am very sorry for her. . . . I am quite tired of so many children" (Letter, March
23-25, 1817). Austen, herself, referred to her books as her children. The
birthing process for books was much safer.

Understanding why some folks (including Austen) broke with tradition

In spite of the pressure to marry, many young women remained single in Jane Austen's day, including Austen herself. What if a gentleman decided not to marry? Not good. England expected every man to do his duty: marry, have children, and thereby add to the economy and the strength of the nation. As the following sections explain, the reasons for breaking tradition vary from having unusual financial independence to never being asked (for women).

Choosing not to marry

Once in a while society produces someone to go against the flow: an independently wealthy single woman who doesn't choose to marry. How might she be independently wealthy? Her mother may have left her daughter a large amount of money that is secured in such a way as to allow her to remain singleFor instance, the only Austen character who doesn't have to marry to continue her high standard of living is Emma Woodhouse, from *Emma,* and she is introduced as "Handsome, clever, and rich" (1:1). She has £30,000 to her name and no brothers. Her sister is married to a gentleman-lawyer, whose bachelor brother, Emma assumes, will leave his estate to his eldest nephew. So Emma can stay in her lovely home for the rest of her life. In fact, Emma even says she has no desire to marry. In real life, Austen's good friend Alethea Bigg of Manydown never married. While the reason remains unclear, she came from a wealthy family — probably wealthier then Emma's — and certainly did not need a husband to enable her to live well.

Emma is so unique in Austen's gallery of heroines that she's the only heroine whose name is also the title of the novel in which she appears. (So if you wish to impress your friends, say that Emma is the *eponymous* heroine, which means having the name that is used as the title or name of something else.)

Sometimes gentlemen also chose not to marry. In literature as in life, the man may not meet the right woman or for some reason, be averse to marriage. Readers never learn the reason that old Uncle Dashwood in *Sense and Sensibility* remained a bachelor. Some men simply waited for "Miss Right." Mr. Knightley was 16 when Emma was born. Knowing that his younger brother was married with sons, Mr. Knightley probably felt under no pressure to marry for inheritance's sake: Donwell Abbey, his estate, would remain in the Knightley family by going to his brother's eldest son. But Mr. Knightley's not being averse to marriage is hinted at when he tells the bossy Mrs. Elton that the only woman who will ever be able to invite guests to Donwell is "'Mrs. Knightley;—and , till she is in being, I will manage such matters myself'" (E 3:6). Emma eventually becomes Mrs. Knightley.

Austen also would have heard of a gay man, John Chute, who owned a wonderful neighboring estate, The Vyne, and died without issue. (He was the lover of Horace Walpole, who wrote the first Gothic novel, *The Castle of Otranto,* and who designed the famous Strawberry Hill castle.) Because none of John's siblings had any surviving children, the Chute estate went to a male relative whose mother was a Chute, Thomas Lobb. The Lobbs moved to The Vyne, changed their surname to Chute, and became great friends with the Austens. Jane Austen danced at many a ball with their son, Tom, and her brothers hunted with the Chute males on the estate for two generations (brother James and his son, James Edward).

Never being asked to marry

Some women never find Mr. Right. The same was true in Austen's day just as it is today. But in Austen's day, the need to marry was so strong for gentry women that those who were never asked to marry were likely connected by a common denominator: the lack of sufficient dowries. This may account for Jane Austen's not marrying. But she may have remained single by preference, as well. This, like many parts of her life, remains a mystery. Her sister Cassandra was engaged, only to have her fiancé, Tom Fowle, die of fever. She never sought to develop another relationship, remaining true to Tom Fowle even in death. Austen's letters include several unmarried females. But the reasons for their being so are not explored. Unless they were wealthy, one can assume they lacked the required dowry.

In *Pride and Prejudice,* Mr. Collins tells Elizabeth Bennet after she has rejected his proposal that "'In spite of your manifold attractions, it is by no means certain that another offer of marriage may ever be made you. Your portion [the amount she will get for her dowry] is unhappily so small that it will in all likelihood undo the effects of your loveliness and amiable qualifications'" (1:19).

The insufficient dowry dilemma weighs heavily on the sisters in "The Watsons" — a fragment that Austen began and never finished back in 1805. The sisters are the daughters of a retired clergyman who hasn't much money and who's very ill. While one sister has married, some of the remaining sisters actually plot against each other because they're so desperate to marry. Of course, where Austen left off the manuscript, the text indicated that the heroine, the lovely 19-year-old Emma Watson, may become the object of the affections of two men, dowry problem notwithstanding. But this was the exception to the rule.

Rejecting the proposal

In some cases, women did reject legitimate and eligible proposals. Not loving the proposer is obviously one reason! And when the woman was, herself, rich, she could afford to be choosey. Austen, herself, advised her wealthy niece, Fanny, "Anything is to be preferred or endured rather than marrying without Affection" (Letter to Fanny Knight, November 18–20, 1814). In this case, Fanny was contemplating an imminent proposal from a highly serious young man about whose Evangelicalism she had reservations. Fanny waited until 1820 and married a baronet, becoming Lady Knatchbull. (For information on Anglican Evangelicalism, see Chapter 13.)

Another heroine, Anne Elliot in *Persuasion,* rejects a proposal from the eldest son of a prosperous gentry family because she's still in love with someone else (1:4).

Living as a single woman

Unless a woman from the gentry married or had her own comfortable income allowing her to live well as a single woman, like Austen's friend Alethea Bigg, the single woman risked living in genteel poverty. This means that she still associates with the gentry, but lives in a second-class way. For example, Miss Bates in *Emma* is the daughter of a clergyman, and thus she is a gentlewoman. But she lives with her widowed mother in genteel poverty: They reside in the village in an apartment above a business. Likewise, such women's association with the gentry put them in a second-tier group. Thus, when the Coles have their dinner party, Miss Bates is invited only for the after-dinner entertainment (E 2:8).

Jane Austen knew what genteel poverty was. At Mr. Austen's death in 1805, the three Austen ladies — Mrs. Austen and her two adult, unmarried daughters, Cassandra and Jane — lost Mr. Austen's clerical pension (which ended when he died) and basically relied on the kindness of sons/brothers. They lived a semi-nomadic lifestyle, moving here and there at relatives' homes, until in 1808, son/brother Edward came across with the Chawton cottage. This nomadic life existed even with Mrs. Austen's sons chipping in to help their mother and two sisters.

The eldest Miss Watson and her sister live with her ailing, elderly father in genteel poverty. Jane Austen knew what that was. When her father retired from the clergy toward the end of 1800, he turned over the rectory house, where the family had lived, to his eldest son.

Coming to Terms

Marriage was both a romantic attachment and a business deal, so the father or guardian of the bride wanted to ensure that the woman would be well taken care of and protected financially. And the gentleman's parents were concerned that their son married well and that their younger grandchildren (that is, not the male heir) would have financial comfort, something that the bride's parents' money frequently helped to ensure. To effect all of this, both bride and groom were usually represented by their lawyers or agents.

Drawing up the marriage settlement or articles

Assuming the future wife brought a dowry into the marriage, the future husband's lawyer, working with the woman's family's lawyer, would prepare a *marriage settlement,* also called *marriage articles.* This contract stipulated many scenarios to "settle" money on the wife and children:

- ✔ It could allow the husband's wife to inherit his property, permitting her to deal with it as she wished.
- ✔ It could give her a portion of his property.
- ✔ It could state that the wife couldn't inherit the property if she remarried.
- ✔ It could also arrange for certain amounts of money to be given to each of the children, both sons and daughters, on the husband's death.

Having a marriage settlement was important for a woman because after her husband died, the bulk of his estate normally went to the eldest son, who was the heir. The marriage settlement ensured that the widow could continue to live in comfort after she moved from the estate so that her eldest son, with his family, could move in as the new heir. Furthermore, the marriage settlement could help support the younger children so they could live and marry well. This was needed as there was no insurance to support a widow or children.

Jane Austen's novels show that she was very much aware of these premarital legal workings between the bride and groom. In *Pride and Prejudice,* the Bennets' marriage settlement is clearly spelled out: "Five thousand pounds was settled by marriage articles on Mrs. Bennet and the children" (3:8). In Volume 1, Chapter 7 of the novel, Mrs. Bennet's father, Mr. Gardiner, a country attorney (not genteel), "Had left her four thousand pounds." Presumably that was her dowry, and the marriage articles added another thousand pounds from Mr. Bennet: "[I]n what proportions [the resulting 5,000 pounds] should be divided among [the Bennet children] depended on the will of the parents" (3:8). Here is a case, then, with the bride's dowry supplemented by £1,000 from the groom. This may sound like a lot. But consider that the Bingley sisters "had a fortune of twenty thousand pounds," and Georgiana Darcy's fortune is £30,000 (PP 1:4, 2:12).

In *Persuasion,* we also hear of marriage articles but with behavioral stipulations involved instead of property. Mrs. Smith speculates that Mr. William Elliot will marry Anne Elliot and suggests that Mr. Elliot, to preserve the Kellynch Estate and Baronetcy for his future sons, will "'put into the marriage articles . . . that [Anne's] father is not to marry Mrs. Clay'" (2:9). If Sir Walter Elliot, Anne's father, was to marry the young Mrs. Clay, and they were to have a son, the estate and the Elliot Baronetcy would, of course, go to their son, thus cutting off Mr. William Elliot's prospects for both land and title.

Arranging for a jointure

Another item that could be discussed and arranged prior to the marriage was the jointure. A *jointure* is an agreement stipulating that the wife would receive a portion — traditionally one-third of it — of her husband's estate when her husband died. With a sufficient jointure, a widow had control over her property. And for this reason, most widows with ample jointures didn't remarry; otherwise, they would then find their property again controlled by their new husbands. Lady Russell feels the freedom from marriage after her husband dies and she's "extremely well provided for" and has "no thought of a second marriage" (1:1). Freedom at last!

If all of this sounds like a lot of money dealing — and it was — remember that Austen's day didn't have pensions or insurance. So people had to look out for their financial well-beings.

Sealing the Deal

As an Anglican, herself, Jane Austen created characters who were also members of the Church of England (when there was any indication of religious beliefs). Readers never see her characters at the altar, but they do get a few brief insights about the wedding and about how the couple is doing after their marriage. This section explains the wedding plans and Church requirements.

The main thing to note here is that a wedding in Austen's day was a far simpler affair than most weddings are today.

Choosing the wedding clothes and coach

When a gentlewoman married, her parents purchased wedding clothes for her, which was an entire wardrobe including fashionable clothes for all occasions, ranging from ball gowns to riding habits.

Traditionally, the bride was married in a formal white bridal gown, but she did have the option of wearing her best dress instead, which could be white or some other color.

The bride normally wore her best dress, but it did not have to be white. (By the same token, it was not black or red.) White was a popular dress color for young ladies of the gentry because it suggested their wealth: They had maids to keep their dresses clean. Thus, the fashion conscious Mrs. Allen reminds Catherine that Miss Tilney "'always wears white'" and advises Catherine to wear her white gown when she calls on Miss Tilney (NA 1:12). A wealthy bride of the gentry like Maria Bertram was "elegantly dressed" for her wedding, and Fanny, a bridesmaid, wore a white gown with "glossy spots" (MP 2:3, 2:5). But when Emma and Mr. Knightley marry, Austen writes that "the wedding was very much like other weddings, where the parties have no taste for finery or parade" (E 3:19). Mrs. Elton, ever jealous of Emma, even snidely remarks that Emma's wedding is "very inferior to her own," having "'Very little white satin, very few lace veils'" (3:19).

The elaborate white wedding dress with a long train only began with Queen Victoria's marriage in 1840. In Austen's day, young ladies commonly wore for any occasion white muslin columnar or tube-shaped dresses, usually beautifully decorated with needlework. A white chemise or slip was worn underneath, serving as underwear. When Fanny wears her bridesmaid dress to a dinner party, she is concerned that she will appear "'too fine,'" but her cousin Edmund reassures her, saying, "'A woman can never be too fine when she is all in white'" (MP 2:5). While white is traditionally associated with purity, white gowns in Austen's time also reflected the contemporary taste for ancient Grecian and Roman fashion. Austen lived at the end of the English neoclassical age; hence, the taste for the straight, white dresses seen in classical sculpture.

Meanwhile, the groom wasn't just sitting around, although he didn't have to rent a tuxedo. At the wedding, he wore his best clothes, too. Prior to the wedding, the groom's main project was usually to buy a new coach for himself and his bride. But sometimes they fall down on the job. When the newly-wed Maria Bertram and Mr. Rushworth leave Mansfield Park, the neighbors note that they are in the "same chaise which Mr. Rushworth had used for a twelve-month before. In everything else the etiquette of the day may stand the strictest investigation" (MP 2:3).

Announcing the nuptials

In Austen's day, the couple who planned to marry had a choice among three ways to head to the altar in the Church of England. Couples selected their way based on their economic and social status. Because Austen writes about the gentry, it is likely that most of her characters marry by the license, discussed below. But in *Emma* when the farmer Robert Martin and Harriet Smith marry, it is more likely they would choose the banns. Like just about everything else in Austen's world, one's class determined one's choices and conduct.

- **Publishing the banns in the Church of England:** A couple could marry in the Church of England if they "published the banns." This phrase meant that the couple requested the local clergyman to announce their upcoming wedding from the pulpit for three successive Sundays during the service. A bride and groom who lived in different church parishes had the banns read in both of their parishes. If no one objected — for example, if someone knew that the groom was unscrupulous and had a wife stashed in another village — to the wedding then the couple could marry within 90 days of the final announcement of the banns. Because publishing the banns cost nothing, it was the method used by poorer people who wished to marry. But publishing the banns in church did not mean that everyone who heard them became a wedding guest. This was just for the public's approval that everything about the bride and groom was legit.

- **Securing a license:** Couples with money normally chose to be married by license.

  - **Common/Ordinary license:** The duo could purchase a license from a clergyman for about 10 shillings and then get married in the parish where either the bride or groom had lived for a minimum of 15 days. Undoubtedly, this process is how Wickham and Lydia were married in London, for Lydia says that they were married at St. Clement's Church "'because Wickham's lodgings were in that parish'" (PP 3:9).

  - **Special License:** The most expensive way to marry was by Special License, granted by the Archbishop of Canterbury, the head of the Church of England; he issued these licenses at his discretion for between four and five pounds. The nature of this license meant that only the wealthy and fashionable could afford a Special License or even be in a position to contact the Archbishop. With a Special License, the couple could marry in any parish at any time. When Mrs. Bennet learns that Darcy and Elizabeth are to marry, she becomes so excited that she cries, "'And a special license. You must and shall be married by a special license'" (PP 3:17). Mrs. Bennet desires this because it carries social panache. But the wedding appears to occur at Elizabeth's parish church, and so a Special License may not have been used.

With a Special License, the couple had more latitude in terms of choosing the location and time to be married. With the banns or the ordinary license, the couple married in the bride's or groom's parish church. (See the next section on the canonical hours.)

Sharing the big day with family and friends

Weddings occurred only during the canonical hours, between 8:00 a.m. and noon — unless the pair had the Special License, which allowed them to marry later in the day, if they chose. Unless couples were very showy or very important, they invited only family and close friends. After the wedding ended, the bride and groom and their guests adjourned somewhere for the wedding breakfast. The most important thing to note is that people in Austen's day did not have the elaborate weddings we attend today.

The breakfast normally included a wedding cake, which, unlike today's tiered wedding cakes, was similar to a fruit cake with icing. The couple might also use the breakfast as the occasion to distribute little gifts to their guests, which ranged from little trinkets to larger gifts.

Eloping to Gretna Green and avoiding the whole thing

Of course, a couple could simplify the whole marriage process and elope to Scotland. People crossed the border to the nearest Scottish village, Gretna Green, and declared before a witness — any witness — their desire to marry. Usually, the witness was the local blacksmith. This very loose marriage "ceremony" could occur in Scotland because the rules of the Scottish Presbyterian Church were far more lax than those of the Church of England.

In *Pride and Prejudice,* Lydia initially goes with Wickham and writes to her sister Kitty that they are headed to Gretna Green (3:5). While her older sisters, Jane and Elizabeth, are horrified at the news, at least Lydia would have been "married" to Wickham before she started to cohabitate with him. A woman living with a man out of wedlock was simply unthinkable — though it did happen, as Austen, no prude, realized. With the double standard, the shame was thrown on the woman. The reader learns that Wickham had no intention of marrying Lydia and had planned to make "his fortune by marriage, in some other country" (PP 3:10). This would have left Lydia a fallen woman: the "spiteful old ladies" of her village think she has already "come upon the town" (become a prostitute) (PP 3:8). Had Wickham not been forced to marry her, she would have shared the fate of Maria Bertram: being sent to live with an older woman companion on a small allowance to a remote country house.

But elopement was frowned upon as a bad start to a marriage. Austen shows how forced marriages or elopements lead to bad marriages through Lydia and Wickham. Soon after their marriage — after the excitement and physical attraction wear thin — they lead largely separate lives as their marriage falls apart. The eloping couple had no dowries or marriage settlements to support their future. And they were an embarrassment to their families as the elopement was anti-social in the very social gentry world. In Austen's day, there was nothing romantic about eloping.

Taking the honeymoon

Honeymoons date back to the early centuries A.D. In Austen's day, when premarital sex was scandalous, the honeymoon truly meant the first time the couple had marital relations. Like today, the newly married couple went off on a holiday together.

It usually strikes readers as peculiar when they read in *Mansfield Park* that when Mr. Rushworth and his new bride Maria leave for their honeymoon, Maria's sister joins them (2:3). Granted, Rushworth isn't the most entertaining companion, but three on a honeymoon? Yes. And this practice continued well into the Victorian period (1837–1901). Frequently, the bride's sister or closest female friend accompanied the couple. This custom was meant to assist both the bride and the groom socially. The bride, a virgin until her wedding night, had a close female companion to comfort her, as needed, during the holiday. And the groom did not appear too groomlike in public places, walking around with two young women. This is a custom that most readers are probably glad has ended!

While the newlyweds were honeymooning, the groom's mother — if she was a widow and still living in the house that her son had inherited from his father — might graciously depart to her own new home, albeit smaller and less grand than that which she left. Thus, Rushworth's widowed mother "with true . . . propriety" decamps from Sotherton to Bath, so the estate will be ready for her son and his wife when they return from their honeymoon (MP 2:3). But Jane Austen's brother Edward remained in the smaller Rowling house on the Knight family's Kent property even after his adopted father died until his adopted mother chose to leave the Godmersham estate.

If the groom's father was alive and well, it was his right to remain on the family estate as its master until his death or disability. Austen knew well the Bigg-Wither family of Manydown, where the widowed Mr. Bigg Wither lived on his Manydown estate, providing a home for his unmarried and widowed daughters and the latter's children. His married son and heir lived with his wife and young family on another, smaller estate that the family also owned. When Mr. Bigg-Wither died, the son and his family moved to Manydown, and his remaining unmarried sister, Alethea Bigg, and widowed sister, Catherine Heathcote, moved to a house in Winchester.

Breaching the Agreement: Facing the Shame of Divorce

Divorce, which was granted by an Act of Parliament, was very expensive, very public, and very shameful almost always for the woman.

The double standard was alive and well in Jane Austen's day. A husband could sleep around, but his wife couldn't divorce him for his adultery. An adulterous husband could commit the act and even if discovered, just get on with his life. His wife had no legal recourse. On the other hand, if the wife committed adultery, her husband could divorce her. In the divorce proceedings, the wife wasn't permitted to testify on her own behalf. And society and the press branded her a slut. The divorced woman lost her social rank and privileges, and her husband gained sole custody of the children — frequently meaning that she never saw them again. If she was lucky, she had a small allowance on which to live. *Sense and Sensibility*'s Eliza Brandon, a divorced woman because of her adultery (never mind that her husband committed adultery first), winds up in the poor house. When Maria Bertram Rushworth commits adultery in *Mansfield Park,* her husband divorces her, and her father sends her to live "in another country," meaning not abroad, but rather to another county or borough in England, "remote and private" (3:17).

A woman could take action in one instance: spousal abuse. A woman couldn't bring her husband to court for committing adultery or for beating her, but if the husband did both — *and* beat her to a pulp — then she did have a shot at divorcing him, assuming she could crawl to court. Because divorces were very expensive, informal separations were cheaper alternatives.

Chapter 8

Wily Females and Seductive Males

· ·

In This Chapter

▶ Putting on the charm to find a mate

▶ Using flirting as a means to an end

▶ Winning your spouse the right way

· ·

Many readers have long thought of Jane Austen as the sweet spinster writer whose novels carry you away back to the more innocent times of "Merry Olde England" — if there ever was such a place! Some readers still do, and that's fine. As Karen Joy Fowler premises in her delightful novel *The Jane Austen Book Club,* all Austen readers have their own Jane Austen.

Austen was a shrewd observer of the world in which she lived, and a writer of realistic social comedies. (For more on her realistic writing, see particularly Chapter 16.) While she was certainly a moral writer, she was well aware of how young men and women behaved, especially when it came to behaving toward each other when the scents of romance and money were in the air. (See Chapter 7 for info on money and marriage.) Because Austen wrote novels about the relationships between young men and women, it was only natural for her to throw sexual flirtation and even seduction — real or attempted — into her books, though sexual acts, of course, occurred off-stage. Austen used the words "by a Lady" as the byline for her first published novel, *Sense and Sensibility.* The word "Lady" connotes not only her social place as a member of the gentry, but also, like today, moral, courteous behavior and demeanor.

As a realistic writer, she knew that wily females and seductive males could work their arts on many people. She even told her sister that she had a "very good eye at an adulteress" (Letter, May 12–13, 1801). And she can write about one, too! (For more information on the gentry and class structure, see Chapter 2; for information on moral versus immoral behavior in Austen's day and novels, see Chapter 13.) This chapter explores Austen's characters as crafty females, male and female flirts, and male seducers.

Working with What You've Got to Get Your Man

Every work of fiction presents a conflict: within a character, between characters, or between a character and society. Writing about courtship and the emotional growth of her heroes and heroines, who range between 16 (Marianne in *Sense and Sensibility* and Lydia in *Pride and Prejudice*) and 36 (Mr. Knightley in *Emma,* and Colonel Brandon in *Sense and Sensibility*), Austen is bound to have some of them personally deal with or witness others dealing with wily females or seductive males as a crucial part of their courtships and learning experiences. Sometimes, the conflict extends beyond the hero or heroine to other characters in the novel.

Capturing a husband with "youth and beauty"

Young ladies needed a dowry if they expected to marry well or even marry at all. (Chapter 7 explains the whole courtship process and the importance of dowries.) But with or without a dowry, young ladies could be extremely flirtatious in order to get their man. Having just turned 20, Austen, herself, wrote facetiously to her sister about how she and Tom Lefroy behaved at a ball doing "everything most profligate and shocking in the way of dancing and sitting down together" (Letter, January 9–10, 1796).

While Jane Austen was youthfully flirtatious, she certain wasn't a wily man-hunter. Yet she has several crafty females in the novels who win or try to win men with "youth and beauty."

The phrase "youth and beauty" comes from *Pride and Prejudice,* where it's revealed how the apparently incompatible Mr. and Mrs. Bennet ever wound up together: he "had been captivated by youth and beauty, and that appearance of good humour, which youth and beauty generally give" (PP 2:19).

Take a look at the following examples of youthful and beautiful women snagging their men in Austen's novels:

✔ **Miss Gardiner (later Mrs. Bennet, and likely named Jane, as eldest daughters were frequently named for their mothers, just as Jane Austen's sister Cassandra was named for her mother) from *Pride and Prejudice:* Miss Gardiner must have had a good share of beauty: Her eldest daughter Jane, who's beautiful, and Elizabeth, who's "very pretty" must have inherited their looks from their mother, for Mr. Bennet is never described as being anything like *Persuasion*'s Sir Walter Elliot, who having been "remarkably handsome in his youth" is "at fifty-four . . . still a very fine man" (P 1:1). While Miss Gardiner had the beauty and high-spiritedness to attract Mr. Bennet, she had a dowry of £4,000. Granted, this purse is more than each of her daughters will have. But it's still not big-time money, and so you know that Mr. Bennet wasn't looking at Miss Gardiner's finances when he became attracted to her. And to get her man, Miss Gardiner had to be shrewd, as well as beautiful.

✔ **Mrs. Crawford in *Mansfield Park*:** Mrs. Crawford, the wife of Admiral Crawford, isn't as lucky as Mrs. Bennet. Whether Mrs. Crawford attracted her naval husband with youth and beauty is unclear, but his turning to other women when he and his wife don't get along is his choice of comfort. He has a mistress and undoubtedly has enjoyed the favors of many a woman. This implication shows one example of how a man dissatisfied in his marriage as Mr. Bennet is deals with his marital unhappiness. But Mr. Bennet "was not of a disposition to seek comfort . . . in any of those pleasures which too often console the unfortunate for their folly or their vice" (PP 2:19). Instead, luckily for Mrs. Bennet, her husband turns to books and sarcasm for solace.

✔ **Lady Bertram in *Mansfield Park*:** Lady Bertram also attracted her husband, a baronet with a country house and estate, by being "handsome," plus having "luck" (MP 1:1). At the time of their courtship, she was considered £3,000 "short" — in terms of her dowry — of making this great match. The spoiled and lazy Lady Bertram must have captivated Sir Thomas with her looks. For she never displays even a hint of spiritedness or wit — or she expended it all in flirting with him during their courtship!

✔ **Jane Fairfax in *Emma*:** Jane Fairfax is a "remarkably elegant" young woman with "pleasing beauty" (E 2:2). Indeed, Jane is so elegant that it's hard to believe she was ever flirtatious. Though so poor that she's the only one among Austen's young women to have to consider a career as a governess, she has beauty and elegance enough to attract Frank Churchill, heir to great wealth, and captivate him. They manage to continue their courtship secretly in Highbury, with Frank finding any excuse to stop by Mrs. Bates's (Jane's grandmother's) house, where Jane is staying, although there's absolutely no sign that they're using this as "The Bates Motel," as I once heard it described! For as Jane confesses when the engagement is made public, the secrecy has been very hard on her, causing her to be in conflict with herself for having to play the hypocrite. (For the plight of the governess, see Chapter 9.)

Using beauty and trickery when you don't have youth

Austen's *Lady Susan,* written in 1794, is a stunning read because, in the novella (short novel), she presents a character, Lady Susan, who displays all the characteristics of sociopathy. Selfish, vain, guiltless, and loveless, Lady Susan Vernon is known as "the most accomplished coquette [flirtatious woman] in England." Still a beauty in her late 30's, she manipulates younger men with her skills in language, making herself look the victim of others' schemes. Nearly winning the hand of the young heir Reginald De Courcy by her flirtatious, poor-me strategies, she winds up with another young man, the "contemptibly weak" (in Susan's view) and rich Sir James Martin, whom she is able to win away from a much younger woman. Sociopaths usually are victorious over the naïve and weak; indeed, they can even manipulate the smart and strong. Sir James didn't have a chance!

Flirting Your Way to a Husband — Hopefully

Austen's characters demonstrate varied tactics of flirting. Each tactic has a different result — not because of the nature of the tactic, but because of either the female doing the flirting or the man she is trying to catch and sometimes, for better or worse, catches.

- ✔ **Flirting by throwing yourself at the guy:** A thoughtless man-chaser, Lydia Bennet, age 16, flirts with Wickham even as he flirts with her, though their motivations differ: She wants a man; he wants money. Her living with him out of wedlock is as much her decision as his. She thinks it's "a good joke' (PP 3:5). And when Darcy buys Wickham's agreement to marry her, Lydia has no sense of shame and just gushes over her "'dear Wickham.'" The flirting of Lydia brings her into conflict with her father and sister, Elizabeth, as well as with the morals of the day. And the Lydia-Wickham marriage soon sinks into mutual "indifference" (PP 3:19).

- ✔ **Flirting for a husband with shrewd, fake sincerity:** *Sense and Sensibility*'s Lucy Steele has so mastered the art of flirting and manipulating that this crafty young female captures two young men — brothers who couldn't be more different in terms of personality.

  - • **Edward Ferrars:** Her first conquest was the shy and awkward Edward Ferrars, heir to the Ferrars's family wealth. He was a student at her uncle's school before heading to Oxford, so she could start working on him while he was young and inexperienced. She managed to win Edward by feigning sincere interest and affection toward him. Given that both his mother and sister are shrews, Lucy was probably the first female who was even nice to him!

- **Robert Ferrars:** When Edward's mother disinherits him and instead names his younger brother Robert as her heir, Lucy forgets Edward and manipulates the new heir. Seeing that Robert is ego-centered, Lucy manipulates him by turning their discussions to Robert, which was Robert's favorite subject anyway. Feigning a sincere interest in Robert, the new heir, Lucy manipulates him into marrying her.

✔ **Flirting with a moron; flirting with a cad; becoming a moron:** *Mansfield Park*'s beautiful Maria Bertram first allows herself to flirt with and become engaged to the stupid and dull James Rushworth for two reasons:

1. He's worth £12,000 a year.

2. She hates being at home.

But when the dashing, clever, and charming Henry Crawford comes on the scene, she reciprocates his advances. Maria encourages Henry in various ways.

- When she, Henry, and Rushworth walk through the wilderness (a symbolic location of Maria's moral wilderness) together at Sotherton, she urges her fiancé to return to the house to secure the key that will allow them to open the gate and proceed.

- Using the moment, Maria complains that she feels restrained. Ready to free her, Henry lures Maria to slip past the gate with his help. Off they go, deeper into the wilderness together. This is a mutual seduction.

- Maria plays the role opposite Henry's in *Lovers' Vows,* enabling their characters to exchange physically affectionate gestures, which they find they need to rehearse a lot.

Maria is both so flirtatious and so vulnerable to Henry's flirtatiousness that even after she has married the moronic Rushworth, she commits adultery with the suave Henry, expecting him to rescue her from that shame (sort of) by marrying her. (A wife's adultery was a big no-no.) The moron turns out to be not-so-moronic: Rushworth divorces Maria, and she becomes a disgraced fallen woman. Henry disappears. Now who's the moron?

✔ **Flirting with beauty, money, charm, and a harp:** The "remarkably pretty" and witty Mary Crawford of *Mansfield Park* is Austen's most provocative flirt (MP 1:4). With £20,000 to her name and a cynical view

Flirting for fun

Emma Woodhouse — "handsome, clever, and rich" — doesn't need to flirt for a husband. In fact, she's determined not to marry. But she does flirt with Frank Churchill because it's expected of her. Frank flirts back with Emma just to deflect any suspicions from his secret engagement to Jane Fairfax. While Emma doesn't love Frank, she enjoys the attention she gets from him. But eventually it's too much attention when he deems her queen of the Box Hill picnic outing and prompts her to insult Miss Bates. The resulting correction she receives from Mr. Knightley for her poor behavior leads to much-needed self-reflection on Emma's part. Furthermore, the flirtation between Frank and Emma prompts Mr. Knightley to realize his true feelings for Emma. The Emma/Frank flirtation, then, leads to no harm for either and actually brings Emma and Mr. Knightley together. Emma's and Frank's flirting with each other is actually the most harmless and ultimately the most beneficial flirtation in all of Austen's novels.

of marriage as a "take-in," the wily Mary is determined to marry well (MP 1:5). So of course, upon arriving at Mansfield Park, she tries to flirt with Tom, the heir to the estate. But Tom is more interested in gambling than girls and doesn't bite. When Tom leaves, Mary, surprisingly, finds herself attracted to Edmund Bertram, Tom's younger brother. She plays the harp, an instrument that emanates sensuality, to attract his attention, and it works. Edmund regularly visits the parsonage where Mary is staying. She's almost like one of Homer's Sirens in *The Odyssey* whose singing lures unsuspecting men to their death.

✔ But Mary's "song" has a different goal: to lure Edmund away from his planned clerical vocation. Failing that, she doesn't give up on him. After Edmund becomes ordained, she still tries to lure him. When her brother (Henry) and his sister (Maria Bertram Rushworth) commit adultery, Mary and Edmund disagree on the seriousness of their siblings' actions. But Mary makes a last-ditch effort to catch Edmund. As he's leaving her, disgusted with her seeing the adultery as a social indiscretion rather than as a moral failure, she calls him back with, in Edmund's words, "'a saucy, playful smile, seeming to invite, in order to subdue me'" (MP 3:16). What a close call for Edmund!

Flirting and failing

Two of Austen's young women try really hard to win their men. But they fail for one of two reasons: one flirts too much with one too many men, while the other goes into overkill, failing to recognize that her attempts at flirting are consistently backfiring.

✔ **Isabella Thorpe:** If any Austen female character is an outrageously affected flirt, it's *Northanger Abbey*'s Isabella Thorpe, age 21. Her "great personal beauty" is defeated by her "decided pretension" and selfishness (NA, 1:4, 1:8, 1:13). Coming from a "not very rich family," Isabella lucked out in having a brother at the university with a nice, naïve Oxford friend, James Morland, whose father, a clergyman, while not wealthy, is far more comfortable financially than the Thorpes. Isabella and James become engaged after James falls for her beauty and exaggerated sentimental talk. But while he's away from her, she sees what looks like a better financial catch. When James learns of her behavior, all the sentimental talk that Isabella can muster isn't enough to win him back.

✔ **Miss Bingley:** The "I think just like you do" flirtation method is the method of choice for Miss Bingley in *Pride and Prejudice.* When Darcy is reading volume one of a book, she chooses to read volume two: Who reads the second volume before the first? But she makes an even greater mistake in insulting Elizabeth Bennet to Darcy's face — assuming that because he rejected Elizabeth at the Meryton Assembly, he isn't really interested in her. When that tactic fails, Miss Bingley starts insulting Elizabeth's family, an even bigger mistake because Darcy, while highly aware of her family's deficiencies, is bent on marrying Elizabeth. Miss Bingley's many moments of "open mouth, insert foot" flirtations might cause you pain if she wasn't so horrible and if Elizabeth Bennet wasn't so appealing!

Witnessing unconscious flirting

When Elizabeth Bennet, determined to hate Darcy, finds herself dancing with him at the Netherfield Ball, she says to him, "'I have always seen a great similarity in the turn of our minds. — We are each of an unsocial, taciturn disposition, unwilling to speak, unless we expect to say something that will amaze the whole room . . .'" (PP 1:18). Darcy questions this. But they continue as verbal sparring partners for much of the novel. Darcy, who enjoys conversation, is certainly tired of dealing with the Miss Bingleys of his world: young women who dance pirouettes of admiration around him because he's tall, handsome, and wealthy (PP 1:6). Elizabeth Bennet is a refreshing change as a pretty, intelligent young woman with incredible self-possession. The two belong together, even though they appear to be in conflict. They complement each other.

Northanger Abbey's Catherine Morland is another unconscious flirt. She's also a modest flirt. As Austen reveals in the next to last chapter of the novel, where she inserts herself as the intrusive omniscient narrator, Henry's "affection [for Catherine] originated in nothing better than gratitude, or, in other words, that a persuasion of her partiality for him had been the only cause of giving her a serious thought'" (NA 2:15). Her naïve and honest admiration for Henry puts her into conflict with no one except the greedy General Tilney, whose hunger for money allowed him to be taken in by another's lie that Catherine was an heiress. (For information on the narrator and narrative devices, see Chapter 16.)

Mistaken flirting

It's an embarrassing instance when people think others are flirting with them, only to discover this isn't the case. This happens to Elinor Dashwood in *Sense and Sensibility* with Edward Ferrars, who has conveniently neglected to tell Elinor that he's engaged to Lucy. A particular scene highlighting this is the hair ring scene (SS 1:18). Elinor's sister Marianne notices that Edward, who's normally not a ring-wearer, is now sporting a ring, made of hair. (Wearing jewelry made of the hair of one's sweetheart was a common practice throughout the Victorian period. At the home of poet John Keats in London, now a museum, a pin using hair is on display.) When Marianne enquires if the hair is his sister's, Edward "coloured very deeply, and giving a momentary glance at Elinor," replies that the hair is, indeed, his sister's. In reality, the hair belongs to his secret fiancée, Lucy Steele. So Edward blushes out of embarrassment about his secret engagement to another woman, totally unknown to Elinor or Marianne. But Elinor, who "had met his eye, and looked conscious likewise," is immediately convinced by his looking at her and blushing that Edward has somehow retrieved a bit of her hair and had it made into a ring. Poor Elinor: She's wrong about the ring and Edward's blushing, which she thinks are his ways of subtly flirting with her.

Dealing with Dangerous Men

Austen presents plenty of unscrupulous males in her novels. Whether it's money, vengeance, the mere thrill of the hunt, or any combination, seductive men work their dubious charms on a number of young women in Austen's fictional world.

Seducing for the thrill of it

The morally worst seducers or would-be seducers are the men who win a young lady's affections just for fun. In such cases, the male's ego is at work, while his head and heart ignore the feelings of his victim. Austen has two especially selfish men who work at insinuating themselves into the hearts of young ladies.

- **John Willoughby:** *Sense and Sensibility*'s Willoughby has all the tools to be seductive. He's tall, handsome, and friendly; he speaks well, rides and shoots with panache, and dances even better. What a glamour boy! So it isn't surprising that when he happens upon the pretty and naïve Marianne Dashwood, fallen in the mud with a sprained ankle, and carries her home to safety through the rain, that she falls for him. "'Thinking only of [his] own amusement,'" Willoughby "'endeavoured, by every means in [his] power, to make [himself] pleasing to [Marianne], without any design of returning her affection'" (MP 3: 8). Because this was a mere ego thing for Willoughby, he knew exactly how to please Marianne's ego: everything she liked, he liked — poems, artists, music. But Willoughby isn't serious about Marianne because he's out for money.

- **Henry Crawford:** Henry, from *Mansfield Park,* is a complex seducer. At first, the Bertram sisters don't find him handsome or attractive at all. But he grows on them because he's witty, charming, and talented. He also knows how to play up to women, especially those who interest him the most: those who present a special challenge because they're engaged or married. So while he had his sister's London friends falling over themselves for him, they were single, eligible, and therefore un- provocative. But because Maria Bertram — discussed earlier in this chapter — is engaged, he finds her especially challenging. Recognizing that she's seducible, Crawford encourages her interest.

  Henry Crawford also tries to win the heart of Fanny Price. Her failure to show interest in him and her apparent determination not to like him — and she doesn't because she has witnessed the way he toyed with Maria and set Maria and her sister Julia opposite each her by initially flirting with both of them — only arouse his spirit of adventure. As he tells his sister, Mary, he "'cannot be satisfied without Fanny Price, without making a small hole in Fanny Price's heart'" (MP 2:6). This, he admits, is for his amusement. But what he doesn't know is that Fanny is safe from his seductive charm, for her heart is secretly true to Edmund. Ironically, a combination of Fanny's unresponsiveness and her display of sisterly affection for her brother William seduce Henry Crawford into actually pursuing her with some seriousness. He's bound to fail, however, because he's seduced by his own love of the hunt into re-seducing the seducible Maria Bertram Rushworth, causing him to lose any chance with Fanny Price.

- **Captain Frederick Tilney:** The Captain may not be a leading character in *Northanger Abbey,* but he's another cad who flirts with Isabella Thorpe for his own amusement. Unlike Willoughby and Crawford, Frederick's "'vanities . . . have not yet injured himself'" because he has "'a stronger head'" than either of them (NA 2:12). The handsome, flirtatious captain is a better strategist than Willoughby and Crawford. Perhaps his military training has helped him in the battle of the sexes. He knows when to retreat! And his dropping Isabella is no cause for tears because she has been encouraging Frederick while her fiancé, James Morland, is out of town.

Seducing for money

Austen's world was no stranger to young men who married, or tried to marry, for money. Living at a time when a gentleman was a fellow who didn't go to work, many young men sought to maintain or attain the nonworking status through marriage to rich young women. Thus, men were wily, too — here are some examples:

- **John Willoughby:** *Sense and Sensibility*'s Willoughby toyed with Marianne's and Eliza's affections for his ego's sake, but he seduces the very wealthy (£50,000!) Miss Grey in London into marriage because she's rich, and he isn't. In a way, he has been seduced by her money even as he has seduced her with the way he can turn on the charm. Miss Grey, who's described as "'a smart, stylish girl . . . but not handsome,'" could well have been swept off her feet by this handsome cad. The two marry, and Willoughby gets what he wants: a life made comfortable by money.

- **George Wickham:** In *Pride and Prejudice,* Wickham is certainly a money-minded seducer. Knowing Darcy's younger sister since she was a child, he preys on her trust, luring her into going off with him. Certainly, Wickham's plan was to force Darcy to pay him to make an honest woman of her. But Georgiana doesn't suffer the fate of Eliza Williams in *Sense and Sensibility,* whom Willoughby leaves pregnant and alone. Georgiana so loves and respects her elder brother, Darcy, that she notifies him, and he comes to her rescue before "anything" happens.

  With one failure under his belt, Wickham eventually sexually seduces the thoughtless and flirtatious Lydia Bennet, who has been throwing herself at him. While Lydia isn't rich, Wickham gets the economic pay-off that he wants and needs. Darcy, out of love for Elizabeth, pays Wickham to make the proverbial "honest woman" of Lydia, honors his debts, and purchases an army commission for him.

Winning a Spouse with Honesty

Notice that none of the wily females or seductive males is a hero or heroine of an Austen novel. Some of her heroes and heroines do a little flirting here and there, but they come together through mutual understanding and respect. *Pride and Prejudice*'s Darcy and Elizabeth are Austen's most flirtatious couple, even though they don't necessarily realize they're flirting. Darcy is actually the more active flirter. For example, he suddenly asks Elizabeth if she would care to dance a reel when Miss Bingley is playing the pianoforte at Netherfield, and he walks over to Elizabeth and his cousin Fitzwilliam at his aunt's home, Rosings, when Elizabeth is playing the pianoforte (PP 1:10, 2:8). When Elizabeth offers witty retorts to Darcy's remarks, she is, at least consciously, unaware that she's making herself even more attractive to him, for "there was a mixture of sweetness and archness in her manner which made it difficult for her to affront anybody" (PP 1:10). While he's attracted to Elizabeth physically, his ultimate attraction to her is intellectual (PP 1:6, 1:8). He admires her for "'the liveliness of [her] mind'" (PP 3:18).

Part III
Living Life in Jane's World

The 5th Wave   By Rich Tennant

"You know, in Jane Austen's time a little well placed irony would have sufficed."

In this part . . .

Although Austen's heroines may appear to have lives of leisure, the reality lurking over all their heads (except for Emma Woodhouse's, because she's unique in being rich) was pretty grim. Part III explains the limited social, legal, and financial opportunities and choices for ladies. And while men enjoyed all the rights not available to women, a gentleman's family had specific expectations for its sons, especially its elder son. Along with a survey of life for the gentry, this Part also discusses the manners and morals, both religious and secular, of Austen's times.

Chapter 9

Looking at Ladies' Limited Rights and Roles

. . . .

In This Chapter

▶ Examining how to live like a lady

▶ Understanding how to please men

▶ Becoming an accomplished woman

▶ Advocating the feminist outlook

▶ Being single and becoming a governess

. . . .

Ladies' lives in Austen's novels appear to be charmed. After all, after courtship and marriage are achieved, ladies in the novels don't do very much. *Mansfield Park*'s Lady Bertram, the wife of a baronet, dozes on the sofa. Although widowed, Mrs. Dashwood, the heroines' mother in *Sense and Sensibility,* has two female and one male servant, even in her difficult financial circumstances. And *Pride and Prejudice*'s Mrs. Bennet, with a housekeeper, a cook, and assorted maids to take care of the daily routine at Longbourn, makes work for herself in seeking husbands for her five daughters by attending balls and hosting dinner parties. But for all the elegance and ease of their lives, these ladies faced a common dilemma: In marrying they surrendered all of their legal and financial rights to their husbands — not that they missed them, because prior to their marriage, all their rights were controlled by their fathers. So the rights were never theirs to begin with.

While Austen's world was a man's world, she lived at a time when ladies' rights were beginning to be discussed openly and somewhat loudly. But with her usual tact and subtlety, Austen makes herself heard in a quieter, yet steadfast way.

Living as a Lady in a Gentleman's World

Because a female had no legal or economic rights in Austen's day, she had to be careful when choosing a husband. For in surrendering her money and her rights to her husband, she wanted to be as sure as she could that he would treat her with respect, fairness, and love. No law required him to do so. In fact, the law gave him the right not to do so. (For details on marriage, see Chapter 7.) Ladies lived with a set of customs that denied them a great deal. Consequently, women were dependent on men.

Limiting the lady's life by law

Ladies' legal rights were minimal. Under the law a lady could not do things that women today take for granted. She could not

- ✔ Vote
- ✔ Attend a university
- ✔ Enter a profession
- ✔ Control her money and property (including her children and her clothes!)

Rarely did a married lady hold property in her own name. *Sense and Sensibility*'s widowed Mrs. Ferrars is unique in Austen's canon because she controls the family's substantial money and property, and with the stroke of a quill she disinherits her elder son and transfers all of his inheritance to her younger son. The late Mr. Ferrars was highly unusual in leaving his estate to his wife. Likewise, owning The Rosings estate, the widowed Lady Catherine de Bourgh of *Pride and Prejudice* is another unusual female property owner. In her case, her late husband's family didn't think it "necessary" to entail the property on males. (Entails restrict an inheritance line. For more on entails, see Chapter 10.) More frequently, a lady's one option for securing her own property was to place it in a trust. Her husband had

- **Control of their children:** Her husband controlled the kids and could, if he wanted, take them away from their mother.

- **Control over their sex life:** Her husband could demand sex — and even rape her or commit adultery.

- **The right to hit her:** Even if the husband locked her up in the attic, beat her, denied her access to her children, and emotionally abused her, she was his property, and so he could do as he liked. (For information on divorce, see Chapter 7.)

Now that you've read the downside of being a woman in Austen's time, don't think that she lived in a nation of wife-beaters; a majority of marriages were happy or at least satisfactory, and most wives weren't beaten!

Belonging to daddy

A father owned his daughter(s), literally. He was in charge of housing, clothing, and feeding her. As a gentleman, he was responsible for seeing to it that she had the dowry money — money that her mother or even her father brought to the table prior to their marriage — to secure a good husband. But was he required by law to supply the dowry? No.

A girl of the genteel class hoped and trusted that her parents' marriage settlement — money that her parents brought to the table back when their family's lawyers negotiated the finances of their marriage — included dowry money for her future marriage. Her father's wise use of this money would leave his children, younger sons, and widow comfortably provided for financially. (For more on marriage articles or settlement, see Chapter 7.) A father who had failed to use the marriage settlement carefully was pretty much considered a failure as a father.

For a young lady of the gentry, her dowry was key to marrying well. With a small dowry or with no dowry at all, the chances of marriage decreased dramatically, even hopelessly.

So belonging to daddy may have been comforting for a time. But if papa failed to think ahead financially, his daughters and even his younger sons faced financial problems in the future. And the situation was worse for the daughters. For the sons could at least pursue the gentlemanly occupations discussed in Chapter 10, and thus earn their income.

The following list describes the many father characters in Austen's fiction who've essentially failed their daughters financially:

- **Mr. Watson:** *The Watsons* features Austen's most pathetic father — the frail, helpless, elderly, and *poor* Mr. Watson. He's a retired clergyman and a really lovely man, but the clergy had no pension fund to assist the clergyman's survivors at this time. So in terms of helping his daughters to marry well, he's a failure. He has unmarried daughters who appear to be with small, if any, dowries. As a result, sisterly disharmony reigns in the Watson household.

- **Mr. Bennet:** *Pride and Prejudice*'s five unmarried Bennet sisters have £1,000 apiece from their parents' marriage settlement to use as their dowries. While this is a great dowry for each Bennet daughter compared to what the Watson sisters have, Mr. Bennet wishes too late that "instead of spending his whole income, he had laid by an annual sum for the better provision of his children" (PP 3:8). When Mr. Collins taunts Elizabeth by telling her that her chances of marrying are little because "'her portion [dowry, or portion of her parents' marriage settlement] is unhappily so small," he is absolutely correct (PP 1:19). If the Bennet sisters don't marry, they would have an annual income of between 4 and 5 percent on their collective £5,000 or between £200 and £250 annually to live on (roughly $24,000 in 2004); the Bennets' current family income, with Mr. Bennet alive and the Longbourn farm, is £2,000— an income they'll lose to Mr. Collins after Mr. Bennet's death because the Longbourn property is entailed on male heirs.

✔ **Mr. Dashwood:** After *Sense and Sensibility*'s Mr. Dashwood dies, the four females of his household live on £500 a year (SS 1:2). Thus, they have to cut back a lot on everything they were used to enjoying. Mr. Dashwood was so confident that his uncle would leave the family's estate to him, his wife, and daughters, that he made little alternative provision for them. Only because their uncle left each girl £1,000 do they have dowries equivalent to the Bennet sisters' dowries — which as Mr. Collins observed, was "small."

✔ **Sir Walter Elliot:** *Persuasion*'s baronet has been such a spendthrift that when his daughter Anne marries, he "could give [her] at present but a small part of the share of ten thousand pounds which must be hers hereafter" (P 2:12).

Austen also provides a few fathers who provide well for their daughters:

✔ **The Rev. Mr. Morland:** The father of *Northanger Abbey*'s heroine is a sensible father. His daughter, Catherine, has a dowry of £3,000 to bring to her marriage with Henry Tilney.

✔ **Mr. Woodhouse:** In *Emma,* Emma's parents' finances were such that she is worth £30,000, making her quite rich!

✔ **Sir Thomas Bertram:** Although the head of *Mansfield Park*'s Bertram family let his elder son get away with wasting money, Sir Thomas pays an extensive visit to his plantation in Antigua, the West Indies, to recoup his finances.

✔ **Mr. Musgrove:** If *Persuasion*'s Sir Walter is the financially careless father, Mr. Musgrove, a hearty, prosperous gentleman-farmer, faces no financial problem in marrying off two daughters at once.

Relying on the kindness of brothers

If the father didn't leave sufficient financial resources to enable his widow and unmarried daughters to live comfortably, the responsibility fell on his sons. Of course, not all sons did this, but in Austen's personal world, they did. As noted in Chapter 3, when Mr. Austen died, his sons got together and supplied their mother and two sisters with an annual income of £450. (That's about $47,500 in retail power for the year 2004.)

Jane Austen also speaks to the brotherly responsibility in *Pride and Prejudice:* The young Lucas boys are relieved that their 28-year-old spinster sister, Charlotte, marries Mr. Collins. Hypothetically, they would've helped her, but they might never have let her forget it!

Protecting the unmarried, brotherless gentlewoman

What happens when there are no brothers or sons to take care of the women? Unless the ladies have generous friends, they're out of luck.

And friends are just who Mrs. and Miss Bates have to lean on in *Emma.* Mrs. Bates is the widow of the local clergyman, whose death left his wife and unmarried daughter with no pension income — like the Austen ladies. But unlike the Austen ladies, there are no Bates brothers or sons to help the two women. Consequently, the two Bates ladies are now out of the vicarage and living in the village in rented rooms above a business. Because of their residual genteel status, and because Highbury, their village, is a generous one, the Bates ladies are the object of kindness from Mr. Knightley, who sends them apples from his estate, and Emma Woodhouse, who sends them pork from the family livestock. They still get to join the upper set of Highbury but in a secondary role.

Becoming an "Accomplished" Lady

Nearly all families in the gentry class had their own copies of Fordyce and Gregory (see Chapter 12 for more on these books) to give their daughters an education on manners, and they also educated their daughters to become "accomplished" women. Female education took various forms as no standard curriculum existed for women. Girls normally started their education at home with penmanship and reading taught by their mothers or governesses. To this beginning sewing ("work" as it was called, and Jane Austen, herself, had her work table), basic arithmetic, and homemaking were added (***Note:*** Homemaking didn't include scrubbing the floors or cooking — servants and staff in the country house did that for the gentry.) Their education in manners constantly evolved as well, as they read the guidebooks of the times and applied that advice to their lives. Interestingly enough, in Austen's novels, the most uninteresting ladies are frequently the products of the most expensive educations.

Defining the "accomplished woman"

Society expected women of the gentry to have certain social skills and talents so they could be good wives, mothers, and hostesses for their husbands' estates. Austen recites these expectations through Miss Bingley, who certainly thinks of herself as an accomplished woman, in a scene in *Pride and Prejudice:*

> "A woman must have a thorough knowledge of music, singing, drawing, dancing, and all the modern languages, to deserve the word ['accomplished']; and besides all this, she must possess a certain something in her air and manner of walking, the tone of her voice, her address, and expressions." (PP 1:8)

To this list, Darcy responds, "'[A]nd to this, she must yet add something more substantial, in the improvement of her mind by extensive reading.'" His use of the words "more substantial" suggests that Miss Bingley's list is composed of insubstantial learning. Let's face it: How intellectually "accomplished" can Miss Bingley be when she picks up the second volume of a book to read only because Darcy is reading the first volume (PP 1:11)? Yet Miss Bingley and her sister had expensive educations (PP 1:4), which doesn't say much for expensive, fashionable educations for girls.

As for Elizabeth's reading: Yes, she does pick up a book to read while at Netherfield instead of joining a group playing cards, leading Miss Bingley to taunt her by saying that Elizabeth "'despises cards. She is a great reader and has no pleasure in anything else.'" But Elizabeth immediately replies, "'I am not a great reader, and I have pleasure in many things.'" But Elizabeth Bennet could not be the articulate and clever young woman that she proves herself to be (and that attracts Darcy, who wants the accomplished woman to improve her mind!) if she didn't read and think about what she read. To Miss Bingley's and Mr. Darcy's combined list of traits for the "accomplished woman," Elizabeth cleverly retorts, "'I am no longer surprised at your knowing *only* six accomplished women. I rather wonder at your knowing *any.*'" That would include Miss Bingley, herself! Jane Austen felt very much like Elizabeth! For Austen never gives Miss Bingley anything sensible to say, especially around Darcy, whom she is always futilely trying to impress.

Attending a seminary in the city

The most fashionable, educational, and expensive institution for young ladies was the seminary. While the word "seminary" suggests today a place for religious education, these seminaries were just fancy schools for rich girls. At the seminary, the students learned sewing ("work"), reading, writing, mathematics, French, and history. Special dancing, music (instrument and singing), and art classes were also included, sometimes for extra tuition. The seminaries in London were especially desirable because they helped students get rid of their country accents and acquire the posh, southern London accent.

While the wealthy confidently sent their daughters to seminaries, Austen doesn't give high marks to ladies with seminary educations:

- **Bingley sisters:** No wonder the Bingley sisters "had been educated at one of the first private seminaries in town" (PP 1:4). Their father was a newly wealthy man who made his money in trade, a nongenteel profession, in the unfashionable north of England. Yet even accounting for natural wit and intelligence, of which Elizabeth Bennet has a generous amount, the Bingley sisters' education doesn't prepare them to engage in the witty conversations that Elizabeth effortlessly has with Darcy. Not that the Bingley sisters lack skill in talking; it's just what they're able to talk about limits them: "Their powers of conversation were considerable. They could describe an entertainment with accuracy, relate an anecdote with humour, and laugh at their acquaintance with spirit" (PP 1:11). With this limited repertoire of topics, no wonder Miss Bingley grows "tired of a conversation" between Elizabeth and Darcy "in which she had no share" (PP 1:11).

- **Jennings sisters:** Two other females in Austen's novels are the products of seminary educations: *Sense and Sensibility*'s Jennings sisters — Lady Middleton (Mary) and Charlotte Palmer. What do the Jennings sisters have to show for their seminary educations? Lady Middleton is described as "not more than six or seven and twenty . . . though perfectly well-bred, she was reserved . . . and had nothing to say for herself beyond the most commonplace inquiry or remark" (SS 1:6). She dislikes the Dashwood sisters, not only because they fail to flatter her and her kids, but also because they're "fond of reading," which she considers being "satirical: perhaps without exactly knowing what it was to be satirical" (SS 2:14). Her younger sister, Charlotte, is a silly woman who laughs all the time.

Going to boarding school

While seminaries boarded students, regular, less fashionable boarding schools for girls located in the country and in towns and cities other than London also existed. In fact, many girls of the gentry went to boarding schools that weren't seminaries. Because of the absence of any standardized curriculum, schools taught what they wanted to teach. Girls' education was pretty basic. Arriving with some rudimentary knowledge from home (sewing, arithmetic, basic writing, and reading skills), the boarding students continued with reading and writing, as well as history, sewing, arithmetic, and geography. They might also have lessons in dancing, music, and French for extra fees from outside masters brought to the school.

"A real, honest, old-fashioned Boarding school" is shown in *Emma* with Mrs. Goddard's school (E 1:3). Here, Austen continues, "a reasonable quantity of accomplishments were sold at a reasonable price, and . . . girls might be sent to be out of the way and scramble themselves into a little education, without any danger of coming back prodigies." In the novel, the simple and not particularly bright Harriet Smith is the product of Mrs. Goddard's school. The fictional school is likely inspired by Austen's own experience in boarding school as a child. *Persuasion*'s Anne Elliot also went to a boarding school in Bath when she was a young girl. She appears to have been well educated: She reads the latest poets and speaks Italian with such fluency that she can do sight translations of Italian musical lyrics into beautiful English. While Harriet's simplicity and bad grammar — Harriet says Robert Martin's sisters, her fellow students at Mrs. Goddard's, "'are quite as well educated as me'" — don't say much for the training she had there, Anne certainly benefited from her boarding-school education. Austen's depictions of such schools in her novels suggest an affectionate remembrance of her own days at boarding school, especially at the Abbey School. (For more on Jane Austen's education at boarding school, see Chapter 3.)

Having a governess

A highly fashionable way to educate one's daughter(s) was to hire a governess — a female tutor who lived with the family. This live-in staff member accomplished two goals: The family had both a live-in educator and a female companion or chaperone for the girls when they went for walks, carriage rides, and so on. Many girls with governesses had all of their education at home until they were well into their teens. The subjects would be the same as at the seminaries or boarding schools. And again, special masters could be hired to supplement the girls' education in dancing, music, and art.

The governess was so common in families of the gentry that in *Pride and Prejudice,* the officious Lady Catherine de Bourgh is surprised that Elizabeth's mother, with five daughters, didn't have a governess for them. Lady Catherine is, of course, a vocal supporter of governesses: "'I always say that nothing is to be done in education without steady and regular instruction, and nobody but a governess can give it'" (PP 2:6). Ironically, Lady Catherine's only child, a daughter who's about Elizabeth's age, and the product of education by a governess, is quiet, withdrawn, boring, and totally uncommunicative. Of course, we need to keep in mind, however, that having a controlling mother like Lady Catherine might well lead to inhibitions and insecurities in her daughter. (Reading Jane Austen sometimes leads one to play Psychology 101!)

Maria and Julia Bertram of *Mansfield Park* were also educated by a governess, as well as by their Aunt Norris. But while they've been taught art and music, we never see them paint or hear them play. Furthermore, they're "entirely deficient in the less common acquirements of self-knowledge, generosity, and humility" (MP 1:2). That's quite a damning comment about the Bertram girls' education.

Learning ad hoc at home (or not)

Because education wasn't mandatory, many young ladies never went to school or had a governess. But this lack of formal education doesn't mean that children grew up illiterate and ignorant. As Elizabeth tells Lady Catherine, "'[S]uch of us as wished to learn, never wanted the means. We were always encouraged to read, and had all the masters that were necessary'" (PP 2:6). Young Jane Austen spent only short periods at boarding school. Having access to her father's excellent library, she would discuss her reading with her parents and siblings. And with a father who ran a small boarding school for boys, young Jane joined the boys for instruction.

Austen never includes in her novels a father like her own. Her dad was well-educated, clever, intelligent, gentle, and interested in all of his children's learning. Elizabeth Bennet, Catherine Morland, and the Dashwood sisters are all products of educations at the hands of their mothers. But none of these heroines makes the moral errors (the Bertram sisters), shows the personality flaws (Emma, the Bingley sisters), or reveals personal dullness (Anne de Bourgh) that Austen's seminary or governess-educated females do.

Training a lady

The French salon of the 17th century encouraged the development of women's ability to make charming conversation. But as Chapter 12's discussion of the influence of Doctors Fordyce and Gregory (Doctors of Divinity, not medical doctors) emphasized, English gentlewomen were expected to be quiet, to hide their knowledge, to behave with delicacy, to avoid "manly" activities like running, and so forth. The whole point of being a lady meant pleasing her husband. Even the great English bluestocking (member of a mid-18th-century group of women devoted to intellectual conversation and charitable causes), Lady Mary Wortley Montague, though she wrote poetry championing women, advised them to keep their learning hidden from men.

All of Austen's heroines are ladies: They move and dance well; they display gracefulness, moderation, and decorum. And while Marianne Dashwood did fall running down a hill, remember that it was raining at the time and that ladies' shoes were delicate with no traction! However, a closer look at Austen's heroines also reveals that these ladies partake in some unladylike behavior, reflecting Austen's opinion of her day's prescription for mannerly ladies. (See Chapter 12 for more on how ladies learned their manners).

Placing Austen in the Women's Movement

When Jane Austen was in her 20s and writing her first draft of *Pride and Prejudice* under the title *First Impressions,* England was debating the "Woman Question": Are women really meant to be as Fordyce, Gregory (Chapter 12), and others prescribed and described? Women's suffrage was the least of women's problems in the early 1800's. Not only were women considered legally moot, but also they were deemed mindless and even encouraged to appear that way. Irate at such demeaning ideas, 18th-century feminists claimed that women had the same moral rights and capacity to reason as men. (Notice that they weren't even pushing for political and legal rights. All they wanted was the right to be considered rational.)

Austen's advocating the rational female

It's always amusing when people speak of Jane Austen as the simple story-teller of days when women were ladies, men were gentlemen, and true love appeared after some 300 pages of misunderstandings. Besides creating attractive female characters who're athletic, strong minded, well read, clever, and self possessed, Austen also advocates seeing women as rational, which in her day was a feminist view of women. So was Austen a feminist? You bet.

Two of Austen's strongest female characters tell the men to whom they're speaking that they're "rational women," which the average man in Austen's day would consider an *oxymoron,* or self-contradictory pair of words:

- ✔ **Elizabeth Bennet:** In *Pride and Prejudice,* Mr. Collins proposes to Elizabeth Bennet. When she turns him down, he refuses to take "no" for an answer, insisting that "'it is usual for young ladies to reject the addresses of the man whom they secretly mean to accept.'" But Elizabeth rejects such silliness and forthrightly replies, "'Do not consider me now as an elegant female intending to plague you, but as a rational creature speaking the truth from my heart'" (PP 1:19).

- ✔ **Mrs. Croft:** In Austen's final novel, *Persuasion,* Mrs. Croft, the extroverted, sharp wife of a naval admiral, says to her brother, Frederick Wentworth, "'I hate to hear you talking . . . as if women were all fine ladies, instead of rational creatures'" (P 1:8). In fact, before readers even meet Mrs. Croft, they hear about her from the lawyer who negotiates the leasing of Kellynch Hall, which the Crofts wish to rent. Recounting his meeting with the Crofts, the lawyer observes of her "'and a very well-spoken, genteel, shrewd lady she seemed to be . . . asked more questions about the house, and terms, and taxes, than the admiral, himself, and seemed more conversant with business'" (P 1:3). Fordyce and Gregory would faint at the thought of such a lady!

Aligning Jane Austen with Mary Wollstonecraft

The most famous champion of women's rights was a contemporary of Austen: Mary Wollstonecraft, whose book, *A Vindication of the Rights of Woman* (1792), was deemed revolutionary. Austen was 16 when *Vindication* appeared. It is very likely that Jane Austen read Wollstonecraft, and her novels certainly show Wollstonecraft's influence.

Wollstonecraft accuses Fordyce of creating "artificial grace" in females. Wollstonecraft advocates "true grace" arising from "independence of mind" (*Vindication*, 2). She wants women to have power over themselves by cultivating their reason, and she advocates schools for boys *and* girls, where both mind and body are strengthened. Women will be better wives and mothers because of the education. Notice that Wollstonecraft isn't so radical that she wants to see women joining the professions. She wants them to be better qualified for domestic life, life in the home.

As readers come to know female characters like *Pride and Prejudice*'s Elizabeth Bennet and *Persuasion*'s Anne Elliot and Mrs. Sophia Croft, we may wonder what their lives would've been like if professional opportunities had been open to them. In *Rasselas,* a fictional work written in 1759 by Austen's favorite moralist, Dr. Samuel Johnson, a female character, the Princess, plans "to found a college of learned women" (Chapter 49). But it would take over 100 years after Johnson's work appeared for women to get the educational opportunities that would enable then to have professional lives:

- ✔ Oxford University: opened two colleges for women in 1878 and allowed women to attend lectures (but nothing about biology, anatomy, or other fields that would be embarrassing!!), and admitted women as full members of the University in 1920 (http://www.ox.ac.uk/about oxford/history.shtml)

- ✔ Cambridge University: opened a college for women in 1869; allowed women to attend lectures in Cambridge (the town) in 1870, but at the University only in 1921, when women were first awarded "titles of degrees but no associated privileges" in 1921, but admitted them as full members of the University only in 1948 (http://www.cam.ac.uk).

- ✔ The British Bar: admitted its first female barrister in 1922

- ✔ The British Medical Association: admitted its first female member in 1873.

- ✔ Being a "full member of the University," like having "associated privileges," means being allowed to participate and vote in University governance.

Austen's familiarity with *A Vindication* and her ability to adapt its ideas for her own purposes become quite clear when we look at one of the case studies Wollstonecraft presented in the chapter "The State of Degradation to which Woman is Reduced" (Chapter 4). Here Wollstonecraft offers a case of poorly educated females who rely on the "reason" and "bounty" of their brothers. "But when a brother marries," his sister is viewed "as an unnecessary burden on the benevolence" of the brother and his new wife. Describing this wife as "a cold-hearted, narrow-minded woman," Wollstonecraft claims that the wife grows "jealous of the little kindness" and "displeased at seeing the property of her child" being "lavished" by her husband on his "helpless" sister.

Anyone who has read *Sense and Sensibility* will notice that Wollstonecraft's little scenario provides a perfect summary of the crisis that opens the novel. Mr. Dashwood makes a deathbed request of his financially very comfortable son by his first (deceased) wife to look after his stepmother (confusingly called in the novel as she was during Austen's day, his "mother-in-law") and three half-sisters, all under age 21. But in the novel's second chapter, the son's wife (Fanny Ferrars Dashwood) manages to convince her husband to give them nothing because anything he offers his mere half-sisters will deprive their "'poor little boy'" — who ironically, at the age 4, has just inherited a wealthy country estate.

Assessing the Single Gentlewoman's Single Occupation

For a lady who fell on financial hard times and who had neither parent nor brother who could assist her, one occupation existed that was genteel enough for a lady: governess. But the job wasn't exactly like Mary Poppins makes it seem. That's because the governess lived in an isolated world of her own, even though she might be beloved by her little charges. As a lady — and a governess had to be a lady, because she was always with the children of the mistress and master of the estate — the governess was socially well above the household staff. She was well educated because she had to be able to teach. She usually spoke at least one foreign language: French. Frequently she also brought such talents as painting, drawing, and music. After all, the governess was a young lady once, and she had a young lady's education. But she was also a paid employee of the family she served: She was a member of the estate or household staff. This means she's not quite good enough to dine with the mistress and master when the children have outgrown dining in the nursery. But she's socially far above the rest of the staff in terms of birth, breeding, and education.

The typical governess of the day isn't the happy and beloved Miss Taylor, Emma's governess who, as Emma grows up, becomes "less of a governess than a friend" to Emma (E 1:1). Indeed, their relationship had "the intimacy of sisters." Miss Taylor's life is so unusual for a governess that she even becomes a member of the gentry. She marries Mr. Weston who owns the Randalls estate, and she and Emma carry on as if they're sisters, instead of governess and former student. Austen shows society's perception of the governess when Mrs. Elton, albeit vulgar, registers surprise that Miss Taylor, now Mrs. Weston, a former governess, is "'so very lady-like . . . quite the gentlewoman'" (E 2:14).

Miss Taylor is the governess to break all stereotypes. But in the same novel, we meet a young woman, Jane Fairfax, who's to be a governess, for "the very few hundred pounds which she inherited from her father [made] independence impossible" (E 2:2). Austen wrote painfully about a governess's fate in terms of Jane Fairfax: "With the fortitude of a devoted noviciate, [Jane] had resolved at one-and-twenty to complete the sacrifice, and retire from all pleasures of life, of rational intercourse, equal society, peace and hope, to penance and mortification for ever" (E 2:2). Jane Fairfax even describes the offices in town that deal with governess hiring as "offices for the sale—not quite of human flesh—but of human intellect" (E 2:17), connecting being a governess with being a slave. (For information on the slave trade and England, see Chapter 2.)

The loneliness of the governess

Victorian painter Richard Redgrave's painting, *The Governess,* done in 1845 and in the collection of London's Victoria and Albert Museum, touchingly depicts the governess's plight. In it, we see a young woman seated in a shadow at a piano where the music for "Home, Sweet Home," sits on the music rack. Dressed in a heavy black dress with a modest white collar — it is clearly meant to suggest a nun's habits — she holds a letter in her hand and looks forlorn. But in the background, dressed in pastels and in the sunlight, are the young girls, not that much younger than she is, whom she teaches. The differences in the young ladies' situations and futures are clear in the painting as described. My first time seeing this painting was on a paperback edition of Charlotte Bronte's *Jane Eyre* (1847), the classic governess novel.

Chapter 10

Being a Man in a Man's World

*J*ane Austen lived in a patriarchal society: father knows best. So does husband. So does elder brother. So does younger brother. Although this was a man's world, it was a world that held specific expectations for gentlemen or men of the gentry, the class on which about Austen primarily focuses and the class that concerns us in this chapter. If a boy was the first son in a family, he was to the manor born! Only under the most unusual circumstances would a first son not inherit his father's property: Austen shows this in *Sense and Sensibility,* where the late Mr. Ferrars disregarded tradition and left his wealth to his widow (SS 1:3). More likely, he was raised and educated to succeed his father as the master of the family estate. This chapter escorts you through the expectations that his family had for him, explaining a young gentleman's upbringing, as well as the inheritance laws, limited professional choices, and changing nature of gentlemanly status. For men were beginning to attain the rank of gentleman in a new way: by working for it instead of inheriting it. Imagine that!

Being a Gentleman's Son

A gentleman was officially a member of the gentry or landowning, propertied class. (For more info on the gentry, see Chapter 2.) Granted, a man could *appear* genteel by being polite and dressing fashionably: think Wickham in *Pride and Prejudice.* But a true gentleman was a man of property. He owned a country house and estate. (For more on country house life, see Chapter 11.) And very likely, he inherited that country house and estate from his father, who inherited it from his father, and so on. Thus, being a gentleman in Austen's day required *only* inherited rank and wealth; a gentleman didn't have to be suave, smart, or sophisticated (what we, today, would expect in a gentleman) — though it was expected that he would be polite. Austen shows the irony of gentlemanly status in *Mansfield Park* through the character of James Rushworth. Sotherton, a country house and estate that dates back to Queen Elizabeth I (d. 1603), has been in the hands of the Rushworth family for generations, as the family portraits that line the walls attest. Does this make James Rushworth, Sotherton's present owner with an annual income of £12,000 — giving him £2,000 more per year than *Pride and Prejudice*'s Darcy — an outstanding individual? No. For as the book's narrator tells us when she introduces the character, he has "not more than common sense" (MP 1:4). And as the novel proceeds, he actually shows little of that. But being a gentleman's only son, he's the new master of Sotherton and a gentleman in terms of class. And while his neighbor, Edmund Bertram, correctly observes that without the money and property Rushworth would be "a very stupid fellow" (MP 1:4), with inherited riches and rank, Rushworth, jerk that he is, is still a gentleman. In fact, because of his great wealth and status, Maria Bertram, though knowing he's stupid, agrees to marry him. After all, Rushworth is even richer than her father and also has a house in London! So Austen, shrewd observer that she was, saw that one didn't need smarts to inherit wealth and rank! But she didn't paint with a broad brush, either, and so she also shows us gentlemen who are rich, propertied, *and* clever: think Darcy.

Training to a be a gentleman in boyhood

In their infancy and early childhood, all the children were attended by nursery maids. From there, they went into the hands of the governess, who gave the boys in the family their preliminary education of reading and writing, as well as basic arithmetic. Special masters were brought to the home — sometimes from the nearest city or even from London — to teach the children music (the girls, especially) and dancing (the boys and girls). (The sisters could also learn drawing from a master.)

The character of Darcy, the only son in a genteel family, would've learned his dance steps at an early age so that he could participate in formal dances as he became older. In fact, in the 2005 film version of *Pride and Prejudice,* Darcy is shown at a dance looking around hesitatingly at the other dancers and painfully counting his steps. But neither his mother, Lady Anne, nor his father would've let him out of Pemberley without mastering the dances that gentlemen were expected to perform. (And in Volume 1, Chapter 6 of the novel, Sir William Lucas compliments Darcy's dancing.)

Among the gentry, male children especially knew their heritage and sense of family continuity from boyhood, and the eldest son knew that he would eventually inherit his father's estate, thus assuming the roles and responsibilities of his father when the father died. The practice of male inheritance occurred by tradition, not law, and almost every family adopted the tradition. Thus, Mr. Ferrars's decision in *Sense and Sensibility* to leave his wealth to his wife and give her control of what his sons receive is quite an exception to the tradition.

Beginning a more formal education

The gentry frequently sent their sons to boarding schools to start their Latin lessons and begin a more formal education. Jane Austen's father ran a private boarding school that accommodated a few boys at the Steventon Rectory, where Jane grew up. Here the boys studied algebra, geometry, some Greek, some English literature (Shakespeare and Milton, especially), ancient history (Greco-Roman), and geography. The last item was important because England was at war, on and off, in varied places around the globe during Austen's lifetime. They also learned French and became more proficient in their writing. Dancing lessons that started at home continued. Because dancing at balls and assemblies was the major way to meet and sustain a relationship with suitable young women for potential wives, the importance of dance lessons should not be minimized. In Austen's novels, Henry and Catherine (NA), Darcy and Elizabeth, and Bingley and Jane (PP) all meet at dances and end up marrying. (See Chapter 5 for more on dancing, and Chapter 6 for information on courtship.)

In *Sense and Sensibility,* the snobbish Robert Ferrars argues that his brother Edward is socially awkward because he attended a small private school (SS 2:14). Through this character, Austen voices the then prevalent debate of whether educating a boy at a small private school was better or worse than sending him to a "public school." But if Robert Ferrars is any example of what a public school produces, Austen must have favored private schools: Robert, who attended Westminster, an elite "public school," is affected, mean-spirited, impolite, selfish, and dumb — he's even outwitted by Lucy Steele. So much for his attending Westminster!

Heading to Eton or another "public" school

If a family preferred, they sent their sons to "public school." Public school is a particularly English phenomenon and has a long history. These schools are actually private schools, and among the more famous are Eton, Harrow, and Rugby. They were founded by wealthy donors as "independent schools" so that ordinary boys (that is, the public) could learn Latin and Greek. But as time went on, these public schools started to take boys from wealthy and frequently aristocratic, even royal, families, and thus became what we think of as private schools. (Keep in mind that public education as we know it — government supported — only began in the 19th century in both England and America.) Austen had nephews who went to an elite Hampshire public school, Winchester College, which is the original English public school, founded in 1394. Her father attended the Tonbridge School in Kent as a boy.

From a school like Mr. Austen's, a boy could go to a public school or even the university. (Students could enter the university as young as 14.) Or he might even go directly from home tutoring to a public school, sometimes as early as age 7 or 8. It really depended on the family's preferences and boy's maturity.

Boys faced a tough regimen at public school and were expected to keep the proverbial stiff upper lip — even if that lip was on a 7-year-old. While at school, boys studied the following subjects:

- ✔ Mathematics
- ✔ History
- ✔ Latin and Greek
- ✔ English literature
- ✔ Modern languages
- ✔ Public speaking
- ✔ Writing
- ✔ Fencing
- ✔ Networking

The last mentioned item was probably the most important part of the public school student's education: Boys met other boys of their own social class or higher, including sons of noblemen. Today we call this *networking*. The eldest son of a gentleman could possibly even meet the brother of the girl who would become his wife many years later. Boys made connections at public school that served them throughout their lives. Many boys attended the schools of their fathers, thus giving the student body generations of connections among families.

Because the eldest son was the son in line to inherit the family's property and title, a father might send his younger sons to boarding schools designed to prepare officers for the army and navy. Being an army or a navy officer meant having a gentlemanly profession. Two of Austen's brothers, Frank and Charles, went to the Royal Naval Academy in Portsmouth. While Mr. Austen did not have a large estate to pass on, he did have the clerical living of Steventon and the parsonage that went with it: He gave them to James, his eldest son. (See Chapter 3.)

Gaining an "OxBridge" degree

Boys went to the university — Oxford or Cambridge, and so Oxbridge! — when they were ready to do so. So a boy entering Oxford at age 14 wasn't necessarily a prodigy (no offense to Jane's eldest brother, James, who did the same at age 14). They didn't have to take entrance exams like the ACT or SAT in those days, and the prime motive for boys' attending the university was to make connections for their future lives. Socializing was as important as — if not more important than — academics.

Both universities, Oxford and Cambridge, had the same precondition of attending: receiving Holy Communion in the Church of England.

The Oxford and Cambridge student bodies included a good many elder sons of gentry and nobility who would inherit great estates and titles. So why would these young men burn the midnight oil with a book in hand? (By 1800, about two-thirds of Britain's noblemen were OxBridge men.) Socializing was far more enjoyable and profitable than studying. Besides, any academic tests given weren't hard, frequently being on a subject that the student had, himself, requested. Getting an Oxbridge degree in those days wasn't hard!

Of course, some young men at the university did study. George Austen, Jane's father, was one of those. As a poor young man who attended Oxford on scholarship, he knew that he would have to have a profession after earning his degree. His intelligence and scholarship show that he had a strong academic inclination, and his excellence as a teacher indicates that he understood his lessons well.

But from what Austen mentions in her novels, not everyone was successful even at networking, and academics frequently took a backseat to drinking:

- *Pride and Prejudice:* Mr. Collins, "though he belonged to one of the universities, he had merely kept the necessary terms, without forming at it any useful acquaintance" (PP 1:15) — in other words, he failed to network while at either Oxford or Cambridge!

- *Northanger Abbey:* While at Oxford, James Morland, eldest brother of the heroine of *Northanger Abbey,* befriends the lying braggart, John Thorpe. The Thorpes have far more to gain from Morland than Morland has to gain from the Thorpes. Clearly, James Morland didn't network well! When Catherine Morland later meets John Thorpe, she remarks that she has "heard that there is a lot of drinking at Oxford" (NA 1:9). In reply, John brags that at a party in his rooms he and his friends only "cleared about five pints a head" (NA 1:9)!

✔ *Mansfield Park:* Edmund Bertram, another Oxonian, tells Fanny and
Mary that while at Oxford, "'I have been a great deal use to have a man
lean on me for the length of a street'" (MP 1:9). In other words, Edmund —
who is so moral and upright that he would never be inebriated — has frequently had to help a fellow student home after a night of tossing a few
pints back — especially if that friend had been at a party thrown by John
Thorpe!

The famous Oxford/Cambridge rivalry was alive and well in Austen's day. She
had a grandfather, a father, and two brothers (James and Henry) with Oxford
degrees. So is it any surprise that *Pride and Prejudice*'s irresponsible
Wickham went to Cambridge (PP 2:12)?

Taking the Grand Tour

After completing a Bachelor's degree at Oxford or Cambridge, or in lieu of
attending the university after finishing public or private school, a young gentleman might wish to expand his view of the world by making a Grand Tour.
The *Grand Tour* consisted of

✔ A jaunt around western Europe that included Italy and France

✔ The chance to practice spoken French, Italian, German, or other modern
language

✔ An opportunity to meet and network with wealthy and titled folks on the
Continent

✔ The occasion to visit famous sites

✔ An invitation to attend dinner parties serving exotically foreign food

Sometimes a Grand Tour meant three years worth of dinner parties!

What might this young man take with him on his journey? In addition to the
usual items of clothing (including formal attire), shoes, boots, favorite books,
art supplies (particularly a sketchbook if he liked to paint or draw), writing
paper, quill pens and penknife, ink, and toiletries, the traveler could have

✔ **A tutor or older man with him:** He might help the young gentleman with
introductions and language translation, as well as provide tutoring and
company for the traveler.

✔ **Letters of introduction:** The letters, as the phrase "of introduction"
suggests, served to introduce the young traveler to important persons
along the way. After all, with mail service from England to the Continent
slow, the traveler might as well carry his letters of introduction with him.

Young gentlemen on their Grand Tours might be lucky enough to have letters from professors, family members, and even distinguished family friends that would enable them to meet and even stay with foreign aristocracy, clergymen (priests, Bishops, Deans of Cathedrals), professors, and fashionable persons. Being able to present to the doorman a letter from an old friend or business acquaintance addressed to the resident of a mansion was traditionally certain assurance of getting invited inside!

Ideally, for the thousands of pounds spent on this jaunt, the young man came back with broader intellectual horizons and possibly a better French, Italian, or German accent!

Jane Austen's brother, Edward, who'd been adopted by their father's wealthy, childless cousins, Mr. and Mrs. Knight, chose to make his Grand Tour in lieu of attending the university. At age 18, he left England in 1786 for two years and visited Switzerland, Germany, and Italy (Rome). While in the last spot, Rome, he had a life-size portrait of himself painted in oils. Looking at the young man in this picture — it's on prominent display at the Jane Austen House Museum in Chawton (it's so big that you can't miss it) — the viewer immediately sees that the subject won't have to work for a living. Dressed in a dark coat, white ruffled shirt, gold silk or satin breeches, white stockings, and shiny black, buckled pumps (they're so dainty that I just can't call them shoes!), he leans against a column, one leg crossing the other with a smart-looking cane in his right hand. His facial expression is satisfied. The Roman ruins are behind him. Although Edward didn't have the networking experience of Oxbridge, he met several young English gentlemen who were also on the Continent, either touring or living there.

Inheriting Property

Because wealth in Austen's England was based largely on the ownership of land, a way to transmit property ownership needed to exist. The practice of primogeniture and the legal devices involved helped ensure that property stayed in the family. The practice went back to medieval times.

Respecting primogeniture

Primogeniture (derived from *first* [primo] *birth* [geniture]) meant that a family's property and wealth went directly to the eldest son. How important was primogeniture? Extremely! It ensured that property stayed within the family and that the paternal surname would continue in future generations. Sometimes, property belonged to family for many generations — even back to the 1200s. The current family wanted to be sure that ownership of the property extended into the family's future, too. In Austen's day, primogeniture was not required, but it was traditionally practiced.

Making sense of *Sense and Sensibility*'s inheritance muddle

The plot gets moving in the first chapter of *Sense and Sensibility* with a situation revolving around a wealthy country gentleman having no son. The excess of Dashwoods in the first few pages of the novel often confuses the first-time readers. So let me try to set the scene for you.

Mr. and Mrs. Henry Dashwood and their three young daughters move to Norland Park, a large and long-established estate owned by generations of Dashwoods, to care for his aging and ailing Uncle Dashwood — a lifelong bachelor and therefore without any direct heirs. Uncle Dashwood, grateful to his nephew and his family for living with and caring for him for ten years, intends to leave the Norland estate to them. So far, so good, right?

However, Henry's grown son from his first wife (long deceased) visits Norland, accompanied by his wife and their cute little son, Harry (who would be elderly Uncle Dashwood's great-grand-nephew). Uncle Dashwood abruptly changes his will and leaves Norland to the father of 4-year-old Harry, and then to Harry, himself. The novel tells us that old Uncle Dashwood had been charmed by Harry's infant antics during his parents' visits to Norland (SS 1:1). But a logical explanation suggests that Uncle Dashwood was also thinking that leaving the estate to his grand-nephew and then to that man's son ensured that the Dashwood name would continue at Norland. After all, if, as Uncle Dashwood had originally planned, Norland went to his nephew and then to that nephew's three daughters, the estate would (Heaven forbid!) pass out of the Dashwood family name when the girls married.

Uncle Dashwood may have been old and frail, but he wasn't stupid. Elderly Uncle Dashwood understood and valued the concept of male inheritance. So he adjusted his will to ensure that at least two more generations of Dashwoods would reside at Norland. But what about Uncle Dashwood's grandnieces who, with their parents, provided ten years of care and comfort for him? By changing his will in favor of male inheritance, Uncle Dashwood has sentenced the three young Dashwood sisters to live in genteel poverty. And so the novel's plot gets rolling.

Thus, a wife's producing a male heir and a spare son was important in Austen's day. This heir not only ensured continuity of the paternal family name, but also the continuity of family ownership of country houses and estates.

When a member of the gentry class had no children, and particularly no sons, he would frequently take measures to ensure family succession. This was the case when Mr. Austen's cousin, Thomas Knight, asked to adopt Edward Austen. Treated like a son by the childless Knights, Edward, the inheritor of the Knights' estates, even changed his surname to Knight in 1812.

Disentangling the entail

Like primogeniture, the *entail* was a legal device to ensure that property would be handed down in a way that suited the ancestor, normally to a male heir, thus keeping the family estate intact. The restrictions of an entail could include prohibitions on dividing or selling the estate; in essence, living on entailed property was being that property's life tenant. If the property was entailed on male heirs, and the life tenant had no sons, the property — on the tenant's death — would go to the nearest male heir. The only way to end or cut off an entail would be through an agreement of the current tenant and the next male heir.

Entails were customary and popular, but not required. The impulse behind the entail was the same as that of primogeniture: keeping property in the paternal family line. Granted, the surname may eventually change as the male line moves from sons to brothers, and then to cousins, as it does in *Pride and Prejudice,* where at Longbourn the Bennets will be replaced by Collinses. But a certain male vanity— no offense to male readers! — compelled male property owners (with rare exception, the only kind!) to want their land and the house(s) on the land to be inherited by the male line of successive generations because at least the property stayed in the family, even distant family. Because a woman's property went to her husband upon marriage, having a daughter, sister, or niece inherit didn't fill the bill of keeping the property in the original owner's line of descent. While entailing property was a gentleman's personal preference — not a legal requirement — England had a lot of property entailed on males in Austen day. (In *Pride and Prejudice,* Sir Lewis de Bourgh did not entail Rosings [PP 2:6].)

The entail situation is what worries Mrs. Bennet in *Pride and Prejudice.* She and her daughters face being ejected from their home, Longbourn, after Mr. Bennet dies. This situation occurs because the Longbourn estate "was entailed in default of heirs male, on a distant relation" (PP 1:7). In the Bennets' case, Longbourn's being entailed on male heirs means that in the absence of a Bennet son, the estate goes to Mr. Bennet's nearest male relative, the unpleasant and empty-headed Mr. Collins. Mr. Bennet inherited Longbourn for his lifetime; however, he can't change the male entail so that his wife and daughters can remain at their family home after his death without the cooperation of the next male in line, Mr. Collins. And Mr. Collins looks upon Longbourn with too much longing even to think of giving it up for the Bennet sisters' sake! His only plan to help the Bennet women is to help himself to either Jane or Elizabeth Bennet. And Mrs. Bennet, in her desperation about losing her home, is ready to force Elizabeth to accept Collins's proposal.

Being the Eldest Son

Among the gentry, the eldest son in a family knew that he had one career in store for him: being a gentleman estate-owner and running the family estate — the estate he would inherit when his father died. But as early as the Elizabethan period (16th century), England's Lord Chief Justice, John Popham, complained that inheritance laws requiring fathers to leave their entire property to their eldest sons led to a lot of unruly and even sexually irresponsible elder sons! Popham was not the only person to observe that restricted inheritance could lead to prodigal elder sons. In fact, during the reign of Queen Elizabeth's father, Henry VIII, the "Statute of Wills" (1540) permitted you to leave your property to anyone you wanted, provided you had your desires about the passage of your property in a will. (This statute was passed not because of reckless elder sons, but because of the King's desire for land revenues!) But at the same time, Parliament did not abolish the "Statute of Uses" from four years earlier, which supported primogeniture. So primogeniture remained the preferred inheritance method, and eldest sons could be good boys or bad boys — depending on the temper of one's father. Or unless the elder son's mother was *Sense and Sensibility*'s Mrs. Ferrars: Though Edward Ferrars is the elder of two sons, he did not inherit the family wealth when his father died because his father left the Ferrars fortune to his wife (SS 1:3). Throughout the novel, Mrs. Ferrars uses her control of the family's money and property to try to control her two sons: First Edward, the elder, is her heir; then she disinherits him, giving the elder son's role to her younger son; then she disinherits both of them; and finally she gives the "primo" role to her younger son again! Each change depended on how pleased or displeased she was with her sons. But the situation of the Ferrars family was not common. Most families, while knowing primogeniture was not the law, practiced this medieval tradition, thus ensuring the eldest son's future.

Enjoying an elder brother's "rights"

Because there weren't many Mr. Ferrarses around, the eldest son enjoyed a life of complete freedom. Knowing that he would inherit the family estate and title, if there was one, he could be as irresponsible and stupid as he wanted. He knew his future was secure. After all, landowners wanted to see their property stay in the family, and it was tough to break with tradition. But while the son was under age 21, he was still under Dad's legal thumb. And Dad could always stop any allowance money from flowing into Junior's pockets. But it's surprising what fathers put up with!

An example of the carefree heir is Captain Frederick Tilney from *Northanger Abbey*. Captain Frederick Tilney is an officer in the army. Although he's heir to the Abbey, his father, General Tilney, feels that an occupation is worthwhile. A "very fashionable-looking . . . young man," Frederick, nevertheless, appears to the novel's heroine as having "taste and manners . . . inferior" to his younger brother's. Frederick is, indeed, deficient in these areas, but with primogeniture on his side, who needed taste and manners? Interestingly, Frederick's younger brother, Henry, observes that Frederick will not go beyond flirting with Isabella Thorpe — a young woman who sees Frederick as a great catch and needs his money — because he "would not have the courage to apply in person for their father's consent" (NA 2:11). This comment suggests that Frederick might fear action taken by his formidable father, the general, who likes to have his own way and isn't afraid to exert his will. While the general may not disinherit Frederick, he could refuse to send him money, causing him to be financially strapped. But Frederick appears to know that and doesn't want to cause problems with his father, the general.

A really problematic elder son with a father who lets him get away with bad conduct is *Mansfield Park*'s Tom Bertram. He gambles and loses so much money that his younger brother Edmund's future income for "'ten, twenty, thirty years, perhaps for life" is drastically affected by their father's having to sell a church living (the clergyman's salary) with the best income to a stranger, even though Sir Thomas Bertram had been holding it for Edmund for the time he became ordained. While Sir Thomas tries to humiliate Tom into better behavior, Tom's only reaction is to think that his "father had made a most tiresome piece of work of it" and that "he had not been half so much in debt as some of his friends" (MP 1:3). Tom's father even takes him to the family's plantation property in Antigua for a year, but Tom returns and goes back to his same, old irresponsible ways. Sir Thomas clearly does not have the emotional and intellectual power over Tom that General Tilney has over Frederick. So Tom just does what he wants. While Sir Thomas is clearly disturbed by his heir's actions, he never gives any sign of planning to write a will and change inheritance order, even though his younger son, Edmund, is far more deserving than Tom. Tom knows he's safe. It's only after a near-fatal illness that Tom sees the error of his ways and improves.

In Austen's youthful novella (a short novel) *Lady Susan*, Sir Reginald de Courcey is terribly worried that his only son and heir, Reginald, will marry the conniving, sexually notorious and older Lady Susan. But all Sir Reginald does is write a letter to his son and namesake, begging him to rethink his opinions of the woman (Letter 12). Sir Reginald even says in his letter that "it is out of my power to prevent your inheriting the family Estate." After all, Sir Reginald has just one son and wants the De Courcey estate to stay with the De Courceys.

Training to run the estate

One didn't figure out how to run a large country estate by osmosis. In fact, when Edward Austen completed his Grand Tour, he had to return to the Godmersham Estate in Kent so he could discover how to run it.

The country estate was a complex economic ministate on which the survival of the resident family, household staff, tenant farmers and their families, and workers depended. A successful estate owner needed a good head for business. (For more on running the estate, see Chapter 11.)

As Austen illustrates, in literature as in life, characters can be successful, but characters can also fail in their positions:

- **Darcy, in *Pride and Prejudice:*** Darcy, who is 28 in the novel, lost his father when he was 23 (PP 2:12). He immediately became master of the great Pemberley estate because he was of age (over 21). While the character's youth occurs off-stage, it isn't difficult to infer that he was well-prepared to succeed his father at Pemberley. After all, the "intelligent" housekeeper, Mrs. Reynolds, who was with the family since Darcy was 4, enthusiastically testified that he was "'the best landlord, and the best master . . . that ever lived. . . . There is not one of his tenants or servants but what will give him a good name'" (PP 3:1).

  Darcy also handles another episode with maturity, insight, and justice. Shortly after his father's death, Darcy had to deal with the younger Wickham's request that he wanted to study law instead of becoming a clergyman. As Darcy writes to Elizabeth, "I knew that Mr. Wickham ought not to be a clergyman" (PP 2:12). And while Darcy was suspicious of Wickham's desire to study law, Darcy adhered to his father's wishes to help him: He saw to it that Wickham "resigned all claim to assistance in the church" and gave him £3,000, which dissolved all connections between the two men and released Darcy of his promise to his father.

- **Rushworth, in *Mansfield Park:*** For every good character, there has to be a bad, or so it seems. Rushworth is the exact opposite of Darcy. He's too stupid to be a good master. Furthermore, the run-down condition of his tenants' houses on his Sotherton estate attest that the previous Rushworth generation was either too careless or too self-involved to look after those who worked for them (MP 1:8).

- **Sir Walter Elliot, in *Persuasion:*** There's no indication that when Sir Walter Elliot inherited Kellynch Hall and the surrounding property that it was in an unstable financial status. But after the death of his wife, who kept him and his expenses in line, Sir Walter considers only his vain and selfish desires, and he leaves Kellynch in debt.

Neither Rushworth nor Sir Walter had the intelligence and character to be good masters like the real Edward Austen or the fictional Darcy.

Supporting Younger Sons of Gentlemen

With the paternal property customarily going to the eldest son through primogeniture, younger sons, like their sisters, relied on their parents' marriage settlements for their income. But unlike their sisters, younger sons could also pursue gentlemanly careers. Their sisters — unless they benefited from an excellent marriage settlement from their mother — could only hope to marry. Jane Austen's lifelong friend, Alethea Bigg, mentioned in Chapter 3, is an example of the unusual single young woman who could afford to live well on her own. So is the character Emma, who has £30,000 and will inherit the family home, Hartfield, through her father's will. (For details on marriage settlements, see Chapter 7.)

Finding a genteel profession

A younger son from a family of the gentry had the same educational opportunities as his eldest brother: Both the public school and university were his for the asking. And because the major goal of such education was networking with his fellow young gentlemen, attending a public school or OxBridge gave him an excellent chance of meeting the sisters of his fellow students. In *Mansfield Park,* for example, Edmund Bertram visits and plans to be ordained with his friend, Mr. Owen. Because Edmund went to Oxford, you may assume that he and Owen met at the university. When Edmund visits Mr. Owen, Mary Crawford, who has her eye on Edmund, worries that Owen has three grown sisters who might compete with her for Edmund's affections (MP 2:11). After all, what better way for one of the Miss Owenses to find a potential husband than meeting one of her brother's best friends?

Entering the Church

Many OxBridge graduates who were also younger brothers entered the clergy. While ideally a gentleman didn't go to work, younger sons had to find something to live on to supplement whatever money they received from their mothers' marriage settlements. Being a clergyman in the Church of England was an acceptable choice of profession. A clergyman had to have an Oxbridge degree, and while both universities had some scholarship students, like Austen's father, most of the students were from the gentry. A priest was also someone whom society respects by virtue of his being associated with the church. And being a clergyman requires no real physical labor: The priest could hire an assistant, called a curate, and for little pay, have him preach the sermons, visit the ill, and do the bulk of the parish work.

Becoming an officer in the army

Another genteel career appropriate for a younger son of the gentry was being an army officer. A gentleman didn't have to earn a promotion; he could buy a commission. Costs varied, going as high as £1,000, plus the price of the uniform. A gentleman as young as 16 could buy an officer's commission. By accumulating seniority, he rose in rank. He need not attend the Royal Military College, as training was provided on the job.

Austen's novels have several gentlemen army officers who are either younger brothers of heirs or heirs, themselves, awaiting the time of their succession to the estate. In *Sense and Sensibility,* Colonel Brandon's evil elder brother inherits the family's estate from their father; Brandon, as his title tells us, pursues an army career. When his elder brother dies without legitimate heirs, Colonel Brandon inherits the estate and becomes its master, whereupon he leaves the army. In *Pride and Prejudice,* Darcy's cousin, Colonel Fitzwilliam, is the younger son of an earl. The colonel's elder brother inherited the Earldom and the accompanying estate, while the colonel, as he only semi-playfully tells Elizabeth Bennet, "'must be inured [i.e., to become accustomed] to self-denial and dependence'" (PP 2:10).

Becoming a naval officer

In Austen's lifetime, the Royal Navy was the especially heroic branch of the service because of Admiral Nelson's victory in the Battle of Trafalgar (1805). So being a naval officer was another career that society considered appropriate for a gentleman.

Because two of Austen's brothers, Frank and Charles, had highly distinguished naval careers, Jane Austen reflects her respect for naval officers in her novels. For more information on the Austen brothers, check out Chapter 3.

During times of war, naval officers could add to their bank accounts by winning prize money: money the Admiralty gave a ship's crew for capturing an enemy vessel. The higher one's rank, the higher one's proportion of prize money. When *Persuasion*'s Frederick Wentworth — who isn't from the gentry — returns as a captain with over £20,000 in prize money, he's considered quality husband material. So imagine the eligibility of a younger son from a gentry family with a captain's rank and substantial prize money to his name: He's quite the catch (and gentleman), indeed.

Practicing the law

Law was yet another genteel occupation, totally acceptable for younger sons of the gentry or aristocracy (those with titles), as long as they practiced law in London, rather than in the country. To become a lawyer, one first had to get a degree at OxBridge — or if from Ireland, at Trinity. (With so little work and study required for the university degree, I find myself unable to say one *earned* a degree!) Then it was off to one of London's Inns of Court:

- The Inner Temple
- The Middle Temple
- Lincoln's Inn
- Gray's Inn

The four Inns of Court were the ancient buildings where lawyers and would-be lawyers lived, ate, and "studied" the law. The lawyers who resided in the Inns were *barristers:* lawyers who argued or pled in court. They were considered the top guns of the law. Aspiring lawyers had to dine a certain number of times at their respective inn. Legal education back then was not at all like today's law school. The study of law in Austen's day was self-study: The student read the right books, worked at a barrister's or attorney's office, and looked on in the courtroom. After a set number of terms and dinners, the student attained his certificate. As a lawyer, the former student was now a gentleman — provided he practiced law *in the city* (London!). And if he was from the gentry, he was a gentleman even before he became a lawyer who practiced law *in London!*

Austen understood that society deemed London lawyers genteel. When *Sense and Sensibility*'s Edward Ferrars recounts the professions that his mother would've approved for him, he says that the "'law was allowed to be genteel enough; many young men, who had chambers in the Temple, made a very good appearance in the first circles, and drove about town in very knowing gigs'" (SS 1:19). His mother, then, was thinking of Edward's being a barrister. (Gigs were the sports cars of carriages. For more information on carriages, see Chapter 11.)

Likewise, in *Emma,* Mr. Knightley's younger brother, John, is a lawyer in London. He's probably a barrister.

But being a lawyer in the country? That's not genteel enough. Thus, the Bingley sisters of *Pride and Prejudice* include Elizabeth Bennet's Uncle Phillips, a country attorney, among her "low connections" (PP 1:6, 1:8).

Marrying into money

Young gentlemen could also secure their financial future by marrying a young lady who was the beneficiary of her mother's generous marriage settlement. In other words, he could marry a lady with a hefty dowry. Assuming he doesn't waste her money, the husband could supplement his income by wisely investing his wife's dowry. During Elizabeth's conversation with Colonel Fitzwilliam, she infers that Colonel Fitzwilliam may be discouraging any thoughts she might have of their marrying when he states, "'I may suffer from want of money. Younger sons cannot marry where they like'" (PP 2:10). That is, younger sons can't marry where they like *if* they wish to continue living in a genteel way. (For details on marriage settlements and dowries, see Chapter 7.)

Pinch-hitting for older brother

If the oldest son in a family died before his father did or died without a male heir (even a little boy), the family's property normally went to the next older brother. This procedure kept the property in the family. When this situation occurred, the wife and children of the eldest son usually vacated the property. The same thing would occur if the father died, leaving behind his wife and younger children. His survivors would normally vacate the property for the next heir — even if that next heir was the mother's eldest son and her children's eldest brother.

Jane Austen saw these circumstances occur in real life. Her good friends, the Bigg and Bigg Wither family (one family as the males added the surname Wither when, as Biggs, they inherited the Withers' property), lived at Manydown Park, a wealthy estate in Hampshire. (A picture of the country house, Manydown, appears in Chapter 11.) The eldest son and expected heir died at age 14 while attending Winchester College. His sudden death left his younger brother as the heir. When the father died, the younger brother — now a grown man with a wife and children — moved to Manydown Park. His grown, unmarried, and widowed sisters who'd lived with their father at Manydown left the house and moved to nearby Winchester. Having to vacate the family house to make room for the heir and his family wasn't a source of sour feelings. It was just the way things went. And in the case of the displaced Bigg sisters, they had enough money to live very nicely, indeed.

Meeting the New Gentleman in a Rising Middle Class

While the hierarchical society was inherent in Austen's England, she also witnessed more changes in society than had been experienced in earlier generations. (Hierarchical society is discussed in detail in Chapter 2.) These societal transformations became more evident in the Victorian period (1837–1901), after Austen's time. But in her own day, Austen saw that men could become gentlemen not by inheriting genteel status, but by earning it. So while Austen wrote courtship novels, she certainly had her very sensitive finger on the pulse of social change.

Moving up as a businessman

With manufacturing beginning to move from home or cottage industry to early factories, businessmen who owned the new factories or merchants in trade became wealthy. Labor was cheap. Cotton, coming from the New World as the result of slave labor, combined with the development of new machinery and the discovery of steam to run engines, meant that the spinning wheel in the house was replaced by machine spinning and mass fabric production. Factories sprung up sporadically, especially in the north. And their owners got rich, as did the merchants in trade! But what about the factory workers and the men who loaded and unloaded trading ships and moved products around the warehouse? They would appear two to three decades after Austen's death in novels by Charles Dickens *(Hard Times),* Elizabeth Gaskell *(Mary Barton),* Charles Kingsley *(Alton Locke),* and other social reform writers as the wretched working class!

The rise of the new businessman is illustrated by the Bingley family in *Pride and Prejudice.* Austen writes that the Bingleys "were of a respectable family in the north of England," and that the family's "fortune . . . had been acquired by trade," suggesting that the Senior Bingley had grown rich in textile manufacturing (PP 1:4). Because of his wealth, he could provide his daughters with "a fortune of 20,000 pounds" and his son with 100,000 pounds. In addition to the money, he gave his daughters an elite female education in London — enabling them to lose their northern accents and replace them with the fashionable accent of southern England — and possibly sent his son to the university, though Austen does not mention that outright. As a result, his three children — Charles Bingley and his two sisters — are able to associate "with people of rank," and Charles is the wealthy and genteel friend of Darcy, a member of the gentry.

After a gentleman earned enough money, he could purchase property. Everyone in Austen's day knew that owning land (hundreds of acres, and usually more like 1,000+) is what made you part of the gentry. The Senior Bingley "had intended to purchase an estate, but did not live to do it" (PP 1:4). Buying an estate would've raised the Bingleys into the gentry. Now Charles intends to buy a country estate, but his easy temperament suggests that he may continue to rent a country house like Netherfield Park and "leave the next generation to purchase" (PP 1:4). His social-climbing sisters, however, were anxious for their brother to have an estate of his own because they wanted to solidify their position as part of the gentry population.

Without the estate, the rich Bingley sisters can act like gentry and associate with gentry, but they only become gentry by owning extensive property, or having a brother who owns property and in whose country house they can now hang out and become gentry by osmosis. Being a member of the gentry, they are of the right class to marry Darcy.

Being a gentleman through manners and education

A man could be considered a gentleman even if he didn't own property, assuming he had an acceptable profession and behaved well. The meaning of the word "gentleman" was slowly changing to mean what we, today, think when we use the word "gentleman": a well-educated, courteous, man.

Nowhere in Austen's fiction is this new concept of the gentleman more fully represented than in *Persuasion* through the characters of Admiral Croft and Captain Wentworth. In the novel, the phrase "gentlemen of the navy" is used (P 1:3). Keep in mind that neither Croft nor Wentworth is the younger son of the gentry who sought an acceptable career as a naval officer. Both earned their rank and wealth by capturing enemy vessels. Sir Walter Elliot — one of Austen's great voices of snobbery — scorns the navy for "'being the means of bringing persons of obscure birth into undue distinction, and raising men to honours which their fathers and grandfathers never dreamt of'" (P 1:3). Likewise, Sir Walter says he was misled by hearing a clergyman called a "gentleman": as a Baronet, he is too snobby to accept clergymen as gentlemen, though society did, and says, "'You misled me by the term *gentleman*. I thought you were speaking of some man of property'" (P 1:3). Times were changing and so the status of a gentleman could now be earned as well as inherited.

Chapter 11

Experiencing Life at Home in Austen's Day

*T*his chapter takes you to the homes and daily lives that people of the gentry led in Austen's day. Frequently, Austen didn't elaborate on daily events or concepts in her novels — such as that "morning" went from what we know as morning through about 3 to 4 p.m. — because she naturally assumed that her contemporary readers would know exactly what she meant. And because she didn't write with posterity in mind, some of these concepts are unfamiliar to today's reader. By the time you finish reading this chapter, you should be fairly comfortable at the thought of suddenly traveling back in time to 1812, where you might run into Jane Austen putting the finishing touches on *Pride and Prejudice* at 2:00 p.m. — in the morning!

Living in a Country House

Jane Austen lived in England's great age of country houses. A country house isn't merely a house in the country; a true country house is the mansion in which the owner of a great estate (from hundreds to thousands of acres) located in the country lived and presided over his estate. Everything at the estate radiated from the country house — the center of the estate. The estate's farm(s) supplied all the food for the residents of the house in this largely self-sufficient little world.

Austen visited, dined at, and attended balls at many country houses such as nearby Manydown Park, which belonged to the family of Austen's close friends, Catherine and Alethea Bigg, as well as Godmersham Park in Kent, and Hampshire's Chawton House, on the property of which Austen lived in a six-bedroom cottage for the last eight years of her life. In fact, she spent weeks at a time at her brother Edward's estate, Godmersham. And his Chawton estate was just up the road from the Austen ladies' cottage. (For more information on Edward, the Knights, and Jane Austen's background, see Chapter 3.)

Touring country houses

While Austen's parents were at the lower end of the gentry, she knew about country house life intimately because she had close friends and a brother, Edward, who lived at the higher, richer end of the gentry. Jane Austen was a good friend of Catherine and Alethea Bigg, whose father owned the beautiful Manydown Park, a country house and surrounding estate (pictured in Figure 11-1).

Figure 11-1:
Manydown Park was the home of the wealthy Bigg Wither family. Jane Austen spent many a day here as an overnight guest. Unfortunately, the house is no longer standing.

Photo by Isabel Snowden, courtesy of the Jane Austen Memorial Trust

Discovering how life in a country house played out in Austen's time can give you some insight to the behavior (some of which may seem odd to you) of her characters.

Getting an idea of the lay of the land

Country house estates were worlds of their own, with the owner and master at the top. Austen's readers get a good sense of what a country house and the estate on which it sat were like by mentally visiting Pemberley, the grand estate of *Pride and Prejudice*'s hero, Fitzwilliam Darcy, as Elizabeth and the Gardiners approach it (3:1):

- **Woods:** As Elizabeth Bennet and her Aunt and Uncle Gardiner drive up to Pemberley, they first approach Pemberley Woods, "stretching over a wide extent" (PP 3:1).

- **Lodge:** After passing by the woods, they see the lodge — a smaller house built at a distance from the main house that was customarily used for shooting (hunting) parties who hunted deer, rabbits, and various birds in the estate's park. Some estate owners rented their lodges to tenants. In *Persuasion*, Lady Russell lives at Kellynch Lodge on the estate owned by an old family friend, Sir Walter Elliot, who resides at Kellynch Hall (P 1:2).

- **Stream:** As the Gardiners' coach continues, they see that Pemberley also has a well-stocked stream on the property, where Darcy later invites Mr. Gardiner to fish.

- **Country house:** About "half a mile" into the Pemberley property, the occupants observe where "the wood ceased, and they were instantly caught by Pemberley House. . . . It is a "large, handsome, stone building, standing well on high ground" (PP 3:1).

Although Pemberley is Austen's grandest and most famous fictional country house, she includes others in her fiction:

- **Norland Park:** The home of the Dashwood sisters until they're displaced by their half-brother and his family in *Sense and Sensibility*

- **Sotherton:** A country house that dates back to the Elizabethan period (16th century) owned by the Rushworth family in *Mansfield Park*

- **Northanger Abbey:** The Tilneys' house, not as large as Pemberley but also a country house

While Mansfield Park is also a country house, it doesn't have the history of grand old Pemberley, Sotherton, the Abbey, or Norland. Mansfield Park and other newer country houses are discussed later in this chapter under "Picking up Austen's hints about a modern-built house." For Austen, a modern-built house frequently carried a certain significance. While she certainly was not adverse to people making their way up to the rank of gentry by earning the money to buy an estate, she scorned those who let their new riches go to their heads and forgot where they came from, especially when such folks turned into snobs. Think: Mrs. Elton and her in-laws, the Sucklings, in *Emma*.

Getting a glimpse of the inside of a country house

When Elizabeth and her companions visit Pemberley, they ask to see the interior of the house (PP 3:1). This inquiry may seem odd to you because Pemberley is a private home, but in Austen's day when owners weren't home, they often set aside a few rooms for public display.

Nowadays, many great English country houses charge admission for tourists, and many houses have been turned over to the National Trust because the owners can't afford the high taxes owed on the mansion and surrounding estate.

As Elizabeth and her companions proceed from the entrance hall of Pemberley to the interior, readers get a good idea of how vast country houses could be:

- **The dining room:** This space is where the family and their guests ate dinner. In *Sense and Sensibility,* much chatter goes on in the Middletons' dining room (1:20), and when Bingley chooses to sit next to Jane in the Bennets' dining room, Elizabeth is pleased (PP 3:12). In each case, there is no squeeze at the dining-room table, and no one is sitting on kitchen chairs dragged into the dining room at the last minute! The Bennets can sit eight with ease in the scene mentioned, and undoubtedly can sit more easily — and they live in a smaller country house than Sotherton, Pemberley, or Mansfield Park.

- **The breakfast room or breakfast parlor:** Large homes, like Pemberley, likely had separate breakfast rooms just as Mansfield Park and Netherfield Park had (MP 2:11, PP 1:9).

- **The drawing room:** The drawing room was the usual location for after-dinner gathering. This large room hosted after-dinner music and informal dancing. (For more on dancing, see Chapter 5.)

- **The picture gallery:** The space is hung with portraits of family members, past and present.

- **The sitting room or study:** A sitting room was used for morning activities (reading, letter writing, cards, painting, drawing, or sewing). Sometimes the husband had the study, while the wife used the sitting room.

- **The library:** The library was open to all, though at Longbourn, a more modest country house, the library is Mr. Bennet's personal retreat. Pemberley's library boasts a book collection that is the result of generations of the Darcy family's reading.

- **The billiard room:** Jane's brother, Edward, had a billiard room installed at Godmersham, which proved popular with his gentlemen visitors. Austen gives Mansfield Park a billiard room, too (MP 1:13).

✔ **The music room:** Some country house owners used an additional drawing room as a music room. Darcy has just purchased a "'new instrument'" for his sister Georgiana, who plays the pianoforte, the predecessor of the modern piano (PP 3:1). He has had it placed in a separate room, likely the music room, at Pemberley. In fact, every country house was likely to have a pianoforte and a daughter or mother in residence who could play it. In *Emma,* we see the desirability of having a pianoforte: The newly-rich Coles have a fine house in the village, and they have a new pianoforte — though none of the Coles know how to play (E 2:8)! The harp was also becoming a fashionable instrument for young ladies: Louisa Musgrove has a harp in *Persuasion.* And the stylish Mary Crawford from London plays the harp in *Mansfield Park.*

✔ **The saloon or salon:** This room at some houses doubled as a picture gallery. But Pemberley is so large that it has both a gallery and a saloon.

✔ **The conservatory:** Let's detour from Pemberley for a moment. While we don't read of a conservatory at Pemberley, it likely had one as many country houses did. Manydown, home of Austen's good friends, the Bigg (Wither) sisters, had a conservatory with tall, large glass windows. (See Figure 11-1, where Manydown's conservatory is visible.) The conservatory served as a greenhouse without the dampness of a horticultural greenhouse: This sunny room was a place to grow indoor plants at a time when there was no central heating.

✔ **The bedrooms:** The many bedrooms of a country home were located upstairs.

- The bedrooms could have adjoining dressing rooms and closets — actual small rooms with bookshelves, a desk, and a chair.

- A husband and wife usually shared a bedroom, but separate bedrooms weren't uncommon. (This separation was the only sure form of birth control.)

- The master bedroom or master's and mistress's bedroom contained a study and dressing room for him and a sitting room and dressing room for her.

- Some bedrooms had adjoining water closets (WCs) — bathrooms with primitive toilets and plumbing. But water for baths had to be heated separately and poured into the tub. This was a job for the servants.

- Bedrooms for frequent houseguests. Austen writes of the many guests who are staying, coming, and going at Godmersham Park while she is visiting in autumn 1813. It's as if Godmersham is a mini-hotel, and no one is sleeping on the sofa!

✔ **The offices:** Because the country house and estate were places of work, as well as residence and entertainment, the mansion had a part of the house separate from the family's residence that contained rooms called offices — all rooms to carry out the many jobs that kept the country house operating smoothly:

- The kitchen
- The pantry
- The laundry room
- The wine cellar

When the Austen daughters and their mother visited the massive Stoneleigh Abbey in 1806, the wing with the offices was so large that Mrs. Austen suggested posting directional signs!

✔ **The servants' quarters:** Servants, male and female, had their bedrooms in the mansion's attic, basement, or even a separate wing of the house. However, the estate's lady's maid sometimes had a room of her own near her mistress's room. The head butler might also have his own room.

Picking up Austen's hints about a modern-built house

Austen is very careful to note when a house is modern — that is, constructed in the 18th century. With class structures starting to change, the recently wealthy tradesman or newly rich and titled baronet could join the gentry by purchasing a country house and estate. So a modern-built country house signified that the residents weren't an old family of the gentry. They have the money, but not the heritage of someone like Darcy, who comes from "'respectable, honourable, and ancient, though untitled'" paternal ancestors PP 3:14). Not that Austen resented those with new money who bought country estates. On the contrary, a character like *Persuasion*'s Admiral Croft, who earned his money in the Napoleonic Wars, serves Kellynch Hall better as a tenant than Sir Walter Elliot, baronet, with a long family heritage, served Kellynch Hall as its owner. Likewise, she admires the same novel's Captain Wentworth for his professional success and rise in status. While he is still a naval officer on active duty, chances are he will have enough money to retire with his wife to a country house. But Austen's readers can infer her opinion of country-house owners who have let their new status go to their heads.

Here are some examples:

✔ In *Emma:* Mrs. Elton's sister and brother-in-law, the Sucklings, have lived at Maple Grove for 11 years. She considers them among the "old established families," for she's sure that his father, old Mr. Suckling, "completed the purchase before his death" (E 2:18). Obviously, Maple Grove existed long before the Sucklings, who now consider themselves old timers, took possession! From the way Mrs. Elton always refers to her sister Selina Suckling's opinions and behavior, we can infer that the vulgar Mrs. Elton's pride in her in-laws' estate mirrors the Sucklings' pride. (And what a surname: Suckling! Austen is unusually heavy-handed here and in naming the Sucklings' good friends, the Bragges.) In fact, Mrs. Elton looks down upon the Sucklings' new neighbors, the Tupmans, who bought an estate merely a year and a half ago, because they give "'themselves immense airs'" (E 2:18). Look who's talking. . . .

✔ In *Pride and Prejudice:* Charles Bingley, Darcy's friend, plans to buy a country house and estate with the money he's inherited from his father — a wealthy tradesman or manufacturer from a northern English city. When he finally does buy the estate, he will officially become a member of the gentry. In the beginning of the novel, he leases an estate, Netherfield Park, but soon after marrying Jane Bennet, he buys an estate 30 miles from Pemberley (PP 3:19). Bingley, himself, is modest, but his sister, Caroline, can't wait for her brother to buy an estate so she can say that she has a brother who's a member of the gentry. Like Mrs. Elton, Miss Bingley will claim to be gentry herself through a sibling!

Keeping the country house running

Given that the country house was a large family home, as well as a place of business for the surrounding estate on which it stood, it required a staff to keep the place running. Each worker had a specific role to play in ensuring that a house like Pemberley or Mansfield Park was clean, well-stocked, and functioning comfortably for the family and their guests. And just as society was based on a hierarchical structure, so was the household staff.

Respecting the role of the steward

Of all the help working at a country house, the steward was at the top of the heap. A steward worked at the largest estates, and smaller estates or farms employed a bailiff. The steward managed the estate for the owner so that he didn't have to deal directly with tenant farmers who rented acreage or the workers who tended it. Other responsibilities included

✔ Overseeing the estate's accounts

✔ Settling any squabbles that arose among the tenants or workers

✔ Purchasing animals and seed and so on

This position was a highly trusted one, and a concerned estate owner met with his steward regularly. Even a smaller farm like that of the Austens at Steventon had a supervisor, a bailiff, named Bond, James — no — John Bond.

In *Pride and Prejudice,* Austen makes Wickham the son of the steward who worked for Darcy's father. Darcy describes the senior Wickham as a "very respectable man, who had for years the management of all the Pemberley estates" (PP 2:12). (Sometimes, the owners of large estates also owned smaller estates, which they rented out or gave to their elder sons so they and their young families could live nearby. This was true of the father of Austen's friends, the Bigg Withers, whose son and heir lived with his family on a Bigg Wither-owned estate.) The closeness between the senior Darcy and Wickham, Jr. is evidenced in the senior Darcy's being young Wickham's godfather and paying for his godson to attend Cambridge University. After graduation, the senior Darcy held a church living for him. In essence, the senior Darcy was giving Wickham, Jr. the education and life of a gentleman, even though the young man's father was an employee. (For more on the class system, see Chapter 2. For more on church livings, see Chapter 10.)

Appreciating the roles of the housekeeper and lady's maid

The housekeeper was to the lady of the estate what the steward was to her husband. While the steward was actually superior in the household hierarchy to the housekeeper, she acted as his surrogate in his absence. She was the most important female servant who carried some clout. The housekeeper's duties were as follows:

- Hired the other household help
- Oversaw the household accounts
- Supervised the help who weren't reporting to the steward
- Managed the ordering of all the household supplies

Austen talks about Pemberley's housekeeper in *Pride and Prejudice:*

- When Elizabeth and the Gardiners visit Pemberley, the housekeeper, Mrs. Reynolds, escorts them through the house. She's an "intelligent servant," a "respectable-looking, elderly woman," with "manners easy and pleasant" (PP 3:1). She has been the housekeeper at Pemberley since Darcy, age 28 in the novel, was 4 (PP 3:1). So a good housekeeper stayed around a long time as a valued employee.

- While the Bennets aren't as rich as Darcy, they, too, have a housekeeper, Hill (PP 1:13). When Lydia disappears with Wickham, Mrs. Bennet takes to her room and "vents all her feelings" about the situation (PP 3:5). Her brother and sister-in-law recognize that because Mrs. Bennet "had not the prudence to hold her tongue before the servants," she should remain in her room with the "*one* only of the household . . . the one whom they could most trust:" the housekeeper, Hill. Thus, a trusted housekeeper was an important member of the household.

Equal to the housekeeper in household stature was the personal maid to the lady of the house: the lady's maid. She took care of all of her lady's personal needs, from keeping her company to dressing her, looking after her lady's clothes, and styling her hair. In *Mansfield Park,* Lady Bertram thinks Fanny looks so good at the ball that her lady's maid, Chapman, must have helped Fanny dress (MP 2:10).

Meeting the other household help

Below the housekeeper and lady's maid was an army of female household help, ranging from the cook down to the laundry and kitchen maids, with the chamber maids and the housemaids, who respectively cleaned the bedrooms and the rest of the house, in the middle. The country house's male servants included grooms for the horses and a coachman to drive and look after the family's carriage(s). Other jobs included

- **A cook:** The person holding this job could be male or female. Large estates had an array of cooks with specialties like brewing, baking, or pastry.

- **A butler:** This job included overseeing the household china, silverware, glassware, and what went into it: the wine and beer. Most country houses had butlers, too. The Bennets in *Pride and Prejudice* had one, as well.

- **A personal valet:** No, a valet doesn't park your carriage; he was the person who took care of his boss's clothes. The valet is the counterpart of a lady's maid. A wealthy man like Darcy would employ a valet.

- **A gamekeeper:** He oversaw the protecting and breeding of game — after all, the estate owner wanted enough deer on his property to hunt!

- **Footmen:** These servants worked inside the house. They could do any number of jobs, from serving as doormen to serving meals at the table.

- **A coachman:** He was the chauffeur of the period, driving and maintaining the family's carriages.

- **Carpenters, blacksmiths, and huntsmen:** Large estates like Pemberley, Mansfield Park, and Norland Park would also have these employees.

Taking on the Responsibilities of the Lady of the House

While the housekeeper took charge of seeing that the country house was well-run, the lady of the house — the estate owner's wife — really set the tone for the house. This is why a gentleman who owned an estate — if he was smart — looked for the right woman to be his wife and helpmate. Of course,

I said "if he was smart." But as we all know, in matters of love, sometimes the heart rules the head. That's what happened to Sir Thomas Bertram of Mansfield Park: He married the beautiful Maria Ward, who — according to society — didn't even have the dowry worthy of a baronet (MP 3:1)! Miss Ward turns into the lazy, unconcerned Lady Bertram, who lets her sister, Mrs. Norris, run things, only to have dire results.

When Elizabeth Bennet sees Pemberley for the first time, she observes to herself, as noted earlier in this chapter, that being its mistress is "something!" (PP 3:1). She's not pointing out that the material gain must be glamorous but that being mistress of such a vast estate must be a huge responsibility. While Mansfield Park's Lady Bertram spends her life resting on her sofa, oblivious to what goes on around her, we can assume that when Elizabeth becomes Mrs. Darcy, she'll be an excellent helpmate to her husband, who, as Mrs. Reynolds, the longtime Pemberley housekeeper attests, is an excellent master of the estate (PP 3:1).

Overseeing the country house

The mistress of an estate supervised the housekeeper. She met with the housekeeper periodically to discuss menus and purchases for the household. Depending on her intelligence, she might also aid her husband with overall estate business. For example, in *Persuasion,* the late Lady Elliot, whose husband was the master of Kellynch Hall, provided the family with "method, moderation, and economy, which had kept [her husband] within his income" (P 1:1). With her death came the end of all sense in spending.

Country house families with good heads and hearts had a real sense of *noblesse oblige* — that the rich should help the poor:

- ✔ The lady of the house also met with the local clergyman to find out the needs of the local poor to see what could be done. Emma, who functions as the mistress of her father's estate, Hartfield, visits a poor, ailing woman to comfort her and then sends the woman's child back to Hartfield to fetch soup for the family (E 1:10). Emma provides the poor with compassion, as well as financial relief. Knowing that Mrs. and Miss Bates are in need, Emma sends them pork from Hartfield's farm.

- ✔ Austen's older friend, Madam Lefroy, began a school for the poor children of her neighborhood and personally vaccinated everyone in her husband's parish against smallpox. (For more on Madam Lefroy, see Chapter 3.)

As hostess to guests, the mistress of the estate saw to it that her company was comfortable and entertained:

✔ Sitting at the foot of the dinner table, she was expected to keep up her share of the conversation.

✔ She was also expected to dress with taste and keep in fashion, for this showed her family's financial well-being.

✔ After dinner, the lady might play the pianoforte for dancing or for musical entertainment.

Of course, Austen knew that not all ladies of the house would earn top grades in the execution of their duties. While *Sense and Sensibility*'s Lady Middleton is livelier than the ever-dozing Lady Bertram of Mansfield Park — she's dull at conversation and ignores her music. Her main job is to decorate her husband's home. At least she has produced a son. (For the importance of the birth of sons, see Chapter 10.)

Raising the children

Wealthy women had nursery maids to whom they handed over such tasks as bathing and dressing the children and entertaining them during the day. But in Austen's fiction, we are also in a time of childrearing history when children were regarded as children, rather than as little adults. Mothers didn't totally disregard their maternal duties. They frequently breastfed their babies and were encouraged to hold and nurture them. At times during the day, the nursery maids would bring the children to their mother. From everything we see in *Emma,* Isabella Knightley, Emma's sister, is an affectionate mother to her five young boys and girls.

But in Austen's novels, more deficient mothers than model mothers are represented, such as:

✔ **Lady Middleton:** In *Sense and Sensibility,* the children enter the room and immediately act up, and throw a guest's handkerchief out the window and gain attention by screaming and sobbing (SS 1:21).

✔ **Mary Musgrove:** In *Persuasion,* Mary Musgrove can't control her two little boys.

✔ **Mrs. Bennet:** In *Pride and Prejudice,* this mother has been and continues to be a casual mother, who lets Lydia get away with far too much freedom. She also embarrasses her daughters Elizabeth and Jane with her careless talk about Jane and Bingley's relationship.

While children of wealthy families had tutors and governesses at home and also went to school, the mother also may have helped with their early education. She taught them how to read and write, and discover basic geography.

This education really depended on the individual mother. In *Mansfield Park,* for example, Lady Bertram is so lazy that she surrenders her maternal responsibilities to her sister, Aunt Norris. The aunt so spoils her nieces that they grow into self-involved adults with no sense of moral responsibility.

Being a Gentleman Farmer

Country house owners were farmers. But they never did the job of farming. They had workers to do that, and stewards who oversaw the farm's day-to-day business. Yet the conscientious estate owner — like his wife with their house — had the responsibility to take an active interest in his property.

Improving the estate, or not

The ideal estate owner would assume the following responsibilities:

- Consult frequently with his steward
- Advise his young tenant farmers
- Take an interest in the lives of his workers
- See to it that his property (livestock) doesn't inconvenience his neighbors
- Offer assistance to his friends and neighbors

Among Austen's fictional estate owners, Mr. Knightley in *Emma* acts as the model owner of his estate. In real life, Austen's brother Edward was an excellent estate owner. Witnessing Edward's management of his great Hampshire estate, Chawton, she writes to their naval brother Frank that "Chawton is not thrown away upon him," adding that he's doing things to make it "better," such as making a new garden (Letter, July 3–6, 1813).

But not all estate owners act responsibly toward their property, neither in real life nor in Austen's fiction.

- **Mr. Rushworth:** When the Bertram party travels to Mr. Rushworth's estate, Sotherton, they proceed through the woods and then to the village, where Maria Bertram — soon to be Mrs. Rushworth — casually observes that the estate's tenants' cottages "'are really a disgrace'" (MP 1:8). While Rushworth is interested in improving the landscape around his house, he's careless of his tenants' well-being.

- **Sir Walter Elliot:** As another of Austen's incompetent estate owners, Sir Walter Elliot from *Persuasion* overspends his income and must lease out his estate and home to tenants. Sir Walter then rents living quarters in Bath in an effort to earn money from the rental.

Raising the children

When children were away from their nursery maids, they spent time with their mother. But some more proactive fathers enjoyed time with the children, too. A father might teach his sons how to hunt and fish, and with the groom, teach them to ride. In *Emma,* Mr. John Knightley takes his boys for a visit to see their uncle, and the boys enjoy a run home. His sons also have a kite, and their father may well have taught them how to fly it.

Mr. Austen actually ran a small boys' boarding school in the family's home, enabling him to spend teaching time with his sons. Likewise, other fathers did take an interest in their sons' intellectual development. In *Mansfield Park,* Sir Thomas Bertram emphasized good reading with his sons (MP 3:3). As boys, Tom and Edmund had to practice this skill with their father.

Aiding the church

The owner of a country house sometimes had church livings to bestow. This gift meant that he could choose whom he wished to serve as clergy of the church(es) on his property. In so doing, he could give the living as a gift to someone, frequently a family member or friend, who was ordained. He could also sell the living to make money on it.

The sale of the living is exactly what Sir Thomas Bertram is compelled to do with his best living in *Mansfield Park.* He sells it to Dr. Grant because his elder son, Tom, has been a wastrel. Sir Thomas needs the money Grant pays for the living to help pay Tom's debts. The jury is still out on whether Dr. Grant was an effective clergyman, but he sure likes to eat good food and drink fine wine.

Hosting one's guests

While the lady of the house saw to her guests' comfort and entertainment, the master saw to it that the visiting gentlemen, in particular, were well occupied. Ideally, he supplied good conversation, good hunting, good riding, and good wine. Of course, he would have consulted with his butler about the wine, his groom(s) about the horses, and his gamekeeper about the hunting, also known as shooting. He might even arrange a ball to entertain his family, guests, and neighbors.

Austen's novels show several estate owners and their guests, and in so doing, she allows us to assess the owners as hosts.

- Darcy invites his male guests to fish in the well-stocked stream at Pemberley (PP 3:1, 2). When he meets Mr. and Mrs. Gardiner, he is chatty and welcoming. He also encourages his shy younger sister to be hospitable to the visiting ladies, especially Elizabeth (PP 3:3).

- Even the reclusive and sedentary Mr. Bennet, who loves to retreat to his library with a book, invites and accompanies Bingley for a morning of shooting (hunting) on the Bennets' property (PP 3:13). It wasn't unusual for the result of the hunt to appear on the dining room table soon after the gentlemen returned.

- In *Sense and Sensibility,* Sir John Middleton of Barton Park is Austen's liveliest host. A man who hates being alone — even with his own wife — Sir John gathers young people to his home and hosts impromptu balls, making him the favorite of the neighborhood's young people. (For more on impromptu balls, see Chapter 5.)

Entering Parliament

Many a country house owner stood for Parliament, which ran the government. Being among the richest and most prominent men in the neighborhood, estate owners usually won. In the best circumstances, the winners, Members of Parliament — MPs — helped the nation and their home regions and counties. In the worst circumstances, the winners helped themselves and their pals.

People in Austen's day were delighted to have friends who were MPs because they could frank their mail. Ordinarily, the recipient of a letter paid the postage on it. But because Members of Parliament had a lot of official correspondence with their constituencies, they could sign their name on the envelope part of a letter, and the recipient wouldn't have to pay postage. This courtesy service was all well and good for the MPs, but the practice was abused, even by Austen, herself, who sought a frank for a letter whenever she could. (For more on letters in Austen's day, see Chapter 6.)

In Austen's fiction, three of her estate owners are either sitting MPs or candidates: *Northanger Abbey*'s General Tilney and Sir Thomas Bertram of *Mansfield Park* are the former, while *Sense and Sensibility*'s Mr. Palmer, owner of the Cleveland estate, plans to run for a Parliament seat in the House of Commons. Of course, being an MP meant spending the time that Parliament was in session in London, away from one's estate. So while the master was away to serve in Parliament or for other reasons, his son might step in for him at home, from consulting with the steward to carving the roast at the dinner table, as Edmund does in *Mansfield Park* while his father and elder brother are in Antigua (MP 1:4). This also reminds us of the importance of having a good steward, who would responsibly look after the estate's workings in the absence of his master. While the steward, of course, wouldn't carve the roast while his master was away — the butler did that if no son was available — the steward saw to it that the gamekeeper shot a deer for roast venison.

Participating in local government

Traditionally, the village's wealthy estate owner became the local magistrate, overseeing any criminal cases that arose in the area. But the funny thing was that the estate owner didn't have any formal legal training. He just simply learned the law as he went along and used his own sense. While today we might find this upsetting or unjust, the people in Austen's day accepted this long-standing practice. After all, they lived in a hierarchical society and accepted the main estate owner as the BMOC — the Big Man of the Country!

Consider Mr. Knightley, the principal landowner of Highbury: He is the local magistrate in *Emma*. Fortunately, not only does Mr. Knightley have intelligence and integrity, but also he has a brother who's a London lawyer. Thus, whenever John Knightley comes to visit, his brother, George, "had generally some point of law to consult [him] about, or, at least, some curious anecdote to give" (E 1:12).

Evening Entertainment

Evening was the time of day for the family and their guests to be together. As noted earlier in this chapter, dinner, the main meal, was usually served between 5:00 and 6:00 p.m. Between breakfast and dinner, a lot had gone on: Father may have shot a deer when hunting at break of day, met with his steward to discuss prices of wheat and livestock, presided over a session at court in the nearby town, and written business letters, while Mother has written personal letters to her sons at Eton and Oxford University, met with the housekeeper to plan the menu for next week's houseguests, helped her youngest daughter with her reading, and enjoyed a visit from the local clergyman's wife to discuss helping the village poor. At dinner, the family convened in the dining room for a big meal and conversation. Young children ate dinner in the nursery with their governess, but might be brought to their parents before or after dinner. After dinner, activities ranged from reading and quiet conversation to lively, even noisy, dancing.

Dining with guests

Dinner was the main meal of the day and was the one meal served in the dining room. When dinner time struck (5:00–6:00 p.m.), the hosts and their guests walked from the drawing room, possibly through other rooms, into the dining room, with the gentlemen escorting the ladies in order of precedence. Titled people went before untitled, and married ladies before single ladies. (For the hierarchy of titles, see Chapter 2.)

Of course, the master of the house presided at the dinner table, because etiquette required it, and still does, especially at formal dinners. After all, who carves the Thanksgiving turkey in most homes? As noted earlier in this chapter, if the master wasn't available for dinner, one of the sons could step in, as Edmund does at Mansfield Park during his father's and brother's absences.

Dinner was a formal meal, for which ladies and gentlemen "dressed." Not that the gentry walked around like slobs during the day! Far from it! But dinner was the time for the family to be together, and so members of the gentry freshened up and donned their good clothes to dine. (After all, father and the boys were out hunting and riding!) Nowadays, people might "dress" for Thanksgiving dinner; in Austen's day, for the gentry, every dinner was Thanksgiving. For example, when General Tilney's party — his family and Catherine Morland — arrive at Northanger Abbey from Bath, they dress for dinner (NA 2:5). While Austen doesn't specify what they wore, her contemporary readers understood that gentlemen wore white cravats, white shirts and vests (known as waistcoats), coat (their version of a man's suit jacket would be a coat with tails), and black or tan breeches. Having left their riding boots to be cleaned, they wore shiny black shoes. The young ladies changed from their traveling dresses to more formal gowns and shoes and re-did their hair.

Dinner was served in courses. When Mrs. Bennet contemplates inviting Darcy and Bingley to dinner, "though she always kept a very good table, she did not think any thing less than two courses, could be good enough" for them (PP 3:11). A typical meal consisted of soup, roasted meat and/or fowl, fish, and various side dishes. After dinner was eaten, the gentlemen remained in the dining room for cigars, wine, and "men's" talk, while the women recessed to the best drawing room (if the house had more than one) where the gentlemen later joined them for dessert and coffee or tea. When both the ladies and gentlemen were in the drawing room and had finished dessert, the evening's entertainment began.

Playing cards

Playing cards was an extremely popular evening pastime because people could talk while playing. Card games included Whist, Loo, Canasta, Piquet, and Speculation.

Like today, people at all economic levels in Austen's day enjoyed cards — from the servants to the mistress and master of the house. Even children love and loved to play cards. Austen enjoyed playing, and she taught her young nephews how to play Speculation, and they had great fun with the game. Her pleasure in cards carried over to her novels where she showed people at cards. Here are some examples of the various card games her characters play:

✔ In *Mansfield Park,* at the Grants' parsonage, the guests break into two groups: the whist players (the serious group) and the speculation players (the chatty group, plus Lady Bertram, who can't remember the rules!) (MP 2:7).

✔ In *Pride and Prejudice,* a group plays a game called "lottery tickets," using cards and "fish" — the equivalent of today's chips (no, not "fish and chips," but poker chips) — at Elizabeth's Aunt Philips's home (PP 1:16). Bingley joins Mr. Hurst, his brother-in-law, playing piquet (PP 1:10), while during another evening at Netherfield, Bingley, his sisters, his brother-in-law, and Darcy play Loo (PP 1:8).

Reading and writing

Post-dinner entertainment could be something as simple as reading aloud. Gentlemen were expected to read well aloud. As Austen was growing up at Steventon, her father and her brothers, as they became older, would read the latest novels to the family circle during the evening. Hearing good reading may well have sharpened the budding novelist's ear for language. As an excellent reader, Henry Crawford entertains the ladies during an evening at Mansfield Park by reading selections from Shakespeare's *Henry VIII* to them. Moreover, discussing what you read enriches your reading. In *Mansfield Park,* Edmund "made reading useful by talking to [Fanny] of what she read" (MP 1:2).

Of course, many people simply liked to read to themselves.

✔ The Dashwood sisters are readers.

✔ Elizabeth Bennet enjoyed reading.

✔ Fanny Price is an avid reader.

✔ Mr. Bennet may enjoy reading too much because he withdraws from his parental responsibilities by withdrawing to his library to read.

While others read and play cards, one might quietly write a letter, as Darcy does in *Pride and Prejudice* (1:10). Austen, herself, recalls an evening when after dinner, she and her brother Edward sit together, each writing his or her own letter, awaiting Edward's eldest daughter, Fanny, to join them with her own letter writing.

Chatting with family and friends

Jane Austen lived in the great age of conversation. Her favorite moralist from the previous generation, Dr. Samuel Johnson, was widely known and respected for his remarkable conversational abilities. Conversation wasn't just mindless babble. Austen enjoyed intelligent, informed discussion with her family and close friends. During a visit to Godmersham, Austen, her brothers, their wives, and her grown niece Fanny sat in the library to talk, while other guests headed to the billiard room. In her novels, particularly in *Emma,* she connects having information — being a man or woman "of information" — with being sensible (E 1:8, 2:2). While the best conversations between characters in her novels are not about the depths of philosophy or the heights of literature, the conversations are thoughtful — whether talking about human persuadability (PP) or the nature of women's feelings (P). *Persuasion*'s intelligent and sensitive heroine Anne Elliot has a conversation with her cousin, Mr. William Elliot, that undoubtedly conveys Austen's feelings on the topic:

> "My idea of good company, Mr. Elliot, is the company of clever, well-informed people, who have a great deal of conversation; that is what I call good company." "You are mistaken," said he gently, "that is not good company, that is the best." (P 2:4)

Listening to music

Society expected all young ladies to play an instrument well enough to provide evening entertainment. Usually, the instrument was the pianoforte, the predecessor of today's piano, but the harp was also becoming popular in Austen's day. In several of Austen's novels, the young ladies play for after dinner entertainment. The pianists include

- ✔ Marianne Dashwood in *Sense and Sensibility*
- ✔ Elizabeth Bennet in *Pride and Prejudice*
- ✔ Emma and Jane Fairfax in *Emma*

The young ladies also sing while accompanying themselves. *Mansfield Park's* Mary Crawford and *Persuasion*'s Musgrove sisters also play the harp.

But just because someone played an instrument didn't guarantee a polite audience. When in *Sense and Sensibility,* Marianne plays at Barton Park, some of her listeners talk through her music. Only Colonel Brandon pays her "the compliment of attention" (SS 1:7). While it takes the entire novel and near-fatal illness for Marianne to appreciate him (because he's not lively!), they marry at the end of the book.

Dancing at home

Many an evening at home ended with an informal dance. Throw together a pianist, some people who like to dance, some people who like to watch, and — Violà! — a dance was born! (For more details on dancing, see Chapter 5.)

Traveling Away from Home

As beautiful and luxurious as country homes were, people still liked to travel to visit friends and relatives and see new sites. And of course, sometimes people traveled for business, too. There were several ways to travel in Austen's day:

- **By foot:** Austen and her friends thought nothing of traveling by foot. They frequently found themselves "crossing field after field at a quick pace, jumping over stiles and springing over puddles" as Elizabeth Bennet did when she made the three-mile walk from Longbourn to Netherfield (PP 1:7). (A *stile* is a set of three or four wooden steps built to help people over a wall or fence constructed in a field to keep animals enclosed.)

- **By coach:** Horse-drawn carriages were the popular way to travel in Austen's day, but mostly the wealthier people had carriages because they were the only ones who could afford them. The Austens, themselves, gave up their carriage in 1798. People with titles, from knight up to the Royal Family, had their coats of arms emblazoned on their carriage doors below the windows. In *Persuasion,* William Elliot, heir to the Elliot Baronetcy, has the family arms on the door of his curricle, and Lady Russell, the widow of a knight, has his arms on her carriage (P 1:12, 2:5). Nothing like calling attention to yourself! (Read on in this chapter for models of carriages.)

- **By horse:** Gentlemen rode horseback if they were traveling a short distance that was too long to walk but not long enough to ride in a carriage. And sometimes ladies, too, rode horseback, but normally just in the neighborhood. Jane Bennet in *Pride and Prejudice* takes a 3-mile horseback ride from her home to Netherfield because the Bennets' coach horses are being used on the farm — probably to pull wagons (PP 1:7). Ladies mostly took carriages and left the horseback rides to the men. Horses, like carriages, were not for those watching their money. When Willoughby plans to give a horse to Marianne, Elinor tells her she must not accept it on the grounds of expense — stable, hay, and groom to care for the horse (SS 1:12).

Roads in the period of Austen's novels were getting better than they had been because Parliament passed a series of acts to build and maintain turnpikes. Turnpikes were toll roads, with the tolls used to maintain the roads. As a result, people could travel long distances by carriage.

Showing that you are what you drive

Many of Austen's characters travel in or drive various types of vehicles. People could own their own carriage or rent one. If the traveler had his own horses and was making an extralong journey, he could use them until the first stop; then, he would send his horses home and rent new horses for the next leg of the journey. Having a personal carriage showed you could afford it and signified status. Emma Woodhouse is upset that Mr. Knightley does not use his carriage much; in fact, he doesn't even keep carriage horses. So she is happy when she sees him in his carriage pulling up to the Coles' house for dinner: "'This is coming as you should do . . . like a gentleman'" (E 2:8). It turns out that Mr. Knightley, ever the thoughtful gentleman, has used his carriage only so that it could be used to pick up poor Miss Bates and her niece, who have been invited for only the entertainment part of the evening. But many other Austen characters not only own carriages of their own, but actually use them. Austen deliberately assigns particular carriages to certain characters to make associations between the person and the carriage he drives, just as we might today characterize one person driving a cheap little car from another driving a large luxury auto.

Chaise

One of the most popular carriages for travel was the chaise, which could hold up to four passengers, although it was a squeeze: The chaise had two seats, but it also had two extra seats that could be pulled out. The chaise was a closed carriage: It had a roof and doors, along with a place where packages and luggage (usually trunks) were strapped or "fastened" on the back (PP 2:15). Hand baggage could be stored within the passenger section. When Catherine Morland, Eleanor Tilney, and Eleanor's maid enter General Tilney's chaise to travel to Northanger Abbey, they see that "the middle seat of the chaise was not drawn out, though there were three people to go in it," causing great crowding for the three passengers (NA 2:5). Instead of having a driver's box up front, the chaise was controlled by a *postilion* (or post boy, who sometimes wasn't a boy at all, but an adult male) riding the left of two horses pulling the vehicle. The "chaise-and-four" was a chaise drawn by four horses, and thus moved faster than the chaise drawn by two. A chaise-and-four could have as many as three postilions, one on each of the two lead horses, which were at the front of the chaise, and a third on one of the two "near wheel" horses, these being the horses next to either front wheel. As Catherine Morland looks out the window of General Tilney's chaise, she admires "the fashionable chaise-and-four—postilions handsomely liveried, rising so regularly in their stirrups" (NA 2:5). ("Liveried" means wearing distinctive uniforms.) Four horses also showed that the owner had money as it was expensive to keep horses. Plus, one had to pay those postilions! Because the chaise was a narrow vehicle, it did not tip over easily and thus was safer on the roads than wider vehicles. (Carriage accidents, where the carriage tipped over, were common; Austen's cousin Jane Cooper died in such an accident at age 28.)

Many of Austen's characters ride in chaises. In *Pride and Prejudice,* Bingley has a chaise-in-four, which is not surprising because he is very rich (PP 1:1). In *Sense and Sensibility,* Mrs. Jennings owns a chaise, and Mr. and Mrs. Robert Ferrars also travel by chaise (SS 2:3, 3:11). In the same novel, Willoughby uses a chaise to go from London to Cleveland in an attempt to see Marianne (SS 3:8). In haste to make the journey because he thinks Marianne is dying, Willoughby probably used a chaise-in-four for speed. *Mansfield Park*'s Mr. Rushworth owns a chaise, though several of the guests at his wedding to Maria Bertram notice disparagingly that he hasn't bought a new one for him and his bride (MP 2:3). Lady Bertram's carriage in the same novel is also a chaise (MP 1:7). In *Persuasion,* "The last office of the four carriage-horses" owned by the vain and financially straitened Sir Walter Elliot is to draw the chaise that takes him to Bath when he leases his country estate to the Crofts (P 1:5).

The chaise was not the grandest vehicle, but it got its passengers where they needed to go. And with four horses mounted by liveried postilions pulling it, the chaise could look pretty good, as Catherine Morland notices in *Northanger Abbey* — even though she is squeezed in! Looking at all the examples of chaise owners in Austen's novels, you can tell that it was a popular vehicle.

Curricle

A curricle was a light, two-wheeled carriage with a convertible top. Drawn by two horses, it was the snazzy sports car of the day, driven by its owner. It is not surprising that Willoughby, a devil-may-care hunk of a male, drives a curricle (SS 1:10). And the way he drives it tells a lot about him: "He drove through the park very fast" as he took Marianne for an all-day excursion (SS 1:13). Because the curricle was light, it tipped over easily and thus required good driving skills. So Willoughby was showing off. *Northanger Abbey*'s Henry Tilney also drives a curricle, but he drives very "well—so quietly—without making any disturbance" (NA 2:5). *Persuasion*'s Charles Hayter, another clergyman, also drives a curricle, and as a highly serious young man, he, too, shows no signs of driving like a show-off (P 1: 11). The curricle was the fashionable young man's vehicle, and like the sports car today, the way one drove it said different things about different drivers.

Gig

The gig (see Figure 11-2) was similar to the curricle, but it was cheaper to own as it required only one horse to draw it. *Northanger Abbey*'s John Thorpe, who likes to think of himself as a snappy man about town, drives a gig. He would probably rather have a curricle, but he's short on cash and can only afford one horse. Like the curricle, the gig was driven by its owner. Thorpe, whip in hand, brags about how fast he drives and how well he controls his wild horse — though Catherine Morland notices when she goes with him that "the animal continued to go on in the same quiet manner, without shewing the smallest propensity towards any unpleasant vivacity" (NA 1:9). *Persuasion*'s Admiral and Mrs. Croft drive a gig in a manner that reflects their marriage: They avoid the danger of hitting a post by Mrs. Croft's "coolly giving the reins [held by the Admiral] a better direction herself" (P 1:10).

Figure 11-2:
A gig such as John Thorpe drives in *Northanger Abbey*.

Phaeton

The phaeton was also a light carriage pulled by one or two horses and used for pleasure driving. It had a convertible top. When Lady Catherine's daughter and her companion, Mrs. Jenkinson, pull up in front of Mr. Collins's parsonage, they're in a low phaeton, which they use to drive around Rosings Park (PP 2:6). A low phaeton had seats lower to the ground than a high phaeton, making the high phaeton more dangerous to drive as the height of the vehicle made it more likely to tip over. Mrs. Jenkinson must have been the driver. When Elizabeth's Aunt Gardiner learns of her niece's marriage to Darcy, she writes to her advising the purchase of a "low phaeton, with a nice little pair of ponies" for driving around the Pemberley estate (PP 3:10). In both cases of Austen's using phaetons, the passengers are ladies and their driving is in a restricted area: around the estate, rather than on public roads.

Chair

Another one-horse carriage was the chair. This light and agile vehicle appears only in Austen's fragment *The Watsons;* the Watsons own a chair because it's very inexpensive, and they're quite poor, living at the very lowest edge of genteel poverty.

The Watsons' chair shouldn't be confused with the sedan chair used in Bath: The sedan chair is a rickshaw-like enclosed chair with two poles, carried by two men, one at the front of the poles, another at the back of the chair holding the rear poles. If you visit the Pump Room in Bath, you'll see a sedan chair there, as well as at Number One, Royal Crescent. Sedan chairs were very popular in Bath during Austen's time, and there was even a sedan chair queue near the Royal Crescent that you can still see — minus the chairs — today: sort of the Regency version of a taxi stand. The sedan chair took its single passenger from one part of town to another and for no very great distance as men, rather than horses, provided the power. At the conclusion of her first assembly, Catherine Morland is carried home from the Upper Rooms in a sedan chair (NA 1:2).

Coach

Coaches were large vehicles that could hold six or more passengers, depending on the coach's size: Usually the coach had two rows of seats (each row held three passengers) facing each other, along with at least one side seat that pulled out. The coach was a strong, closed vehicle with front and back axles connected by a "crane neck" — a long curved iron bar. This bar also supported the body of the coach. The crane neck supposedly acted like springs to alleviate the bumpiness of the ride. Four horses pulled the coach, which had a driver's box at the front. The horses were controlled or driven by the coachman. The Bennets of *Pride and Prejudice* have a coach, as do the Musgroves of *Persuasion* (PP 1:7, P 1:11). Each is a large family and needs a large carriage to get around. With four horses needed to pull the coach, and a coachman to drive and maintain it, the owners showed they had the money to see to its upkeep. But the coach was also the most practical vehicle for a large family who could afford it.

Chariot

Another four-horse vehicle was the chariot, holding four people facing the front, as opposed to facing opposite each other. The chariot was lighter than a coach and provided comfortable and speedy travel. John and Fanny Dashwood in *Sense and Sensibility* have a chariot, as does Mr. Rushworth's mother in *Mansfield Park* (SS 3:2, MP 2:3). The chariot was a classy vehicle, as appropriate for the wealthy Dashwoods as for the widowed, wealthy Mrs. Rushworth, who behaves with "propriety."

Barouche

The most distinguished and showy of carriages was the barouche (see Figure 11-3) — a heavy vehicle drawn by four horses, but light-looking. The barouche had no storage box: Anyone who owned a barouche preferred having his luggage or purchases delivered! (Horse-drawn carts and even farmers' wagons served delivery purposes.) The barouche came in two models, the regular barouche and the barouche-landau. The barouche-landau's roof covered all four of the passengers, who sat facing each other as couples; the roof could also be arranged to cover just parts of the vehicle. In other words, the landau was the Regency's answer to the convertible car. The barouche's folding roof covered only the back part of the vehicle. But whatever the roof configuration, the barouche was the carriage of style. In *Persuasion,* the Dowager (widowed) Viscountess Dalrymple owns a barouche, as does *Mansfield Park*'s eligible bachelor Henry Crawford (P 2:7, MP 1:8).

Henry drives his own barouche, seated in the barouche-box, which accommodated the driver and another person, for a total capacity of six. With its folding roof down, Henry's barouche is the perfect vehicle for the characters to use for their trip to Sotherton on a pleasant, warm day. While the barouche had no place for storage, Henry offers to pick up his sister's harp in his barouche: He could put it in the passenger area.

The Viscountess, as a lady, has a driver, so the three ladies who accompany her ride inside (for a total of four passengers). *Emma*'s Mrs. Elton brags repeatedly of her in-laws, the Sucklings, who own a barouche-landau. Interestingly, there are a lot of other carriage owners in *Emma,* but their carriages are called simply that: carriages. Only the Sucklings' barouche-landau is mentioned by model name — and it's Mrs. Elton who mentions it over and over again!

Figure 11-3:
A barouche.

So while you could drive only one other person in your gig, you could take the whole family plus their baggage and purchases in your coach.

Austen's showing that you are what you drive

Austen knew her carriages, just as she knew her characters. She places people in the vehicles that are most appropriate to their personalities, which is a nice touch that her contemporary readers would recognize.

The curricle drivers are all young gentlemen. Darcy has a curricle, as do Willoughby and Henry Tilney (PP, SS, NA). Charles Musgrove and Mr. William Elliot of *Persuasion* also drive curricles. They are rich enough to have two horses. But as noted earlier, John Thorpe drives a one-horse gig, and he drives it so fast that he nearly knocks down Isabella and Catherine as he races it into Bath (NA). In a later time, John Thorpe would be one of those drivers who love to screech his brakes. In *Persuasion,* Admiral and Mrs. Croft drive around the Kellynch area in a gig; as naval people, they are probably more comfortable on a ship! But they would have hired a larger, sturdier carriage to take them to Bath.

Emma's Mrs. Elton, Austen's most boastful character, brags repeatedly that her sister and brother-in-law, the Sucklings of Maple Grove, drive the ostentatious barouche-landau. The Sucklings are Austen's version of the nouveaux riche, and being "riche" is what the Sucklings want to show the world.

Chapter 12

Minding Your Manners

· ·

· ·

*B*efore the Renaissance (14th- to 17th-century Europe), gentlemen, in the form of courteous men, were nonexistent. Whether in the royal court or on a street corner, men burped, spat, picked their teeth, grabbed food and ate it with their fingers, sulked and showed anger openly, and sneezed without using a handkerchief in a public place or at home. Who needed a handkerchief, anyway? The guy had his hand and sleeve.

And women? The Renaissance also prescribed a code of behavior for ladies as the counterpart of gentlemen. For example, skills with weaponry and horseback riding were deemed unbecoming for ladies of the court. Ladies were expected to be affable, gracious, and charming. And it's hard for a lady to be all that while out riding around and hunting with the guys.

Étiquette is the French word for ticket. Think about it: good manners and polite behavior as the ticket to social acceptability.

Eighteenth-century England inherited polite practices from two sources: Renaissance Italy, for both gentlemen and ladies, and 17th-century France for ladies, who, in turn, were influenced by the ladies of Renaissance Italy. In this chapter, I explore the behavioral changes that both men and women made during the Renaissance to become more mannerly, at least more mannerly according to the theories of the day. In this chapter, I also show you just how Austen's characters behaved, which gives you a glimpse into how Austen felt about the mannerly behavior of her time.

Thank heavens for the Renaissance! It gave us not only da Vinci and Michelangelo, but also it gave men manners. And handkerchiefs.

Using a handkerchief

In the 1996 film of *Sense and Sensibility* starring Emma Thompson and Hugh Grant, Grant's character, Edward, gives a monogrammed handkerchief to Thompson's weeping Elinor. She treasures it as a keepsake and takes it out when she feels all hope for Edward and herself is gone. (For more on the film adaptations of Austen's novels, see Chapter 15.) While using the handkerchief to clean the nose dates back to 300 A.D., this use for a small square of cloth really only became commonplace in the Renaissance. It began in places where courtesy started to matter: the courts of Italy and France, particularly in the mid-16th-century court of King Henry the II of France. Using the handkerchief for nasal purposes began to spread so much among fashionable people that the Dutch philosopher Erasmus of Rotterdam (1466–1536) is said to have commented that wiping one's nose with one's sleeve was boorish.

Making a Gentleman

Gentlemen, in terms of their genes and bloodlines, were, of course, *born* into families of the gentry and aristocracy. (If you need details on who the gentry and aristocracy were, please read Chapter 2.) But gentlemen, in terms of polite men, were *made*. The gentlemen with the genes and the bloodlines who were belching in public needed to be made into polite men. They made this transition by reading courtesy books — publications that advised on the education and conduct of a courtier (a man of the royal court) or a prince. While Castiglione was writing about how a man could become the perfect courtier, his behavior prescriptions also taught men how to become perfect English gentlemen. (See the nearby sidebar for more information on the publications of the time.)

By Austen's period (1775–1817), English gentlemen had a good idea of how to behave. Politeness was so ingrained in the genteel classes that boys were bred to be well bred practically from birth. And if he needed to check something, conduct books were still around.

Training an English gentleman

In Austen's day, boys from the gentry and aristocracy were taught courtesy and decorum before they could pronounce those words. Their nursery maids, tutors, governesses, and parents made sure that their children behaved properly. Good breeding was emphasized at schools. If a young gentleman failed to behave properly, he was promptly corrected by his family, teachers, and fellow students, who of course, were gentry just like he was.

Making everything look effortless and graceful was an Italian notion called *sprezzatura*. Though dating from the Renaissance, Castiglione's sprezzatura was still in the air of Austen's England. Men were expected to dance gracefully, walk gracefully, sit gracefully, and so on. Taught from childhood, gracefulness became second nature by adulthood. A male's outward behavior reflected his good breeding. A member of the gentry should behave like one:

- ✔ Speak and act with modest confidence *(sprezzatura)*

- ✔ Maintain emotional control and don't sulk in public like the big babies of the Middle Ages (1100 until the Renaissance)

- ✔ Use proper language (decorum, meaning suiting the style to the subject)

- ✔ Be well educated in literature, the arts, history, and dancing

For more information on a gentleman's education, see Chapter 10.

Assessing Austen's gentlemen heroes

According to Castiglione, the courtier (or courteous man) had specific characteristics:

- ✔ He should be educated from youth to behave well in the company of others like him.

- ✔ The courtier should be poised and pleasant.

- ✔ The courtier should master weapons (this was 16th-century Italy, remember).

- ✔ His attire should be clean and neat.

- ✔ He should be well read in Latin and Greek and knowledgeable about music, world affairs, dancing, art, and literature.

- ✔ An excellent and affable conversationalist, the courtier should also be modest and considerate of others' feelings. (And having accomplished the task of the previous asterisk, the courtier has the material for good conversation.)

- ✔ He shouldn't show off his knowledge or act in an affected manner. (Boasting and acting in a way that calls attention to oneself are the opposite of *sprezzatura*.)

- ✔ The courtier should be effortless and graceful in his mannerisms.

- ✔ And yes, he should use a handkerchief, too!

Reading your way into manners

The most famous courtesy book is *Il Cortegiano* by Baldassare Castiglione, published in 1528. The trouble for English gentlemen was, it was in Italian. But this guide to protocol in a social context soon became so popular that by 1538 it was translated into Latin, and in 1561 Sir Thomas Hoby translated it into English as *The Book of the Courtier*. So self-help books are nothing new; they've been around since the Renaissance!

As a result of the immense popularity of *Il Cortegiano,* which besides being translated into Latin and English, was soon translated into French and German, courtesy books appeared all over western Europe. In England, other popular courtesy books for men included Sir Thomas Elyot's *The Book of the Governor* (1531), Henry Peacham's *Compleat Gentleman* (1622), and Richard Braithwait's *English Gentleman* (1622).

Castiglione had clear expectations of how a *gentle*man should behave, and judging by Austen's portrayal of genteel men, she agreed with Castiglione's definition:

✔ **Mr. Knightley:** As the hero of *Emma,* Mr. Knightley most consistently portrays the genteel man. He practices conversational decorum:

- He converses well with everyone, including those who are below him in terms of social and economic class.

- He speaks with kindness and respect to old Mr. Woodhouse and to poor Miss Bates.

- He converses politely but firmly warding off the irritating attempts at control of Mrs. Elton when she tries to push her own ideas (and housekeeper) on him for his strawberry party.

- His mere walk reveals to Emma "in how gentlemanlike a manner, with what natural grace, he must have danced, would he but take the trouble" (E 3:2). When he finally dances — and this occurs when he heroically rescues the wallflower Harriet at the Crown Inn Ball — he shows himself to be an "extremely good" dancer. Now, this is an English gentleman with a healthy dose of *sprezzatura!*

- Mr. Knightley is sensitive to the needs of others.

- He firmly corrects Emma for insulting and hurting Miss Bates at Box Hill.

- He quietly sends apples to the Bates family.

- He uses his carriage only so Miss Bates and her niece can use it to go to an evening party and return home in it — "'the sort of thing that so few men would think of,'" correctly says Miss Bates (E 2:8).

✔ **Colonel Brandon:** *Sense and Sensibility*'s Colonel Brandon comes in second to Mr. Knightley.

- His speech is well mannered.

- He tends to be "silent and grave," but during his silence, he's dealing emotionally with the sudden and mysterious eighth-month disappearance of his 16-year-old ward, Eliza, which worsens the "gloom" he feels over Eliza's mother's disgraceful sexual conduct (SS 2:9).

- He's polite enough not to raise these subjects to call attention to his own worries while exerting emotional control.

- When he learns that Willoughby is responsible for his ward's disappearance and unwed pregnancy, he handles the situation with a quiet private duel and makes no attempt to ruin Willoughby's reputation among his friends.

- While he never dances in the novel, he's the only person to listen to Marianne play the pianoforte without talking over her performance: "He paid her only the compliment of attention" (SS 1:7). (What a great line for Austen to have written, too!)

✔ **Henry Tilney:** *Northanger Abbey*'s Henry Tilney is also a gentleman.

- He dances well.

- He converses with ease, humor, and wit.

- He shows without bragging that he's well educated and well read.

- He behaves politely and pleasantly to everyone.

- He stands by Catherine Morland when his greedy and misled father, General Tilney, demands that Henry drop her.

- And as Catherine notes, he drives his carriage and handles his horses well, unlike the show-off driver in the novel, John Thorpe.

Austen is also quick to portray characters that don't exemplify the characteristics of Castiglione's gentleman:

✔ **Darcy:** You may wonder why Darcy doesn't fit into the category of "gentleman." By birth and by the ownership of the vast Pemberley Estates, making him a member of the gentry, he qualifies as a "gentleman" in terms of social class. But while he dances well, converses with ease, and bows nicely, he displays some ungentlemanly characteristics as well:

- He was extremely inconsiderate of the feelings of others when he caught Elizabeth's eye at the Meryton Assembly, and then he said that she wasn't pretty enough to choose as a dancing partner.

- He interfered with his friend Bingley's relationship with Jane, telling Bingley that Jane wasn't really interested in Bingley — even though Darcy was unaware of Jane's placid, composed demeanor and "uniform cheerfulness of manner" (PP 1:6).

- When he proposed to Elizabeth the first time, he mentioned in his proposal all of the reasons that she and her family were beneath him and how he was lowering himself to marry Elizabeth. He behaved in a way that contradicted the way he was bred. His decorum flew out the window.

✔ **Edward Ferrars:** In *Sense and Sensibility,* Ferrars isn't adept socially. He doesn't converse with ease, and this isn't just because he's awkward. He's a liar and lies with considerable *sprezzatura!* (But Castiglione, while advocating ease, didn't advocate ease in lying!) For when Marianne, in the company of Elinor, notices Ferrars wearing a ring made of human hair (a common love token) and asks whose hair it is, though he momentarily colors with embarrassment, he says the hair belongs to his sister and even adds that the setting changes its appearance (SS 1:18). The hair really belongs to Lucy Steele, to whom he's secretly engaged. Even though Edward momentarily blushes before his big fat lie, Elinor still thinks that the hair, which he somehow acquired, is hers. So Edward scores low marks in the gentleman test.

✔ **Captain Frederick Wentworth:** As *Persuasion*'s naval hero, Wentworth certainly appears to be a gentleman. He must have even handled arms with skill, given that naval battles of the day frequently led to shooting guns at close distances and engaging in sword fights on deck. He's also friendly with the Harvilles, Musgroves, and Crofts, and he converses well. But he doesn't have his emotions under control, and he's playing games with people's feelings:

  - Anne Elliot rejected his proposal eight years earlier, so he's friendly to everyone except her, treating her with cold and formal politeness. He shows he's hurt! He even comments to the Musgrove sisters that Anne has changed so much for the worse that he hardly recognizes her. He knew that his comment would get back to Anne.

  - He behaves improperly, spending so much time with Louisa Musgrove that his close friend Captain Harville considers him "'an engaged man. . . . I was hers [Louisa's] in honour if she wished it'" (P 2:11). Sorry, folks, but the brave naval hero Wentworth is like — of all people — the dull and awkward landlubber Edward Ferrars. By paying attention to another woman (Edward to Lucy and Frederick to Louisa), about whom he doesn't really care, each man hurts the woman he really loves and who really loves him.

✔ **Edmund Bertram:** Bertram is the hero of *Mansfield Park,* and from everything the reader can surmise, he's a polite and well-cultured young man. And he's generally considerate of others' feelings. But he doesn't really know himself. He becomes enamored of the sexually attractive Mary Crawford and — unaware of Fanny's love for him because he is too self-involved — he unloads all his emotional burdens on her, causing Fanny to feel extreme emotional pain. Castiglione today would probably send Edmund to a good shrink to be able to claim his status as gentleman.

Training a Lady in Her Duty: Pleasing Her Man

Because marrying a gentleman was a lady's primary goal, learning to please him was considered a lady's duty. Books were available to teach young women how to behave and what was right for them in terms of manners and conduct. The information in these books echoes Castiglione, who said that the lady should be charming, gracious, and pleasing to gentlemen. Austen subtly shows in her work her thoughts regarding women's behavior.

Ignoring the prescription of Dr. Fordyce

The most famous book of Austen's day is the one that Mr. Collins begins to read to the five Bennet sisters in *Pride and Prejudice:* Dr. James Fordyce's *Sermons to Young Women,* published in 1765 and many times reprinted (PP 1:14). Dr. Fordyce's book, which sold by the thousands, explained within a Christian framework the main lesson that society believed females had to master: how to please men in order to marry them in a time that deemed women inferior to men in every way.

Fordyce's book encourages woman to act in the following ways:

- He instructed women to be docile, meek, soft, obedient, and even submissive to neglect.

- He emphasized beauty over education, noting that nature made men naturally smarter than women, and he concluded that men prefer quiet, delicate, charming women. (Interestingly, Castiglione was far more liberated because in *The Courtier,* he advocated the same education in literature, music, painting, and dancing for both males and females — though he also stressed that a woman's primary aim was to be charming. On that last matter, Fordyce echoes Castiglione.)

- He encouraged ladies to avoid exercise, which he considered manly and ungraceful. (Remember that Castiglione advised women to avoid such physical activities as horseback riding and hunting!)

Austen shows her views on Fordyce's female ideals with subtlety, charm, and humor. In fact, she challenges his ideas both overtly and covertly. *Pride and Prejudice* offers her most specific opinions on the subject. Jane Austen subtly answers his prescription for women by creating active heroines and other female characters who behave in an un-Fordyce-like manner, and their physical activity adds to their feminine allure:

- ✔ While Fordyce discourages young ladies from being robust and doing physical exercise, Elizabeth does her own version of a three-mile workout when she walks across the fields "at a quick pace" to visit Jane at Netherfield. "[J]umping over stiles and springing over puddles," Elizabeth arrives at her destination "with weary ankles, dirty stockings, and a face glowing with the warmth of exercise" (PP 1:7). Elizabeth is fit for this strenuous walk, because as Austen later slips in, she is "in the habit of running" (PP 3:7).

- ✔ When Elizabeth reaches Netherfield Park, the jealous Miss Bingley criticizes her appearance, saying snippily, "'Why must *she* be scampering about the country. . . . Her hair so untidy, so blowsy?'" (PP 1:8). But the gentlemen have a very different reaction, and it is far from what Fordyce expects. Both Messieurs Bingley and Darcy admire the effects of the "Elizabeth Bennet Workout": The former thinks she "'look[s] remarkably well,'" and the latter admires her eyes, which "'have been brightened by the exercise'" (PP 1:8). Elizabeth's cross-country jaunt has enhanced her physical beauty and sexual attractiveness. The Jane Austen Workout for Elizabeth Bennet preceded the "Jane Fonda Workout" by over 150 years!

- ✔ What Austen thought of Fordyce is also communicated by the physical activities — albeit unladylike — that several of her female characters enjoy. In *Northanger Abbey,* the adolescent Catherine Morland loves rolling down hills, horseback riding, "running about the country," and playing baseball and cricket (1:1). More female athleticism appears in *Sense and Sensibility:* Marianne (17) and Margaret (13) are thrilled to have the chance to ignore "propriety" by "running with all possible speed" down a hill towards home when it rains (SS 1:9).

Undermining Dr. Gregory's advice

An equally popular book, written by Dr. John Gregory, in Austen's lifetime was *A Father's Legacy to his Daughter,* published in 1774, one year before Jane Austen's birth. Dr. Gregory thought women should hide their knowledge and wisdom to avoid coming across as superior, and he also felt men may be jealous of such knowledge and find intelligent women irritating. Thus, he encouraged women to retain their innocence of the world, especially when speaking.

As for Dr. Gregory's prescription for female ignorance and passivity, all of Austen's heroines in her six completed novels undermine that notion:

- ✔ **Catherine Morland of *Northanger Abbey:*** Austen's youngest heroine at age 17 says she "'cannot speak well enough to be unintelligible'" (NA 2:1). And she's absolutely right. Unlike those who use their facility with words to deceive and mislead, Catherine is always a straight shooter. So when she tells her brother and his friends, the Thorpes, that she can't join them for an outing because she already has a walking engagement date with her friends, the Tilneys, she's rightfully angered when the Thorpes and her brother, who's wrapped around Isabella

Thorpe's finger, verbally attack her with phony reasons for canceling the Tilney walk in order to accompany them. And when John Thorpe goes after the Tilneys to say that she is pre-engaged to walk with him, his sister, and Catherine's brother — which is, of course, a boldfaced lie — Catherine breaks away from her brother and so-called friends, and "almost" runs after the Tilneys, following them breathlessly into their house to declare the truth, oblivious to the protocol of footmen and announcements (NA 1:13). No wonder Henry Tilney finds her charming!

✔ **Elinor Dashwood of *Sense and Sensibility:*** She maintains stoic self-control. When she learns that Edward Ferrars, who has certainly appeared romantically interested in her, is engaged to another woman, she keeps such a stiff upper lip that even those closest to her are fooled by her appearance. By an act of sheer will, she lives her code of general civility and shows great physical and emotional courage. Marianne sincerely despises the ways of the gossipy, insensitive society in which they live, preferring a code of personal morality on the grounds that "'we always know when we are acting wrong'" (SS 1:13). Both young ladies have strong wills.

✔ **Elizabeth Bennet in *Pride and Prejudice:*** Elizabeth Bennet isn't playing games with Mr. Collins when she refuses his marriage proposal based on the fact that she wants to be considered "'as a rational creature,'" instead of the "'elegant female'" he thinks she is (PP 1:19). Angered by her rejection, Collins verbally throws her meager dowry in her face, saying that her "'portion is unhappily so small that it will in all likelihood undo the effects of [her] loveliness and amiable qualifications'" for marrying well (PP 1:19). For once, Collins is absolutely correct. But notwithstanding her dowry's negative effect on her marriage ability, she refuses to dance pirouettes of admiration around the wealthy, handsome Darcy as other women, such as Miss Bingley, do. When Elizabeth and Darcy are together at Netherfield Park and at Rosings, she wittily challenges him in conversation, making the two verbal sparring partners. And she rejects his first proposal on the grounds that he has not acted like a gentleman. So is it any surprise that when Elizabeth and Darcy finally get together and rehash the ups and downs of their relationship that Darcy tells her that his admiration and love for her are based on "'the liveliness of [her] mind'" (PP 3:18)?

✔ **Fanny Price of *Mansfield Park:*** Fanny is frequently considered Austen's weakest heroine. Physically frail, she's treated by her uncle's family, with whom she lives at Mansfield Park, as a semi-servant, as a person with no feelings, as a fool. But when pressed to act in a family play, she stands her ground, insisting that she can't and won't act. If her resolution here doesn't exemplify her moral and intellectual strength, her refusal to marry Henry Crawford certainly proves that she's neither weak nor passive. She knows her own heart. Her strength is in her quiet willingness to persist, though others in the novel wrongly see her as obstinate or weak.

✔ **Emma Woodhouse of *Emma*:** Emma Woodhouse must never have read Fordyce or Gregory! She's the boss and as a result suffers from one major problem: Thinking too well of herself. This characteristic makes her a proactive doer, especially as a matchmaker. Refusing to acknowledge mistakes, she faces one humiliating experience after another. Only Mr. Knightley is willing or able to correct her. But even he can't get through to her until she recognizes that she's been her own worst enemy. Her final humiliation doesn't weaken her; instead, it strengthens her because it teaches her about herself.

✔ **Anne Elliot of *Persuasion*:** As Austen's oldest heroine at age 27, Elliot has already experienced the plot of a courtship novel before the action in *Persuasion* begins. Eight years earlier she'd fallen in love with Frederick Wentworth and he with her. But she refused to marry him because she truly felt that marriage at that time in Wentworth's early naval career wouldn't be in his best interests (P 1:4). Yet as time passed, she remained so true to Frederick that she refused a proposal from a gentleman and heir to considerable property that would've at least released her from the unpleasant life she had with her selfish and vain father and older sister at home. Only Anne, "with an elegance of mind and sweetness of character," could've displayed such constancy and emotional strength (P 1:1).

Knowing Your Place and Rank

With Austen's England structured according to class, knowing your place was a required social convention. And your place was quite literal, depending on your age, gender, marital status, and social class. You had to know when to bow, how to enter a room, and to whom you could and could not introduce yourself. But all this protocol was so engrained in people that they didn't have to carry a pocket-sized etiquette book with them. Austen is careful to observe this protocol in her novels: She follows it both seriously and humorously — the latter when a character overdoes protocol in a futile and foolish effort to look genteel and impress others. (For details on the class structure, see Chapter 2.)

Honoring rank when entering a room

Even an act as simple as walking into a dining room was actually a little parade of superiority: People walked in couples, with the gentlemen escorting the ladies whose age, marital status, and social rank determined the walking order. The pecking order, known as precedence, was as follows:

1. **Aristocracy (everyone from the rank of baron and baroness upward) entered before commoners (baronets, knights, and all others without titles).**

2. **Titled commoners (baronets and knights, the lowest of the titles) and their offspring went before untitled folks.**

3. **Married women went before single women.**

Ranking people in your speech

Chapter 2 details the social ranks with which people — and I mean *all* people, from the poorest and most humble to the richest and most aristocratic — in Austen's day were familiar. The ranks were the foundation of the hierarchical society in which they lived. While Austen deals with titled folks as nothing more than secondary characters, when they do appear, other characters know precedence. But even among nontitled characters, knowing rank among commoners and within families was a social necessity. You needed to know when to speak — or not — and how to address someone. Failing to treat people of rank correctly was a major social blunder.

Addressing young ladies

Rank was important in the way young ladies were discussed and/or addressed. In a family of daughters, the eldest is Miss X, and those younger than she are spoken of as Miss Mary X. In *Pride and Prejudice,* for example, Jane Bennet, the eldest, is called Miss Bennet. Her younger sisters, however, would be introduced as Miss Elizabeth Bennet, Miss Mary Bennet, and so forth. Speaking in direct address, Collins recognizes that Miss Bennet (Jane) isn't available for a proposal, and so he proceeds in birth order to propose to the next eldest, "Miss Elizabeth" (PP 1:19).

Talking with friends

Outside the family, only close friends of equal or near equal status use their first names with each other. Thus, Miss Elizabeth Bennet and Miss Lucas (not Miss Charlotte Lucas, because she's the eldest Lucas sister) address each other as Elizabeth and Charlotte. But in *Emma,* though the heroine befriends Harriet Smith, because Harriet is of a lower class (even though Emma believes, on no grounds, that Harriet is a gentleman's daughter!), she addresses Emma as Miss Woodhouse, while Emma calls her Harriet. (If you're wondering why Emma, as the younger of the two Woodhouse sisters, is not called Miss Emma Woodhouse in the novel, remember that her elder sister Isabella is married and out of the house.)

The same naming rule applied to gentlemen. Thus, in *Emma,* Mr. Knightley is called such because he's the elder of the two Knightley brothers. But people speak of his younger brother, though an adult, as Mr. John Knightley.

Notice that close male friends frequently call each other by their last names. Fitzwilliam Darcy calls Charles Bingley "Bingley," instead of Charles, and Bingley calls his friend "Darcy" (PP). Sir John Middleton refers to his old friend "Brandon" (SS). Edmund Bertram calls Henry Crawford "Crawford," and Crawford calls Edmund "Bertram" (MP).

Speaking with married people

Married people of Austen's day often referred to each other in a more formal way. Traditionally the older generation of society stuck to these rules, while the younger couples felt free to break free from the convention. Here are some examples:

- Married women, unless they were very close friends, called each other Mrs. X or Y. In *Persuasion,* the newly acquainted Mrs. Musgrove and Mrs. Croft refer to each other in just that way.

- Even spouses, especially older spouses, call each other "Mr." and "Mrs." because that was traditional. On the opening page of *Pride and Prejudice,* Mrs. Bennet addresses her husband of more than 23 years as "Mr. Bennet."

- In *Sense and Sensibility,* the younger John Dashwood speaks of and to his wife as "Fanny" instead of Mrs. Dashwood.

- Younger people always respected their elders. So in *Sense and Sensibility,* Elinor and Marianne Dashwood, both in their late teens, would never think of calling their London hostess anything other than "Mrs. Jennings."

Conversing with a "courted" lady

A gentleman courting a lady addressed her as Miss X until the courtship had proceeded to the engagement stage. Likewise, a lady called him Mr. X until that same time. In Austen's novels, the only exception to this is Emma, who insists that she'll always call Mr. Knightley "Mr. Knightley," and only use his first name, George, when they take their wedding vows (E 3:17).

For information on using titles like Sir and Lady, see Chapter 2.

Remembering rank in introductions and greetings

To meet and greet properly, those in Austen's time had to remember the following rules:

- **People of a lower social class had to wait to be introduced to those of a higher class, unless the higher class person introduced himself to the lower class person.**

  In *Pride and Prejudice,* Elizabeth Bennet, learning from Mr. Collins that he plans to introduce himself to Darcy, asks him with utter disbelief, "'You are not going to introduce yourself to Mr. Darcy?'" (PP 1:18). Although

Collins replies to her that he "'consider[s]the clerical office [that is, being a clergyman] as equal in point of dignity with the highest rank in the kingdom,'" he's completely wrong. So it's neither a surprise nor a sign of Darcy's snobbery that Darcy, the higher in rank, shows astonishment and "unrestrained wonder" and replies to Collins "with an air of distant civility" when Collins "attack[s]" him. Collins has committed a major social blunder, which embarrasses Elizabeth because Collins is her relation, albeit (thankfully for her) a distant one.

✔ **When not properly introduced, you must be silent.**

In *Northanger Abbey,* when Catherine Morland and Mrs. Allen enter the tea room at a ball, and unacquainted with anyone, they find themselves suddenly at the table of strangers, they feel extremely awkward. Mrs. Allen says to her young companion, "'The gentlemen and ladies at this table look as if they wondered why we came here — we seem to be forcing ourselves into their party'" (NA 1:2). Mrs. Allen isn't being paranoid. But I am pleased to report that the strangers at the table finally share their tea with Catherine and Mrs. Allen. So common sense could intervene with protocol in order to alleviate social awkwardness.

✔ **After you were introduced, you always acknowledged each other when seen.**

This practice went on forever: once an acquaintance, always an acquaintance. When Anne and Admiral Croft walk together in Bath, he quite properly diverts his attention from Anne for a moment to say "How d'ye do" to Captain Brigden, and when Sir Archibald Drew spots the Admiral, he waves and kisses his hand to Anne, mistaking her for Mrs. Croft (P 2:6). Failure to acknowledge an acquaintance, even with a man's slightly tipping his hat or nodding his head, was a breach in conduct. To do this deliberately was to "cut" someone. (See the sidebar at the end of this section for more information on cutting.)

✔ **Bow and curtsey when formally introduced and reserve your handshake for when you want to show a sign of real friendship.**

Shaking hands hadn't yet outdated bowing and curtseying for many occasions. When introduced to someone older or of higher rank, the people of lower rank bowed or curtsied. Gentlemen bowed and ladies curtsied when formally introduced to each other and again when parting. After Darcy hands Elizabeth his letter of explanation at Rosing, he makes "a slight bow" and departs (PP 2:12). In *Sense and Sensibility,* Mr. Palmer bows to the Dashwood ladies upon leaving Barton Cottage (SS 1:19). *Mansfield Park*'s Tom Bertram says that when he met Mrs. Sneyd and her daughters, "'I made my bow in form'" (MP 1:5). Sometimes, a man bowed simply in acknowledgement of someone or something. Such bowing occurs when *Northanger Abbey*'s Henry Tilney bows to Sarah for pointing out the Allens' home to him, or when Mr. Hurst bows to Jane Bennet who is finally well enough to join the others downstairs after spending time ill upstairs (NA 3:1, PP 1:11). Even Elizabeth Bennet answers Darcy "with a slight bow," when he informs her at Pemberley that the Bingleys will soon be arriving (PP 3:1). A gentleman bowed to the lady when asking her to dance (and she curtsied to him) and after escorting her back to her seat. Even if he knew the lady previously, he sometimes bowed when joining her company and when departing from her, as both Mr. Elton and Frank Churchill do (his is specifically "a graceful bow") when they leave Emma (E 1:9, 2:6). But while the bow and curtsey were alive and well, men and women were not bowing and curtseying all the time to each other! Upon entering and leaving rooms, good friends and family members were not expected to be always bowing and curtseying! Common sense prevailed.

While nowadays people shake hands when they're introduced, in Austen's day, handshaking was a sign of real friendship. So Harriet Smith, who has seen Emma Woodhouse several times, but is now invited to Emma's home, is thrilled when at the end of the evening's little party, "Miss Woodhouse had . . . actually shaken hands with her at last!" (E 1:3). When Catherine Morland and Isabella meet and seem to be immediate best friends, they shake hands at parting (NA 1:4). Only gentlemen who knew each other well and were of about the same class shook hands.

Shaking hands with a person of the opposite sex was less frequent and less proper. But when Emma asks Mr. Knightley to shake hands with her both as an old family friend and as a gesture of their making up from an earlier disagreement, she's perfectly polite and proper (E 1:12). Similarly, Marianne Dashwood asks Willoughby, "'Will you not shake hands with me?'" when she unexpectedly encounters him at a London party. This question is perfectly acceptable after they've already spent a lot of time together back at Barton (SS 2:6).

Causing pain by "cutting"

Cutting causes pain in *Sense and Sensibility*. At a London party, Willoughby sees Marianne — the last person he wants to see as he's about to be married to another woman — and so he curtly bows to Marianne and then immediately ignores her (SS 2:6). She can't understand why he has cut her, responding in such a formal and mechanical way after the affection he expressed toward her earlier. Similarly, at the concert in *Persuasion*, Frederick Wentworth, jealous of Mr. William Elliot's attentions to Anne, plans "only to bow" to Anne and "pass on," when Anne's graciousness causes him to stop and chat. Meanwhile, Anne's father and elder sister, who disapprove of Wentworth, finally make, respectively, a "simple acknowledgement of acquaintance" (probably a curt bow) and "a slight curtsey" (P 2:8). Another dutiful acknowledgement of acquaintance occurs in *Pride and Prejudice* when Darcy and Wickham see each other in Meryton. Wickham "after a few moments, touched his hat — a salutation that Mr. Darcy just deigned [forced himself] to return" (PP 1:15). Witnessing this minimal acknowledgement of each other's presence, Elizabeth wonders what "the meaning of it" was: Each nearly cut the other, indicating that they're acquainted (otherwise Wickham wouldn't have touched his hat to Darcy), but obviously not friends anymore.

Conversing pleasantly and politely

Recognizing that everyone has lighter moments of humor and idle talk, society still expected conversation to be substantive or at least intelligent, informed, and if appropriate, clever. But not all of Austen's characters talk politely and pleasantly. In fact, Austen uses their conversation as signs of their personalities and moral values. The following list gives you some examples of how characters converse:

✔ **Speak in poor taste:** When it comes to poor taste, *Sense and Sensibility*'s Mrs. Jennings wins this award hands down. The nosey and somewhat vulgar Mrs. Jennings teasingly presses Elinor for the name of her beau, so Lady Middleton suddenly mentions "'that it rained very hard,'" an interruption for which Elinor is grateful and which she believes proceeds from "her ladyship's great dislike of all such subjects of raillery as delighted her husband and mother" (SS 1:12). Sensing Elinor's discomfort, Colonel Brandon continues to talk of the weather, to Elinor's relief.

✔ **Shock genteel listeners with rude or suggestive comments:** *Mansfield Park*'s Mary Crawford is guilty of just such behavior. Mary puns on the various admirals' ranks in the navy and the sodomy for which the navy was infamous when she says, "'Certainly, my home at my uncle's [and admiral] brought me acquainted with a circle of admirals. Of *Rears* and *Vices*, I saw enough. Now, do not be suspecting me of a pun, I entreat'" (MP 1:6). Hearing this, the highly proper and moral Edmund "looks grave." Austen's giving Mary this pun is the novelist's way of showing Mary's blemished character. To enforce her point, Austen has Edmund ask Fanny in the next chapter, "'But was there nothing in her conversation that struck you Fanny, as not quite right?'" (MP 1:7). The innocent and proper Fanny replies that Mary "'ought not to have spoken of her uncle as she did. . . . An uncle with whom she has been living for so many years, and who . . . treat[s her brother] . . . quite like a son.'" Edmund concurs, not even referring to the bawdy pun that Mary shockingly made.

✔ **Break decorum by being overbearing:** Being pushy, loud, and boastful was also frowned upon, as was monopolizing a conversation or interrupting others. *Emma*'s Mrs. Elton displays all of these characteristics and couldn't be more vulgar:

  • She interrupts Emma.

  • She constantly brags about her brother-in-law and sister's (significantly named Mr. and Mrs. Suckling!) spiffy carriage and estate.

  • She manages always to turn the conversation to herself.

  • She drops hints for compliments.

  • She has a loud voice.

Likewise, Mrs. Jennings (surprise, surprise) has a loud voice and promotes gossip, especially about Colonel Brandon, another *faux pas.* And while Lady Catherine de Bourgh is the daughter of an earl, she brags, monopolizes conversations, speaks like a know-it-all, and even interrupts a conversation occurring across the room between Elizabeth Bennet and Colonel Fitzwilliam.

Exposing Bad Manners

Austen clearly saw beyond appearances. And she expects her readers to be able to do this, too. Sometimes even other characters — often the hero or heroine — are fooled by a person's good manners. But Austen expects us to be on our toes. To help her readers discern those who *appear* good from those who *are* good, she frequently uses manners as a signal.

Listening to the ungrammatical and the insecure

A genteel person, like an educated person today, should speak in a grammatically correct way. So when Austen has grammatical errors tumbling out of a character's mouth, she's warning us that all is not what it seems. For example, when the Steele sisters arrive at Barton in *Sense and Sensibility,* it doesn't take long for either Elinor or the reader to hear that Lucy Steele is poorly bred:

- ✔ Showing Elinor a miniature portrait of Edward in order to discourage Elinor's interest in him and show that he's already taken, Lucy talks of having her own portrait painted for him: "'I am determined to set for it the very first opportunity'" (SS 1:22). Her use of "set" instead of "sit" is an immediate tip that Lucy may well not be a suitable match for the educated Edward.

- ✔ A few lines later, as Lucy attempts to work her charms on Elinor, she says, "'[A]s soon as I saw you, I felt almost as if you was an old acquaintance.'" Again, Lucy's failing to use the correct verb form — "were" instead of "was" — emphasizes her lack of gentility. Even dull characters whose conversations are meaningless speak with correct grammar if they're truly genteel.

Another example from Austen's fiction is Harriet Smith from *Emma.* Harriet Smith is a poor advertisement for the grammar skills she was supposed to learn at Mrs. Goddard's school as seen early in her acquaintance with Emma. She tells Emma that Robert Martin's sisters "'are quite as well educated as me'" (E 1:4). Her lack of grammar prowess is exceeded by her lack of confidence and lack of ability to make a decision. She can neither figure out a riddle nor determine where to send goods purchased at Ford's store without Emma's help. And so it's not surprising that later in the novel Emma can talk Harriet out of marrying the man she really loves because Harriet can't make a decision to save her life. Such characteristics should warn Emma that Harriet isn't the gentleman's daughter that she believes her to be.

Discerning the liars through their charming manners

Frequently, the lesson that Austen's heroines must learn is how to see past a character's manners in order to find the truth about a person. Encountering people who are not really at all what they appear to be is an everyday occurrence.

Jane Austen reflects this experience in *Emma*'s Mr. Knightley in two ways: in terms of differentiating between manners and conduct and between the French word *aimable* (to "have very good manners and be very agreeable") and the English word *amiable,* which he defines as "having delicacy toward the feelings of other people" (E 1:18).

Even Castiglione in *The Book of the Courtier* says that the courtier should be considerate of others' feelings. Those who aren't considerate of others think only of themselves. See the sidebar "Reading your way into manners" earlier in this chapter for more information on Castiglione.

Austen's novels have a number of characters who are what Mr. Knightley would call *aimable* as opposed to *amiable.*

> ✔ **Frank Churchill:** He's the man of the graceful bows. He's a charming conversationalist, a polite companion, and a good dancer. He's just about everything *aimable,* but he draws Jane Fairfax into a secret engagement — a social no-no — because he fears that his adopted mother, who controls his purse strings, won't approve of his marrying a young lady with very little money. He manipulates Jane, his father, his new stepmother, his aunt and uncle, and Emma so that things go his way. And he gossips with Emma about Jane and Mr. Dixon — Jane's friend's young husband — simply to throw Emma off the "Jane and Frank" scent. The gossip flatters Emma's ego, but it's unbecoming to a gentleman. And his insisting that Jane maintains the secrecy of their engagement puts a great emotional and physical strain on her, causing her headaches and tension. Frank lies and makes another lie: He is anything but "frank."

- ✔ **George Wickham:** *Pride and Prejudice*'s Wickham initially wins over Elizabeth Bennet by flattering her ego. On first meeting her, he draws her into a conversation about Darcy right after saying to her, "'I have no right to give my opinion . . . as to his [Darcy's] being agreeable or otherwise. I am not qualified to form one. I have known him too long and too well to be a fair judge'" (PP 1:16). Having said he won't give his opinion of Darcy, Wickham then perverts the truth about Darcy, making Darcy look like a vengeful and unfair man. But Elizabeth at this point is too blinded by prejudice because Darcy hurt her pride to notice the discrepancy between Wickham's talk and behavior. Besides, Wickham is attentive, polite, and friendly — everything that Darcy wasn't when he insulted Elizabeth at the Meryton Assembly.

- ✔ **Henry Crawford:** *Mansfield Park*'s Henry Crawford is also a charmer: He's a persuasive talker, a man of much information, a dancer, a horseback rider, and a polite escort. And when he says he loves Fanny, he plays the role with great flair. But just as he was challenged to attract Maria Bertram's interest when he learned she was an engaged woman and challenged to make "a small hole in Fanny Price's heart" because she seems impervious to his charms, so too, he's challenged to return to the newly married Maria and have an affair with her. He ruins Maria's life.

- ✔ **John Willoughby:** In *Sense and Sensibility,* this character walks out of a fairy tale — at least he appears this way to Marianne Dashwood. After rescuing her from a bad fall and carrying her home, he seems like a knight in armor. He's well read; he knows music and sings; he knows poetry and reads it well aloud; he's polite; he dances up a storm; and he's friendly to all the Dashwood women. And his behavior to Marianne makes her fall in love with him. But his armor isn't shining. It's tarnished by his lies and seduction of another young woman who's pregnant with his child, and he's a financial egoist.

- ✔ **William Elliot:** Austen's charmer in *Persuasion* is the heir to Sir Walter Elliot's baronetcy and estate, and he once ignored Sir Walter, causing a breach in the relationship — a relationship that has no bearing on inheritance laws that make William the heir whether or not he and Sir Walter like each other. When he resurfaces, he's respectful to Sir Walter, courteous to one and all, clever and witty in conversation, and kind and attentive to the heroine, Anne. But William Elliot's whole demeanor is a cover for his plan to keep the widowed Sir Walter from remarrying so that Sir Walter Elliot II Jr. doesn't appear, thus keeping the inheritance from him.

Chapter 13

Following Religion and Morality for Jane Austen and Her Times

*I*n Austen's Georgian England, spiritual life was, for the most part, a private matter. Many clergymen walk in and out of the pages of Austen's novels, but for Austen, herself, she's quiet about her specific religious beliefs and rarely, if ever, preaches to her readers. Austen is a moral writer who uses her characters to comment about human choices — choices that we still make every day.

Members of The Church of England were and are also known as Anglicans. When Austen mentions her characters attending church, you can assume that the place of worship was Anglican. Jane Austen, her characters, her friends, and her gentry neighbors were all Anglican members of The Church of England.

In this chapter, I discuss the evolution of Anglicanism to Austen's time, Austen's brand of Anglicanism, and her presentation of religion and morality (or immorality) in her novels.

Shaping Anglicanism

Austen, herself, was an Anglican and was surrounded by folks who also followed Anglicanism: Her father and two of her brothers were Anglican clergymen, her sister, Cassandra, was engaged to an Anglican cleric, her cousin Edward Cooper, and her niece, Anna, married an Anglican priest. Rumor says that Austen had a brief seaside courtship with an Anglican priest. Being the national religion, Anglicanism was the most practiced religion of the day in England. To understand Jane Austen's religious life and how it affected her writing, you must understand the basics of Anglicanism. (For more on Jane Austen's life, see Chapter 3.)

Forming the Church of England

Remember Henry the VIII (1491–1547, reigned 1509–1547) and his six wives? Instituting the Church of England is how he managed to marry wives numbers two, three, four, five, and six. Henry's main desire was to have absolute authority over the Catholic Church in England so that he could annul his marriage to his first wife in the hope of producing a son and heir with a subsequent wife.

The Anglican Church's organization and theology was really a compromise between Roman Catholicism and non-Calvinist Protestantism.

- The *liturgy* (the service and rituals of worship found in the *Book of Common Prayer*) was said in English rather than Latin. The Austens used the 1662 edition of the *Prayer Book*.

- The Anglican Church retained the medieval Catholic organization.

  - Bishops and archbishops governed the church.

  - Church-taxes (tithes) were paid by landowners.

  - The church contained a parish structure (ecclesiastical districts had their own church and clergy and determined the structure of the local government).

- Anglicanism held that salvation came from faith, good works, free will, and God's grace.

The Test Act, passed in 1673, required holders of public office to take the Holy Eucharist according to the Anglican rite (denying the Roman Catholic belief in transubstantiation that at Holy Communion, when one takes the bread and the wine, these substances miraculously become the body and blood of Christ). This act remained in effect until 1828 and greatly affected English education and politics because to attend Oxford or Cambridge University, to hold a government office, or to be a military officer, you had to be Anglican. Therefore, Anglicanism permeated all walks of public life in Austen's day.

Altering Anglicanism by Austen's day

The Anglican Church was and remains a living structure that witnessed change in its fabric. By the late 17th century

- ✔ The High Church group within Anglicanism emphasized its Catholic or apostolic nature and denied toleration to Dissenters (religious sects that weren't Anglican, such as Methodists). High Churchmen held to the sanctity of the Scriptures and the *Book of Common Prayer*.

- ✔ The Low Church element stressed the Church's Protestantism, tolerated Dissenters, and supported *Latitudinarianism* or latitude within the church.

Latitudinarians respected reason and allied themselves with progress in the intellectual world. They worked to harmonize Scriptures with reason and emphasized practical morality assisted by society's institutions, including both the government and church. This attitude led to a more secularized Church of England in the 18th century and during most of Austen's lifetime. The Church of England had become "enlightened."

Sleeping in on Sunday

For many people in Austen's time, being an Anglican meant being one in name only. People skipped church or slept through the sermon when they did go. The worst offenders in this category were the city dwellers of London. In fact, in Austen's day, many people who lived in the country considered London a place of corruption, while many Londoners deemed the country boring and boorish. The attitude was known as the city versus the country debate.

Attendance was normally better in the country, where Austen's characters resided and where she, herself, lived. But living in the country didn't guarantee attending church or even attending services in one's private chapel. While Austen, as the daughter of a clergyman, went to church every Sunday (two services in one day), she knew that for as many fellow parishioners sitting in the church pews around her, some people only made it to church for Easter and Christmas. She shows that even a family of the gentry, who should be setting an example for their tenants, thinks so little of religion that they have discontinued services in their family chapel. In *Mansfield Park,* a group of characters visits Sotherton, a large country house, which like many other great country houses had its own chapel. At Sotherton, the chapel dates back to 1685–1688, but it has lately fallen to disuse: "'Prayers were always read in it by the domestic chaplain. But the late Mr. Rushworth [i.e., the speaker's late husband] left it off'" (MP 1:9). Hearing this, the worldly Mary Crawford, a Londoner, quips, "'Every generation has its improvements.'" While a case could be made that the Rushworths closed the private chapel in order to attend their parish church, the future Mrs. Rushworth is delighted that the previous generations of Rushworths who saw to the church's construction didn't have it built near the Great House, where they lived: "'The annoyance of the bells must be terrible,'" comments the future Mrs. Rushworth (MP 1:8). Judging from the future Mrs. Rushworth's later adultery, the reader may assume she would've done better to obey the bells and head to church!

Why do we go to church?

Even if Austen's age showed a lax attitude about religion, among the gentry, at least, going to the parish church was something they regularly did on Sundays. When the master and mistress of a country estate and their children and household staff went to church, they set a good example for their tenants. Austen's characters are shown attending church with varying degrees of religious feeling. Many, like Jane Austen and members of her family, went to church with sincere hearts. When Austen doesn't comment in the novel about characters at church, readers can make educated inferences about the attitudes with which her varied characters attend church:

- ✔ *Persuasion*'s Anne Elliot goes to church, and judging from her conduct throughout the novel, she must be thoughtful and devout (P 1:11).

- ✔ *Northanger Abbey*'s Catherine Morland goes to a chapel on Sunday morning while in Bath, and judging from her good and innocent nature, we can assume she devoutly prays (NA 1:4).

- ✔ *Emma*'s Mr. Knightley is active in church business, and as the largest landowner in the area, surely attends church regularly.

- ✔ *Pride and Prejudice*'s Jane and Elizabeth leave Netherfield Park "after morning service" (PP 1:12). It is reasonable to assume that everyone in residence at Netherfield, the Bingleys, the Hursts, and Darcy, attended morning service together. But witnessing these characters' behaviors throughout the novel, readers can assume that Miss Bingley dropped her handkerchief to get Darcy's attention and Mr. Hurst dozed through the sermon!

- ✔ *Persuasion*'s Mary Musgrove attends church just to look at people (P 2:11).

- ✔ Isabella from *Northanger Abbey* undoubtedly prays only in a materially devout way for a rich young man to cross her path (NA 1:4).

- ✔ *Pride and Prejudice*'s Lady Catherine de Bourgh attends church on Sundays, and Mr. Collins, being the clergyman of that church, advises Elizabeth Bennet that she will be impressed when she sees her (PP 2:5). Knowing Lady Catherine's controlling personality, readers can assume she will find something to criticize about everyone else in attendance!

Learning morality at home

For Austen, morality, like charity, began at home. Parents must pay attention to their children and set an example for both manners and morals. (For etiquette in Austen's day, see Chapter 12.) Austen clearly believed that an immoral or a lax home adversely affected children into adulthood:

✔ In *Pride and Prejudice,* Austen says that Mr. Collins's "self-conceit" and "weak head" are the result of being raised by "an illiterate and miserly father," who raised his son under "subjection" (PP 1:15).

✔ When *Mansfield Park*'s Edmund Bertram seeks Fanny's advice about Mary Crawford, who says she will never marry a clergyman, he blames "'the influence of her former companions'" for "'the tinge of wrong'" and "'evil'" that frequently occur in her speech. Fanny replies simply, "'The effect of education,'" and Edmund agrees, blaming Mary's immoral uncle ("a man of vicious conduct," who brought his mistress into his home as soon as his wife died) and ill-used aunt for injuring and tainting Mary's mind (MP 1:4, 2:9).

For more information on failed parents, see "Lust: Failing parents of fallen daughters" later in this chapter.

Assessing Austen's Anglicanism

Although dissenting religious sects grew in England during the 17th and 18th centuries, the Anglican Church remained the national religion and had the highest membership. With the Anglican parish system determining the structure of local government, even non-Anglicans were influenced by the Church of England. In Jane Austen's lifetime (1775–1817), just about the entire gentry and aristocracy were Anglicans. Even the wealthier people in trade, manufacturing, commerce, and the elite professions were Anglican. After all, with the Test Act in effect, what other way was there to get ahead? (For information on the Test Act, see "Forming the Church of England" earlier in this chapter.)

As the daughter of an Anglican clergyman, Jane Austen absorbed her father's moderate Anglicanism. The Rev. Mr. George Austen's Anglicanism balanced salvation through faith, good works, and God's grace, along with attention to and belief in the *Book of Common Prayer* and the Bible and the exercise of practical common sense, reason, and prudence. Jane believed in the importance of attending church and taking Communion. She lived at a time when the national church promoted patriotism. And with two brothers in the Royal Navy during the Napoleonic Wars, she was certainly patriotic. Her beliefs are supported in her brother Henry's "Biographical Notice" of his late sister: "She was thoroughly religious and devout. . . . On serious subjects she was well-instructed, both by reading and meditation, and her opinions accorded strictly with those of our Established Church" (RWC, 5:8).

Reviewing Austen's Clerical Characters

Part of the public's casual attitude about church (see the section "Sleeping in on Sunday," earlier in this chapter) may well be the result of the informal way clergymen were selected. Young men of the gentry, especially younger sons who wouldn't inherit the family estate, needed genteel professions, and the role of clergyman provided that. Whether or not young men felt "called" to serve, becoming a clergyman was a social and career move. For more information about the clergy, check out Chapter 10.

A priest didn't have to live in the parish that he served, meaning he could delegate duties to his curate assistant, who made much less of a living than the priest. Therefore, with the priest having others do his work, he wasn't a regular presence in the lives of his parishioners.

In the period in which Austen wrote, novels didn't really delve into a character's spiritual awakening or epiphany. Overt moralizing and preaching in novels belonged to later writers in the Victorian period (1837–1901): Charles Kingsley's *Alton Locke,* George Eliot's *Adam Bede,* and *Silas Marner,* Anthony Trollope, and even Charles Dickens. Why not in Georgian England, Austen's period? Go back to the first paragraph of this chapter! (Okay, you don't have to turn pages: I wrote at the beginning of the chapter that in Austen's day, religion was a private affair.)

None of Austen's fictional clergymen expressed any spiritual beliefs or appeared among parishioners in the pages of the novels. When *Sense and Sensibility*'s Edward Ferrars tells Elinor of the various professions open to him, he mentions a preference for the church, but lists it along with the law and the army without stating any reason for preferring the church (SS 1:19). And he only goes to Oxford to be ordained after his mother disinherits him so that he'll be in position to try to secure a church living so he can marry Lucy and have a parsonage in which to live (SS 2:2). For more on church livings, flip back to Chapter 10.

While many sincere, exemplary clergymen existed — including Jane Austen's father — Austen's novels show young men entering and practicing the clerical professional with about as much spirit as they would show entering law school or practicing the law. But of course, she includes some exceptions. Jane Austen implies that the following young men will do fine as clergymen:

✓ **Edmund Bertram:** *Mansfield Park*'s Edmund Bertram receives a church living from his father, who has two of them to bestow. He's the only one of Austen's clergyman characters to speak about the role of a clergyman:

- • In large cities like London (the old city versus the country debate arises here!), he says, "'The clergy are lost in the crowds of their parishioners'" (MP 1:9). So a clergyman's private life is not witnessed by his flock. Edmund doesn't like that as explained in the next quotation.

- • Clerics, he says, have the "'duty to teach and recommend'" good principles and Christian doctrine: "'[I]t will . . . be every where found, that as the clergy are, or are not what they ought to be, so are the rest of the nation.'" So Edmund sees the ideal clergy as models of moral behavior.

✔ Edmund's father, though not a clergyman himself, also speaks of the role of the priest and his parishioners:

- • "'A parish has wants and claims, which can be known only by a clergyman constantly resident'" (MP 2:7).

- • Determined to live in his country parsonage, Edmund fully understands his father's saying that if a parish priest "'does not live among his parishioners and prove himself by constant attention their well-wisher and friend, he does very little either for their good or his own.'"

✔ **Henry Tilney:** *Northanger Abbey*'s clergyman, Henry Tilney, holds a church living that is a gift from his father. Henry doesn't always live in his parsonage, which was common. He's probably paying his assistant to carry out his everyday work:

- • Visiting the sick, elderly, and poor

- • Providing spiritual counsel to his parishioners

- • Offering religious instruction to the children of his parish

- • Finding help for the poor and hungry

Henry appears more frequently at home or on the ballroom floor than he does in the church — though his intelligence and integrity suggest that he's a good priest to his flock when he's in residence.

Aside from the younger sons who receive church livings from their fathers or friends, men who didn't have such connections could buy livings from patrons who wanted to sell them, especially if the patrons needed the money. Another way of securing a living was for the clergyman to beg, plead, charm, flatter, or in any other way finesse a living from a patron. Austen gives no indication that any of the three clergymen who bought or flattered to secure their livings — Grant, Collins, or Elton — are from genteel families. And none is particularly promising as a clergyman the way the genteel Edmund Bertram or Henry Tilney are:

✔ **Grant is gluttonous.** As soon as he is introduced in *Mansfield Park,* we learn that "Dr. Grant was very fond of eating" (1:3). At the end of the novel, he dies of "an apoplexy" caused by stuffing himself at "three great institutionary dinners in one week" (MP 3:17). Sir Thomas Bertram sells the better of two livings at Mansfield Park to Dr. Grant (a Doctor of Divinity) to help defray the expenses of his wastrel elder son. Grant leaves only when he gets a clerical position at London's famed Westminster Abbey. During his residency at Mansfield Park, his eating is discussed, while we learn nothing of his preaching or other clerical duties. But gluttony is one of the Seven Deadly Sins!

✔ **Collins is stupid and self-important.** Shortly after meeting *Pride and Prejudice*'s Mr. Collins, we read that "Mr. Collins was not a sensible man, and the deficiency of nature had been but little assisted by education" (PP 1:15). When he speaks, he utters "pompous nothings." Collins undoubtedly flattered Lady Catherine when "A fortunate chance had recommended him to Lady Catherine de Bourgh when the living of Hunsford was vacant" (PP 1:15).

✔ **Elton is egotistical and cruel.** Angry that Emma had supposed him in love with Harriet Smith, the illegitimate daughter of "somebody," *Emma*'s Mr. Elton later refuses to dance with Harriet, who is the only young woman without a partner (E 1:3, 3:2). As he strides away, "smiles of high glee passed between him and his wife." Both he and Mrs. Elton enjoy seeing Harriet humiliated. Granted, early in the novel he heads to visit a poor and ailing family, but he turns around to accompany Emma, who has already been there (E 1:10). Some priest! Austen gives us no idea how *Emma*'s Mr. Elton secured the living of Highbury — though flattering someone is in character for Elton, too.

The single clergyman in Austen's fiction who is said to have "zealously" performed "all the duties of his office" "for more than forty years" is *Persuasion*'s Dr. Shirley — though in the novel, he has reached a point where he has grown "too infirm" to continue (P 1:9). This is all we know about him. But his presence certainly shows that Austen knew good, devoted clergymen as well as careless, self-involved clergy.

Serving Up the Seven Deadly Sins

Austen's realism as a novelist included moral realism. Knowing human nature as well as she did, she showed a world that for all its etiquette, decorum, and tea drinking was also a fallen world. At age 20, while visiting Bath and attending a ball in the Upper Rooms, she wrote to her sister, "I am proud to say that I have a very good eye at an Adultress" (Letter, May 12–13, 1801). Yet even with her eye for picking up on the sins of the day, she doesn't sermonize to her readers in her novels.

Instead, Austen writes about sin through examples in her novels without stating her opinions of the sin. Her readers are to come to their own conclusions about moral and immoral behaviors. Through Austen's background in the church and her keen insight into her characters, she deals with each of the "seven deadly sins," as portrayed in the Bible, in her fiction.

Pride: Thinking you're the cat's meow

Proverbs 16:18 states: "Pride goeth before destruction, and an haughty spirit before a fall" (King James Version, which is the Bible edition Austen knew). Austen sharply discerns between the good pride that's healthy self-confidence and the bad pride that encompasses an excessive ego and self-importance. Some of Austen's self-important characters find themselves thwarted, while others learn from having mistaken pride or too much pride.

Pride and Prejudice immediately comes to mind when speaking of pride. The novel doesn't present the two characteristics of the title as a simple dichotomy, with — as the 1940 film version of the novel emphasized — Darcy representing pride and Elizabeth prejudice. On the contrary, they both have their share of pride and prejudice. For example:

✔ The proud Darcy hurts Elizabeth's pride when he says she isn't pretty enough to ask for a dance.

✔ The proud Elizabeth, in the sense of having healthy self-esteem, doesn't become weak in the knees and submissive when introduced to the boorishly proud Lady Catherine de Bourgh, who presumes to know more than everyone and whose presumption leads to outright rudeness.

✔ Lady Catherine's pride in her noble ancestry (her father was an earl) takes a real beating when Elizabeth refuses to follow her orders not to marry her nephew, Darcy. Not only do Lady Catherine's plans for Darcy to marry *her* daughter amount to nothing, but also her interference leads to Darcy's having "hope" that Elizabeth will accept his second proposal.

✔ In Darcy's second proposal, he admits to Elizabeth that her earlier disapproval of his ungentlemanly ways "'properly humbled'" him. But Elizabeth has also been humbled: She believed Wickham's lies about Darcy only to learn that she'd been deliberately misled by Wickham's charm. "'How humiliating is this discovery,'" she says to herself, blaming her own "'vanity'" (PP 2:13).

Emma also presents another example of pride. Emma Woodhouse is also humiliated — not just once, but several times — because Austen claims that Emma has "the power of having rather too much her own way, and a disposition to think a little too well of herself" (E 1:1). Emma's ultimate humiliation leads to her learning that she has been "totally ignorant of her own heart" in denying that she loved Mr. Knightley as someone more than a brother. She grows "ashamed of every sensation but the one revealed to her — her affection for Mr. Knightley. Every other part of her mind was disgusting" (E 3:11).

The pride of minor characters is also appropriately demolished. For example, in *Sense and Sensibility*

✔ Mrs. Ferrars thinks she can use her power over her son Edward's inheritance to force him to marry a rich young woman, whose only attraction is the money she'll bring to the marriage. But Edward sticks with the poor Lucy out of duty and ends up with the less poor (but in now way rich!) Elinor out of love. Likewise, Mrs. Ferrars's younger son fails to gain the Morton money for the family because he winds up marrying the poor Lucy Steele just to spite his mother! Finally, Lucy uses her manipulative skills to worm her way into Mrs. Ferrars's favor, despite her pride.

Greed: Wanting it all (and then some)

Greed is unpleasant and frequently inflicts pain on the less fortunate in Austen's novels.

✔ ***Sense and Sensibility:*** Fanny Dashwood is a greedy woman. While her husband has inherited wealth from his mother, and she has wealth from her family, she convinces him to neglect his father's deathbed wish to use some of the money and estate he just inherited to care for his poor half-sisters and stepmother and give them nothing (SS 1:2). Fanny Dashwood won't part with a shilling for her sisters-in-law.

✔ ***Northanger Abbey:*** This novel is full of greedy people:

• Isabella dumps Catherine's brother in an attempt to secure a richer man. The money-hungry Isabella winds up losing both men.

• General Tilney is misled by the lying John Thorpe into believing that Catherine is an heiress. Thus, he encourages the romance between her and his younger son, Henry. But the General evicts her from the Abbey when he believes Thorpe's new lies that Catherine's family is deeply in debt. Henry, however, refuses to give up Catherine, who's neither very poor (much to his father's relief) nor very wealthy (much to his father's dismay).

In *Northanger Abbey,* Austen takes potshots at the Gothic novels — books full of mystery and horrors — that were highly popular at that time. She paid particular attention to Ann Radcliffe's bestseller, *The Mysteries of Udolpho,* which Catherine reads voraciously and which leads her to suspect murder and torture where there is none. Radcliffe was known for writing "the rationalized

Gothic," where all the seemingly supernatural horrors have natural, reasonable explanations that she holds back until the end of the book. In *The Mysteries of Udolpho,* the villainous Montoni, for all his threats, turns out to be nothing more than a greedy man who wants the heroine's inheritance from his late wife, her aunt. So Montoni and General Tilney are cut from the same Gothic cloth: both are greedy!

Lust: Failing parents of fallen daughters

Some people think of Austen as a gentle, genteel, and ever-ladylike writer. But she was a realist who clearly knew the world. And she uses her worldly knowledge to add to the moral realism of her novels, especially relating to lust. Austen presents parents whose lax upbringing of their children negatively affects their children as adults:

✔ *Mansfield Park:* Coming from a home where parents didn't pay serious attention to them, the Bertram sisters were educated and bred to show good manners. But Maria and Julia are "entirely deficient in the less common acquirements of self-knowledge, generosity, and humility" (MP 1:2).

  • Maria, the elder, becomes an adulteress.

  • Julia elopes with a young man who "had not much to recommend him beyond the habits of fashion and expense, and being the younger son of a lord with a tolerable independence" (he has money to his name) (MP 1:13).

  • The girls' mother and father weren't involved in their education, moral or otherwise.

  • Their father, Sir Thomas, is a great spokesman for morality and prudence. But he's so distant from his daughters that they're uncomfortable talking with him.

  • Their mother pushes all her maternal responsibility to her sister who's selfish herself and spoils her nieces.

Sir Thomas Bertram punishes his adulterous daughter by providing a minimally sufficient income for her; he also sends her to live "in another country [county or borough] — remote and private" (MP 3:17). There Maria, who "had destroyed her own character," and her Aunt Norris reside as each other's "mutual punishment."

✔ *Pride and Prejudice:* The character of Lydia flees and lives with Wickham while they are unmarried. Both Mr. and Mrs. Bennet are responsible for Lydia's immoral behavior with Wickham:

- Mrs. Bennet overindulges Lydia and even encourages her in chasing the militia officers, announcing that she, too, "'liked a red coat myself very well — and indeed so I do still at my heart'" (PP 1:7).

- When Lydia begs to be allowed to go on her ill-fated trip to Brighton, her mother supports her, saying, "'A little sea-bathing would set me up for ever'" (PP 2:18).

- Mr. Bennet, for all his witty charm, also shoulders responsibility for Lydia's actions. Discussing her sister's disappearance with her Aunt Gardiner, Elizabeth bemoans "'my father's . . . indolence and the little attention he has ever seemed to give to what was going forward in his family. . .'" (PP 3:5).

- Spoiled by her mother and ignored by her father, Lydia shows she is, indeed, "'so lost to every thing but love of [Wickham], as to consent to live with him" out of wedlock (PP 3:5).

- Lydia, later married to Wickham, returned home and felt neither shame nor guilt for her earlier behavior, and her actions add to her poor reputation. She proudly shows off her marriage ring, adding pride to her sin of lust.

✔ *Sense and Sensibility:* Eliza Williams, the unmarried ward of Colonel Brandon, becomes pregnant with Willoughby's child (SS 2:9). In this case, Brandon sends his ward into the country to have her child as a protective measure, so Eliza will be away from the sneers of those who know her and the snares of other men, who, like Willoughby, indulge in irresponsible sexual behavior. Eliza's moral fall repeats that of her mother, Eliza Brandon (the colonel's sister-in-law), who had her daughter out of wedlock. Eliza Brandon died, poverty-stricken and shamed when her daughter was just an infant. Society would see her daughter's fall as an example of "like mother, like daughter."

Anger: Forgetting to hold your tongue

Austen's angriest characters are women, and they're ladies of wealth or at least financial comfort and position. But material comfort doesn't promise happiness. And these women show their unhappiness by lashing out at others:

✔ **Aunt Norris:** Aunt Norris is an active child abuser, who continues to abuse the heroine of *Mansfield Park,* Fanny Price, into her young adulthood. Whether sending Fanny to walk repeatedly between Mansfield Park and her home in the hot sun, stipulating that Fanny's room is never to have its fireplace lighted (even in the coldest weather), or verbally humiliating Fanny in front of others by telling her that she'll always be the "lowest and last," Aunt Norris frightens Fanny and treats her with unreasonable cruelty.

- ✔ **Mrs. Ferrars:** In *Sense and Sensibility,* when Mrs. Ferrars can't convince her elder son, Edward, to marry the wealthy Miss Morton, she becomes so angry that she cuts him off completely — financially and personally.

- ✔ **Lady Catherine de Bourgh:** In *Pride and Prejudice,* Lady Catherine de Bourgh plans to unite the wealthy de Bourgh estate with the even wealthier Pemberley estate by having the heiress to the first (Lady Catherine's daughter) marry her cousin, the owner of the other (Darcy). Greed again rears its ugly head! Lady Catherine's anger at Elizabeth's possibly marrying her nephew Darcy leads her to threatening and insulting Elizabeth, talking *at* her, and telling her that she'll pollute Pemberley (PP 3:14). Catherine may be a Lady, but she's no lady.

Gluttony: Tipping the scales

Gluttony in any area (money, power, or control) is the opposite of moderation: gluttony is excess and out of balance. We normally associate gluttony with eating. While Austen never offers dieting advice, she does mention two characters, in particular, who are heavy:

- ✔ **Mr. Rushworth:** Austen describes Rushworth of *Mansfield Park* as "a heavy young man, with not more than common sense" (MP 1:4). Other characters see him as "stupid," "inferior," and "ignorant" (MP 1:4, 2:3).

- ✔ **Mr. Collins:** Collins, of *Pride and Prejudice,* is "a tall, heavy-looking young man," with the "Self-conceit of a weak head" (PP 1:13, 15).

Physical size, of course, has no connection with mental ability. But Austen suggests that there is one for Collins and Rushworth.

Envy: Casting a jealous eye

Jealousy in Austen's novels most clearly appears in matters of love. That was also true in Shakespeare's *Othello,* where jealousy is called a "green-eyed monster" (III:3:1816–1817). Indeed, the jealous can become monsters!

- ✔ **Lucy Steele:** When Lucy meets Elinor and gets a reaction out of her by mentioning the Ferrars family, Lucy is "eyeing Elinor attentively," giving her a "side glance," and "fixing her eyes upon Elinor" (SS 1:22). Jealous of Elinor as competition for Edward Ferrars, who has clearly mentioned Elinor favorably to her, Lucy, "her sharp little eyes full of meaning," forces Elinor into a game of mutual hypocrisy that causes Elinor to exert painful self-control (SS 2:2).

✔ **Miss Bingley:** She shows her jealousy of Elizabeth as a competitor for Darcy — a competition of which Elizabeth is completely unaware as she claims to hate Darcy (PP 1:18). (But as one of my students reminded our Austen class a few years ago, the opposite of love is not hate; it's indifference!) Miss Bingley consistently makes cutting remarks about Elizabeth to Darcy, and they frequently backfire. For example, at Sir William Lucas's party, Darcy finds himself admiring Elizabeth's face, particularly how "it was rendered uncommonly intelligent by the beautiful expression of her dark eyes" (PP 1:6). Miss Bingley comes over to him, remarking on the dullness of the evening and asking what he has been contemplating. He replies, "'I have been meditating on the very great pleasure which a pair of fine eyes in the face of a pretty woman can bestow.'" Miss Bingley "immediately fixe[s] her eyes on his face," and asks to whom he's referring. "'Miss Elizabeth Bennet,'" is his firm answer. You can almost "see" the fire leaping from Miss Bingley's eyes.

Sloth: Being a bad parent

Sloth and unawareness can lead to unpleasant, even dangerous results. One duty of parents was to instill and model moral behavior for their children. Austen focuses on a few instances of lazy and neglectful parents who fail to meet their responsibilities to their daughters.

✔ Mr. Bennet withdraws from his family into his library so that he can escape them. As an absentee father in his own home, he hasn't exercised parental duty in raising his daughters, particular the three younger Bennet sisters. We can speculate that he was a more involved, dutiful father when the two elder girls, Jane and Elizabeth, were growing up. For they are mature and responsible young women. But he clearly neglected the three younger daughters, Mary, Kitty, and Lydia. The youngest, Lydia, who ran off with Wickham, certainly needed more guidance from both of her parents.

✔ While Mr. Bennet withdraws to his library, *Mansfield Park*'s Lady Bertram reclines on the sofa in the drawing room, either sewing useless fringe or dozing off. As noted earlier in this chapter, she played no part in the raising of her daughters, leaving that to her obnoxious sister, the angry Aunt Norris, who spoiled her nieces. Lady Bertram's laziness and lack of involvement extend to Aunt Norris's bad treatment of their niece, Fanny Price.

Outweighing the Bad by Doing Good

Austen was as aware of the goodness in people as she was of their flaws — mental or moral. Charity to one's neighbor was an important facet of Georgian life, and it was especially important to the gentry. For the master and mistress of the estate were to exercise *noblesse oblige* — the idea that people born into the nobility or upper social classes must behave in an honorable, generous way toward those less privileged.

Jane Austen took care of the poor. She and her sister sewed clothes for them, so in turn, Austen would want to create characters who look out for the poor and ailing, too. Austen shows this most visibly in *Emma:*

- ✔ For all of Emma's self-centeredness, she visits the poor and sick in her village and sincerely provides comfort, as well as soup.

- ✔ She sends pork from her family's farm to the Bates ladies, who live in genteel poverty.

- ✔ Likewise, Mr. Knightley sends the Bates family apples from his farm — even his last basket instead of keeping the apples for himself — and uses his carriage for a party just so Miss Bates can ride to and from the party in it.

Persuasion's Anne Elliot is also kind to the less fortunate. In spite of her egotistical father's objections, she visits and cheers an old school friend from her youth, Mrs. Smith, who is not only "widowed, and poor," but also suffers from "a severe rheumatic fever which finally settling in her legs, had made her, for the present, a cripple" (P 2:5). Mrs. Smith, herself, while confined to bed, knits items that are sold to the rich to benefit the poor.

Austen also praises *Pride and Prejudice*'s Darcy for his charity. His housekeeper tells Elizabeth and the Gardiners that he, like his late father, is "'affable to the poor'" and the "'best landlord, and the best master.'" She goes on to say, "'There is not one of his tenants or servants but what will give him a good name'" (PP 3:1).

Part IV
Enjoying Austen and Her Influence Today

The 5th Wave   By Rich Tennant

"Here's a lesser known Jane Austen novel that you might enjoy. It's about carpentry and lawn care, called 'Fence and Fencibility'."

In this part . . .

*P*oor Jane Austen! She didn't live long enough to earn royalties on all the films, television shows, stage productions, and books that are either based on or inspired by her novels. This part surveys the Austen-related productions, in both print (literary classics and pop culture) and other media. Chapter 14 even gives you tips on reading Austen.

Chapter 14

Reading Jane Austen

. . . .

In This Chapter

▶ Studying each of Austen's six major novels

▶ Forming a study group and having some discussion

. . . .

Many of you reading this book read Austen's novels for pure pleasure, and that's just fine. But Austen put a lot of effort into her writing, and she deals with much more than courtship. So this chapter suggests some ways of approaching each of the six novels so that perhaps you can get more out of them than you have. The nice thing about this is that there are no papers and no grades!

Keep in mind that readers come to Austen's novels at different ages and with different life experiences. Speaking for myself as a lifelong Austen reader, I can say that as a teenager, I read her books for their romantic stories. But as I got older and became more informed about my own world and Austen's, I became more aware of her as a social satirist. I found myself laughing with her more than I did as a teenager.

So as you — yes, you! — read Austen, you will approach and come away from her with different reactions. But her novels are always vivid and meaningful. For this reason, she's a classic.

Reading Northanger Abbey

Northanger Abbey shows its early place in her writing because at the end of Volume 1, Chapter 5, Austen defends the novel as a form of literature. It's as if she has to reinforce for both her readers and herself that novels are quality literature. This book is the only time that she ever defends her chosen form of literature, the novel.

Knowing the background

Austen's writing this novel, first as *Susan* and then as *Catherine*, undoubtedly came about as her reaction to the popular "Gothic novels" of her day — fiction that set a young heroine in scary, mysterious circumstances with ghosts and spirits, or what seemed like ghosts and spirits, making noises and frightening her as she loses sleep in a dark room with no candle or fire (both have been blown out) and no lock on her door. The most popular Gothic novel and the one that most influences Austen's reading heroine, Catherine Morland, is Ann Radcliffe's *The Mysteries of Udolpho*.

Radcliffe's *Udolpho* deals with a young lady, Emily, who's orphaned and compelled to live with her aunt, who marries the striking, but scary, Montoni. He takes his new wife and her impressionable niece to his fortresslike castle of Udolpho high in the Italian mountains. He's accompanied by a gang of threatening-looking thugs. Hearing all kinds of strange noises, Emily snoops around the castle, scares herself, and spends many sleepless nights. After reading several hundred pages, the reader discovers that Montoni is after Emily's inheritance, which the aunt has left to Emily. Montoni tries to scare Emily into signing papers that will turn her inheritance over to him, but Emily doesn't budge. She's finally saved, and Montoni's plan fails.

Linking Northanger Abbey to Udolpho

Not only does Catherine Morland love scaring herself by reading *The Mysteries of Udolpho*, but Henry Tilney, who has also read the book — his "'hair standing on end the whole time,'" as he jokes — teases Catherine on their way to Northanger Abbey by taking some of Emily's Udolpho adventures and suggesting that Catherine may experience something similar at the Abbey. But this is only the most obvious way Austen uses Radcliffe's book in her novel.

While Catherine expects to find that the severe General Tilney, father of her friends Henry and Eleanor, is Montoni-like in having locked up his wife and deprived her of care, she learns that the general is actually only greedy: He thinks Catherine is rich and dismisses her from the Abbey when he incorrectly believes that she's a poor fortune-hunter. But in reviewing *The Mysteries of Udolpho*, you see that Montoni — though a murderer — is also greedy. So Catherine's suspicions that the general is like Montoni aren't really that far off the mark.

Watching Catherine learn

Naïve and inexperienced, Catherine goes to Bath with family friends, Mr. and Mrs. Allen. Bath was the popular spa city where people went not only for their health but also to introduce their marriage-aged children to the whirling social life and perhaps to meet a future spouse. More interested in fashion than Catherine, Mrs. Allen means well, but she's a poor guide for Catherine. But Catherine has good instincts. And so she doesn't allow herself to be guided by the dangerous yet attractive Isabella Thorpe into doing things that aren't right, such as breaking promises. Likewise, Catherine always senses that General Tilney's children are uncomfortable around their father (something is strange about the general). Catharine is, of course, correct, but she learns it the hard away — by being suddenly sent home — and not knowing until later how misled the general's greed has allowed him to be.

Catherine's coming to learn more about herself and others begins a pattern in Austen's writing. Her heroines achieve better self-knowledge, as well as better knowledge of the world through their mistakes.

Hearing the narrator's irony in Northanger Abbey

The *narrator* of a novel is the voice that tells the story. In this early novel Austen speaks quite overtly in her own voice — for example, in her defense of the novel as a literary form or genre. Elsewhere in the book, Austen is unusually heavy-handed in her narration, dripping with *verbal irony,* which is when you say something, but mean something else. Here's an example of verbal irony from *Northanger Abbey:*

> Where people wish to attach, they should always be ignorant. To come with a well-informed mind, is to come with an inability of administering to the vanity of others, which a sensible person would always wish to avoid. A woman especially, if she have the misfortune of knowing any thing, should conceal it as well as she can. (NA 1:14)

This passage occurs when Catherine and the Tilneys are walking together, and the Tilneys begin to praise the scenery, using language that shows their familiarity with art. Catherine feels "ashamed of her ignorance," and the implication is that she will defer to the Tilneys' views. But does Austen really want females to be ignorant? While Doctors Fordyce and Gregory, discussed in Chapter 12, prescribed female ignorance as a way of catching a husband, Austen certainly doesn't uphold this view in her other novels. So what's with Catherine? And what's with Austen? Austen is being ironic.

Readers should contemplate another irony in the novel. Catherine is Austen's most inexperienced heroine and one of her two youngest heroines at age 17. (*Sense and Sensibility*'s Marianne Dashwood is the other young heroine.) And Henry Tilney is her most teacher-ish hero, ready to instruct Catherine, who thinks that he's always right. After all, he's "about four or five and twenty," and a university graduate (NA 3:2). But by the end of the book, it turns out

that Henry is wrong in not suspecting his father of greed, and Catherine is
right in sensing a villain lurking within the general — a villain who allowed
himself to be duped by another character's conflicting stories about
Catherine Morland. Who's the most ignorant person now? Not Catherine! So
much for the general.

Reading Sense and Sensibility

Sense and Sensibility is one of those titles that lead a reader to think, at first
glance, that these two traits are going to be opposed by two characters.
Sense is common sense, practicality, intelligence, and reason. *Sensibility,* in
Austen's time, meant relying on one's feelings as a guide to behavior, as a
guide to truth. Is Austen preparing to advocate one over the other?

Erring with either sense or sensibility

The two Dashwood sisters, Elinor and Marianne, are sometimes seen as representing sense (Elinor) and sensibility (Marianne). But each heroine has
some of each trait, and each heroine suffers by letting one trait dominate.
Austen shows us that neither sense nor sensibility is the right way to go. A
person needs to be balanced.

Elinor's sense

Elinor seems to be the one with sense:

- ✔ She advises her mother about saving money and living economically.

- ✔ She advises Marianne to reject Willoughby's present of a horse on the
  grounds of its expense.

- ✔ She knows how to play the social game and is always polite, responsive,
  and pleasant, even to those who try her patience, because she sees that
  practical good sense is the best way to achieve the "general civility" that
  she desires all to practice.

Yet her sense that Edward Ferrars loves her and not Lucy causes her great
emotional pain because Edward has neither the sense nor the sensibility to
come out and tell his true feelings and personal circumstances. Elinor has
strong feelings, "but she know how to govern them" — by sense (SS 1:1). But
with Edmund's odd behavior — he hangs around her, but looks gloomy and
acts like a friend, rather than a boyfriend — Elinor still maintains a calm exterior. Puzzled, Elinor arrives at a conclusion drawn from common sense:
Edward's behavior is the result of his mother's pressuring him to marry a

wealthier young lady. But Elinor's sense takes a real hit when the manipulative and money-hungry Lucy Steele confides in Elinor that she, Lucy, has been secretly engaged to Edward for four years. No wonder Edward's behaving oddly!

Elinor's stiff upper lip gets only stiffer from acting as though she's not in love with Edward and doesn't care about his engagement to Lucy. Instead of looking gloomy and hurt, Elinor puts up a good front: She acts coolly and behaves reasonably, as if all is well. She shows no emotion and tells no one of her feelings. Forced into a role of constant game-playing by and with Lucy, Elinor doesn't make sense look very appealing. While emotionally certain that Edward truly loves her and is tired of Lucy — this is Elinor's sensibility at work — her senses show her that everything conspires to get Lucy and Edward married:

- He keeps the engagement even though his mother disinherits him for it.

- Lucy sticks to him like glue, even though he has been disinherited (after all, his little money is far more than she has!).

- He unexpectedly gets a church living with a house from Colonel Brand on — when it looks like nothing will be available for him — that will enable him to save money to marry Lucy.

Yet this makes no sense to her: She can see that Edward is trying to get out of his Lucy entanglement.

Marianne's sensibility

Marianne uses her feelings (sensibility) as her guide.

- She flaunts convention and decorum, going off with Willoughby for an unchaperoned carriage ride to explore a house where she has no permission to be.

- She insists she has done no wrong because her feelings would've told her if her actions were incorrect.

- Her senses tell her that Willoughby loves her:

  - He pays attention only to her.

  - He asks for a clipping of her hair as a love token.

  - He likes everything she likes.

  - He acts like a hero of sensibility, a man of feeling who adores her.

What makes more sense than to think he's truly caring, based on such evidence? But Willoughby uses a selfish sense to guide his actions. He deserts Marianne because his financial sense tells him he needs to marry money. His sense of self-preservation also told him to desert the pregnant Eliza Williams so he wouldn't get stuck with her and their baby. If Willoughby's sense dictated such behavior, can sense be all that desirable? Meanwhile, Marianne, unable to find meaning in Willoughby's conduct and unwilling to control her emotions with even a little sense, is left to suffer: Her feelings betray her body, and she slips into a deeper and deeper depression until she nearly dies from a resulting infection brought on by an extended period of neither sleeping nor eating. Willoughby's cruelty to her makes no sense for a long time, and so her sensibilities go on overload, weakening her body. Marianne believed her feelings for Willoughby and Willoughby's feelings for her. But feelings turned out to be an unreliable guide without some sense to temper them.

Just as Elinor suffers from repressing her sensibilities with too much sense, so Marianne suffered from refusing to let any sense temper her sensibilities.

Seeing other characters' sense and/or sensibility

Elinor and Marianne aren't the only characters in the novel to get tangled up in sense and sensibility.

- ✔ At the opening of the novel, Uncle Dashwood disinherits the Dashwood females and gives his estate to a 4-year-old grandnephew. Now is that sense or sensibility?

  - On the one hand, the uncle was charmed by the child's antics (sensibility).

  - On the other hand, the uncle undoubtedly sees that leaving his estate to the little boy ensures male Dashwood occupancy for several more generations (sense).

  Similarly, when Fanny and John Dashwood assist each other in arguing away John's promise to his father to assist his stepmother and sisters, are they using sense or sensibility? Certainly, Fanny's financial sense is at work as she pressures her husband's sensibility in saving everything for their little boy.

- ✔ Mrs. Ferrars disinherits Edward, her elder son and heir, because he honors his engagement to Lucy: Is that Mrs. Ferrars's sense at work in protecting the Ferrars money from a gold-digger or her emotional reaction of anger prompting her to punish Edward monetarily?

Neither sense nor sensibility is always right. Either can lead people to cruelty, greed, selfishness, or goodness. The two characteristics need to be balanced so that neither is perverted by the other.

Reading Pride and Prejudice

This novel's title is another one that suggests that two traits are going to be opposed and represented by two different characters — usually seen as Darcy's pride and Elizabeth's prejudice against him. But Austen isn't that simple. And the novel reveals that

- There are many kinds of pride and prejudice.
- Different characters display these characteristics for better or for worse.

Getting past the first line of the novel

Before examining how pride and prejudice vary in the novel, it's worthwhile to examine the book's famous first line: "It is a truth universally acknowledged, that a single man in possession of a good fortune, must be in want of a wife." Sounds true, yes? But after reading the first chapter, the reader sees that the reverse is true: that single women desire single men with money. Austen has written the line with *verbal irony* — saying one thing, while meaning its opposite. The single rich man is considered the "rightful property" of the women, and so the game is on. Neither Darcy nor Bingley came to Meryton with the intention of marrying. But by the end of the novel, they both marry daughters of the village.

Determining who's proud and who's prejudiced

At one time covers of paperback editions of *Pride and Prejudice* frequently bore the profiles of a young woman and man (Elizabeth and Darcy), with her profile under *Prejudice* and his over *Pride*. And in the Meryton Assembly scene, when Darcy refuses to dance with Elizabeth and says so within her hearing, he certainly seems proud, and she certainly develops a prejudice against him.

But right from the first page of the novel, readers begin to encounter pride and prejudice in many forms:

- Mr. Bennet is prejudiced in favor of Lizzy (Elizabeth), who is clever like he is, and Mrs. Bennet is proud of Jane's beauty and her own.
- Mrs. Bennet is prejudiced in favor of Lydia and ridiculously proud when Lydia, who has been shamelessly living with Wickham, comes home a married woman after a Regency version of a shotgun wedding.

- Elizabeth is prejudiced in Jane's favor when her sister questions whether Bingley really loves her.

- Elizabeth is proud of her prejudices against Darcy, until she learns that Wickham lied to her; then, her pride is deflated.

- Collins is proud of his patroness Lady Catherine's "condescension" to him.

- Charlotte Lucas, desperate at being 27 years old and still unmarried, casts pride to the winds and accepts Collins as her husband.

- Lady Catherine is prejudiced against Elizabeth and tries to stop her from becoming engaged to Darcy.

- Miss Bingley is proud of her new money and new status, while she's prejudiced against those in trade — ironically forgetting that her father's being in trade gave her the new money and status she now has.

- Miss Bingley is prejudiced against Elizabeth because she sees that Darcy is interested in her.

- Wickham says Darcy is prejudiced against him.

- Elizabeth takes pride in her Aunt and Uncle Gardiner's appearance and personalities.

- Elizabeth has sufficient pride not to be cowed by Lady Catherine's pride.

Notice how at times pride and prejudice are *good* things.

Understanding Mr. Collins

Mr. Collins exemplifies unpleasant, even ridiculous pride because he is proud of Lady Catherine's "condescension" to him. While "condescension" in Austen's day had a positive meaning in referring to how higher class people could be pleasant to lower class people, Lady Catherine's "condescension" is more like the typical use of the word today: patronizing people, acting towards your inferiors in a way that shows you think they're inferior and you're a lot better than they are. Collins is proud that Lady Catherine gave him a church living. He brags of having Lady Catherine's patronage and praises her "condescension" to him. This condescension turns out to include advising him to marry, as well as to rearrange the furniture in his house and install shelves in his upstairs closets. But Collins is too stupid to take any offense at her being a busybody. That he gratefully accepts her interference in his personal life was probably why she selected him for the church living he now occupies. The Collins–Lady Catherine relationship is Austen's subtle way of telling her contemporary readers — who knew all about how the

Anglican Church gave out its local jobs — that selecting priests for a parish by private patronage might lead to giving spiritually and intellectually unqualified men the responsibility for many innocent souls. Austen's treatment of Collins is certainly merciless. For example, when he writes to the Bennets after Lydia's disgrace, advising them to turn her away from their family, Mr. Bennet dryly comments, "'*That* is his notion of Christian forgiveness!'" (PP 3:15). From that, the reader can only think, "His poor parishioners, having Collins as their spiritual adviser." (For details on church livings, see Chapter 10.)

Reading Mansfield Park

Many readers have traditionally been disappointed with Fanny Price, the heroine of *Mansfield Park*. The meek Fanny seems wimpy after reading about *Pride and Prejudice*'s Elizabeth. Yet when pressured by her cousins to act and by her uncle and cousin Edmund to accept Henry Crawford as husband material, she defies all of them, holding her ground and refusing to submit. So what's the matter with Fanny Price? Why does she make readers uncomfortable?

Dealing with abusive behavior

It's uncomfortable to watch Fanny because she's the victim of abuse. Her Aunt Norris, whom the Bertrams allow to have free reign at Mansfield Park, constantly berates her. She gives her a room with the maids and tells the little girl that she will never be equal to her cousins. She prohibits the maids from lighting a fire in Fanny's study on even the coldest days, and she makes Fanny walk back and forth between her home and Mansfield Park on the hottest day. Aside from this physical abuse, Aunt Norris practices psychological abuse on Fanny, making demeaning comments about her to her face or to others while Fanny is in the room. The abuse is uncomfortable to witness, even on the page of a book.

Likewise, Sir Thomas and Lady Bertram are abusers, but they're passive. By handing over their respective parental responsibilities to Aunt Norris, they allow her to get away with what she does. As readers, you may sometimes want to tap Sir Thomas on the shoulder and say, "Why don't you call Aunt Norris on this?" But you have to take yourselves out of the novel and read with what 19th-century poet and critic Samuel Taylor Coleridge called "a willing suspension of disbelief."

Accepting a passive heroine

Coming as she does between Elizabeth Bennet and Emma Woodhouse, each of whom is anything but passive, Fanny Price's passivity can be surprising and even irritating to the reader. Yet when she reasserts her passivity by insisting that she can't "act" during the scenes when everyone pressures her to be in the play, she, ironically, is acting here. She is claiming for herself the right not to act which — ironically — is an act of will.

However, reading about the way people treat Fanny is painful. Many readers say that Fanny is the last Austen heroine with whom you'd want to have dinner! But Fanny is also the Austen heroine who endures the most misunderstanding, thoughtlessness, and abuse from others. How can you not be happy when Edmund marries her at last?

Hearing a very intrusive narrator

Not since *Northanger Abbey* have the readers of Austen's novels encountered such an intrusive narrator as they hear in *Mansfield Park*. Austen begins the final chapter saying, "Let other pens dwell on guilt and misery. I quit such odious subjects as soon as I can, impatient to restore everybody, not greatly in fault themselves, to tolerable comfort, and to have done with all the rest" (MP 3:17). Austen could not be more obvious in showing who is in charge of the novel! And she then talks of "My Fanny," showing her affection for and attachment to her heroine.

Reading Emma

For most readers, *Emma* is two different books.

- ✔ The first time you read it, you may be duped by Frank Churchill's behavior and have little or no suspicion about why he behaves the way he does.

- ✔ Subsequent readings have readers marveling at the way Austen plants her clues and hints about Frank Churchill all along the way. Each reading uncovers another clue, and the book puts the reader in the role of detective. (Notice that I am not giving away the surprise here!)

Attending to the first line and first paragraph of the novel

Austen sets up her heroine for error in the opening line:

> Emma Woodhouse, handsome, clever, and rich, with a comfortable home and happy disposition, seemed to unite some of the best blessings of existence; and had lived nearly twenty-one years in the world with very little to distress or vex her. (E 1:1)

The line promises a delightful heroine, suffering none of the problems and pains that her chronological predecessor Fanny Price did. But Austen slips in the word "seemed," tipping the reader that the rest of the novel may not be smooth sailing for Emma.

By the end of the third paragraph, the reader discovers that Emma has been "directed chiefly by her own" judgment. And then Austen drops the heavy shoe, saying, "The *real* evils, *indeed,* of Emma's situation were the power of having rather too much her own way, and a disposition to think a little too well of herself." (I have italicized the words "real" and "indeed" to call attention to the way Austen tells of Emma's big problem: Her egoism is a real evil, and Austen underscores that by using the intensifying word "indeed.") So the reader knows why Emma makes the blunders she does from the outset.

Bringing in Mrs. Elton

Austen uses Mrs. Elton (the former Augusta Hawkins) for at least four reasons:

- ✔ By marrying Augusta Hawkins soon after being rejected by Emma, Mr. Elton shows that he wasn't really in love with Emma. Here Emma was right in assuming that if he couldn't get Miss Woodhouse with her £30,000, he would go after Miss Somebody (anybody) with £20,000 or £10,000. He gets the £10,000.

- ✔ She has the fancy first name "Augusta" derived from the Latin word *august,* meaning grand or sacred. Then she has the ordinary surname Hawkins, suggesting that she "hawks" or is "hawking" or advertising in the loud way that hawkers do. She brags about herself in every way she can: from her courtship with Mr. Elton to her sister's marriage to Mr. Suckling, who drives a barouche-landau carriage, a very ritzy vehicle. (To see a barouche-landau carriage, see Chapter 11.) Is it any wonder that the Sucklings' good friends are named the Bragges?

Austen rarely uses names symbolically. But she had a good time with this in *Emma*. In addition to the names mentioned above, she uses the name Frank Churchill to remind readers in the second or later go-round of this novel that Frank Churchill is anything but frank in his interactions with everyone.

✔ Mrs. Elton is an exaggerated version of Emma's egoism and desire to control others. She swoops — like a hawk — into Highbury, fastens hers claws to poor Jane Fairfax, and runs her life, despite Jane's awkward protests. What Emma did to Harriet Smith, Mrs. Elton does in a more vulgar way to Jane.

✔ Augusta Hawkins Elton comes from Bristol, a thriving commercial port connected to the slave trade. When Jane Fairfax connects being a governess to being a slave, Austen wants you to remember that Mrs. Elton, who's busy trying to get her into a family as a governess, is, in effect, dealing in the sale of Jane Fairfax. (For more on slavery during this period, see Chapter 2.)

So Austen gets a lot of mileage out of this obnoxious character, who, ironically, gets the last lines of speech in the novel as she criticizes Emma's wedding for having "'Very little white satin, very few lace veils.'" But doesn't it always seem like the pushiest people get the last word?

Reading Persuasion

Austen's final novel has the most social commentary in it. She was witnessing a changing society, where the long-established gentry was being nudged by a rising middle class, where men like Captain Wentworth, who actually earned money and status, were becoming players. Thus, *Persuasion* deals with men named in two different books:

✔ *The Baronetcy*, which is Sir Walter's favorite book because he sees his name and the land and title he inherited printed in it

✔ *Navy List*, which includes the names and ships of naval officers who have earned their rank by fighting courageously in a time of war and who have made themselves by *doing*

Austen shows the titled man who inherited his property and title to be vain, insipid, and irresponsible, while the naval officers are just the opposite. The subsequent Victorian age would vindicate her ideas with the rise of the middle class and the new concept that people should work for wealth and status. See Chapter 2 for more information on inheritance and earning status.

Meeting "Only Anne"

Minimized by her father and sisters, heroine Anne Elliot is "only Anne" to them, a mere nothing. Having "lost her bloom" in the eight years since her romance and break-up with Captain Wentworth before the novel begins, Anne is wispy and quiet, still in love with Wentworth, but feeling helpless to do anything about it because he hasn't attempted to contact her again, and protocol of the day says she can't make the first move in contacting him.

Yet as the novel proceeds and Anne moves farther away from her demeaning family, her stock with people goes up. She moves from being "only Anne" in the minimal sense to being "only Anne" in the unique sense. When she's at the Musgroves' two homes, *only Anne* can tend to the children well and listen patiently to everyone's complaints. At Lyme, Mr. Elliot looks admiringly at *only Anne*. When Louisa has her accident at Lyme, *only Anne* keeps her head as all about her lose theirs and Louisa hurts hers: Anne offers smelling salts and sends the proper individual — the one who lives in Lyme — to find help. At Bath, *only Anne* can translate the Italian songs. *Only Anne* regains her lost "bloom." Austen's use of the word "bloom" likens Anne to a flower that miraculously revives after eight years of dormancy. And at the end of the novel, Anne is the only heroine over whom Austen casts a shadow by writing in the final line that "She gloried in being a sailor's wife, but she must pay the tax of quick alarm": her contemporary readers saw in hindsight that in setting her novel before Napoleon's escape from Elba, Austen was deliberately placing Wentworth in future danger with the revival of war with France.

Facing reader frustration

Some readers of this novel complain that the final section drags, beginning with the question the narrator poses on behalf of Anne: "How was the truth to reach him?" (P 2:8). The truth refers to Anne's lack of interest in Mr. Elliot as a husband and her true love for Wentworth: How will Anne convey this to Wentworth, who seeing Anne and Mr. Elliot together, has become jealous and shows Anne only formal courtesy? Nowadays, Anne would invite him for coffee and explain things. But in Austen's day protocol said that the woman should be passive, letting the man make the first move. Thus, in the novel's concert scene, she can make room on the bench for Wentworth to sit next to her, but she cannot, as a lady, say, "There's room here; why not sit down with us?"

As readers go along the slow and torturous route with Anne in subtly getting the "truth" to Wentworth, Austen has Anne accomplish her task cryptically. Anne converses with Captain Harville about female constancy, which Wentworth overhears as he writes a note to Captain Benwick. While Anne is speaking directly to Harville, she's also communicating indirectly with Wentworth. As Wentworth is writing to Benwick, he's cautiously listening to Anne. Hearing her speak with passion and force of women's constancy in love, Wentworth now has the emotional permission he needed from her to write the passionate note he leaves for her to find. While all of this is highly romantic, Austen was also having Anne behave as a lady should in her day. She can't approach the man; it's his move.

In the 1995 film of *Persuasion,* Anne runs after Wentworth when he abruptly and jealously leaves the concert and stops him to ask if there's anything worth staying for. Anne is acting not only out of character in this added scene but also against the rules of behavior of the day. So when you think about it in the film: if Anne is willing to break with decorum and physically run after Wentworth at the concert, why wouldn't she come right out and tell him the truth? Adding that scenes undercuts Anne's real dilemma in the novel of "How was the truth to reach him?" in terms of the etiquette of the day.

Discussing Austen's Novels

So you want to form a Jane Austen reading group. How do you go about it? Here are some tips:

- Decide whom you want in your group — people you know from work, school, or the neighborhood? Do you prefer meeting new people? Do what's most comfortable for you.

- Most reading groups have about ten members — a number that allows for discussion and lets everyone have a chance to talk. If you desire new people to join the group, post a notice in the library, at local bookstores, at work, and at schools, colleges, and universities. Now, be smart: Don't put personal info on the notice (just announce the meeting place and time and its purpose), and plan to meet in a public place, such as a library, a bookstore (many bookstores have pleasant areas for book clubs to meet), a coffee shop, and so on. If your book group is comprised of people you already know well, you can let friends know of your plans by e-mail, phone, and word-of-mouth. With friends, you can also meet at someone's house. Be sure to divide responsibilities so that people know what to bring: cookies? cold veggies and dips? teas? juices? napkins and paper plates? paper cups? You get the picture!

- At the first meeting, come up with a plan for meetings: How frequently will you meet? Will one person "run" the book group or will the leadership role rotate among members? How will books be selected — for

Austen, do you want to start with her youthful works and move forward? Will you also read her letters?

✔ Be sure no one dominates the group. Encourage everyone to talk. Help the quiet people to speak up without embarrassing them.

After your group is formed, tackle the questions and topics in the following sections to get the discussion moving in your new group.

General questions

Here are few topics for a group that has read all of Austen's novels:

✔ Readers sometimes call *Persuasion* Austen's book of second chances because after an eight-year hiatus, Anne and Wentworth get together. How might her other novels also be considered books of second chances?

✔ Analyze if there is a progression in the way Austen's heroines behave from the earliest novel through her final work.

✔ Create Austen's ideal man using characteristics from various male characters. Create different ideal males for different age groups.

✔ Create Austen's ideal woman using characteristics from various female characters. Create different ideal females for different age groups.

Discussing Northanger Abbey

These questions will get you going on *Northanger Abbey.* If you really want to get the most out of this novel, you might want to begin with reading Ann Radcliffe's *The Mysteries of Udolpho,* so you know what Austen is spoofing and why Austen's heroine Catherine is so terrified!

✔ From the opening pages of the book, what do you think Austen is spoofing in terms of the way heroines from earlier novels were presented?

✔ Analyze what makes Henry Tilney attractive to Catherine. Is he attractive to you? Why or why not?

✔ What lessons do Isabella's so-called friendships teach Catherine?

✔ How does Catherine's friendship with Eleanor differ from her friendship with Isabella?

✔ Analyze the failures of John Thorpe as a gentleman.

✔ Analyze General Tilney; the way his children react to him; the way Catherine reacts to him.

Discussing Sense and Sensibility

You might want to begin your discussion of this novel by creating, on a large pad, a family tree of the Dashwoods, because the book opens with a lot of them! Once you have the family structure and characters' identities down, you'll be set to get going on these questions:

- Analyze Mrs. Dashwood (the mother of Elinor, Marianne, and Margaret) as a mother.

- After reading the novel and watching the Emma Thompson film version of this novel, discuss what she gains or loses in casting Hugh Grant in the role of Edward Ferrars. How does Austen present Edward, and why does she do it in the way she does? What does Thompson add to Edward's characterization? Do her changes in any way affect your impressions of him? If so, how?

- Analyze Colonel Brandon as a romantic character. Who gets the better deal at the end of the novel, Marianne or Brandon? Explain.

- Analyze the way Lucy Steele plays the games of society to suck up to others.

- Discuss the characters in the novel in terms of all aspects you can think of regarding sense and sensibility.

Discussing Pride and Prejudice

Many people of your group may have seen the recent *Pride and Prejudice* television series and films, and so they will come to the novel with pre-conceived ideas about how characters look and behave. (See Chapter 15 for the film and television versions.) As the people in your group read this book, ask them to note any physical descriptions Austen gives of the characters.

- Does Mrs. Bennet get a fair deal from the narrator? Is she as stupid as she appears? Explain your answer.

- Discuss Darcy's friendship with Bingley: Speculate why they're friends. Can you forgive Darcy for meddling in the Jane/Bingley relationship? Why? Why not?

- Compare Charlotte Lucas Collins and Mr. Bennet in terms of how each deals with an unhappy marriage.

- Why are Elizabeth and Darcy a good couple?

✔ Watch the 1995 television miniseries of *Pride and Prejudice,* and then discuss the following:

  • Is Jennifer Ehle well cast in the role? Why? Compare her looks and actions to what Austen says in the novel.

  • Is Colin Firth well cast in the role? Why? Compare his looks and actions to what Austen says in the novel.

  • Notice the scenes that script writer Andrew Davies added to the series that weren't in the novel. What purposes do they serve?

✔ Watch the 2005 film of *Pride and Prejudice* and discuss the following:

  • How does the film change the setting of the novel? What purpose did it serve?

  • Compare the way Matthew MacFayden plays Darcy to the way Austen presents Darcy in her novel. Is Macfayden's portrayal accurate?

  • Compare the way Donald Sutherland plays Mr. Bennet in the film to the way Austen presents him in her novel. Is Sutherland's portrayal accurate.

Discussing Mansfield Park

If any of your group members have seen Patricia Rozema's film of *Mansfield Park,* and have not yet read the novel, they're in for a big surprise! Start your discussion with these questions:

✔ What is Austen showing through the Bertram sisters, Maria and Julia?

✔ Find a copy of the play *Lovers' Vows;* read it; then discuss why Austen chose that play for *Mansfield Park.*

✔ Analyze Mary Crawford. She's one of Austen's most complex characters. Determine her good and not-so-good traits. Why does Edmund fall in love with her?

✔ Henry Crawford starts his attentions to Fanny with the purpose of making a small hole in her heart. How do his feelings for Fanny change? Do you agree with the narrator at the end of the book that Henry truly loved Fanny? Why?

✔ Apply the traits of pride and prejudice to characters in this novel.

Discussing Emma

This is the novel that your group might wish to discuss twice: once the first time they read it and then again, after everyone re-reads it, noting all the clues Austen plants about the book's secret that causes Emma to be "duped."

- Austen said of this heroine that nobody but she, Emma's creator, would much like her. Do you like Emma? Why or why not?

- What are Emma's good qualities?

- How do you interpret Emma's interfering with people's lives? What are her motivations? Can you forgive her? Why?

- Emma and her father appear to be highly different. How are they alike?

- Trace the clues Austen presents regarding Frank Churchill's real reason for visiting Highbury. In so doing, trace how Frank covers his tracks.

- Watch Amy Heckerling's updating of *Emma* in the film *Clueless*. How does she change some of the characters to make them more relevant to your own time? Does the change work in still presenting the basic Austen character on whom the Heckerling character is modeled? Why?

- Watch the Gwyneth Paltrow *Emma* film. What is gained or lost in the presentation of Harriet Smith, played by Toni Collete? How does the film present Emma and Mr. Knightley's relationship? Is it effective? Why?

- Watch the Kate Beckensale television miniseries of *Emma*. This version is closer to the book. Compare and contrast the way the lead characters are played in this version and in and the Paltrow version.

Discussing Persuasion

Austen never had the chance — because of her fatal illness — to go through this book and revise it after letting the manuscript sit for a while. But she did make some changes in the final chapters of Volume 2: Revising her original Chapter 10 to what it is now, she wrote a new Chapter 11, and made changes in her old Chapter 11 to make it the current Chapter 12. Most editions of *Persuasion* have what are called "Austen's cancelled chapters" in an appendix at the end of the novel. Ask the group to read those chapters so that you can discuss and evaluate her changes.

- What was Lady Elliot like? Why did she marry Sir Walter?

- How do persuasion and persuading operate in the novel?

✔ Why did Lady Russell persuade Anne to drop Wentworth back in 1806? Can you justify Lady Russell's actions?

✔ What are your feelings about Mrs. Clay? What hints does Austen plant earlier in the novel for Mrs. Clay's final action?

✔ Evaluate the Crofts as a married couple.

✔ What do the senior Musgroves represent?

✔ Wentworth seems very romantic and heroic. Yet a case could be made for his being wimpy and unpleasant. Make that case *or* argue against it!

✔ Analyze the changes in Anne Elliot: how she goes from being "only Anne," as in "just Anne," to "only Anne," as in "uniquely Anne!"

Chapter 15

Bringing Austen Novels to Stage, Screen, and Television

*B*esides being free of copyright restrictions, Austen's novels are attractive to producers for several good reasons. Great works of literature — and Austen's novels are great works of literature or "classics" — have long been used by film studios as sources for movies. Just think of Audrey Hepburn in Tolstoy's *War and Peace,* Henry Fonda in Dickens's A *Tale of Two Cities,* Cary Grant in *Gunga Din,* or Ralph Fiennes in *The English Patient,* and we remember how many popular and critically acclaimed films have their source from novels or poems (Rudyard Kipling's *Gunga Din*). In fact, coming from a classic literary text gives a film or television show a certain cachet. And when to that cachet we add (for the ladies) Colin Firth emerging from a dip in a lake wearing a clingy, sheer white shirt, or (for the gents) Jennifer Ehle breathing heavily in her décolleté dress, is there any wonder that 1995's *Pride and Prejudice* miniseries had viewers of both genders glued to their TVs? This chapter explores the reasons for Austen's dramatic adaptability and provides an annotated list of all the productions for stage and screen (TV and film) that exist up to the point of this book's writing.

Assessing Austen's Adaptability

Because Austen's novels are public domain, there are no royalties to pay: this lack of an extra expense means that using one of her works for a play or film is cheap. Austen's literary classics have a high stature, so using one of her works is a sign of classiness. But Austen's novels are adaptable for other reasons than just cost and borrowed elegance.

Creating attractive and admirable heroines

As I observed in Chapter 1, Austen tells a great story. All of her novels deal with young and (usually!) attractive men and women looking for true love, and what's more, they find it after overcoming odds of various types — mutual pride and prejudice in one book (you know which one!), overcoming blinding self-absorption in another *(Emma),* and reuniting with a suitor eight years after rejecting him in still another *(Persuasion).* So while all Austen's novels are courtship novels, the courtships and the lovers involved in them all differ. And who doesn't like a love story? If you don't, and you're still reading this book, think again!

Austen's heroines appeal particularly to females, whether readers or movie-goers or both.

- ✔ Elizabeth Bennet, Austen's most popular and possibly most admirable heroine, has a sense of self-possession about when and whom she chooses to marry that was unusual in a young woman for her time and still admirable in ours.

- ✔ Even Austen's most passive heroine, Fanny Price of *Mansfield Park,* holds out for true love despite numerous pressures to the contrary.

Such heroines are attractive to women, young and not-so-young. In fact, Austen's heroines can be viewed as prototypes of feminism. But they aren't the strident bra-burners of the 1970s. Jane Austen is far more subtle than that! Instead, Austen's heroines show that the events and thoughts of a woman are worthwhile — worthwhile enough to read about for 300 or more pages.

While all Austen readers have their own mental pictures of how these characters look — keeping in mind that she gives relatively little physical description — to see how they're portrayed on screen is always fun. For me, personally, two of the best portrayals in terms of Austen's verbal descriptions of them are as follows:

- ✔ Elizabeth Garvie as Elizabeth Bennet in the 1980 BBC miniseries of *Pride and Prejudice* because, for me, Garvie looks and acts just as I perceive Austen's depicting Elizabeth in the novel.

  - Garvie has beautiful bright eyes (such as Darcy admires in the novel), along with wit and charm.

  - Garvie is extremely petite, and in the novel, Mr. Bennet talks of his "little Lizzy," suggesting that while she is not the youngest Bennet sister, she may well be the most petite of the five (PP 1:1).

  - Garvie's petite physique makes her look as though she could be "crossing field after field at a quick pace, jumping over stiles [fences] and springing over puddles," as well as running "gaily off" as Elizabeth does in the novel (PP 1:7, 10).

- Garvie has a look of mischief in her eyes that Elizabeth *must* have when she plays Miss Pert to Darcy!

✔ Gwyneth Paltrow as Emma in the 1996 commercial film of *Emma*

- Paltrow is handsome in this film and looks to the manor born. (*Emma* opens with a description of its heroine as "Handsome, clever, and rich.")

- Her performance is marked by the sad, almost hangdog look she shows whenever Emma realizes that all of her good-willed planning to help others doesn't work out. This reaction reminds even the film viewer who hasn't read *Emma* that our heroine's meddling interference is usually — at least in her mind — well, even kindly, meant and that she is chagrined when she fails.

- Paltrow looks both "Handsome" and sweet — an important combination for the film version because Emma's meddling can really irritate the reader or viewer.

- Paltrow has what Emma has: in the words of the novel's Mrs. Weston, "'regular features, open countenance with a complexion! oh! what a bloom of full health, such a pretty height and size; such a firm and upright figure'" (E 1:5). Paltrow looks the part.

Finding ready-made dialogue in the novel

One of Austen's greatest skills as a novelist is delivering her plot in dialogue. This way of presenting the story is a much livelier and more realistic way than doing straight narration. Dialogue is more realistic because it replicates the way we come to know people and deal with situations in everyday life: by conversing with others. When and how a person talks tells a lot about the character who's speaking, sometimes more than the character even realizes. This aspect of fiction is called dramatic irony. For example, in *Pride and Prejudice,* Miss Bingley attempts to demean Elizabeth by saying in front of Darcy that Elizabeth's uncle lives in Cheapside, London, a commercial, rather than fashionable, area, in the city. But she conveniently forgets — though the reader remembers — that Miss Bingley's father made his money in trade, too (or commercially, instead of inheriting it as Darcy did his) (PP 1:8).

When you're reading *Pride and Prejudice,* you come across pages when dialogue occurs without even a "he said" or "she said." Austen, herself, noted this when she received her copies of her newly published novel. While noting that adding these words would clarify the dialogue, she then remarked, "[B]ut 'I do not write for such dull Elves'" (Letter, January 29, 1813).

Austen's speech lines can be rather long. In fact, when Jennifer Ehle played Elizabeth Bennet in the 1995 *Pride and Prejudice* TV miniseries, she observed that Austen's lines were harder to memorize than Shakespeare's because of their length and structure of (grammatically) complex sentences with the subject sometimes coming at the end of the sentence. But listening to witty, well-spoken talk — whether in our mind's ear while reading or from the mouths of actors on the screen — is always a pleasure to the mind or ear. As a result, most adaptations of Austen for the screen — commercial or home — borrow whole sections of her dialogue from her novels. So while Emma Thompson won a highly-deserved Oscar for Best Screenplay for her 1995-adaptation of *Sense and Sensibility,* she shared that award with Austen — a fact Thompson, herself, graciously noted when she made her acceptance speech for Best Screenplay at the 53rd Annual Golden Globe awards in 1996.

Looking for courtesy in an increasingly impolite world

Austen's world is a polite world where adhering to decorum and courtesy was a given for the gentry characters who inhabited her novels. (For more on the class known as the gentry, see Chapter 2.) So after a long day at work where you get doors slammed in your face all day, going home to watch ladies and gentlemen dressed in beautiful early-19th-century British costumes, bowing to each other, is a nice change of pace.

Even insults in Austen are delivered with class. For example, in the Box Hill scene in *Emma,* Frank Churchill facetiously declares that Emma desires to hear everyone say "'one thing very clever . . . or two things moderately clever — or three things very dull indeed.'" The innocent, well-meaning Miss Bates immediately replies (because she can't resist a chance to speak), "'Three things very dull indeed. That will just do for me. . . . I shall be sure to say three things dull things as soon as I open my mouth, shant't I?'" The narrator then inserts that "Emma could not resist," saying with "mock ceremony," "'Ah! Madam, but there may be a difficulty. Pardon me — but you will be limited as to the number — only three at once'" (E 3:7). Miss Bates is, of course, devastated by Emma's cruel comment, but you have to admit that Emma's language was quite polite!

Watching costume drama to experience armchair travel

Costume drama has a wide appeal because it transports the viewer to days gone by when men wore breeches and bowed to ladies dressed in lovely gowns. Watching costume drama provides an occasional escape from everyday life. Add to the costumes, the scenery of the beautiful, green English countryside and the indoor scenes filmed in glorious 18th-century country houses (mansions), and a cold, rainy day in New York City becomes a vicarious trip to the late-18th- and early-19th-century English countryside in springtime.

While some earlier television versions of Austen novels have been shot on location, instead of inside a studio, all of the Austen-based films and TV miniseries since 1995 have been filmed on historical sites in England, painstakingly chosen to represent scenes in the novels. The 1995 film *Sense and Sensibility* used the gorgeous Double Cube Room in Wilton House, Salisbury, for an indoor ballroom scene, and Saltram House, near Plymouth, built and landscaped in the 18th-century by the two foremost architects and landscape artists of the day, Robert Adam (founder of the neoclassical Adam style) and Lancelot "Capability" Brown, was used for the exterior and interior of Norland Park. Seeing such sites delights the sight of the viewer.

Dealing with difficulties in adapting Austen

While Austen's novels are popular sources for screenplays, they're also difficult to adapt in their own way. One of Austen's great strengths as a novelist is her skill in narration, where her narrator is frequently a source of the irony for which she's famous. (For more on the narrator in Austen, see Chapters 1 and 14.)

But in a film, using a voiceover for a narrator can be awkward. While director Tony Richardson brilliantly used the camera to replace the narrator's voice in his 1963 film version of Henry Fielding's novel *Tom Jones,* the technique wouldn't work with Austen because *Tom Jones* is a broad comedy. So the hero turns to the camera and speaks directly to the audience, and it works. But Austen's novels are far too subtle in their use of irony, usually for comic effect, to sustain that type of narrative substitution. For example, the famous, ironic opening line (ironic because, as the novel shows, just the opposite is true: single women are looking for men of good fortune as husbands) of the novel *Pride and Prejudice,* which is delivered by the narrator — "It is a truth universally acknowledged, that single man in possession of a good fortune, must be in want of a wife" — is usually given to a character as part of a normal dialogue, but directors have to adapt this line in different ways:

- In the 1995 miniseries version of the novel, Elizabeth speaks the line in conversation with her sisters.

- In the 1980 BBC miniseries, Elizabeth says it to her practical friend Charlotte Lucas.

- The 2005 *Pride and Prejudice* omitted the line altogether, though Austen uses the line to preview what the following pages show.

✓ The 1999 *Mansfield Park* adaptation resorted to actors facing the camera and speaking directly into it, causing reason in film viewers to believe the interpretation detracted from the film's Austen-ness.

Another difficulty is taking Austen's 300-plus pages of the novel and compressing them into a commercial film, which normally has a running time of less than two hours. Each of Austen's words and lines are deliberate, so deciding what to cut and/or compress is a tough choice.

Finally, Austen's talent for getting into the heads of her characters is hard to show on screen. A prime example of this is Elizabeth reading Darcy's long letter in *Pride and Prejudice* several times. She speaks to herself, debates the letter's meaning, examines her own behavior, and reassesses his behavior (PP 2:11). Capturing on stage the interior conversation that Elizabeth has with herself in the pages of the novel is difficult, leading to the awkward use of voice-overs or the heroine's talking out loud to herself.

Staging a Jane Austen novel

While a staged production of a novel can't provide the gorgeous location sites that a film does, it can, when based on an Austen plot and characters, of course, offer the playgoer an entertaining evening at the theater. *Pride and Prejudice* is the only Austen novel adapted for the stage: five times (as far as I could find) as a play and twice as a musical — and more are undoubtedly coming.

✓ Mary Medbury MacKaye (Mrs. Steele MacKaye) was the first to adapt the novel for the stage in 1906; it played in both NYC and London.

✓ Next came Helen Jerome's *Pride and Prejudice — A Sentimental Comedy*, published and performed as a Broadway hit in 1935. This version has seen recent revivals in productions performed by university theater groups.

✓ In 1936, A. A. Milne adapted the novel for the London stage under the title *Miss Elizabeth Bennet*. And no, Winnie the Pooh did *not* play Darcy.

✓ Fifty years later, an American, Christina Calvit, also adapted the novel; it is available through the Internet as a reader's theatre production audio tape (1986), starring Kate Burton, Miriam Margoyles, and Steve Toland.

✓ A newer version by James Maxwell and revised by Alan Stanford is part of the famous Guthrie Theater's National Tour repertoire for spring 2007. Internet browsing is likely to reveal more dramatic renderings for local theater groups.

In addition, the novel has been frequently adapted for radio drama, especially in the UK.

Most interesting are the musical versions of the novel. One was called *Pride and Prejudice*. But the second, called *First Impressions* after Austen's early rendition of the book, is better known. (For more details on Austen's early *First Impressions,* an epistolary novel or a novel told through letters, see Chapter 3.) Playwright and columnist Abe Burrows based *First Impressions* on Jerome's play, with music and lyrics by

Robert Goldman, Glenn Paxton, and George Weiss. The musical had 92 performances between March 19 and May 30, 1959, at Broadway's Alvin Theater. Actress Polly Bergen played Elizabeth; Farley Granger, known for his romantic film roles in the 1940s and 1950s, was Darcy; Phyllis Newman, who went on to star in many Broadway plays, played Lydia; and the great character actress Hermione Gingold played Mrs. Bennet. The show's original cast recording has been remastered and is available on DVD over the Internet. It features such numbers as "Five Daughters" sung by Mrs. Bennet (Gingold), "This Really Isn't Me," sung by Elizabeth (Polly Bergen), and one piece called "Polka/The Assembly Dance," which must be the novel's Meryton Assembly — though Austen's characters never oom-pah-pah to a polka! What personally intrigued me was seeing that the show's musical director was Frederick Dvonch — he was music director for the first Broadway version of *The Sound of Music,* and the father of my delightful and lively childhood camp counselor Peggy!

Checking Out Austen Adaptations

The first Austen adaptation for film was the 1940 MGM *Pride and Prejudice* starring Greer Garson, who despite her beauty, was at least a decade too old to be a believable Elizabeth Bennet. As of this writing, the latest versions of Austen's novels will be new television versions of *Persuasion, Mansfield Park,* and *Northanger Abbey* that are in the works by Britain's ITV for autumn 2006 airing in the UK, as well as a new BBC *Sense and Sensibility* series, which will be shown in the United States on PBS's *Masterpiece Theatre* in 2007. Whether the three ITV Austen productions will be shown in the U.S. is yet unclear. The following sections include the current, most complete, listing of television and film versions of Austen's novels.

Seeing villains in Northanger Abbey

The BBC/A&E television version of *Northanger Abbey* (1986, 90 minutes), shown in the United States on PBS-TV's *Masterpiece Theatre* series, was directed by Giles Foster from a screenplay by Maggie Wadey, produced by Louis Marks. Here are some of its features:

- ✔ It features eerie music, which includes very high and scary female voices, by Ilona Sekacz.

- ✔ The music is undoubtedly meant to underscore the fears experienced by heroine Catherine Morland, skillfully played by Katharine Schlesinger, who in this version has an even more vivid imagination than the novel's Catherine.

- ✔ The TV Catherine imagines herself wearing heavy eye makeup and seeing the hero's father placing a sword across her arm. No wonder the female chorus sounds scared!

- ✔ The hero, Henry Tilney, is played by Peter Firth (not related to Colin).

This Gothic *Northanger Abbey* is still available on VHS and DVD.

The upcoming ITV film of *Northanger Abbey* is by the grand master of literary adaptations for television, Andrew Davies, and is sure to be closer to the novel.

- ✔ The story goes that Davies had written the adaptation in 1998 and that Miramax was going to begin production the following year. Nothing happened.

- ✔ Davies speculated to a group at a Humanities Festival at the University of Wisconsin-Madison that because of the poor critical and audience response to Miramax's *Mansfield Park,* discussed later, the production company was reluctant to invest in the filming of another Austen novel.

- ✔ However, Davies's script is finally coming out of moth balls. Britain's ITV is using it for its series of three Austen productions.

- ✔ Sue Birtwistle, the producer of the successful 1995 *Pride and Prejudice* miniseries, is producing. Her involvement, like Davies's, suggests close adherence to the novel.

Scoping Sense and Sensibility

Adaptations of *Sense and Sensibility* go back to June 1950:

- ✔ In 1950, NBC *Philco Television Playhouse* presented a one-hour live rendition of the novel, in which Marianne Dashwood was played by a very young Cloris Leachman.

- ✔ In 1971, BBC-2 TV broadcasted in the UK a four-part miniseries of the novel in which the role of Elinor Dashwood was played by Joanna David, who in the 1995 *Pride and Prejudice* miniseries played Mrs. Gardiner. Robin Ellis, later seen as the title character of the PBS *Masterpiece Theater*'s *Poldark* series, was Edward Ferrars. David Giles directed a screenplay by Denis Constanduros. Martin Lisemore was the producer.

- ✔ In 1981, the BBC's seven-part miniseries of the novel broadcast in the United States on PBS TV's *Masterpiece Theater*. Denis Constanduros again wrote the screenplay, with Alexander Baron. Rodney Bennett directed.

Constanduros's involvement with this screenplay undoubtedly accounts for its similarities to the 1971 version. The big difference between the two adaptations is setting. In 1971, most of the series was shot on indoor sets. But in 1981, the crew and cast went to locations. Irene Richards played Elinor, and Tracey Childs was Marianne. It's available on VHS and DVD.

✔ The 1995 Columbia Pictures/Mirage commercial film version of the novel is based on Emma Thompson's screenplay, with direction by Ang Lee. Lindsey Doran produced. Thompson, though at least ten years older than Elinor, played the role beautifully, capturing Elinor's conflicted interior nature. Kate Winslet played Marianne; Alan Rickman was Colonel Brandon; and the charming Hugh Grant played the novel's unremarkable Edward Ferrars. The casting of Grant in the role was the least of the changes Thompson made in the story to make Edward, who in the novel is described as "not handsome, and his manners required intimacy to make them pleasing," and who causes Elinor great emotional pain for about 95 percent of the book, attractive to moviegoers (SS 1:3). But the production values of the movie are excellent, with costumes that capture the period of the novel and beautiful on-location sites. The film is available on VHS and DVD, and Patrick Doyle's score can be heard on a CD.

Casting characters correctly

The curious point about the Mariannes that I've seen on screen — Tracey Childs and Kate Winslet — is that they're fair-skinned blondes. But Austen writes that Marianne's "skin was very brown . . . and . . . her eyes . . . were very dark" (SS 1:10). I tend to think that Marianne might be considered Austen's "dark lady" — the woman of deep feelings or sensibility that critic Leslie Fiedler discusses in his classic book on American literature, *Love and Death in the American Novel*.

Only the future will tell the type of actress the BBC will cast in its new adaptation of *Sense and Sensibility* by Andrew Davies. We will get to see her when it is shown on PBS-TV in the 2007 television season.

In 2000, India's Bollywood tried its hand at adapting *Sense and Sensibility* in a film called *Kandukondain Kandukondain*, or *I Have Found It*. When I first viewed this long film, I thought I had the wrong film in the DVD case: It began with a group of Indian soldiers in a jungle creeping toward a schoolhouse, where they're riddled with bullets fired by children who've suddenly pulled out automatic weapons. The officer who's rendered lame from his wounds turns out to be the Colonel Brandon character. The beautiful Aishwarya Rai stars. Enough said. Directed and written by Rajiv Menon, it features lots of gorgeous musical numbers and fabulous scenery. Don't worry about the novel! Enjoy!

Perpetuating Pride and Prejudice

Because Jane Austen is so popular, filmmakers love to retell her stories. Check out these versions that read like a timeline of the classic *Pride and Prejudice:*

✔ **1940:** The 1940 MGM film of *Pride and Prejudice* is a hoot to watch! Lawrence Olivier and Greer Garson star as a chronologically mature Darcy and Elizabeth, who tell each other that he represents pride and she prejudice. While this is too simple an understanding of the complexities that Austen pulls out of the title — with Elizabeth, Darcy, as well as other characters displaying both pride and prejudice of varying types — the film was a resounding success when it came out, breaking and holding the box office record when it was shown at NYC's Radio City Musical Hall, which originally always showed a film *plus* the Rockettes. (Ah, the good old days.) Watch the film and count the anachronisms!

✔ **1949:** In 1949, NBC's *Philco Television Playhouse* offered a one-hour black-and-white production of *Pride and Prejudice*.

✔ **1952:** Not to be outdone, in 1952, the BBC showed a live six-part miniseries, in which Peter Cushing, later of horror film fame, played Darcy. Cedric Wallis did the script.

✔ **1958:** Six years later (1958), the BBC used the same screenplay, but with different actors, for another six-part go at the novel.

✔ **1967:** BBC's miniseries industry continued with yet another six-part miniseries, this time with a script by Nemone Lethbridge, in 1967.

✔ **1980:** The BBC didn't come up with another *Pride and Prejudice* miniseries until 1980 with a five-part screenplay by the British novelist and Austen fan Fay Weldon. U.S. television viewers saw this on PBS-TV's *Masterpiece Theatre*. Elizabeth Garvie rendered (for my money!) the definitive portrayal of Elizabeth Bennet. The excellent actor David Rintoul is Darcy. Irene Richard, who would be Elinor in the BBC's 1981 *Sense and Sensibility,* plays Charlotte Lucas in this production. It's on DVD or VHS.

✔ **1995:** Then in 1995 came the mother of all television — indeed, even commercial film — versions of *Pride and Prejudice:* Andrews Davies's adaptation of the novel as a six-part, 300-minute miniseries, for the BBC and the Arts & Entertainment network in the U.S. For many viewers, Jennifer Ehle's Elizabeth and especially Colin Firth's Darcy are definitive. When the final episode was shown in the UK, London suffered horrible traffic jams as people hurried home to catch the show, which broke viewing records. Sue Birtwistle produced the series. DVD and VHS versions? Of course. And there is a CD of Carl Davis's score.

✔ **2001:** Helen Fielding's riff on *Pride and Prejudice, Bridget Jones's Diary,* was turned into a film of the same name in 2001. Fielding collaborated with Andrew Davies, the veteran novel adapter of the 1995 *Pride and Prejudice* and other films drawn from classic novels, on the screenplay.

Renee Zellweger stars as Bridget, a far-from-self-possessed and confident Elizabeth Bennet. Colin Firth, from the 1995 *Pride and Prejudice*'s Darcy, plays Mark Darcy, and Hugh Grant plays Daniel Cleaver, the Wickhamesque character. The cast reprised their roles in Fielding's 2004 *Bridget Jones: The Edge of Reason, very* loosely based on *Persuasion*. Both are out on DVD. When you're watching the films, try to catch all the little references to Austen's novels: Pemberley Press is named for Darcy's estate, for example. Both are on DVD.

✔ **2003:** Another, less well-known film version of *Pride and Prejudice* appeared in limited release in 2003. The posters added the words "*A Latter-Day Comedy*" with a colon after the PP title. Set largely in Utah, the film integrates an updated storyline from the novel with Mormon (or the Church of Latter-Day Saints) beliefs. The screenplay credits Jane Austen, Anne Black, Jason Faller, and Katherine Swigart; the director is Andrew Black. It's on DVD.

✔ **2004:** Gurinder Chadha's good humored 2004 *Bride and Prejudice: The Bollywood Musical* is a visual and musical delight. Placing the story in India, London, and Los Angeles, Chadha, who with Paul Mayeda Beyes wrote the script, also directed the movie. She pays homage to Austen and shows us that the Regency English culture about which Austen wrote is not that different from a contemporary Indian culture in terms of mores regarding the marriage "choices" of young people. While not trying to represent the novel, the movie uses Austen's work as an inspiration. It's on DVD.

✔ **2005:** So what chance did the 2005 commercial film of *Pride and Prejudice* have? With memories of Colin Firth as Darcy, the dour, scowling Matthew MacFayden seemed more like Heathcliffe who'd missed the stop for *Wuthering Heights* and got off the train by mistake in Austenland. While many viewers loved the film, many devoted Austen readers were disappointed with the Brontefication of the story in terms of its darkness, placing scenes outside in storm and wind borrowed from *Jane Eyre*. The DVD is out if you'd like to buy or rent it.

Moving to Mansfield Park

ITV/BBC was the first to tackle *Mansfield Park* in the form of a miniseries, shown in the U.S. on PBS-TV's *Masterpiece Theater*. The telling of the story sticks closely to the novel. Nick Farrell played the hero, Edmund Bertram, to Sylvestra Le Touzel's appropriately sensitive and introspective Fanny Price. Anna Massey is terrific as the cruel and insinuating Aunt Norris. Angela Pleasance as the placid Lady Bertram has a great moment when, hearing that her dangerously ill son Tom has just been brought home, her sedentary character leaps from her sofa and runs down a flight of stairs. It's on VHS and DVD.

I had the pleasure of hearing Ms. Le Touzel speak about Fanny at the 2003 Annual General Meeting of the Jane Austen Society of North America in Winchester, England, where I found her insights penetrating and sensitive.

Patricia Rozema's 1999 *Mansfield Park,* which is called just that — "Patricia Rozema's *Mansfield Park*" — is a fine movie in its own right. It's just not Austen's *Mansfield Park.* Written and directed by . . . you guessed it, Patricia Rozema, this film reinvents the passive heroine Fanny Price into a self-possessed young woman who writes stories (using Austen's own juvenile works) and — like Richardson's cinematic *Tom Jones* — talks directly to the camera. Clearly influenced by late-20th-century neocolonial academic literary criticism, the film emphasizes in varied ways that the wealth of Mansfield Park comes from the slave trade. Nobel-prize-winning British playwright Harold Pinter plays a villainous and creepy Sir Thomas Bertram — who in the novel isn't particularly villainous and creepy.

Mansfield Park is on Britain's ITV's list of new Austen television productions slated for UK release in the fall of 2006. Maggie Wadey, who did the eerie *Northanger Abbey* 1986 miniseries, is doing the screenplay. I'm hoping that Wadey stays close to this intriguing, deep, and different Austen novel — different because the heroine is unusually passive and timid.

Getting clues about Emma

Emma continues to receive popular coverage in the media as well:

- *Emma* was first in the hands of adapters for a 1948 live, BBC television show that ran for almost two hours.

- In 1954, NBC's *Kraft Television Theater* did a live, one-hour version, starring Felicia Montealegre in the title role, with Roddy McDowell, graduating from child roles to playing Mr. Elton.

- Three years earlier, Miss Montealegre became the wife of the prominent conductor and composer of the musical *West Side Story,* Leonard Bernstein. That fact has nothing to do with Austen, but may help you win a game of trivia.

- In 1960, the BBC did a six-part, 180-minute miniseries based on *Emma.* The same year CBS's *Camera Three* series offered a one-hour *Emma.*

- The novel finally received more coverage in 1972, when BBC-2 offered a five-part miniseries by our old friend Denis Constanduros (of the two *Sense and Sensibility* miniseries, discussed earlier). It's on DVD and VHS.

- The screen then had to wait 25 years for another *Emma* adaptation, but it was worth the wait. Amy Heckerling wrote and directed the hit film *Clueless,* the title of which perfectly describes Emma, star and centerpiece of her own novel, *Emma.* Resetting the novel in a contemporary Beverly Hills High School, Heckerling's film reminds us that the experiences that

Austen's Emma endures are so universal that *Clueless*'s Cher, played by Alicia Silverstone, endures similar events. As Austen knew, human nature never changes. When the news finally came out that *Clueless* was, indeed, based on the 1815-novel *Emma*, teenagers who loved the film were shocked that Jane Austen could be relevant. It's on DVD.

✔ Placing the novel back in its historical context, Doug McGrath's 1996, two-hour commercial film, *Emma*, starring Gwyneth Paltrow, was also a hit. With gorgeous costumes and wonderful location settings, the film makes occasional departures from the novel — such as turning the timid little Harriet Smith, who's Emma's project in the novel, into the bull-in-the-china-shop Toni Collette, who gained weight to play the role. Placing Emma and Mr. Knightley (played by the suave, but too-short-for-the-role Jeremy Northam) outside shooting arrows at a target is a nice little tip of the hat to the 1940 MGM *Pride and Prejudice*, where Elizabeth (Greer Garson) surprises Darcy (Lawrence Olivier) with her skill with the bow. (And no, the bow and arrow scene is not in the novel.) Ewan Macgregor plays Frank Churchill. But departures from Austen's novel aside, Paltrow is a charming Emma, showing how sincere Emma is in trying to help those around her, while remaining clueless. And she does a great British accent. It's on DVD.

✔ Another *Emma*, this time a 107-minute television version produced by Britain's ITV and the U.S. Arts & Entertainment cable station, came out in 1996. A young Kate Beckinsale plays Emma in this film, written by Andrew Davies. The petite Samantha Morton is more like the novel's Harriet Smith than Toni Collette's in the McGrath film. Mark Strong is an appropriately tall Mr. Knightley. This is available on VHS and DVD, and it will be re-released on British TV for ITV's Austen extravaganza.

Performing Persuasion

Austen's last finished novel, *Persuasion*, has seen three versions.

✔ In the 1960–1961 winter holiday season, BBC presented a four-part mini-series on videotape.

✔ Then in 1971, Britain's ITV/Granada offered a 225-minute miniseries, available on VHS and DVD.

The oddest point about the 1971 version is that the actress playing the heroine, Anne Elliot, always looks the same. In the novel, Anne is said to have lost her bloom during the eight-year period since she had rejected a proposal from Captain Wentworth, the novel's naval hero. She then regains her bloom at Lyme Regis — so much so, that her father, who never pays attention to her, notices how much better she looks when he sees her again in Bath.

✔ The 1995 version of *Persuasion,* starring Amanda Root as a wonderful Anne, emphasizes the change in Anne by showing her rather frumpy early in the film, and then rather attractive later. This adaptation of the novel had two lives as both a television production (seen in the US on PBS-TV's *Masterpiece Theatre*) and a commercial film. It was produced by the BBC and Sony Pictures. Nick Dear wrote the script, and Roger Michell directed. Ciaran Hinds plays Captain Frederick Wentworth. The film does well in showing more realistically than other Austen-based films what life was like back then.

- Dinner is in a darkish room because it's lighted only by candles.

- The naval officers' uniforms are well worn.

- Their faces sport five o'clock shadows.

The only disappointing part of the film comes near the end: Nick Dear used Austen's cancelled chapters about the reunion of Wentworth and Anne. When you read the book with both the cancelled and Austen's revised final chapters, you see why Austen changed them. You can get this as a DVD or VHS.

✔ A new television version of *Persuasion,* with a screenplay by Simon Burke, is to be part of Britain's ITV Austen series to be shown in the UK in August 2006. So we'll just have to wait to see if the new Anne Elliot loses her bloom or not.

"Inventing" Austen's Life On Screen

A new film docudrama, *Becoming Jane,* a fictionalized account of Austen as a young woman, is in the works for a 2007 release. It presents the highly controversial and unsubstantiated story of Jane Austen's reunion with Tom Lefroy in London. (For more on Austen and Tom Lefroy, see Chapter 3.) Anne Hathaway plays Jane Austen and James McEvoy plays Tom. A person I know who read the script reports the film has a lot of "invention" in it: This means, if your teacher assigns you to learn about Austen's actual life, reading *this* book will get you a much better grade on the test than seeing the film. But the film is said to be fun — truth aside! The Irish Film Institute is supporting the film.

Chapter 16

Determining Austen's Literary Descendents

*J*ust as Jane Austen's writing was influenced by those who came before her, so her writing influenced and continues to influence those who follow her. First-tier writers — and by first-tier, I mean those who are in the canon of British and American writers whose works are considered by scholars as the best literary representatives of their time — such as George Eliot, Henry James, Oscar Wilde, and Edith Wharton all show in their work that they knew and respected Austen, another canonical writer. Austen's work has also inspired a vast number of sequels in the past 40 years for those readers who are interested in such hypothetical matters as how Darcy and Elizabeth function as a married couple or how Emma, as Mrs. Knightley, raises her own children. Then there are the authors who've been inspired to use Jane Austen as a literary character to flesh out her personality. Some writers and reviewers see Austen as the founder of *chick lit,* which in its best sense is literature written for women that shows women fulfilling themselves like Elizabeth, Emma, Elinor, and other Austen heroines do. And finally, nowadays advertisers and reviewers occasionally deem the author of a novel that can loosely be called a "comedy of manners" because it reflects a contemporary, recognizable social scene, the "new Jane Austen." ("As if!" as Cher says in the clever film *Clueless,* an *Emma*-based story).

Obviously, Jane Austen has had a wide, deep, and broad influence on her readers.

From canonical works of literature to fluff, and all kinds of books in between, you can identify Jane Austen's presence, and this chapter explores just that.

Influencing Later Canonical Writers

Among the first-tier novelists (see Table 16-1) whom Austen influenced are those who write in the realistic tradition. Austen's novels present realistic situations and experiences that reflect the world of the gentry in the England of her times. In so doing, she presents characters whose psyches she explores so that her readers can come to understand them, sometimes better than those readers understand themselves. (For more on early realistic writing, see Chapter 4, especially the section on Henry Fielding.) The witty dialogue seen particularly in *Pride and Prejudice* influenced the dramatist Oscar Wilde, who wrote comedies of manners for the stage as Austen did for the novel.

Table 16-1	Jane Austen's Canonical Heirs in Chronological Order
Novelists	*Dramatists*
Gaskell	Wilde
Eliot	
Trollope	
Flaubert	
James	
Wharton	
Forster	
Woolf	

Speaking of Austen's "realism" refers to her realistic portrayal of life among the English gentry in the late-18th and early-19th centuries. Used in this broad sense, the term realism isn't to be confused with the later 19th-century movement called "Realism" in American, British, and especially French literature, where novelists sought subjects related to middle-class life and placed less emphasis on traditional plotting. Austen crafted her plots with great care and focused on the gentry of her time. But Austen's realistic writing, as well as Fielding's and Richardson's, which strongly influenced Austen's, certainly contributed to 19th-century Realism. And many of those realistic writers, such as George Eliot, Henry James, Edith Wharton, and Gustave Flaubert, learned the elements of realistic writing from Austen and will be discussed as her literary heirs in this chapter. (For more on the class structure of Austen's day, see Chapter 2.)

Examining types of narrative technique

The narrator is the "voice" that tells the story, as opposed to the actual author, though the two are often one in the same. (The narrator and the author are noticeably different when an author chooses to present the novel in the voice of a particular character: for example, a male author tells the story in the voice of a young girl.) The narrator can tell the story from different perspectives or points of view. Austen uses two of these perspectives or narrative techniques:

Omniscient, third-person narration occurs when the narrator is all-knowing and speaks of the characters in the grammatical third person (he, she, they, Elizabeth, Darcy). Jane Austen uses an omniscient, third-person narrator, applying free indirect discourse and even mediating omniscient narration. Austen is also occasionally the intrusive omniscient narrator commenting on events, as she does in the final chapters of *Northanger Abbey* and *Mansfield Park*. For example, in the final chapter of *Mansfield Park,* she writes of "My Fanny," showing affection for the novel's heroine, Fanny Price. Reading that phrase, we know she'll treat her with tenderness is that chapter.

Objective narration is also known as "fly on the wall." Characters speak to each other with no intermediary words from the narrator. This technique can be applied to dramatic presentation. Austen uses dramatic presentation, when she offers, without interceding, the ongoing conversation among characters, as in the drawing-room scenes at Netherfield in *Pride and Prejudice,* where Darcy and Elizabeth engage in extensive dialogue, with occasional comments from other characters like Bingley. In so doing, Austen sometimes doesn't even insert "he says" or "she says."

Looking at some of Austen's novelizing heirs

Austen's heirs in the top tier of literature were influenced by her writing in multiple ways. Not only did they follow her in presenting a realistic view of their contemporary society, but also in choosing the types of characters and societies they treat, as well as in narrative technique.

Austen almost always uses an all-knowing narrator that speaks of the characters in the third person (he, she, they, and so on) — see the sidebar, "Examining types of narrative technique."

Austen used both an omniscient narrator and a dramatic presentation of characters through conversation. Among Austen's many important contributions to the novel form, which was developing as she wrote, is the narrative technique she used to present a character's thoughts and feelings called *free indirect discourse.* This term means that Austen writes so readers can slip into the character's head and understand what the character has been experiencing intellectually and emotionally. By dramatizing the character's consciousness, Austen advances the action. For example, in *Emma,* Mr. Knightley recognizes his romantic love for the heroine: "He had been in love with Emma, and jealous of Frank Churchill, from about the same period, one sentiment having probably enlightened the other. It was his jealousy of Frank Churchill that had taken him from the country. . . . He had gone to learn to be indifferent" (E 3:14). Today, readers are used to reading passages of free indirect discourse. But Jane Austen was key in developing and using it in her novels.

Henry James

Literary scholars frequently think of Henry James and Jane Austen as a pair. Rudyard Kipling's short story, "The Janeites," published in 1924, encourages this practice. "The Janeites" is about a small group of British soldiers in World War I, all of whom are masons, who form a subsidiary Masonic group based on their knowledge and admiration for the works of Jane Austen, which comfort them in the trenches. Told largely in a British Cockney dialect, the story has one soldier, Hammick ('Ammick), say of Austen, " . . . what a pity 'twas Jane 'ad died barren," to which Macklin counters, "She *did* leave lawful issue in the shape o' one son; an' 'is name was 'Enery James." Here's a translation from the Cockney English: Hammick says that Austen, who was unmarried, died without children ("died barren"). Macklin disagrees, saying that Austen left one heir, a literary one: Henry James. (For more on Kipling's "The Janeites," see Chapter 1.)

Henry James was influenced by Austen, whom he admired greatly. James's presentation of the thoughts of major characters owes much to Austen's narrative technique, especially how she goes into the minds of Emma Woodhouse and Elizabeth Bennet, though James's style is more complex than Austen's. In fact, James criticized Austen for her occasional overt narrative intrusions because they subvert realism, such as the final chapter of *Mansfield Park,* where the narrator quickly wraps up the novel, dispensing poetic justice all around. Readers have noted the similarities — deliberate or unconscious — between Kate Croy in James's *The Wings of the Dove* and Mary Crawford in *Mansfield Park.* Many of his novels, such as *The Ambassadors,* are regarded as comedies or novels of manners in the vein of Austen, who learned about comedies of manners from the brilliant plays of the masters of this type of writing, William Congreve and Richard Brinsley Sheridan. (For more info on comedies of manners, go to Chapter 4.)

Other writers

Canonical writers of both novels and plays before and after James are also indebted to Austen. Here they are in chronological order; for James's place in the chronology, see Table 16-1 in this chapter.

✔ **Elizabeth Gaskell:** While far more concerned with presenting social problems overtly than Austen, the Victorian novelist Elizabeth Gaskell focuses on domestic life in country villages in the manner of Austen, where the events within a family are the material for novels. Among Gaskell's novel in this vein are *Cranford* and *Wives and Daughters.*

✔ **George Eliot (pen name Marianne Evans):** Eliot's most famous work, *Middlemarch* (1871), is a novel of epic proportions with a cast of characters far larger than any Austen novel. But its subtitle, "A Study of Provincial Life," the center of which is the village of Middlemarch, is reminiscent of Austen's focus on country life. Eliot, like Austen, delves into the psychological lives of her characters. In fact, early reviewers of Eliot's writing noted the similarities between hers and Austen's. Nowadays as novel readers, you expect to find the author dealing with the inner lives or psychology of characters. Keep in mind that Austen was one of the early novelists to bring her readers into characters' minds without having them write letters to express their feelings. *Middlemarch*'s heroine, Dorothea Brooke, may also be likened to Austen's heroines as she, too, is looking for personal fulfillment. Austen handled this type of female character so successfully that she is sometimes credited with founding the noncanonical but currently popular chick lit.

✔ **Anthony Trollope:** The great Victorian novelist Anthony Trollope, who called *Pride and Prejudice* the best English novel, was also an heir of Jane Austen, particularly as he, like Austen, was a novelist of manners. Both novelists look acutely at their respective societies and quietly satirize parts of it. On this subject, Trollope, with his six-novel Barsetshire series, presenting the lives of ordinary people in the fictional English county of Barsetshire, is a good example.

✔ **Gustave Flaubert:** Flaubert, whose best-known novel is *Madame Bovary,* is a social, psychological, and moral Realist. Like Austen, he uses free indirect discourse. The consciousness of the characters advance the action in his works and put readers into intimate contact with the characters' thinking.

✔ **Oscar Wilde:** Victorian playwright Oscar Wilde succeeded Sheridan as the master of comedies of manners with his plays *Lady Windermere's Fan, A Woman of No Importance, An Ideal Husband,* and *The Importance of Being Earnest.* Joking in a letter to her sister about her newly published *Pride and Prejudice,* Austen foresaw her readers' "delight in the playfulness & Epigrammatism of the general stile (sic)" (Letter, February 1813). By "Epigrammatism," Austen means clever, witty, terse comments, such as Darcy's saying, "'Every savage can dance,'" or Mrs. Bennet's, "'Those who do not complain are never pitied,'" or Elizabeth's "'Is not general incivility the very essence of love?" (PP 1:6, 1:20, 2:2). Likewise, Wilde, in his comedies of manners for the stage, is also skilled at clever one-liners, as well as lively repartee between hero and heroine in the vein of Darcy and Elizabeth.

✔ **Edith Wharton:** An American novelist, Wharton offers in her novels ironic studies of turn-of-the-century (from the 19th to the 20th century, that is!) New York City society, complete with young heroines who have much to learn. She, too, wrote comedies of manners. Examples of her work are *The House of Mirth* and *The Age of Innocence*.

✔ **E. M. Forster:** Forster wrote, "I am a Jane Austenite." He follows Austen in writing comedies of manners set on the domestic stage, paying attention to decorous behavior (behaving according to one's class) and stressing individual morality. His novels include *A Room with a View* and *Howard's End*. (For decorum and morality in Austen, see Chapter 12.)

✔ **Virginia Woolf:** Woolf wrote influentially about Austen in her important essay, "Jane Austen," in *The Common Reader* (1925). Like Austen, Woolf experimented with narration, but Woolf's narration is the modern stream of consciousness technique (following the mind of a character in a continuous flow of thought). While in many ways, Woolf and Austen are very different types of writers — because they come from very different worlds, with Woolf living through the physically and psychologically cataclysmic Word War I — Woolf, like Austen, dealt with the ordinary experiences of women.

✔ **Barbara Pym:** While not a canonical writer, British novelist Barbara Pym has been called "the twentieth-century Jane Austen." Pym writes subtle, quiet comedies set in country villages (sound familiar?). Her main characters tend to be single women, but their stories tend not to have the happy endings that Austen's heroines enjoy. Her heroines also tend to be spinsters — more like Miss Bates (in *Emma*) than Elizabeth or Emma. Readers find parallels between Pym's *A Few Green Leaves*, with its heroine named Emma, and *Emma*. Other have suggested that *A Glass of Blessings* is Pym's version of *Emma*. Because *Some Tame Gazelle* deals with two sisters, readers have found parallels with *Sense and Sensibility*.

✔ **Anita Brookner:** A distinguished art historian at Cambridge University and London's prestigious Courtauld Institute, Anita Brookner also has a highly successful career as a novelist, whose carefully crafted works are considered comedies of manners, like Austen's, though they are darker. But unlike Austen's characters, her female characters frequently experience disappointed love and loneliness. While literary reviewers and critics frequently align her with Austen, Brookner denied it in a January 28, 2001, interview with London's Sunday *Observer* newspaper! Brookner's *Hotel du Lac* won England's highest literary award, the Booker Prize, in 1984.

Sequelizing Austen's Novels

Austen characters are so vividly real for many readers that readers want to continue the characters' lives after the novels end. Sequels to *Pride and Prejudice* and *Emma* are especially numerous, perhaps because the marriages of such attractive characters as Elizabeth and Darcy and Emma and

Mr. Knightley pique readers' curiosities. Others just need more Jane Austen(ish) novels. I have to admit that when I need more Jane Austen, I just reread Jane Austen. But for those readers who seek sequels, I refer you to the Republic of Pemberley Web site (www.pemberley.com), which has a link to sequels.

As you can tell from the previous paragraph, I am not a fan of sequels. But many lovers of Austen's novels are, and I would never attempt to convince them not to read the sequels. I've never read one because I'm content to let Austen's characters' lives end with her novels — although Austen, herself, would tell family members, when they asked, what happened to her characters after the book ended! But that's the point: The characters are *her* characters, presented in her inimitable way with her uniquely infectious wit and subtle irony. And I can leave them in her novels without the least concern about what happens to them after the last pages of her books. Now all the Austen sequel writers — which is a genre in and of itself — will hate me!

Finishing Austen without Austen

Austen left two works incomplete: her early (1805) *The Watsons* and *Sanditon,* a hysterical send-up of hypochondriacs that she wrote, with sad irony, while dying and left unfinished because she could no longer manipulate a pen or pencil.

According to Austen's nephew, James Edward Austen-Leigh, his aunt left *The Watsons* unfinished while living in Bath, a conclusion reached from the 1803 and 1804 watermarks on the paper on which it is written. (See Chapter 3 for Austen's Bath residence.) Austen-Leigh actually gave the manuscript, which was in his sister Caroline's possession, its title when he printed it for the first time in the second edition of his *Memoir of Jane Austen* (1871). According to Austen's family, her plan for continuing the work included the death of elderly Mr. Watson, causing his daughter, Emma (the work's heroine), to live with her brother Robert and his obnoxious wife. Emma would then turn down a marriage proposal from Lord Osborne, whose sister, in turn, was to be in love with the charming Rev. Mr. Howard, who loves Emma. (And in the part written by Austen, Emma appears interested in Mr. Howard.) True love would finally prevail when Emma and Mr. Howard marry.

By selectively using this information, two modern authors have attempted continuations.

> ✔ John Coates rewrote much of the beginning (Austen's actual material!) and finished it, publishing the book in 1958; it was reprinted in 1977. His work changes Austen's lovely heroine, Emma Watson, into a rather unpleasant character! I read this out of scholarly duty back in graduate school. The whole work was un-Austen to me.

✔ Joan Aiken, who has written Austen sequels and complements (such as *Jane Fairfax,* which as its subtitle states is "Jane Austen's *Emma,* Through Another's Eyes"), tried her hand at another version called *Emma Watson,* published in 1975. Because I'm not a sequel reader, I cannot comment on this work.

The incomplete *Sanditon* was completed in 1975 and published with the byline "Jane Austen and Another Lady." Two different authors have attempted to complete this book.

✔ An Austen sequelizer, Juliette Shapiro, is responsible for a more recent continuation, published in 2004.

✔ Fay Weldon is currently writing a script for *Sanditon.*

Attributing "chick lit" to Austen

Chick lit is a term used to describe a form of popular fiction marketed to single young working women in their 20s. The term chick lit is derived from the slang *chick* for a young woman, as well as from the gum brand, Chiclets suggesting that chick lit is reading candy for young women. Many chick lit books are printed with candy-colored covers (pastels). Intending to make Austen novels more appealing to the young female eye, a British publisher is planning to bring out her novels in the summer of 2006 in a paperback edition for which all the covers will be in pastels, giving the books the appearance of chick lit. But if chick lit is more narrowly defined as literature dealing with a woman's fulfilling her needs and desires, then Jane Austen certainly is the mother of the genre. For all of her heroines' experiences are geared toward greater self-knowledge and self-fulfillment.

Popular culture critics normally credit Helen Fielding's novel, *Bridget Jones's Diary* (1996) with starting the chick lit genre. Fielding noted that her book was inspired by *Pride and Prejudice. Bridget Jones's Diary* offers many superficial connections to Austen's novel.

✔ The surname of both heroes is Darcy.

✔ The personalities of Elizabeth's and Bridget's fathers are similar.

✔ The relationship between Austen's Darcy and Wickham inspires that of Fielding's Darcy and Cleaver (the Wickham-like character).

✔ The publication for which Bridget works is Pemberley Press — the name of Austen's Darcy's estate.

Being "Austenesque"

In Alexander McCall Smith's novel, *The Sunday Philosophy Club* (Knopf Publishing Group), the philosopher and heroine philosophizes that "It is a great honor as a philosopher or as a writer to become an adjective" (166). (McCall Smith, himself, is called Austen-like in his writing.) Readers can be Austenesque through books that enable them to have tea with Jane Austen and to cook foods mentioned in her novels (like the white soup Bingley promises to serve at the Netherfield Ball in *Pride and Prejudice*) and letters using *The Jane Austen Cookbook* (McClelland and Stewart, Ltd.).

Novelists can also write Austenesque books.

✔ The aristocratic Dame Emily Eden (1797–1869) wrote two novels, now published in one volume, *The Semi-Attached Couple* and *The Semi-Detached House* (Bantam Doubleday Dell Publishing Group, Virago Modern Classics Series), that are social comedies like Austen's novels. Both of these books are concerned with love, money, and manners. Indeed, novels that focus on these themes or that are social comedies tend to be viewed as Austenesque.

✔ *The New Yorker's* review of Ian McEwan's *Atonement* (2002) called it "semi-Austenesque." In fact, *Atonement* (Knopf Publishing Group) quotes a few lines from *Northanger Abbey* as its epigraph.

✔ The cover of the U.S. paperback edition of Susanna Clarke's international bestseller, *Jonathan Strange and Mr. Norrell* (publisher Bloomsbury USA), quotes a review from *Time* magazine saying the book "combines the dark mythology of fantasy with the delicious social comedy of Jane Austen. . . ."

✔ For readers interested in going back, imaginatively, to the Regency period in which Austen lived and about which she wrote, the most Austenesque novelist is Georgette Heyer (1902–1974), queen of the Regency Romances, a style that she created. The Regency Romance is a sub-genre of the genre "romance," in which a man and woman find romantic love and live happily ever after. Regency romances subscribe to the mores and conventions of the Regency period (1811–1820), as seen in such Heyer titles as *Regency Buck* and *Sprig Muslin*. (For information on the Regency/Georgian period relevant to Regency romances, see Chapters 2 and 12.)

The heroine of Fielding's novel, however, is falling apart most of the time, making her totally dissimilar to the incredibly self-possessed and clever Elizabeth Bennet. Fielding's second *Bridget Jones* book, *The Edge of Reason* (1999), very loosely parallels *Persuasion*. Both books were made into successful films in 2001 and 2004. The movies further emphasized Austen parallels by having Colin Firth, who played Darcy in the 1995 television miniseries of *Pride and Prejudice*, play Mark Darcy. Close viewers of the films also see other actors who've played characters in other Austen-based films and television series doing roles in the *Bridget Jones* films, making the films more of an "in" joke for Austen fans.

Appropriating Austen in Popular Culture

Jane Austen is so popular today that even people who've never read her novels (gasp!) know her name and recognize at least the title of *Pride and Prejudice,* her most famous book. People may even recognize who Darcy is — or at least know that Colin Firth played Darcy in the televised miniseries of the novel. Because Austen's books are "courtship novels," dealing with how men and women relate to each other and connect, they've been used as source material for advice manuals on the contemporary dating scene:

✔ *Dating Mr. Darcy: The Smart Girl's Guide to Sensible Romance*

✔ *Jane Austen's Guide to Dating*

Anything to do with Jane Austen is an eye-catcher nowadays because she's extremely popular. So some books use Austen's name in the title just to gain attention:

✔ *Jane Austen in Boca*

✔ *Jane Austen in Scarsdale*

Other titles focus on issues other than dating. For example, Karen Joy Fowler's *The Jane Austen Book Club* is a charming novel set in contemporary California about six readers who form the reading group of the title. Given that Austen writes about human nature, which is always the same, Fowler's characters experience events similar to those experienced by several of Austen's characters. The reader also attends the book club's six meetings — one for each Austen novel — and listens to Fowler's characters discuss the novels. (For info on forming a book club — on Jane Austen, of course — go to Chapter 15.)

Other writers sometimes give Austen a little tip of the hat, acknowledging their delight in her work. In the Harry Potter books, J. K. Rowling calls the cat at Harry's school Mrs. Norris after the nasty, controlling Mrs. Norris (Aunt Norris) in *Mansfield Park*. And in *Harry Potter and the Sorcerer's Stone,* when Dumbledore first appears in Chapter 1, his eyes are "light, bright, and sparkling" — the phrase (minus Austen's "&" between "light" and "bright") Austen used in her letter to Cassandra when she joked about needing to make *Pride and Prejudice* a darker novel (Letter, February 4, 1813).

Part V
The Part of Tens

The 5th Wave   By Rich Tennant

"The chef was flirting with our English nanny
in the garden the other day, so she tied him to
a tree and stuck a watermelon over his head.
I'm sure there's an 'Austenism' that would
describe the scene perfectly, I just can't think
of what it is."

In this part . . .

Lists, list, lists: I don't know about you, but I'm always dealing with lists of things to do. But the lists in this part shouldn't be a burden to you. As both President of the Jane Austen Society of North America and as a professor of English who teaches three — count 'em, three! — different Austen-based courses, people frequently ask me all sorts of questions about Austen. So, I've created these lists to give you some quick info, along with my personal views, about Austen topics, trivia, and treats. In the following pages you can find my thoughts, evaluations, and recommendations about Austen's ten most memorable characters and quotations, ten best Austen places to visit in England, and ten best books (besides this one, of course!) about Jane Austen.

Chapter 17

Ten Most Memorable Austen Characters

In This Chapter

▶ Being memorable doesn't necessarily mean being good

▶ Noting the worthy characters of Austen's fiction

Austen's works have so many great characters that it's hard to select just ten. It's almost like having to select your most memorable friends! So I've tried my hardest to pick the characters most worthy of the honor. (One section is a tie, so although I only have nine sections, I do indeed list ten people!) Check out the following sections for my top choices and see if you agree!

Austen's Most Memorable Child

Austen doesn't populate her novels with many children, and when they're on the page, they're usually annoying like the Middleton children in *Sense and Sensibility*. But she has one truly wonderful child character in her fragment *The Watsons*. Charles Blake is a 10-year-old boy who loves to dance — so much so that he accompanies his mother and the noble Osborne family to the ball. Having lined up Miss Osborne as his partner for the first dance, he awaits the opening dance with excitement and joy. But as the dance is to begin, Miss Osborne dumps Charles for Colonel Beresford, promising Charles she will dance with him after tea. Charles now stands "the picture of disappointment, with crimson'd cheeks, quivering lips, and his eyes bent on the floor." Suddenly, Emma Watson saves the day (and evening!) and offers to dance with Charles.

Charles puts on his new dancing gloves and proceeds to the floor with Emma. When Miss Osborne sees him dancing with Emma, she says, "'Upon my word Charles . . . you have a better partner than me'" — to which the happy Charles answered "'Yes.'" And he's not just speaking of Emma's dancing quality.

Austen's Most Memorable Leading Lady

And the award goes to . . . *Pride and Prejudice*'s Elizabeth Bennet, hands down. She's clever and quick, but she shows that being clever and quick is both a strength and a weakness. On the positive side, Elizabeth is quick and snappy in conversation: When Darcy claims that country life offers little variety in people, she immediately counters, "'But people themselves alter so much, that there is something new to be observed in them for ever'" — just like Elizabeth Bennet (PP 1:9)! Yet having been insulted by Darcy's saying she was just okay-looking, but not pretty enough to ask for a dance, she quickly forms and nurtures a prejudice against him, egging him on about Wickham. Taking everything that Wickham says at face value allows her to be duped by his lies. But Elizabeth is also honest with herself and others. When she studies Darcy's explanatory letter and reflects both on its contents and the behaviors of Jane and Wickham, she is totally frank about her errors, saying "'Till this moment, I never knew myself'" (PP 2:13). Elizabeth is also athletic, a good dancer, and modest about her accomplishments. No wonder Darcy falls for her!

Austen's Most Memorable Leading Man

Pride and Prejudice may be racking up some honors in this most memorable list. But, hey, it's a delicious book! Fitzwilliam Darcy is the next character from *Pride and Prejudice,* but he may be a bit misunderstood. Misunderstood? Yes. Actors play him dour, sullen, and serious. While he does look grave once in a while, he does so because he has a lot at stake in choosing a wife to become the next mistress of Pemberley, his fabulous estate. He frequently smiles at Elizabeth appreciatively and is remarkably patient when she's being pert with him. He enjoys conversation and is "clever," as the author points out. Did I say he's tall and handsome? Most memorably, however, is the way he learns from his mistakes, which are biggies. He insults Elizabeth Bennet, meddles in the Bingley/Jane romance, and first proposes to Elizabeth outlining all the ways she's inferior to him. Even with an annual income of £10,000, he wasn't charming his way into Elizabeth's heart and mind by insulting her. But he's always in movement, trying to explain himself to Elizabeth, and he learns more about himself because Elizabeth (a strong character herself — that's why she's the most memorable leading lady) corrects him and puts him in his place. Later, Darcy admits to her how she has helped him to be a better man and a gentleman. He's an honest man who admits his faults, a wonderful hero, and for my money, the most memorable hero in Austen's novels.

Austen's Most Memorable Female Flirts

It's a tie here, but each female flirt is different from the other. *Pride and Prejudice*'s Miss Bingley loves to flirt with Darcy, but she goes about it in the wrong ways. She can't stop putting her foot in her mouth, and her flirting seems to gratify the reader because the flirting always boomerangs on her. For example:

- She asks Darcy what's on his mind, expecting him to insult the company at the Lucas party; he answers that he's contemplating how Elizabeth Bennet's fine eyes enhance her pretty face.

- She asks him how tall his sister is: He first says she's about Elizabeth Bennet's height — which shows he has been paying attention to Elizabeth!

- She picks up to read the second volume of a work because Darcy's reading the first. She doesn't realize how dumb that makes her look. No one reads the second volume before the first.

Miss Bingley's nasty attempts at flirting with Darcy by demeaning Elizabeth and her family either fall flat or ricochet on her. She can't win. It's almost a pleasure to watch her fail.

Mary Crawford from *Mansfield Park* is a memorable flirt for a very different reason than Miss Bingley is. The pretty, witty Mary is a dangerous flirt because she nearly gets her man, Edmund, who finds this daring, good-looking, harp-playing city girl physically attractive. He has never seen any woman quite like her. She's flirty, athletic (soon after learning to ride the horse, she breaks into a canter, while poor Fanny can hardly make it walk!), and she has an attitude: "'Selfishness must always be forgiven you know, because there is no hope of cure,'" she says, apologizing for monopolizing Fanny's horse. But Mary's character is also made complex and interesting because the narrator speaks of "the really good feelings by which she was almost purely governed" (MP 1:15). Austen says this when Mary is the only person in the room to rescue and comfort Fanny when the mean Aunt Norris yells at her for being stubborn and "ungrateful" in refusing to act in the play (MP 1:15).

Austen's Most Memorable Cad

Austen's fiction has a good number of flirtatious males, but her cads are her most provocative flirts because cads behave irresponsibly with women. The most memorable cad is Henry Crawford, brother of one of the most memorable female flirts — what a family! Crawford has money and an estate, and so is unlike cads from other novels who flirt to win a wealthy wife. Because Crawford is actually reluctant to marry, and a wife, even a rich wife, is neither appealing nor necessary to him, he flirts for the thrill of the hunt. This behavior makes him, like his sister, a more dangerous character than his fellow cads.

- ✔ Henry flirts with Maria Bertram simply because she's engaged to Mr. Rushworth.

- ✔ He seduces Mrs. Maria Bertram Rushworth into adultery simply because he can: If an engaged woman is a challenge, a married woman is a real challenge.

- ✔ He wants to put a small hole in Fanny Price's heart and make her love him because she makes her disapproval of him obvious. He insinuates himself with his target, coming, for example, to Fanny's home in Portsmouth just at the time when the noise and the dirt are getting to her.

This morally reprehensible behavior makes him a little scary. These traits don't bode well for his character's improvement, even under the near saintly power of Fanny Price.

In the final chapter of *Mansfield Park,* the narrator, tidily wrapping up all the loose ends, states that had Crawford "persevered . . . uprightly, Fanny must have been his reward" (3:17). This statement implies that had Crawford not "attack[ed]" Maria and led her into adultery, Edmund would've married Mary, and Fanny would've "voluntarily bestowed" herself on Crawford. Yet the reader may question this neat conclusion because of Henry Crawford's callous treatment of women. All of this makes Crawford Austen's most memorable cad.

Austen's Most Memorable Dupe

If you want to give out awards for characters who are easily deceived or used as tools for someone else's power, you would have to look no further than Emma Woodhouse. Although she's certainly "Handsome, clever, and rich," she lets her clever side slip and allows herself to be deceived by Frank Churchill.

Frank, who's anything but frank, leads Emma into having sexually suspicious thoughts about Jane Fairfax (not fair facts about Jane!) and making unflattering remarks about her, suggesting that Jane is feeling "all the dangerous pleasure of knowing herself beloved by the husband [Mr. Dixon] of her friend" (E 2:8). Emma attributes Jane's failing to accompany her friends to Ireland (where the Dixons live) and suddenly receiving a beautiful pianoforte as an anonymous gift to her imagined Jane-Dixon affair. When Emma learns of the Frank/Jane engagement, she complains to Mrs. Weston about their coming "'among us with professions of openness and simplicity. . . . Here we have been . . . completely duped'" (E 3:10). But Emma has been the biggest dupe of all, allowing herself to think that Frank was in love with her and that Jane was in some type of relationship with her friend's husband. Too clever for her own good, Emma, as she herself complains, has been duped by Frank and Jane. But mostly, she has been duped by her romantic imaginings (E 3:10).

Austen's Most Memorable Talker

Hands down, the honor of most memorable talker goes to Miss Bates, from *Emma,* who says quite openly, "'I am a talker, you know; I am rather a talker'" (E 3:5). The good-hearted Miss Bates talks incessantly, moving from one topic to another without stopping to catch her breath, and never letting anyone get a word in edgewise! Thus, she enters, talking, the Crown Inn Ball, and seeing Frank Churchill says:

> "Oh! Mr. Frank Churchill, I must tell you my mother's spectacles have never been in fault since; the rivet never came out again. My mother always talks of your good nature. Does not she, Jane?—Do not we talk of Mr. Frank Churchill" Ah! Here's Miss Woodhouse—Dear Miss Woodhouse, how do you do — Very well I thank you, quite well. This is meeting quite in fairyland!" (E 3:2)

This speech consists of 65 lines of her talking solo!

Austen's Most Memorable Couple

Elizabeth Bennet's Aunt and Uncle Gardiner from *Pride and Prejudice* aren't only Austen's most memorable couple, but also they're her most elegant. Through the Gardiners, Austen shows that a man (Mr. Gardiner) can live in London within sight of his warehouses — a fact the Bingley sisters laugh about as a sign of his presumed lack of gentility — and still be an utter gentleman. His wife is a perfect match for him: She's a true lady. Thus, when Elizabeth and the Gardiners visit Pemberley and are surprised by the unexpected appearance of the estate's owner, Darcy, Elizabeth is proud when the couple talks so politely and intelligently with Darcy that he "takes them for people of fashion" (PP 3:1). They are at ease with the rich Darcy: courteous without flattering him and sensible in their conversation without showing off.

Austen's Most Memorable Abnormal Personality

Writing at the beginning of the 19th century, Austen created a number of characters who displayed abnormal personality disorders nearly two centuries before they were identified as such. *Mansfield Park*'s Aunt Norris and Lady Catherine of *Pride and Prejudice* are controllers. Lucy Steele of *Sense and Sensibility* is passive aggressive toward Elinor Dashwood. And in the same novel with Lucy, the charming John Willoughby is a sociopath. But with all of these characters vying for the prize of most abnormal, it's John Willoughby who takes the cake.

Sociopaths are superficially charming and amiable. They tend to engage in casual sex and feel no guilt for any wrong they've done. Rather, they feel themselves to be victims. Now look at Willoughby:

- He's attractive and charming; the Dashwood women think he's marvelous.

- He impregnated Eliza Williams and promptly forgot her.

- He admits to first paying attention to Marianne simply for the fun of it.

- He feels that Mrs. Smith (his rich relative) has disinherited him simply because she's a prude and wants him to accept Eliza and their child as his wife and child. He complains of Mrs. Smith's victimizing him.

- He blames his wealthy wife, the former Miss Grey, for making him write the callous break-up letter to Marianne.

With Willoughby's unprincipled and dishonorable behavior, he could be placed in the cad category, but he has crossed too many lines with the Eliza pregnancy and abandonment. Cad would be too generous of a term.

Chapter 18

Ten Best Austen-Related Books (Besides This One!)

▶ Looking at other books for background on Austen
▶ Finding some fun facts about Austen

*O*f course, I expect you to read all of Austen's fiction, but beyond this book, you can find even more information on Jane Austen and her world that can enhance your experience reading Austen time and again. In this chapter, I list the best publications to continue your knowledge of Jane Austen. I include six biographical works, two that discuss Austen's world, one just for fun, and one about the making of the 1995 miniseries *Pride and Prejudice.* (The last has pictures of Colin Firth in it!) You can get all of the books and resources through the Internet by using search engines or popular book Web sites, or at your local bookstores.

In the following sections you will notice one name popping up repeatedly: Deirdre Le Faye. Le Faye is the most knowledgeable individual today about Austen's life, works, and letters. Formerly employed for many years at the British Library, Le Faye started in 1970 to research all things Austen in archives all over England. She is thorough, accurate, and detail-oriented, yet she also sees the big picture of Austen's life. For those reasons, you'll find her name with biographical books, letters, a quizbook, and even a cookbook — all, of course, related to Jane Austen!

Checking Out the Relatives' Writings

Jane Austen's nephew, James Edward Austen-Leigh, wrote *A Memoir of Jane Austen,* published in England in 1870 and as a revised edition in 1871. Known in the family as Edward, he knew his Aunt Jane very well. While Jane Austen, her sister and mother, and their friend Martha Lloyd lived in the cottage at

Chawton (1809–1817), Edward lived in the nearby Steventon rectory (Jane Austen was born and raised there), where his father, Jane's eldest brother James, was the rector. Edward was 10½ when his Austen aunts and grandmother, as well as his Aunt Martha (Edward's mom's sister) moved to Chawton. He spent many a happy day with them, and as he grew up, his Aunt Jane advised him on writing his own novel. In a letter to her old friend, Alethea Bigg, Austen conveyed her affection for him, saying that she and her sister "have just had a few days' visit from Edward. . . . He grows still, & still improves in appearance, at least in the estimation of his aunts, who love him better & better as they see the sweet temper & warm affections of the Boy confirmed in the young Man" (Letter January 24, 1817). Six months after his Aunt Jane wrote this letter, Edward served as a pall-bearer for her funeral. At the request of friends and acquaintances who admired his aunt's novels, he wrote the *Memoir,* the first full-scale biography of Jane Austen, with the help of his sisters, Anna and Caroline, and letters by Jane Austen provided by various family members. In the second edition (1871), he placed in print for the first time his aunt's early, unpublished works *Lady Susan* and *The Watsons,* along with sections of her final fragment *Sanditon,* and the chapters of *Persuasion* that she had originally written before changing them for the published novel. The *Memoir* is the virtual starting point and basic resource for all biographical work about Jane Austen. Consisting of 11 chapters, the *Memoir* follows Jane Austen from birth to death, providing personal anecdotes about her and her family and details about the writing and publication of her novels. This book triggered a new interest in Austen's works when it was published. Out of print for a long time, the *Memoir* was edited by Kathryn Sutherland and published in 2002 in paperback format as *A Memoir of Jane Austen: And Other Family Recollections* (Oxford World's Classics). This handy paperback edition also includes other resources. Each of the other works is a small pamphlet in and itself:

- "Biographical Notice of the Author," by Henry Austen (1818), which originally appeared, unsigned (without a byline) in the four-volume *Northanger Abbey* and *Persuasion* set. Henry Austen's brief biography of his sister, written shortly after her death, was the first published account of Jane Austen. This work is nowadays frequently reprinted in even paperback editions of *Persuasion,* Austen's last completed novel.

- "Memoir of Miss Austen," by Henry Austen (1833). In 1832, Henry Austen expanded the "Biographical Notice" and retitled it "A Memoir of Miss Austen" when Bentley's Standard Novels Series requested a biographical piece about his sister for their re-publication of Jane Austen's novels in 1833. Bentley's Standard Novels Series reprinted popular novels in nice, hardbound editions and sold them at prices that families could afford, thus enabling them to add novels to their home book collection.

✔ "Recollections of Aunt Jane," by Anna Austen Lefroy (1864). Anna Austen Lefroy was James Edward Austen-Leigh's half-sister: Anna's father was Jane Austen's eldest brother James, whose first wife died when Anna was only two. In 1864, she wrote the "Recollections" for Edward to assist with his *Memoir*. Though only consisting of a few pages, Anna's work contains some charming reminiscing about her aunt, including Jane Austen's being a favorite of the local children as a teller of stories. Anna married Ben Lefroy, the youngest child of Jane Austen's adult friend, Madam Lefroy, mentioned in Chapter 3.

✔ "My Aunt Jane Austen," by Caroline Austen (1867). Caroline Austen was the younger sister of James Edward Austen-Leigh. Though just 4 years old when her Austen aunts and grandmother, along with Martha Lloyd (also Caroline's aunt, as Martha's sister Mary was Caroline's mother), moved to their cottage in Chawton in 1809, she spent a lot of time with them. As a grown woman, Caroline frequently visited her Aunt Cassandra (Jane Austen's sister). From "My Aunt Jane Austen," Austenites learned many details of the Austen ladies' routines at Chawton cottage. In 1951, the British Jane Austen Society printed Caroline's work as a small paperback book; they reprinted it in 1991.

Opening Austen's Letters

Jane Austen's Letters (Oxford University Press) is now available as a paperback book, edited by Deirdre Le Faye. Le Faye's edition of Austen's *Letters* is called the 3rd or New Edition because R. W. Chapman's ground-breaking editions of Austen's letters are the first (published in 1932) and second (published in 1952) editions. Le Faye's edition is now the definitive edition of Austen's known remaining letters, which are the closest we can ever come to hearing her speak in her own voice. The edition is comprised of 161 letters written by Jane Austen, mostly to her sister, Cassandra, but also to her publisher for *Emma*, John Murray; nieces Anna, Caroline, and Fanny; her brother Francis (Frank), and others. Running from January 1796, when Jane Austen was 20, to May 1817, shortly before her death at age 41, the letters range in subject matter from attending dances and gossiping about neighbors to articulating ideas about writing fiction. Austen's letters are an invaluable resource. The edition concludes with three letters by Cassandra, informing friends and family of Jane Austen's death. Le Faye's "Biographical" and "Topological" Indexes are worth their weight in gold: the alphabetical "Biographical Index" provides mini-biographies, with birth and death dates, of all the persons mentioned in Austen's letters, while the "Topographical Index" is an alphabetical listing of the places mentioned in the letters with facts about those places.

Following the Austen Family's History

Other than *Memoir,* among the best books about Austen and her family are

- *A Chronology of Jane Austen and Her Family, 1700–2000* **(Cambridge University Press):** This book by Deirdre Le Faye presents three decades of Le Faye's research regarding Jane Austen's ancestors, immediate family, and the novelist, herself, in over 10,000 entries. The book was published in February 2006, and so at the time of this writing, it is available only in hardback.

- *Jane Austen: A Family Record* **(Cambridge University Press):** William Austen-Leigh was James Edward Austen-Leigh's (JEAL, the *Memoir* writer) youngest son and the uncle of Richard Austen-Leigh, who was JEAL's grandson. The uncle and nephew collaborated to publish in 1913 *Jane Austen: Her Life and Letters, A Family Record,* which included letters and information gleaned by the family since the 1871 publication of the *Memoir.* R. A. Austen-Leigh's descendants, the Impey family, inherited his copy of the 1913 book, the pages covered with many handwritten notes and the book, itself, overloaded with numerous papers about Jane Austen. The Impeys concluded that their Uncle Richard was planning an updated edition of the book he wrote with his Uncle William. So the Impey family contacted Deirdre Le Faye to carry out the revised edition, which was published by The British Library in 1989. It is now available, with further revision by Deirdre Le Faye, in paperback. The book is what the title says: a family record or history of Jane Austen and her family.

- *Jane Austen's "Outlandish Cousin:" The Life and Letters of Eliza de Feuillide* **(The British Library):** *Jane Austen For Dummies* discusses Eliza, but if you want the full scoop on this spirited young woman who certainly influenced her young writing cousin, this book is the place to go. Deidre Le Faye is the editor.

- *Portrait of Jane Austen* **(Farrar, Straus, and Giroux):** This book by David Cecil is a detailed reconstruction of Austen's life supplemented by numerous pictures from various archives.

Sailing Away with Austen — or at Least Her Brothers!

Jane Austen and the Navy (National Maritime Museum) by Brian Southam focuses on Austen's relationship with her naval brothers, ultimately Admirals Frank and Charles Austen, during the Napoleonic Wars, especially, as well as the naval references in her novels.

Creating a Dinner Austen Would Be Proud of — and Probably Ate!

The Jane Austen Cookbook (McClellan and Steward) includes about 75 recipes on everything from Mrs. Dundas's Biscuits to Mrs. Fowle's Orange Wine. (I personally like the less exotic-sounding but tasty salmon recipe the best.) One source for some of the recipes was the personal cookbook of Martha Lloyd, who lived with Jane, Cassandra, and Mrs. Austen at Chawton cottage. So it's very likely that the Austens ate what Martha cooked. Maggie Black and Deirdre Le Faye have taken the time to put together an appealing book that gives you the urge to create a Jane Austen dinner. Measurements are given for both British and American cooks, so if you don't have a cup for measuring 50 grams of melted butter, don't worry: they tell you that 50 grams = 4 tablespoons!

Kicking Back with Jane Austen

Kick back and relax while you discover some fun facts about your favorite author, Jane Austen. Check out these two books:

✔ *So You Think You Know Jane Austen? A Literary Quizbook* (Oxford World's Classics Paperback): After you've read all of Austen's novels *and* this book *(Jane Austen For Dummies),* of course, test yourself and your Austen-loving friends with the progressively harder quizzes in the quizbook by John Sutherland and (who else?) Deirdre Le Faye.

✔ *The Making of "Pride and Prejudice"* (Penguin): Meant to accompany the 1995 television miniseries of Austen's most famous novel, this book, by Sue Birtwistle (who produced the miniseries) and Susie Conklin, follows the making of the series, from deciding to make the series to casting actors to creating costumes and hairstyles to finding appropriate locations. It includes interviews with many of the series' actors and with Andrew Davies, who wrote the script. Great photos!

Chapter 19

Ten Best Austen Places to Visit

In this chapter, I list the best Jane Austen sites to visit, and I even give you directions on how to get there. The best sites include places where artifacts are kept; places where she lived or visited; and places that provide locations for the novels or films of the novels. When you get to your hotel or bed and breakfast in London, find one of the many free maps with the underground and train stations clearly marked on them (each underground/ subway line is in a different color!), and prepare to immerse yourself in all things Austen.

The British Library at St. Pancras, London

The British Library in London is the official library of the United Kingdom, and they have Jane Austen's writing desk. Not to be confused with a conventional desk, her writing desk is about the size of a portable typewriter case (anyone remember typewriters?). Made of wood, the desk is sloped at an ergonomically correct angle for writing. If you lift up the top (which you won't be able to do because the desk is encased in glass), you can store desk items inside. Austen placed this desk on top of a small round table, which is at the Jane Austen Museum, and wrote her novels and letters.

The British Library is at 96 Euston Road, London NW12DB. You can't miss it: a huge redbrick complex with excellent signs. To get there, you have a few options:

1. **Take the Northern or Victoria Line Tube to the King's Cross/St. Pancras station; turn right upon exiting on Euston Road, and just walk for about two blocks straight ahead. The library is between Midland and Ossulton streets.**

2. **Or take the bus; buses 3, 10, 30, 73, and 91 all go to or near the British Library. The bus drivers are always helpful and call out the stops. You'll be getting off around Euston Road and Upper Woburn.**

   For more information, visit `www.bl.uk/`, and at "Quick Links" click the link "Visit Us."

Originally, the British Library was within the British Museum. There is still a library within the British Museum, but it is just a general reference library now. The actual British Library moved out of the museum several years ago. There is wonderful stuff at the museum. But for Jane Austen's writing desk, you need to go to the new British Library, as directed.

The descendents of Jane Austen's eldest brother James, the Austen-Leigh family, were in possession of the desk until the fall of 1999. The late Joan Austen-Leigh kept the desk safe in an old suitcase in a closet in her home in Canada. In 1999, Joan Austen-Leigh and her eldest daughter traveled to London and generously donated the desk to the British Library at a lovely ceremony.

No. 10 Henrietta Street, Covent Garden

Covent Garden isn't a garden at all. It is an area of shops and restaurants and is where the Royal Opera House is located. Jane Austen's brother Henry lived at No. 10 Henrietta Street in Covent Garden while he was a banker, and Jane Austen stayed with him when she visited London.

To get to Covent Garden:

1. **Take the Northern Line Tube to Covent Garden and then follow the signs to the London Transport Museum.**

2. **The Transport Museum is between King and Henrietta streets. Head to Henrietta and No. 10. It's the house with the green and gold plaque on it.**

(*Note:* If you're at the British Museum, you can walk to Covent Garden in about 10 to 15 minutes. Leave the museum by the main entrance and cross Great Russell Street. Follow the signs to Covent Garden.)

Jane Austen's House Museum in Chawton

Jane Austen wrote her novels at her home in Chawton. This home has been turned into the Jane Austen House Museum. Jane, Cassandra, Mrs. Austen, and Martha Lloyd moved to Chawton in 1809, and Austen resided there for the rest of her life, until weeks before her death 1817. (For details on the Austen ladies' move here, see Chapter 3.) While living here, she revised *Elinor and Marianne* into *Sense and Sensibility* and *First Impressions* into *Pride and Prejudice,* wrote *Mansfield Park, Emma,* and *Persuasion,* and began *Sanditon.* The house contains many artifacts: the table on which she set her writing desk (now at the British Library), a quilt she helped make, and the Topaz crosses that her brother Charles brought back for his sisters from Gibraltar (which are the models for William Price's giving an amber cross to his sister Fanny in *Mansfield Park*). You can find more about the Jane Austen House Museum before you go to England by visiting www.jane-austens-house-museum.org.uk/.

The museum also contains a shop where you can buy all things Austen. The house has a lovely garden, where you can sit and enjoy the flowers or even eat your picnic lunch; www.jane-austens-house-museum.org.uk.

Directions are as follows:

1. **Take a taxi or the Tube (Bakerloo, Northern, or Jubilee Lines) to the Waterloo Train Station. This is a big, busy, but manageable station, and if you're in a taxi, tell the drive you want "country trains" — otherwise he'll drive you to the side of the station for the popular trains that go under the English Channel to France!**

2. **At the ticket counter for "country trains," buy a ticket for Alton; the trains go to Alton about twice an hour. You will see the train times on the big board, Also, pick up an ALTON schedule, so you will have the times for the return trains.**

   The trip takes about 1 hour and 20 minutes.

3. **Get off at Alton and take a taxi from the station to the Jane Austen House Museum (about 5 minutes).**

   If you're hearty, walk to the house by following the signs. It's about a 20- to 25-minute walk.

St. Nicholas Church and the Chawton House Library

When you've finished with the Jane Austen House Museum, visit the sites under this heading: They are just a short, pleasant walk on a sidewalk from her house.

While living at Chawton, the Austens worshipped at St. Nicholas Church, and the two Cassandras — Mrs. Austen and Jane's sister — are buried behind the church. You can enter the church and also see the graves.

The Chawton House Library (formerly called the Chawton Great House) is where Edward Austen lived when in Hampshire county; during part of Jane Austen's life at Chawton, her brother Frank and his family lived here, too. The Chawton Great House became the Chawton House Library for the Study of Early Women Writers in 2003, and only pre-arranged users with appropriate credentials can enter the library. But it's a beautiful building to view from the outside, and the landscaping around the house has been re-planted to look like what it did in Austen's day.

Get to these attractions by following these directions from the Jane Austen House Museum:

1. **Cross the road to the Cassandra's Cup side, and turn right, staying on the curving road (has a sidewalk) past the parking lot and continue walking.**

   You will see cricket fields on your left as well as other houses and a farm. Just before the end of the road, you will see on your left the signs for St. Nicholas Church and Chawton House Library.

2. **Turn left into the driveway and follow the signs to the library and the church.**

   You can walk down the driveway and then veer slightly down the path to your right (there's a sign!) to the church through its little gate. Walk into the church (it's tiny) and then around the back to the graves of Jane Austen's sister and mother. One of the staff members (Anne) from the Jane Austen House Museum typically leaves flowers from the house's garden on the graves. When you've returned to the driveway, you can gaze at this lovely large home that Austen and her family knew as the Great House, but which is now the Chawton House Library. There may be sheep grazing in the field and horses being exercised!

Steventon

Jane Austen was born and raised in Steventon, living there for 25 years, until Spring 1801. While the rectory house is gone, you can still see the beautiful, small 12th-century church where her father preached and where she attended in her childhood until the family moved to Bath. The church has many Austen-related plaques inside. This is another site in the immediate area of the Jane Austen House Museum.

To get there:

> Take a taxi from the Jane Austen House Museum. The folks at the house will call a cab for you. Ask the driver to take you to St. Nicholas's Church, Steventon (not to be confused with St. Nicholas's Church, Chawton!). Ask the taxi to wait for you at Steventon while you walk around for 5 to 10 minutes. The church may be open, and I suggest you go inside, walk around this tiny building, look at the Austen plaques, and then sit in a pew. It's also interesting to walk around the little graveyard (okay, the meter will be ticking, but, hey, you're in Austenland!).

Winchester Cathedral

Jane Austen is buried in the nave, in the north aisle of Winchester Cathedral. While there, visit the catacombs, see the Roman ruins, browse the gift shop, and eat at the refectory. Before leaving for England, go the Cathedral's Web site at `http://www.winchester-cathedral.org.uk/` for all kinds of information, including services.

To get there from London:

1. **Go to Waterloo Station (following all the tips given for the visit to the Jane Austen House Museum!) and head to the ticket counter for "country trains."**

2. **Get a ticket for a train to Winchester.**

3. **Depart the train at Winchester and take a taxi from the station to the Cathedral. (You can walk if you're hearty, but it's quite the little hike! Head for the town center or centre, as the English spell the word.)**

But if you're already at the Jane Austen House Museum, you can call for a taxi to drive you the 20 minutes to Winchester, visit the Cathedral and No. 8 College Street (the next site on this list), and then take a train from Winchester back to Waterloo Station in London. What a great Austen day that would be! And think of the time you'll save doing all this in one day!

No. 8 College Street, Winchester

Jane Austen spent the last weeks of her life at No. 8 College Street, Winchester. The yellowish house has the official blue oval plaque on it, saying Jane Austen died there. No. 8 College Street is now a private residence. But you can look up and see the bay window, which was in Jane Austen's room. The folks who own the house are used to tourists taking photos of the exterior of their house. So snap away!

1. **If you're beginning your Austen sites in Hampshire with No. 8 College Street, follow the instructions for taking the train from London's Waterloo Station to Winchester, and once in Winchester, ask the taxi driver to take you to No. 8 College Street.**

2. **If you're at the Cathedral, the previous site, exit by the main doors, and go left, walking through the Cathedral Close (the Close is a road backing on to a cathedral, where staff buildings and houses are located) and under the medieval stone arch; turn left; H. P. Wells Bookstore will be across the street; cross to that side and walk about 100 feet and there's No. 8 College Street.**

Bath

Jane Austen lived in Bath between 1801 and 1806, visited Bath several times, and set sections of *Northanger Abbey* and *Persuasion* here. You can visit several different Austen-related places while you're in Bath. Must-see sites include

- **The Pump Room:** This place is in the lower part of the city. In the Pump Room, you see the clock mentioned in *Northanger Abbey,* as well as a "sedan chair," like Catherine Morland used, also in *Northanger Abbey.*

- **Laura Place:** Across Pulteney Street Bridge is where *Persuasion*'s Dowager Viscountess Dalrymple lived.

- **No. 4 Sydney Place:** Located at the eastern end of Pulteney Street, this house is where the Austens lived when they first moved to Bath in 1801. Now a private home, it is the only one of the Austens' Bath residences that has a blue plaque on it, announcing her connection to the house.

- **Assembly Rooms:** *Northanger Abbey*'s Catherine Morland danced in the ballrooms of the Assembly Rooms, and the concert in *Persuasion* is given in the Octagon Room. Austen, herself, attended balls.

- **The Costume Museum:** This museum traces the history of fashion, and you can see clothing from Austen's day. It's located below the Assembly Rooms, in the same building.

- **Royal Crescent:** The Crescent is a fabulous curved row of houses. Jane Austen and her characters in Bath walked here. Number 1 Royal Crescent (on the far right as you look at the Crescent) is open as a museum of a home of Austen's time, and like the Pump Room, it has a sedan chair on display. To take a photo of the whole Crescent, you'll need a panoramic lens!

To get to Bath, take a taxi or the Tube (District, Circle, or Hammersmith and City Lines) to London's Paddington Station, and buy a ticket to Bath Spa. Travel time one way is about 1 hour and 30 minutes.

Portsmouth Harbor

Although Portsmouth was largely rebuilt after World War II because of bombing damage, visit here to take the Royal Navy's tour of the Lord Nelson's ship "HMS *Victory*". This excellent tour around the ship focuses, of course, on Nelson and the Battle of Trafalgar. But taking this tour gives you an idea of the ship life lived by Austen's two navy brothers, Frank and Charles. *Mansfield Park*'s Price family also lived in Portsmouth. Go to the waterfront and look across to see the Isle of Wight or as little Fanny Price calls it "the Island."

To get to this destination:

1. **Follow the directions for getting to the Jane Austen House Museum about getting to London's Waterloo Station.**

2. **Head for "country trains" and buy a ticket for Portsmouth Harbour. This trip takes about 1 hour and 30 minutes.**

3. **Once there, take a taxi to the HMS *Victory;* it's one of Portsmouth's *big* attractions!**

4. **Before leaving for England, visit the Web site at** `http://www.hms-victory.com/`**.**

5. **If you're in Winchester and have spent the night there in one of the several hotels, you can take a train from Winchester to Portsmouth Harbour for an hour. If you've stayed the night in Bath (and it's worth it!), there's no need to go back to London to go to Portsmouth Harbour; instead, take the train from Bath to Portsmouth Harbour (about 2 hours and 20 minutes).**

Lyme Regis

Not only did Jane Austen visit Lyme Regis twice, in 1803 and 1804, but she set a major section of *Persuasion* there. In the novel, Louisa Musgrove jumps down the old steps (known as "Granny's Teeth") a second time from the Cobb to the beach, misses Captain Wentworth's arms, and hurts her head. But have no fear: Today there are roomy, modern steps down to the beach. If you walk along the nearby street called Marine Parade, you will see a small stone bust of Jane Austen and Bay Cottage, now a café but thought to be originally the little house used as Captain Harville's residence in the same novel.

Travel to Lyme Regis by the following means of transportation:

1. **Again, following the train tips for going to the Jane Austen House Museum, go to London's Waterloo Station, go to the "country trains" ticket center, and get a ticket for the Exeter Line as far as Axminster.**

   The train to Axminster takes 2 hours and 30 minutes.

2. **From Axminster, take a taxi to Lyme Regis.**

   It is worthwhile to spend the night at one of the hotels in the town. Walk along the Cobb, look out at the water, and dine on fish.

Chapter 20

Ten Best Austenisms (and What They Mean)

In This Chapter
▶ Looking into Austen's words of wisdom
▶ Using her characters to send messages

Austen really knew how to turn a phrase, and she never wrote a throw-away line. In this chapter, I offer some of her best lines, including one at the beginning that doesn't sound like it should appear engraved on a wall of inspiring sayings, but instead shows how keenly aware she was of how her readers sometimes feel.

Speaking for the Homebodies

In *Emma,* John Knightley, the family-loving lawyer-brother of the book's hero, Mr. Knightley, has "reserved manners which prevented his being generally pleasing; and capable of being sometimes out of humour" (E 1:11). He straightforwardly tells Emma, his sister-in-law, how he feels about being compelled to leave the warm fireside at home on a cold night to attend a dinner party at Mr. and Mrs. Weston's house on Christmas Eve:

> **"A man . . . must have a very good opinion of himself when he asks people to leave their own fireside, and encounter such a day as this, for the sake of coming to see him. He must think himself a most agree-able fellow; I could not do such a thing. It is the greatest absurdity — Actually snowing at this moment! — The folly of people's not staying comfortably at home when they can! If we were obliged to go on an evening such as this, by any call of duty of business, what a hardship we should deem it."** (E 1:13)

Haven't you felt this way at one time or another? John Knightley speaks for the homebody in everyone. And no, he's not Scrooge from Dickens's *A Christmas Carol*. Keep in mind that the celebration of Christmas is really a Victorian invention, helped along by Dickens. In Austen's time, Christmas was more a *holy*day than a *holi*day.

Acknowledging Differences

"'One half of the world cannot understand the pleasures of the other'" (E 1:9). In *Emma*, Emma's nervous father, Mr. Woodhouse, worries about Mr. Knightley's tossing his nephews in the air and then catching them — a game they love, so Emma explains that the same pleasures aren't enjoyed by everyone.

Each person likes his own tastes best. But Emma is right, of course, when she makes this observation to her father, who barely leaves his chair and can't understand a child's pleasure in being gently tossed and caught by a loving (and very tall!) uncle. In the novel, another scene demonstrates Mr. Woodhouse's egocentric nature that prevents him from understanding others' preferences that differ from his own: Just because wedding cake disagrees with his stomach, he feels nobody should eat it. Likewise, just because he loves a bowl of nice thin gruel in the evening, he expects everyone to want one, too! This characteristic of Mr. Woodhouse connects him to his daughter, Emma, who though totally opposite to her father in her youth, liveliness, good health, and cleverness, is also egocentric and expects others to feel as she does, particularly regarding their romantic attraction to others.

Expressing Sympathetic Understanding

"'It is very unfair to judge of anybody's conduct, without an intimate knowledge of their situation. Nobody, who has not been in the interior of a family, can say what the difficulties of any individual of that family may be'" (E 1:18). From *Emma*, Emma says this quote to Mr. Knightley when he complains about Frank Churchill's not coming to Highbury to meet his new stepmother. Emma defends Frank's conduct, noting that his aunt, Mrs. Churchill, is known to be a difficult personality.

Austen's sympathetic understanding of personal problems caused by family members, both loved and at the same time sometimes trying, is clear. And Austen demonstrates this understanding when she writes *Mansfield Park*. Fanny Price's passivity is better understood when seen against the way she's treated at Mansfield Park, especially by her Aunt Norris. Likewise, in *Sense and Sensibility*, Marianne Dashwood's excessive emotionalism reflects what she has learned from her mother. Throughout her novels, Austen shows us that we understand many characters more fully when seen in light of their families and upbringings.

Embarrassing Moments

"Their straightforward emotions left no room for the little zigzags of embarrassment" (E 1:15). In another example from *Emma,* Elton shocks Emma by proposing to her in the coach, and Emma silences him, rejecting the notion that she was ever interested in him, just as he rejected her plan that he marry Harriet Smith. Both Elton and Emma are embarrassed by what they've said and what they've done. In a closed coach going along the snowy road, there's no physical room for one to be separated from the other. At the same time, there's no psychological room to separate Emma and Elton, either. Each is embarrassed!

Revealing Wrongs with Subtle Ease

"'I do not pretend to set people right, but I do see that they are often wrong'" (MP 1:5). Mary Crawford, from *Mansfield Park,* has one-liners to spare. This one happens to also apply to her creator, Jane Austen, as much as it does to her. In the scene in the novel where Mary utters this snappy line, she and Tom Bertram are discussing the varied behaviors of young ladies, depending on whether they are "in" or "out." Mary has very decided opinions to offer Tom, who reports facing embarrassing situations where he treated a young lady who was not "out" as if she was "out": In another words, he actually spoke to her! (Young ladies who were not yet "out" were supposed to remain quiet when around adults.) Mary blames the mothers of girls who aren't "out," but who act like they are. But she would never tell those mothers how she feels. (See Chapter 6 for info on young ladies coming "out.")

As a novelist, Jane Austen, like her creation, Mary Crawford, doesn't "pretend to set people right," but she does see "that they are often wrong." So instead of telling readers that certain societal practices are wrong, thus overtly instructing her readers, she simply lets the characters who exemplify the practices call those practices into question. In *Persuasion,* Sir Walter Elliot, a baronet and the owner of a great estate, is so careless about his money and property that he has to lease the estate out because he's in debt. His tenants, Admiral and Mrs. Croft, are a navy officer and his wife; the admiral has money that he has earned (*not* inherited, as Sir Walter has), and he and his wife are far better occupiers of the Elliot mansion than Sir Walter was. Even doing little things around the house to improve its livability shows that they are superior stewards of the house than Sir Walter was. Austen never preaches a word about the unfairness of the inheritance system, which gives wealth and property to the vain and silly Sir Walter. But she sees the occasional problems with the inheritance system, and she slips them into her novel.

Ending on a Happy Note

"Let other pens dwell on guilt and misery" (MP 3:17). Austen begins the final chapter of *Mansfield Park* with this quote. While what follows is a rather heavy and unusual dispensing of poetic justice all around, the quotation reminds readers that Austen's novels are *comedies* in the purest sense of the word: works with happy endings. So you can deduce that reading an Austen novel leaves you happy. So go read one!

Seeking Good Fortune — Big Bucks, That Is

"'It is a truth universally acknowledged, that a single man in possession of a good fortune, must be in want of a wife'" (PP 1:1). The first line of *Pride and Prejudice* is Austen's most famous line. Its proverbial sound has taken the first seven words of this quotation into advertising (for computers), college catalogues (for meal plans), and various other places. Here are some samples:

- For computer products: "It is a truth universally acknowledged, that a consumer in possession of a small form factor PC must be in want of a media centre system. . . ." Found at www.shoebox computers.com/ product -reviews_info.

- From *The Oxford Student* (Official Student Newspaper, April 30, 2006, in a feature called "Food, Glorious Food." and "Food, Glorious Food!" by the way, is a song title from Lionel Bart's "Oliver," the musical version of Dickens's *Oliver Twist*!): "It is a truth universally acknowledged that Oxford has many great restaurants." Found at www.oxfordstudent. com/tt2003wk7/features.

In the novel, however, Austen uses the line ironically. For as the reader discovers moving beyond the first sentence, the real truth is that young women are seeking men of good fortune.

Making Sure Money Isn't Everything

"'Do anything rather than marry without affection'" (PP 3:17). In *Pride and Prejudice,* Jane says this quote to Elizabeth, who has just told her of her engagement to Darcy. Austen said the same thing to her niece, Fanny Knight, and Austen, herself, withdrew her acceptance of a proposal from an old family friend whose wealth would have given her widowed mother and unmarried sister a life of ease (Letter to Fanny, November 18–20, 1814; for Austen's turning down an advantageous proposal, see Chapter 3 of this book). Austen was like her heroines: They never married without some money, but they never married *for* money. They *must* love their husbands.

Watching Your Step

"'Run mad as often as you choose; but do not faint'" (source *Love and Freindship* [sic], Letter 14). Austen's youthful work, *Love and Freindship* (purposely misspelled) ridicules the sentimental novels that flooded the market of her youth. In the middle of Letter the 14th, Laura recounts how her dear friend Sophia died after catching an infection caused by constantly faint- ing on wet grass. Sophia's final words to her friend Laura were the words from the quote above. Laura sensibly accepts this advice, saving herself from the danger of wet grass by running back and forth in a frenzy.

Austen, of course, is poking fun at the ever-present fainting habits of the heroines in sentimental novels. She was about 14 or 15 when she wrote this, showing her early skills at humor and mockery.

Trusting the Right People

"'Those who tell their own Story . . . must be listened to with Caution'" (S 3). In *Sanditon*'s hysterical send-up of hypochondriacs and health resorts of which Sanditon is one, filled with broad, physical humor that is unchar- acteristic of Austen, she has Mr. Parker, Sanditon's greatest supporter, say these words. Said another way: Never trust the teller; trust the tale. Mr. Parker's comment reminds the reader of the tendency to present an experience in terms of personal prejudices.

Jane Austen Chronology

. . . .

1775

Jane Austen, the seventh of eight children and second daughter of the Rev. Mr. George Austen and Mrs. Cassandra (Leigh) Austen, is born in the family home, the Steventon Rectory, in Hampshire, England, on December 16. Jane's siblings at this point are James (1765–1819), George (1776–1838; born epileptic and possibly also deaf and mute, George is sent to live with a local family under his parents' watchful eyes), Edward (1767–1852), Henry (1771–1850), Cassandra, "Cassie" (1773–1845), and Francis, "Fly" as a boy for his speedy movement, later Frank (1774–1865).

1777

George Austen's widowed sister, Philadelphia (Austen) Hancock, and her 16-year-old daughter, Elizabeth Hancock, leave London for Paris to live more economically. Elizabeth was born in India, and her parents call her Betsy. But moving to the more sophisticated Paris, Elizabeth drops Betsy for the French-sounding Eliza.

1779

On June 23, Charles Austen is born at the Steventon Rectory. Austen and her sister Cassandra call Charles their "own particular little brother." During this year, James, Austen's eldest brother, heads to St. John's College, Oxford University. Meanwhile, Mr. Austen allows his wealthy cousin, Mr. Thomas Knight II, and his wife to take his 12-year-old son, Edward, on their honeymoon with them.

1781

In France, Eliza Hancock marries the Comte de Feuillide, Jean-François Capot, and becomes the Comtesse de Feuillide. They attend many balls at Versailles hosted by King Louis XVI and his queen, Marie Antoinette.

1782

The Austen family and Mr. Austen's students from his rectory school perform their first traditional home theatrical under James's direction. Young Austen enjoys watching.

1783

Austen, Cassandra, and cousin Jane Cooper attend Mrs. Cawley's school in Oxford. Mrs. Cawley inexplicably moves the school to Southampton, a port town with much disease, and a typhoid epidemic breaks out, threatening the girls' health. Mrs. Austen and her sister Mrs. Cooper arrive in Southampton in time to nurse the girls, but Mrs. Cooper soon succumbs to the fever. The Knights formally adopt Edward Austen as the heir to their extensive estates in Kent and Hampshire. The Lefroys move to Ashe, near the Steventon area; Mrs. (Madam) Lefroy, seeing something special in Jane, though only 8, will become a beloved adult mentor to the young Austen.

1784

Another Austen family play is performed in the spring: Sheridan's famous comedy of manners, *The Rivals.*

1785

Austen and Cassandra board at the Abbey School in Reading, probably the model for Mrs. Goddard's school in *Emma.*

1786

Edward Austen departs on his Grand Tour of Europe, which lasts until 1790. Francis (Fly) Austen, age 12, enters the Royal Naval Academy at Portsmouth, beginning an illustrious naval career. James goes to the Continent. In December, Austen and Cassandra come home from school, ending their formal schooling experience.

1787

Austen starts writing short fictional works, later known as her *Juvenilia,* as gifts for family members. James returns from the Continent and, in December, produces another play for the family: Susanna Centlivre's comedy, *The Wonder: A Woman Keeps a Secret.* Eliza, Comtesse de Feuillide, who's visiting Steventon with her baby son (born 1786) plays a role. She charms the Austen boys, especially Henry.

1788

With the continuing winter holiday, James produces another play, *The Chances,* in January, and in March does *Tom Thumb.* Austen performs in a small role in the latter. Henry heads to Oxford University in July, and soon thereafter Mr. and Mrs. Austen take their daughters to Kent and London. Their Kent visit may have coincided with Edward's returning from his Grand Tour and staying at the Knights' Godmersham Estate in Kent to learn more about running it. In September, Eliza returns to France with her mother and son. On December 23, Frank, age 14, leaves Portsmouth's Royal Naval Academy and signs on board the *Perseverance,* heading to the East Indies. Over the winter holidays, James produces *The Sultan* and *High Life Below Stairs.*

1789

At Oxford, on January 31, James publishes the first issue of *The Loiterer,* which appears weekly until March 1790. It appears that James is the writer of the family. The Lloyd family moves into Deane parsonage; Austen becomes close friends with the daughters, Martha and Mary.

1790

James becomes a curate. In June, Austen writes and dedicates to her cousin, Eliza, a fictional piece called *Love and Freindship* (yes, she spelled it that way) that brilliantly ridicules sentimental fiction. (For more on this work, go to Chapter 4.)

1791

Eliza's husband, the Comte de Feuillide, fights against the French Revolutionary forces on the side of the Royalists (supporting the King). In July, Charles Austen, now 12, follows his brother Frank as a student at Portsmouth's Royal Naval Academy. James rises in the clerical profession, becoming the vicar of Sherborne St. John in September. On December 27, Edward marries Elizabeth Bridges of Goodnestone, Kent.

1792

The year begins with the Lloyds leaving Deane to live at Ibthorpe. Austen and Cassandra visit them in October. On March 27, James marries Anne Mathew. The newlyweds move to the Deane parsonage, which the Lloyds had vacated for them. In August, Austen writes the dedication of *Catharine; or, The Bower* to her sister. (For more info on *Catharine,* see Chapter 3.) Sometime in the winter, Cassandra becomes engaged to the Rev. Mr. Tom Fowle, whose brother had been a student at Mr. Austen's school at the Steventon Rectory.

1793

On January 21, Louis XVI is guillotined in Paris. On January 23, Edward and his wife have their first child, Francis (Fanny); as she gets older, Austen and Cassandra will consider Fanny almost like another sister. On February 1, the French Republic declares war on Great Britain. Henry enlists in the Oxfordshire militia as a lieutenant. Mr. and Mrs. James Austen have their first child, Anna. Austen writes her final piece of *Juvenilia,* a poem called "Ode to Pity," dated June 3, found at the end of *Volume the First* of her youthful writings, of which there are three volumes. Frank returns home from the Far East in December.

1794

Eliza's husband, the Comte de Feuillide, is guillotined on February 22. On October 23, Edward's adoptive father, Thomas Knight II, dies, and Edward takes over his estates as the heir. Austen possibly composes most of *Lady Susan* in the fall but without writing a conclusion.

1795

Austen writes *Elinor and Marianne,* the epistolary version of what would later become *Sense and Sensibility*. (See Chapter 4 for info on epistolary writing.) On May 3, James's wife suddenly dies, and little Anna, age 2, is sent to live temporarily at the Steventon rectory with her grandparents and aunts. Between December 1795 and January 1796, Austen meets Tom Lefroy, who's visiting his Aunt and Uncle Lefroy at the Ashe rectory. She writes about him in her first existing letter.

1796

Austen's first existing letter is dated January 9–10, 1796. At this time, Cassandra's fiancé, the Rev. Mr. Tom Fowle, sails for the West Indies as the private chaplain of his kinsman, Lord Craven. During the summer, the widowed James courts the widowed Eliza de Feuillide, but nothing comes of it. In November, he gets engaged to Mary Lloyd of Ibthorpe. In October, Austen begins *First Impressions,* an epistolary novel, which is the forerunner of *Pride and Prejudice*.

1797

On January 17, James marries Mary Lloyd. The following month, Cassandra's fiancé dies of tropical fever at San Domingo, but she only learns of his death in May because news travels slowly. In August, Austen completes *First Impressions,* which on November 1, her father offers by mail to the London publisher Cadell and Company. They return his letter without even opening it. Meanwhile, Austen returns in November to *Elinor and Marianne* and begins transforming it into *Sense and Sensibility.* In the same month, Austen and

Cassandra accompany their mother to Bath to visit her brother and sister-in-law, Mr. and Mrs. James Leigh-Perrot. Edward and Elizabeth move their family from Rowling into the splendid Godmersham country house, also in Kent, that he has inherited from the Knights. On December 31 in London, Henry marries Eliza de Feuillide, who's ten years older than he is.

1798

During the summer, Austen begins *Susan* (later called *Catherine,* and finally published posthumously as *Northanger Abbey*) while visiting Edward at his new estate with her sister and their parents. The Austens remain at Godmersham between August and October 24, when Austen and her parents return home, while Cassandra remains with Edward and his family. Meanwhile, Mr. Austen gives James his curacy of Deane and closes his school at the Steventon rectory. He also gives up his carriage, which hinders personal travel for the family. Mrs. Austen is ill in October and November, and Austen nurses her. On November 17, James's son, James Edward, is born; he becomes an important biographer of his aunt in 1869, though the title page of the first edition of his *Memoir of Jane Austen* gives 1870 as the publishing year.

1799

Mrs. Austen and Austen visit Bath in May with Edward and Elizabeth and remain there until the end of June. Austen is finishing *Susan* (*Northanger Abbey*) around this time but will work on it again later (1803). Frank is on a ship in the Mediterranean Sea. On August 14, Mrs. Leigh-Perrot, Mrs. Austen's sister-in-law, is formally, but falsely, accused of shoplifting lace from a Bath shop and sent to jail.

1800

On March 29, after spending time in jail, Mrs. Leigh-Perrot is tried and acquitted at the court in Taunton. In late November, Austen visits Mrs. Lloyd and Martha at Ibthorpe. When she returns home in December, she learns that her father has decided to retire and that her parents plan to leave the Steventon rectory to James and his family and move to Bath with her and her sister. Rumor has it that Austen fainted when she heard the news.

1801

In January, Henry Austen begins a business in London as an army agent and banker. He and his wife, Eliza, and her sickly son Hastings de Feuillide (1786–1801) live in London on Upper Berkeley Street. Later in the month, Austen visits her great friends Catherine and Alethea Bigg at Manydown Park in Hampshire. In early May, Mr. and Mrs. Austen, Jane, and Cassandra move to Bath on No. 4 Sydney Place. The four Austens then take their first summer seaside holiday from Bath — which becomes a tradition to escape that city's heat — and visit Sidmouth and Colyton. Austen's supposed short summer romance with a young clergyman who later died occurred at Sidmouth, sometime between this visit in 1801 and the family's visits in 1804. The Austens then visit Steventon (James and his family) and Ashe (the Lefroys), finally returning to Bath in the cool of autumn on October 5.

1802

The Peace of Amiens, ceasing French/England hostilities, is declared on March 25, and Charles and Frank come home. Charles joins the four Austens for the summer. In September, Charles escorts Austen and Cassandra to Godmersham, where they remain until the end of October. Austen's Godmersham visit enhances her understanding (she had already spent much time at other country houses, like Manydown Park) of what country house life is like for the richer gentry. On November 25, Austen and Cassandra visit their old friends, Catherine and Alethea Bigg at Manydown Park. On the evening of December 2, Harris Bigg-Wither proposes to his sisters' old friend, Austen. Harris is the unexpected heir to Manydown, as his older brother died at age 14 in 1794. She accepts. But after a restless night, Austen rejects Harris's proposal, and she and Cassandra immediately leave Manydown for Steventon and then, escorted by their brother James, for Bath. Austen spends the remainder of 1802 revising *Susan* (later *Northanger Abbey*).

1803

In spring, Austen, with Henry's help, sells *Susan* to the publisher Crosby & Company in London for ten pounds. He promises to publish it but never does. On May 18, Napoleon breaks the Peace of Amiens, and Charles and Frank are back at work in the navy. In September and October, the four Austens are again visiting Godmersham and living in luxury. Returning to Bath near the end of October, they visit Lyme Regis (later used in *Persuasion*).

1804

Charles, now a commander, serves the Royal Navy in the Atlantic to prevent slave trade between the United States and the British West Indies, as well as trade of commercial goods between the U.S. and France. Austen works on *The Watsons,* which is left unfinished. The four Austens, joined by Henry and Eliza, return to Lyme Regis for the summer. On returning to Bath, the Austens move to the Green Park Buildings, far less stylish and far more inexpensive than their Sydney Place home. On Austen's 29th birthday, December 16th, her dear friend and mentor, Madam Lefroy, is killed in a freak horseback-riding accident even though Madam Lefroy was a skilled equestrienne.

1805

Mr. Austen dies unexpectedly on January 21. In March, the three Austen women move to 25 Gay Street, Bath, where they're joined in April by Martha Lloyd after the death of her mother. This little band of ladies remains close friends and housemates. Austen concludes *Lady Susan* this year and also makes a final or "fair" copy of it. With Mrs. James Austen expecting her second child, the Austen ladies take James's elder daughter, Anna, with them to Godmersham in June. Anna's sister Caroline is born June 18. On October 21, the English navy, under Admiral Nelson, defeats the French and Spanish navies in the Battle of Trafalgar. Because Frank's ship is sent back to Gibraltar, he misses the glory of Trafalgar.

1806

In February, Austen and Cassandra revisit Manydown Park, their first visit since Austen's proposal fiasco. On July 2, the Austen ladies leave Bath for good and visit Clifton and Adlestrop, where Mrs. Austen's cousin lives. On August 5, they join him to visit the magnificent Stoneleigh Abbey estate in Warwickshire, which he has inherited, and they remain there until August 14. Meanwhile, Frank marries Mary Gibson in July. In October, the Austen ladies, along with Martha Lloyd, cease their nomadic lifestyle and rent lodgings with Frank and Mary Austen in Southampton.

1807

In March, the Southampton Austen/Lloyd group moves into a house in Castle Square, Southampton. Charles, still on duty in the West Indies, marries 17-year-old Fanny Palmer, daughter of the ex-attorney general of Bermuda.

In September, Edward Austen gets the family together at his Hampshire Estate in Chawton; they all stay at the Chawton Great House for ten days.

1808

Between January and March, Austen again visits the Bigg sisters at Manydown. While there, she joins the Bigg (Bigg-Wither) family in one of their theatricals, playing the role of Mrs. Candour in Sheridan's great comedy of manners, *The School for Scandal.* Austen spends June 14 through July 8 at Godmersham, where Elizabeth Austen is expecting her 11th child in September. Cassandra goes to Godmersham to help with the other children. On October 10, Elizabeth Austen dies suddenly, just days after the birth of her son. Two of Edward's sons stay with their Aunt Jane and grandmother in Southampton, taking time from school in Winchester for comfort and care. In Austen's letter to Cassandra (still at Godmersham) of October 24–25, she first mentions cryptically their plans to move to Chawton, where Edward provides them with a six-bedroom cottage.

1809

In April, Austen writes to Crosby & Company Publishers under the pseudonym Mrs. Ashley Dennis (M.A.D.!) to inquire about *Susan,* which Crosby had advertised but never published. Crosby offers to sell it back to her for the ten pounds they paid her in 1803. Meanwhile, Edward sees to it that the Chawton cottage is remodeled to suit the needs of his mother, sisters, and Martha Lloyd. In May, the female Austen group visits Edward at Godmersham. On July 7, the four ladies arrive at Chawton cottage in Jane's native county of Hampshire. By August, Austen takes out *Sense and Sensibility,* and she continues to rework it. She's back to a regular writing schedule.

1810

For July and August, the two Austen sisters again visit the Bigg sisters at Manydown. In September, Frank resigns his command of the St. Albans in order to spend more time with his wife. That same month, Charles is in command of the *Cleopatra,* which Austen mentions in the scene at Portsmouth Harbor in *Mansfield Park* (MP 3:7). In the winter season of 1810–1811, Austen learns that the London publisher Thomas Egerton accepted *Sense and Sensibility* for publication.

1811

In February, Austen works on *Mansfield Park*. But she's happily interrupted with a March visit to London, where she stays with Henry and Eliza, in order to correct the proofs of *Sense and Sensibility*, which is published on October 30. Meanwhile, in August, Charles and Fanny Austen, along with their two children, return to England after Charles has spent over six years across the Atlantic. Toward the end of 1811, Austen begins extensive revisions of *First Impressions* to make it *Pride and Prejudice*.

1812

Austen spends much of this year continuing her revision of *First Impressions*, the copyright to which she sells to the publisher Egerton in November for £110. During this period, Edward and his eldest child, Fanny, visit Chawton in April. On October 14, Edward's adoptive mother, Mrs. Knight, dies. He assumes the surname Knight, becoming Edward Austen Knight. His children also took the surname Knight.

1813

On January 28, *Pride and Prejudice* is published and goes through two editions in one year. Jane has a big hit! On April 21, Edward and his family come to Chawton to stay at the Great House for four months. But Austen leaves for London on April 22 to nurse Henry's wife, Eliza, who dies three days later. Austen remains with her brother until May 1. She again picks up *Mansfield Park*, finishing it around June or July. On August 17, the Austen and Lefroy families are united when Anna Austen, James's elder daughter, becomes engaged to Ben Lefroy, Madam Lefroy's youngest child. In September, Austen makes her final visit to Godmersham, staying there until November. In October, the 2nd edition of *Sense and Sensibility* comes out. Egerton accepts *Mansfield Park* for publication around this time.

1814

On January 21, Austen begins *Emma*. In March, Henry escorts his sister to London, where she enjoys the theater, seeing the great actor Edmund Kean play Shylock in *The Merchant of Venice*. Napoleon abdicates on April 5 and is exiled to Elba. (This event plays a role in *Persuasion.*) Edward and his family spend two months at the Chawton estate, beginning in April. On May 9, *Mansfield Park* is published; the first edition sells out in six months. In August, Frank Austen and his family move into the Chawton Great House, where they live for two years and then move to nearby Alton, a market town within walking distance of the Chawton cottage. But on September 6, sadness strikes when Charles's wife, Fanny, dies in childbirth. Ben Lefroy and Anna Austen marry on November 8.

1815

In March, Napoleon escapes from Elba, and the 100 Days (the period from March 20 to June 28, when Napoleon again reigns) begin, with fighting between England and France resuming. On March 29, Jane completes *Emma.* On June 18, Napoleon is defeated at the Battle of Waterloo. Austen begins her final complete novel, *Persuasion,* on August 8. Henry escorts his sister to London, where he's negotiating with a new publisher, the famous John Murray (also Byron's publisher), about *Emma.* However, Henry becomes seriously ill, and his sister stays with him to nurse him. During this period, one of Henry's physicians learns that his sister is the author of the novels, which, says the physician, are enjoyed by his royal patient (the prince regent). This meeting results in Austen's November 13 visit to the prince's library at Carlton House, the prince's London residence, where she's shown about by the librarian, James Stanier Clarke, who later draws a female figure that is almost certainly Austen. Austen is then invited to dedicate a novel to the prince regent, whose immoral behavior disgusts her. But this royal invitation is equal to a royal command, and so *Emma* is dedicated to the prince regent. Austen returns to Chawton on her birthday (December 16), and *Emma* is published at the end of the month.

1816

Henry goes to the publisher Crosby, who still has *Susan,* and buys it back for his sister for the ten pounds she was paid for it. She changes the title to *Catherine,* possibly because another novel called *Susan* is out. A second edition of *Mansfield Park* is published, this time by Murray. Henry goes bankrupt on March 16. Austen begins to feel sick, but continues to write *Persuasion.* In May, Cassandra takes Austen to Cheltenham, seeking medical care, and they stay there until June 15. On returning to Chawton cottage, Austen resumes writing *Persuasion,* finishing a first draft on July 18 and then revising the final chapters, which she completes on August 6. Her health is failing. Henry becomes ordained and the curate of Chawton in December.

1817

In January, Austen begins writing *Sanditon,* a satirical novel about hypochondriacs and health spas. She works on this until March 18, when her failing strength doesn't permit her to hold a pen or a pencil. She writes her will of just a few lines on April 27, but has nobody witness it because she's concerned that her family will worry about her declining health. *Pride and Prejudice* is now in its third edition. On May 24, Cassandra escorts Austen to Winchester, seeking new medical care under the well-known Mr. Lyford. Catherine Bigg, who now lives in Winchester, arranges for the sisters to stay near her in rooms at No. 8 College Street, near the Winchester Cathedral. Early on July 18, Austen dies. She's buried on July 24 in Winchester Cathedral. Through Henry's work, *Northanger Abbey* (formerly *Susan* and *Catherine*) and *Persuasion* are published by Murray in December, though 1818 is printed as the publication year. This four-volume set is prefaced by Henry's "Biographical Notice" of his sister, identifying the author of these volumes, as well as *Sense and Sensibility, Pride and Prejudice, Mansfield Park,* and *Emma,* as Jane Austen.

Index

See also Character Index and Quotation Index at the end of the General Index

General Index

• A •

• P •

Character Index

Quotation Index

Notes

BUSINESS, CAREERS & PERSONAL FINANCE

Grant Writing FOR DUMMIES
0-7645-5307-0

Home Buying FOR DUMMIES
0-7645-5331-3 *†

Also available:
- Accounting For Dummies †
  0-7645-5314-3
- Business Plans Kit For Dummies †
  0-7645-5365-8
- Cover Letters For Dummies
  0-7645-5224-4
- Frugal Living For Dummies
  0-7645-5403-4
- Leadership For Dummies
  0-7645-5176-0
- Managing For Dummies
  0-7645-1771-6

- Marketing For Dummies
  0-7645-5600-2
- Personal Finance For Dummies *
  0-7645-2590-5
- Project Management For Dummies
  0-7645-5283-X
- Resumes For Dummies †
  0-7645-5471-9
- Selling For Dummies
  0-7645-5363-1
- Small Business Kit For Dummies *†
  0-7645-5093-4

HOME & BUSINESS COMPUTER BASICS

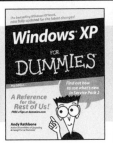

Windows XP FOR DUMMIES
0-7645-4074-2

Excel 2003 ALL-IN-ONE DESK REFERENCE FOR DUMMIES
0-7645-3758-X

Also available:
- ACT! 6 For Dummies
  0-7645-2645-6
- iLife '04 All-in-One Desk Reference
  For Dummies
  0-7645-7347-0
- iPAQ For Dummies
  0-7645-6769-1
- Mac OS X Panther Timesaving
  Techniques For Dummies
  0-7645-5812-9
- Macs For Dummies
  0-7645-5656-8

- Microsoft Money 2004 For Dummies
  0-7645-4195-1
- Office 2003 All-in-One Desk Reference
  For Dummies
  0-7645-3883-7
- Outlook 2003 For Dummies
  0-7645-3759-8
- PCs For Dummies
  0-7645-4074-2
- TiVo For Dummies
  0-7645-6923-6
- Upgrading and Fixing PCs For Dummies
  0-7645-1665-5
- Windows XP Timesaving Techniques
  For Dummies
  0-7645-3748-2

FOOD, HOME, GARDEN, HOBBIES, MUSIC & PETS

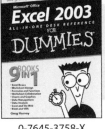

Feng Shui FOR DUMMIES
0-7645-5295-3

Poker FOR DUMMIES
0-7645-5232-5

Also available:
- Bass Guitar For Dummies
  0-7645-2487-9
- Diabetes Cookbook For Dummies
  0-7645-5230-9
- Gardening For Dummies *
  0-7645-5130-2
- Guitar For Dummies
  0-7645-5106-X
- Holiday Decorating For Dummies
  0-7645-2570-0
- Home Improvement All-in-One
  For Dummies
  0-7645-5680-0

- Knitting For Dummies
  0-7645-5395-X
- Piano For Dummies
  0-7645-5105-1
- Puppies For Dummies
  0-7645-5255-4
- Scrapbooking For Dummies
  0-7645-7208-3
- Senior Dogs For Dummies
  0-7645-5818-8
- Singing For Dummies
  0-7645-2475-5
- 30-Minute Meals For Dummies
  0-7645-2589-1

INTERNET & DIGITAL MEDIA

Digital Photography FOR DUMMIES
0-7645-1664-7

Starting an eBay Business FOR DUMMIES
0-7645-6924-4

Also available:
- 2005 Online Shopping Directory
  For Dummies
  0-7645-7495-7
- CD & DVD Recording For Dummies
  0-7645-5956-7
- eBay For Dummies
  0-7645-5654-1
- Fighting Spam For Dummies
  0-7645-5965-6
- Genealogy Online For Dummies
  0-7645-5964-8
- Google For Dummies
  0-7645-4420-9

- Home Recording For Musicians
  For Dummies
  0-7645-1634-5
- The Internet For Dummies
  0-7645-4173-0
- iPod & iTunes For Dummies
  0-7645-7772-7
- Preventing Identity Theft For Dummies
  0-7645-7336-5
- Pro Tools All-in-One Desk Reference
  For Dummies
  0-7645-5714-9
- Roxio Easy Media Creator For Dummies
  0-7645-7131-1

* Separate Canadian edition also available

† Separate U.K. edition also available

Available wherever books are sold. For more information or to order direct: U.S. customers visit www.dummies.com or call 1-877-762-2974.
U.K. customers visit www.wileyeurope.com or call 0800 243407. Canadian customers visit www.wiley.ca or call 1-800-567-4797.

 **WILEY**

SPORTS, FITNESS, PARENTING, RELIGION & SPIRITUALITY

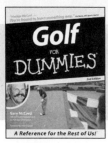

0-7645-5146-9

0-7645-5418-2

Also available:
- Adoption For Dummies
  0-7645-5488-3
- Basketball For Dummies
  0-7645-5248-1
- The Bible For Dummies
  0-7645-5296-1
- Buddhism For Dummies
  0-7645-5359-3
- Catholicism For Dummies
  0-7645-5391-7
- Hockey For Dummies
  0-7645-5228-7

- Judaism For Dummies
  0-7645-5299-6
- Martial Arts For Dummies
  0-7645-5358-5
- Pilates For Dummies
  0-7645-5397-6
- Religion For Dummies
  0-7645-5264-3
- Teaching Kids to Read For Dummies
  0-7645-4043-2
- Weight Training For Dummies
  0-7645-5168-X
- Yoga For Dummies
  0-7645-5117-5

TRAVEL

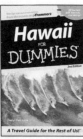

0-7645-5438-7

0-7645-5453-0

Also available:
- Alaska For Dummies
  0-7645-1761-9
- Arizona For Dummies
  0-7645-6938-4
- Cancún and the Yucatán For Dummies
  0-7645-2437-2
- Cruise Vacations For Dummies
  0-7645-6941-4
- Europe For Dummies
  0-7645-5456-5
- Ireland For Dummies
  0-7645-5455-7

- Las Vegas For Dummies
  0-7645-5448-4
- London For Dummies
  0-7645-4277-X
- New York City For Dummies
  0-7645-6945-7
- Paris For Dummies
  0-7645-5494-8
- RV Vacations For Dummies
  0-7645-5443-3
- Walt Disney World & Orlando For Dummies
  0-7645-6943-0

GRAPHICS, DESIGN & WEB DEVELOPMENT

0-7645-4345-8

0-7645-5589-8

Also available:
- Adobe Acrobat 6 PDF For Dummies
  0-7645-3760-1
- Building a Web Site For Dummies
  0-7645-7144-3
- Dreamweaver MX 2004 For Dummies
  0-7645-4342-3
- FrontPage 2003 For Dummies
  0-7645-3882-9
- HTML 4 For Dummies
  0-7645-1995-6
- Illustrator CS For Dummies
  0-7645-4084-X

- Macromedia Flash MX 2004 For Dummies
  0-7645-4358-X
- Photoshop 7 All-in-One Desk
  Reference For Dummies
  0-7645-1667-1
- Photoshop CS Timesaving Techniques
  For Dummies
  0-7645-6782-9
- PHP 5 For Dummies
  0-7645-4166-8
- PowerPoint 2003 For Dummies
  0-7645-3908-6
- QuarkXPress 6 For Dummies
  0-7645-2593-X

NETWORKING, SECURITY, PROGRAMMING & DATABASES

0-7645-6852-3

0-7645-5784-X

Also available:
- A+ Certification For Dummies
  0-7645-4187-0
- Access 2003 All-in-One Desk
  Reference For Dummies
  0-7645-3988-4
- Beginning Programming For Dummies
  0-7645-4997-9
- C For Dummies
  0-7645-7068-4
- Firewalls For Dummies
  0-7645-4048-3
- Home Networking For Dummies
  0-7645-42796

- Network Security For Dummies
  0-7645-1679-5
- Networking For Dummies
  0-7645-1677-9
- TCP/IP For Dummies
  0-7645-1760-0
- VBA For Dummies
  0-7645-3989-2
- Wireless All In-One Desk Reference
  For Dummies
  0-7645-7496-5
- Wireless Home Networking For Dummies
  0-7645-3910-8

HEALTH & SELF-HELP

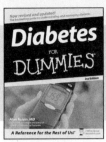

0-7645-6820-5 *†   0-7645-2566-2

Also available:

Alzheimer's For Dummies
0-7645-3899-3

Asthma For Dummies
0-7645-4233-8

Controlling Cholesterol For Dummies
0-7645-5440-9

Depression For Dummies
0-7645-3900-0

Dieting For Dummies
0-7645-4149-8

Fertility For Dummies
0-7645-2549-2

Fibromyalgia For Dummies
0-7645-5441-7

Improving Your Memory For Dummies
0-7645-5435-2

Pregnancy For Dummies †
0-7645-4483-7

Quitting Smoking For Dummies
0-7645-2629-4

Relationships For Dummies
0-7645-5384-4

Thyroid For Dummies
0-7645-5385-2

EDUCATION, HISTORY, REFERENCE & TEST PREPARATION

0-7645-5194-9   0-7645-4186-2

Also available:

Algebra For Dummies
0-7645-5325-9

British History For Dummies
0-7645-7021-8

Calculus For Dummies
0-7645-2498-4

English Grammar For Dummies
0-7645-5322-4

Forensics For Dummies
0-7645-5580-4

The GMAT For Dummies
0-7645-5251-1

Inglés Para Dummies
0-7645-5427-1

Italian For Dummies
0-7645-5196-5

Latin For Dummies
0-7645-5431-X

Lewis & Clark For Dummies
0-7645-2545-X

Research Papers For Dummies
0-7645-5426-3

The SAT I For Dummies
0-7645-7193-1

Science Fair Projects For Dummies
0-7645-5460-3

U.S. History For Dummies
0-7645-5249-X

Get smart @ dummies.com®

- **Find a full list of Dummies titles**
- **Look into loads of FREE on-site articles**
- **Sign up for FREE eTips e-mailed to you weekly**
- **See what other products carry the Dummies name**
- **Shop directly from the Dummies bookstore**
- **Enter to win new prizes every month!**

* Separate Canadian edition also available

† Separate U.K. edition also available

Available wherever books are sold. For more information or to order direct: U.S. customers visit www.dummies.com or call 1-877-762-2974.
U.K. customers visit www.wileyeurope.com or call 0800 243407. Canadian customers visit www.wiley.ca or call 1-800-567-4797.

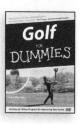